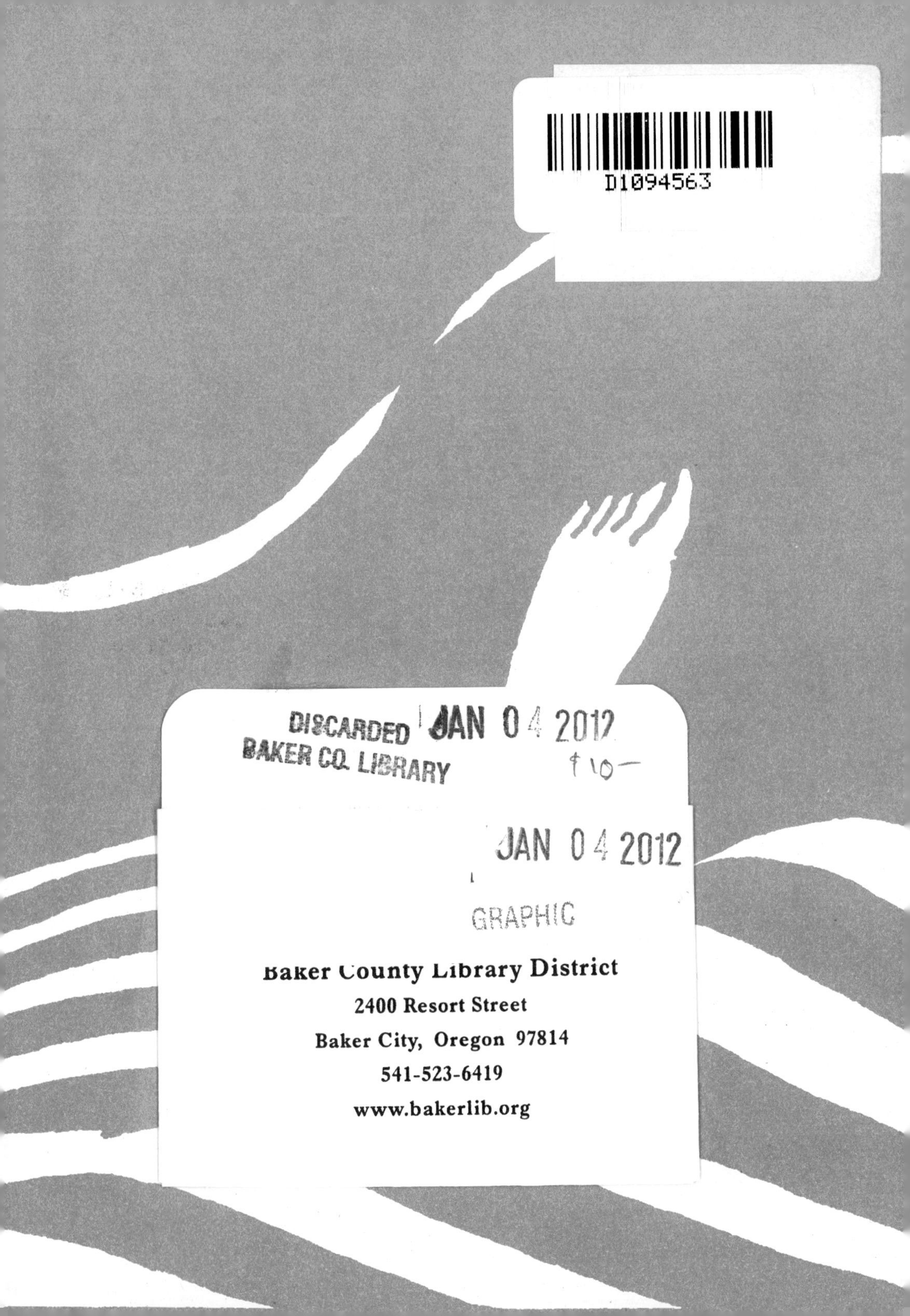

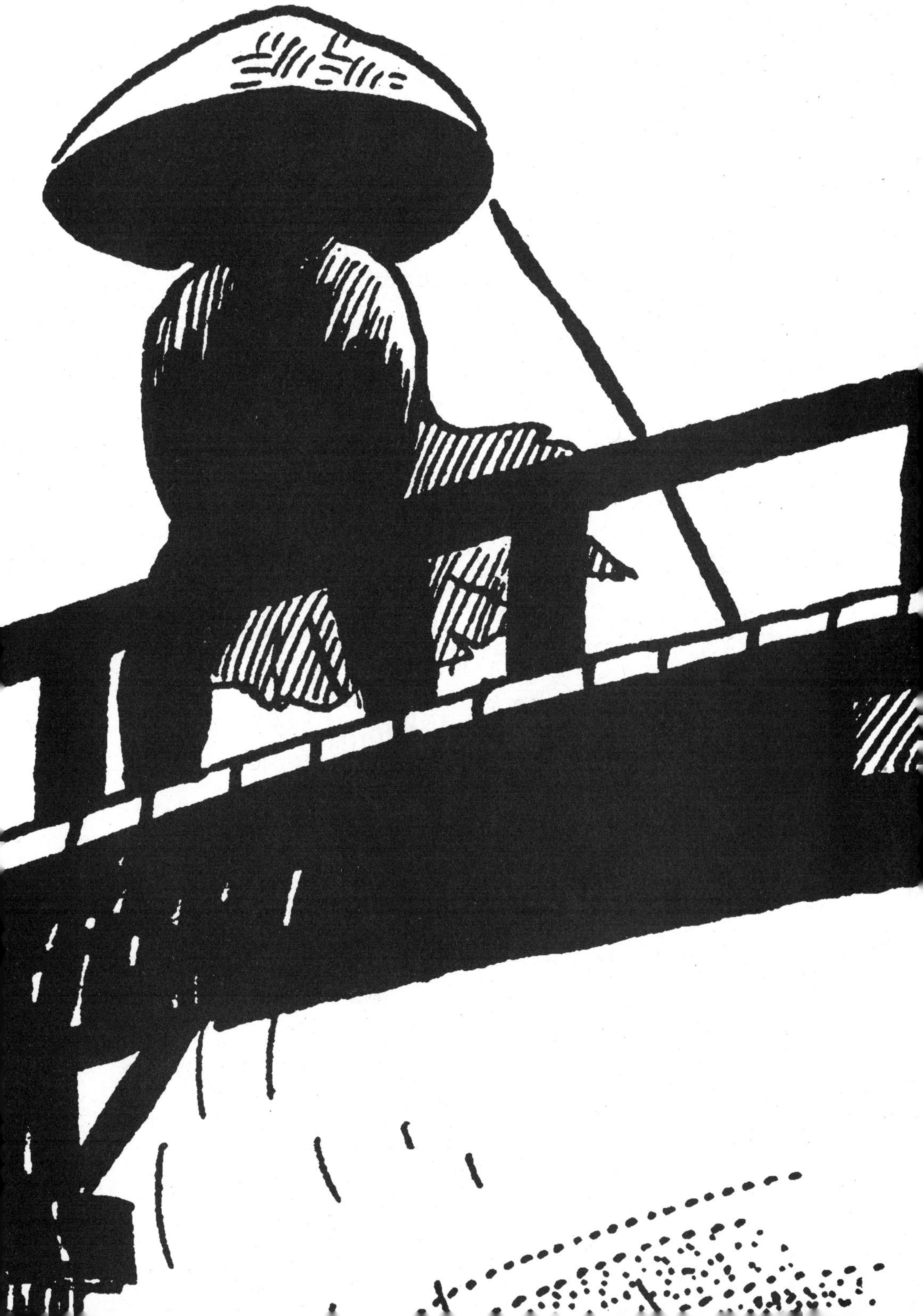

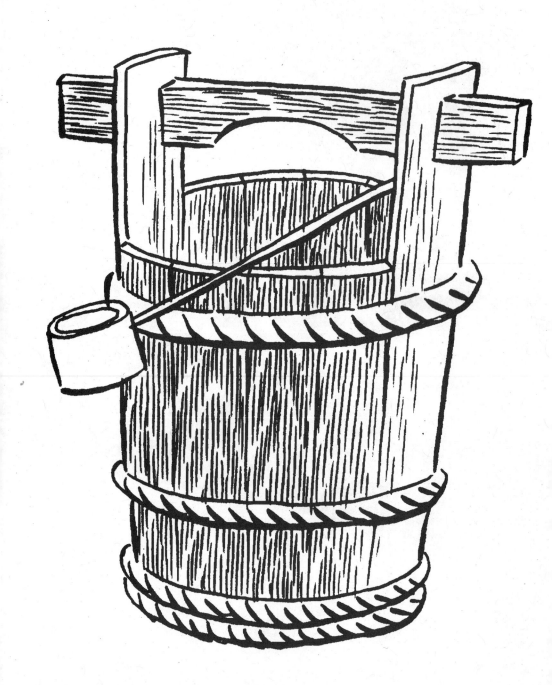

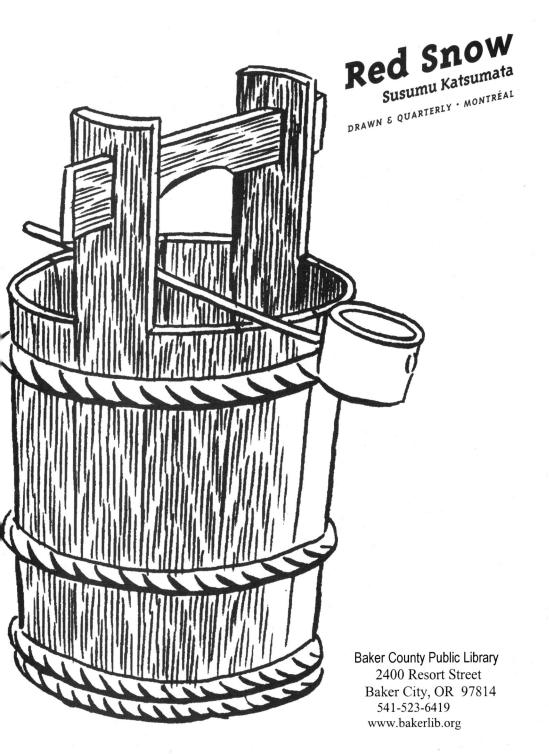

Red Snow
Susumu Katsumata

DRAWN & QUARTERLY · MONTRÉAL

Translation: Taro Nettleton. Font design: Rich Tomasso. Drawn & Quarterly, Post Office Box 48056, Montreal, Quebec, Canada H2V 4S8; www.drawnandquarterly.com; First hardcover edition: September 2009. Printed in Canada. 10 9 8 7 6 5 4 3 2 1 Library and Archives Canada Cataloguing in Publication; Katsumata, Susumu, 1943-2007; Red snow / Susumu Katsumata ; translated by Taro Nettleton. Originally published in Japanese under title Akai Yuki. ISBN 978-1-897299-86-9; I. Nettleton, Taro II. Title. PN6790.J33K379 2009 741.5'952 C2009-901645-1; Distributed in the USA and abroad by Farrar, Straus and Giroux, 19 Union Square West, New York, NY 10003; Orders: 888.330.8477; Distributed in Canada by Raincoast Books, 9050 Shaughnessy Street, Vancouver, BC V6P 6E5; Orders: 800.663.5714

Red Snow

MULBERRIES
ECHO
CRICKET HILL
PULP NOVEL ABOUT A SACK
KOKESHI
THE DREAM SPIRIT
SPECTER
TORAJIRO KAPPA
WILD GEESE MEMORIAL SERVICE
RED SNOW

MULBERRIES

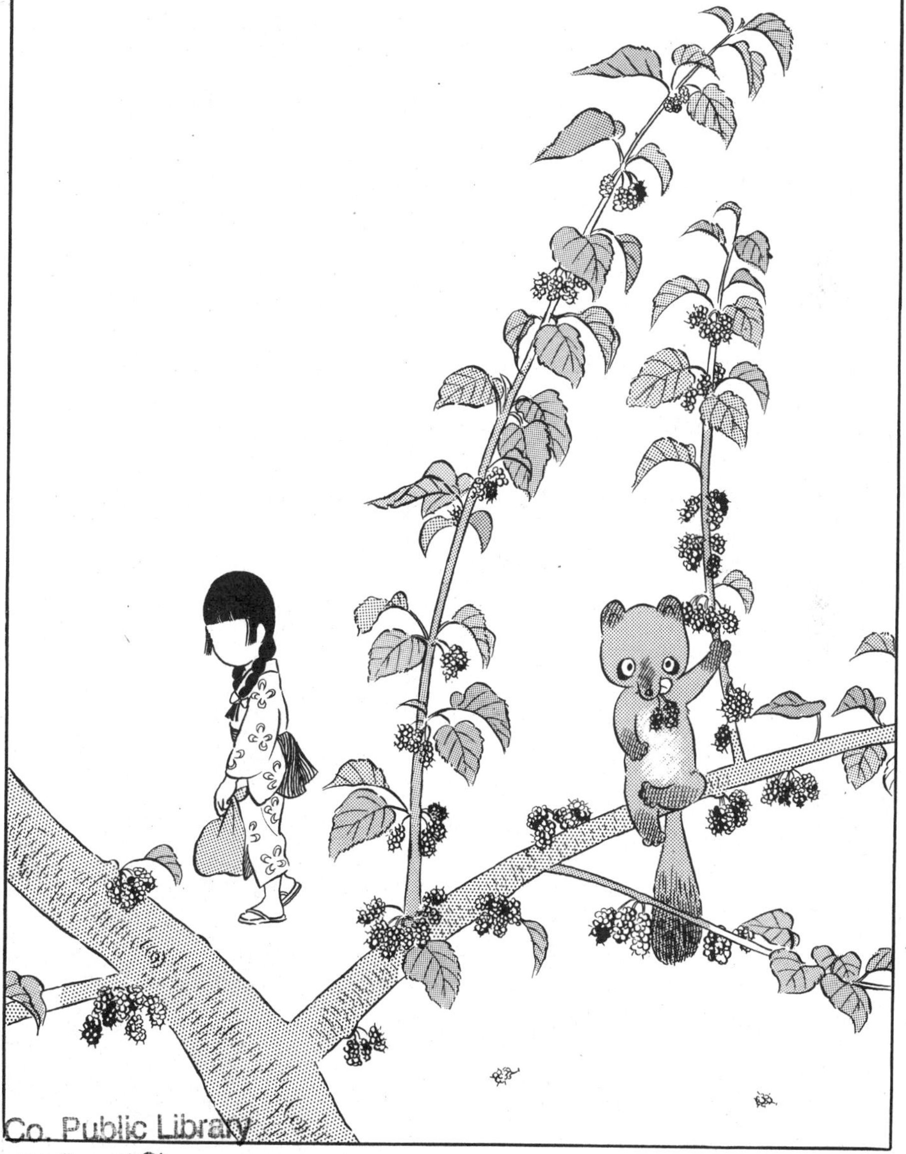

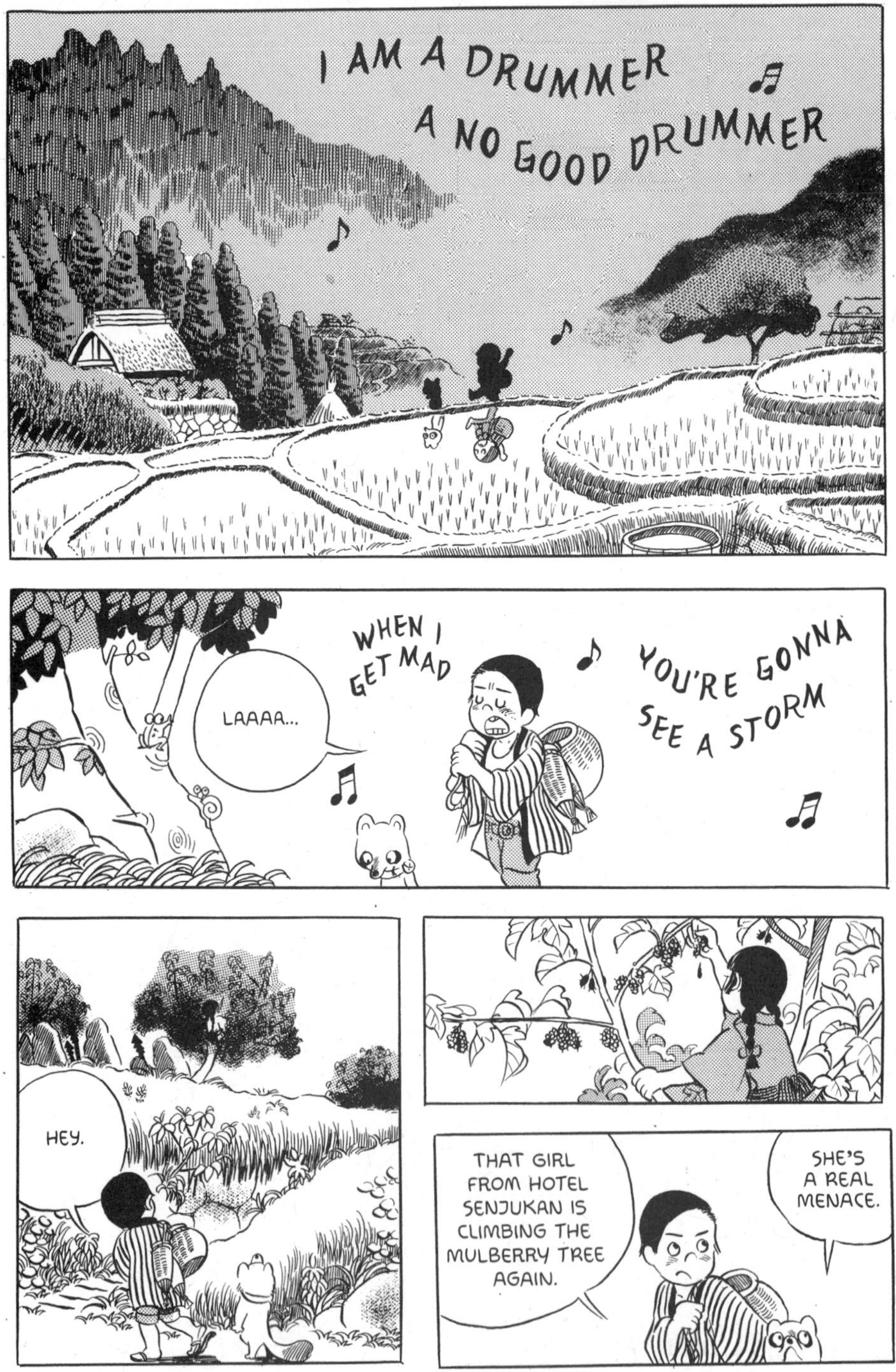
I AM A DRUMMER
A NO GOOD DRUMMER
LAAAA...
WHEN I GET MAD
YOU'RE GONNA SEE A STORM
HEY.
THAT GIRL FROM HOTEL SENJUKAN IS CLIMBING THE MULBERRY TREE AGAIN.
SHE'S A REAL MENACE.

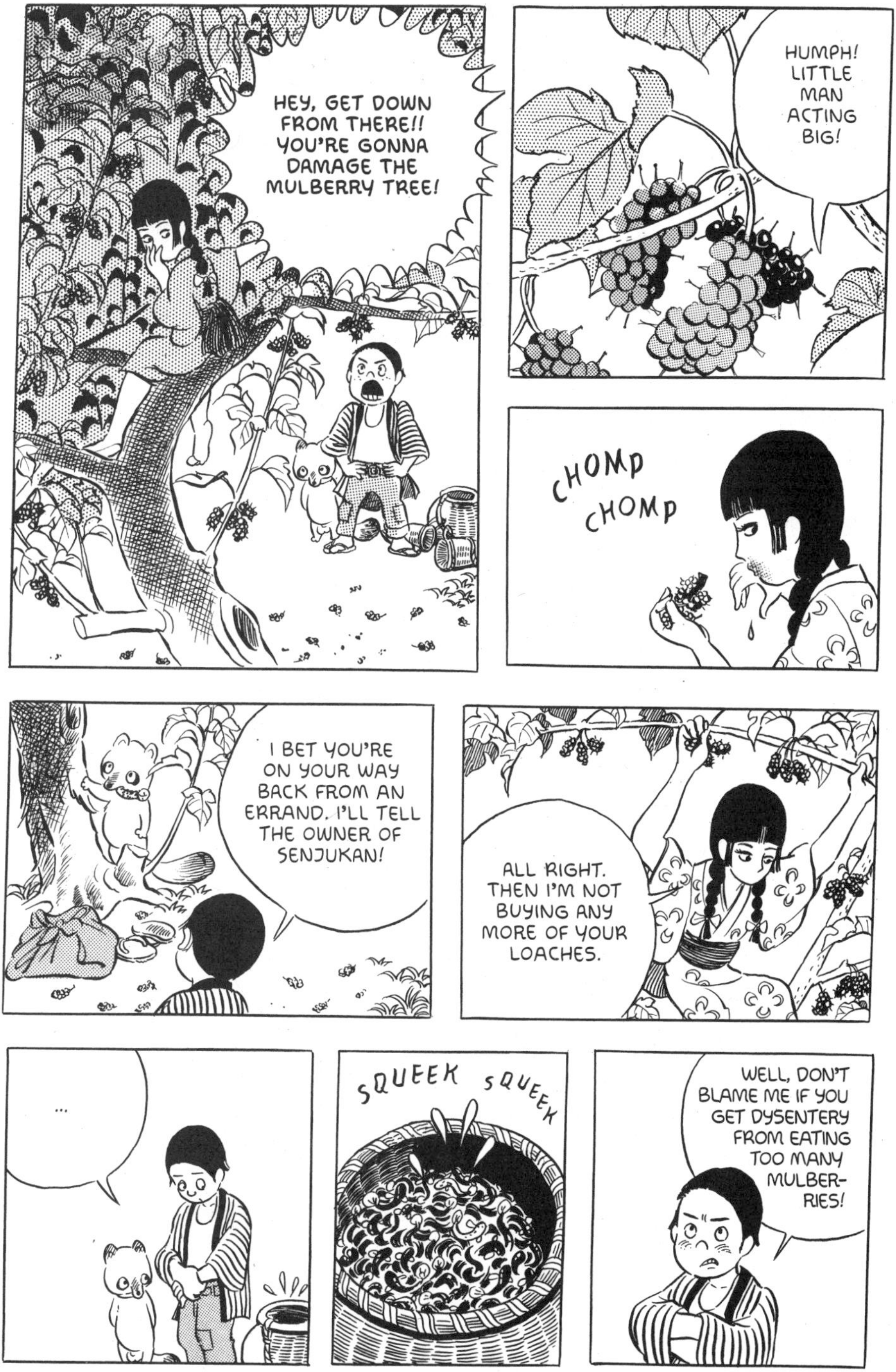
HEY, GET DOWN FROM THERE!! YOU'RE GONNA DAMAGE THE MULBERRY TREE!
HUMPH! LITTLE MAN ACTING BIG!
CHOMP CHOMP
I BET YOU'RE ON YOUR WAY BACK FROM AN ERRAND. I'LL TELL THE OWNER OF SENJUKAN!
ALL RIGHT. THEN I'M NOT BUYING ANY MORE OF YOUR LOACHES.
...
SQUEEK SQUEEK
WELL, DON'T BLAME ME IF YOU GET DYSENTERY FROM EATING TOO MANY MULBER-RIES!

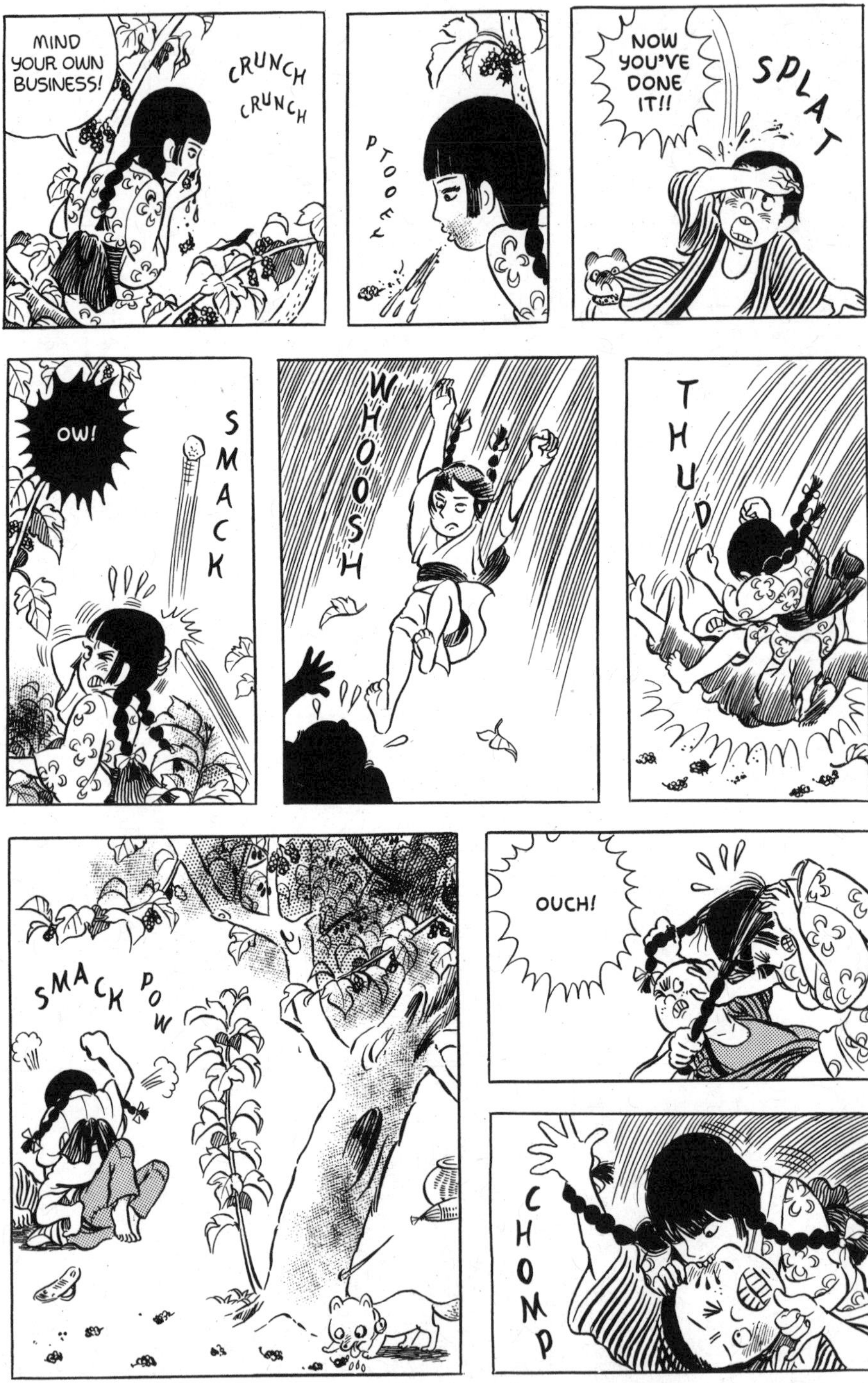
MIND YOUR OWN BUSINESS!
CRUNCH CRUNCH
PTOOEY
NOW YOU'VE DONE IT!!
SPLAT
OW!
SMACK
WHOOSH
THUD
SMACK POW
OUCH!
CHOMP

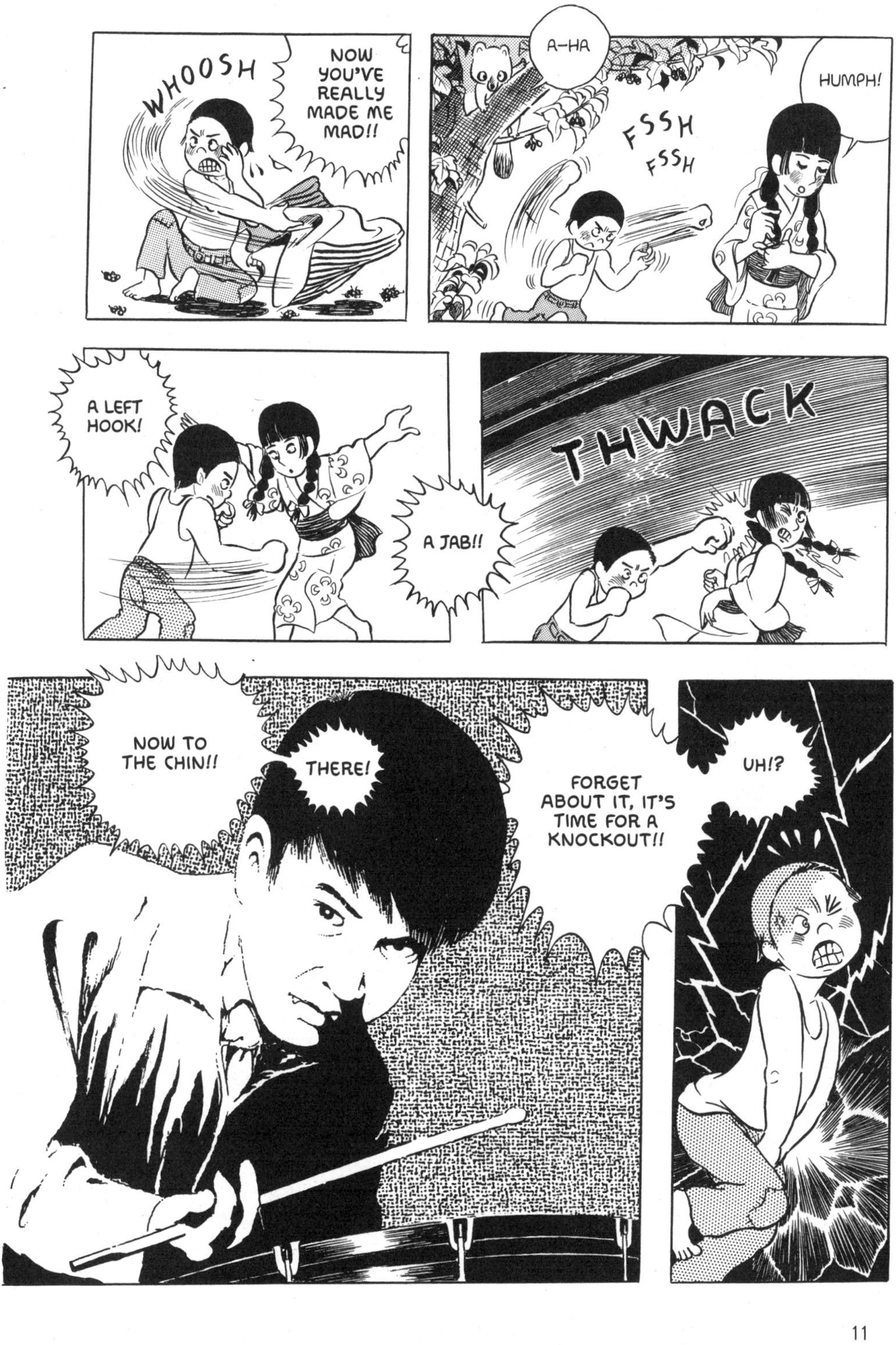
WHOOSH
NOW YOU'VE REALLY MADE ME MAD!!
A-HA
FSSH FSSH
HUMPH!
A LEFT HOOK!
A JAB!!
THWACK
NOW TO THE CHIN!!
THERE!
FORGET ABOUT IT, IT'S TIME FOR A KNOCKOUT!!
UH!?

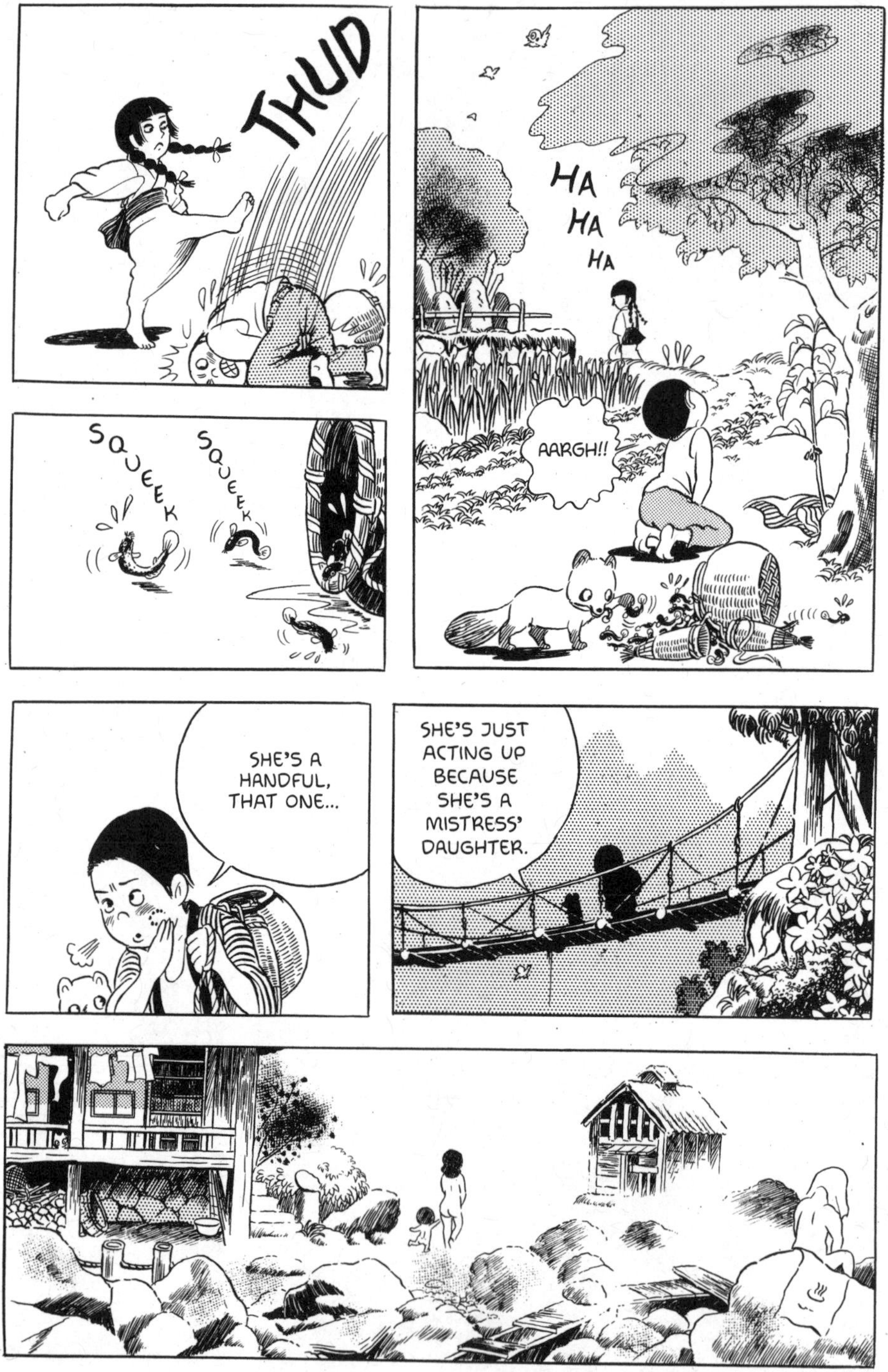
THUD
SQUEEK
SQUEEK
HA HA HA
AARGH!!
SHE'S A HANDFUL, THAT ONE...
SHE'S JUST ACTING UP BECAUSE SHE'S A MISTRESS' DAUGHTER.

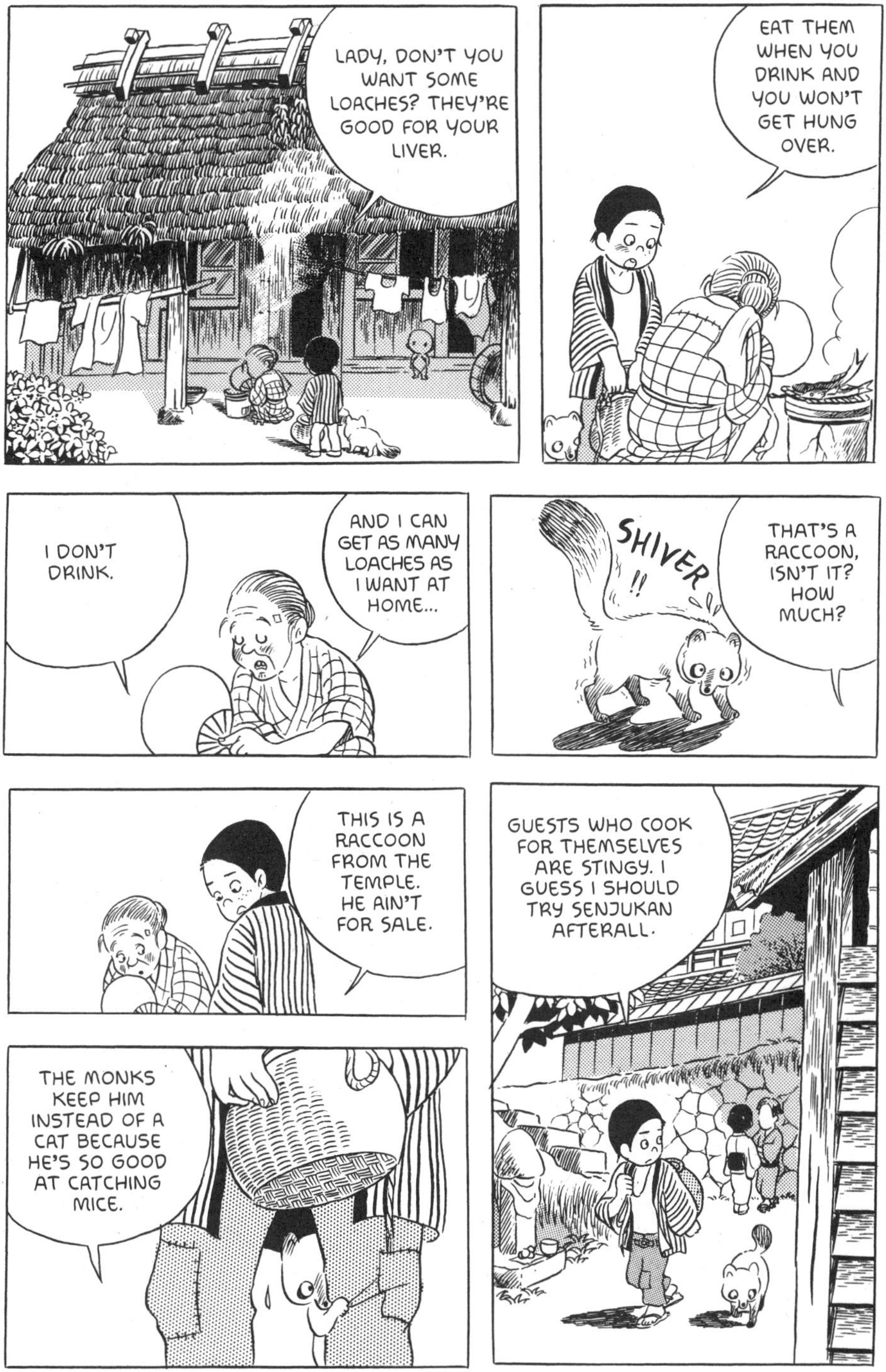
LADY, DON'T YOU WANT SOME LOACHES? THEY'RE GOOD FOR YOUR LIVER.
EAT THEM WHEN YOU DRINK AND YOU WON'T GET HUNG OVER.
I DON'T DRINK.
AND I CAN GET AS MANY LOACHES AS I WANT AT HOME...
SHIVER !!
THAT'S A RACCOON, ISN'T IT? HOW MUCH?
THIS IS A RACCOON FROM THE TEMPLE. HE AIN'T FOR SALE.
THE MONKS KEEP HIM INSTEAD OF A CAT BECAUSE HE'S SO GOOD AT CATCHING MICE.
GUESTS WHO COOK FOR THEMSELVES ARE STINGY. I GUESS I SHOULD TRY SENJUKAN AFTERALL.

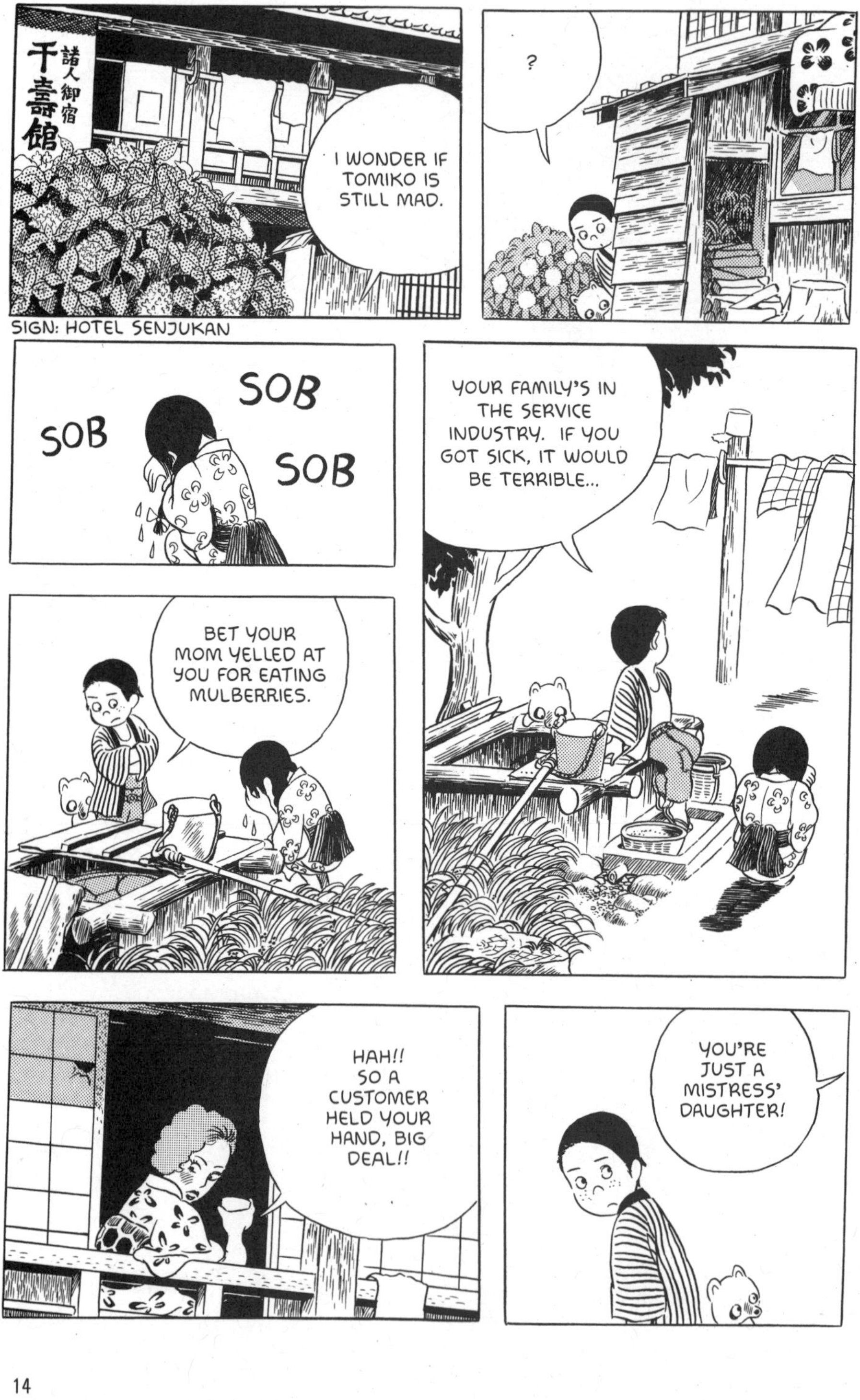
諸人御宿
千壽館
I WONDER IF TOMIKO IS STILL MAD.
?
SIGN: HOTEL SENJUKAN
SOB
SOB
SOB
BET YOUR MOM YELLED AT YOU FOR EATING MULBERRIES.
YOUR FAMILY'S IN THE SERVICE INDUSTRY. IF YOU GOT SICK, IT WOULD BE TERRIBLE...
HAH!! SO A CUSTOMER HELD YOUR HAND, BIG DEAL!!
YOU'RE JUST A MISTRESS' DAUGHTER!

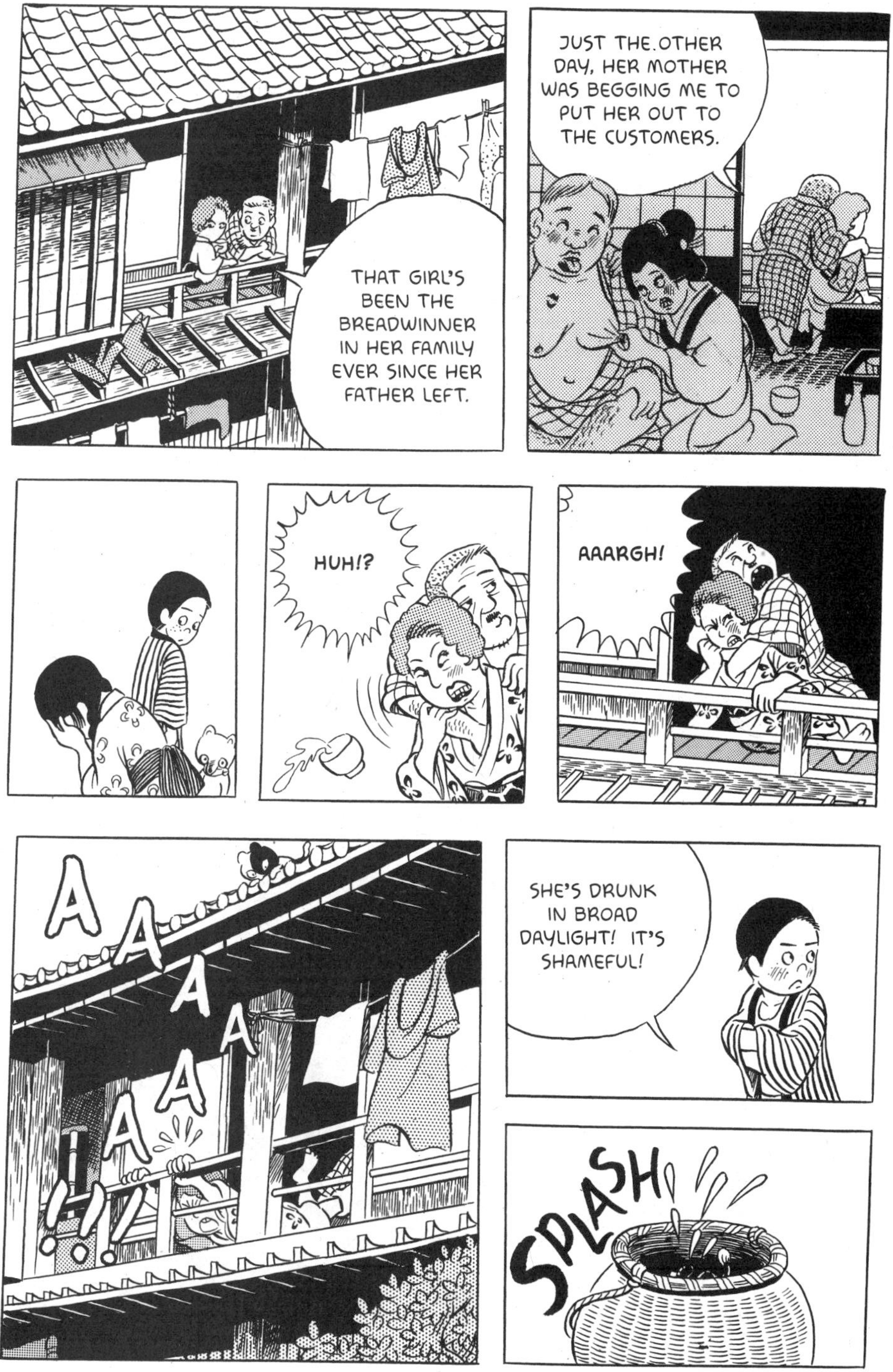
THAT GIRL'S BEEN THE BREADWINNER IN HER FAMILY EVER SINCE HER FATHER LEFT.
JUST THE OTHER DAY, HER MOTHER WAS BEGGING ME TO PUT HER OUT TO THE CUSTOMERS.
HUH!?
AAARGH!
AAAAAA!!!
SHE'S DRUNK IN BROAD DAYLIGHT! IT'S SHAMEFUL!
SPLASH

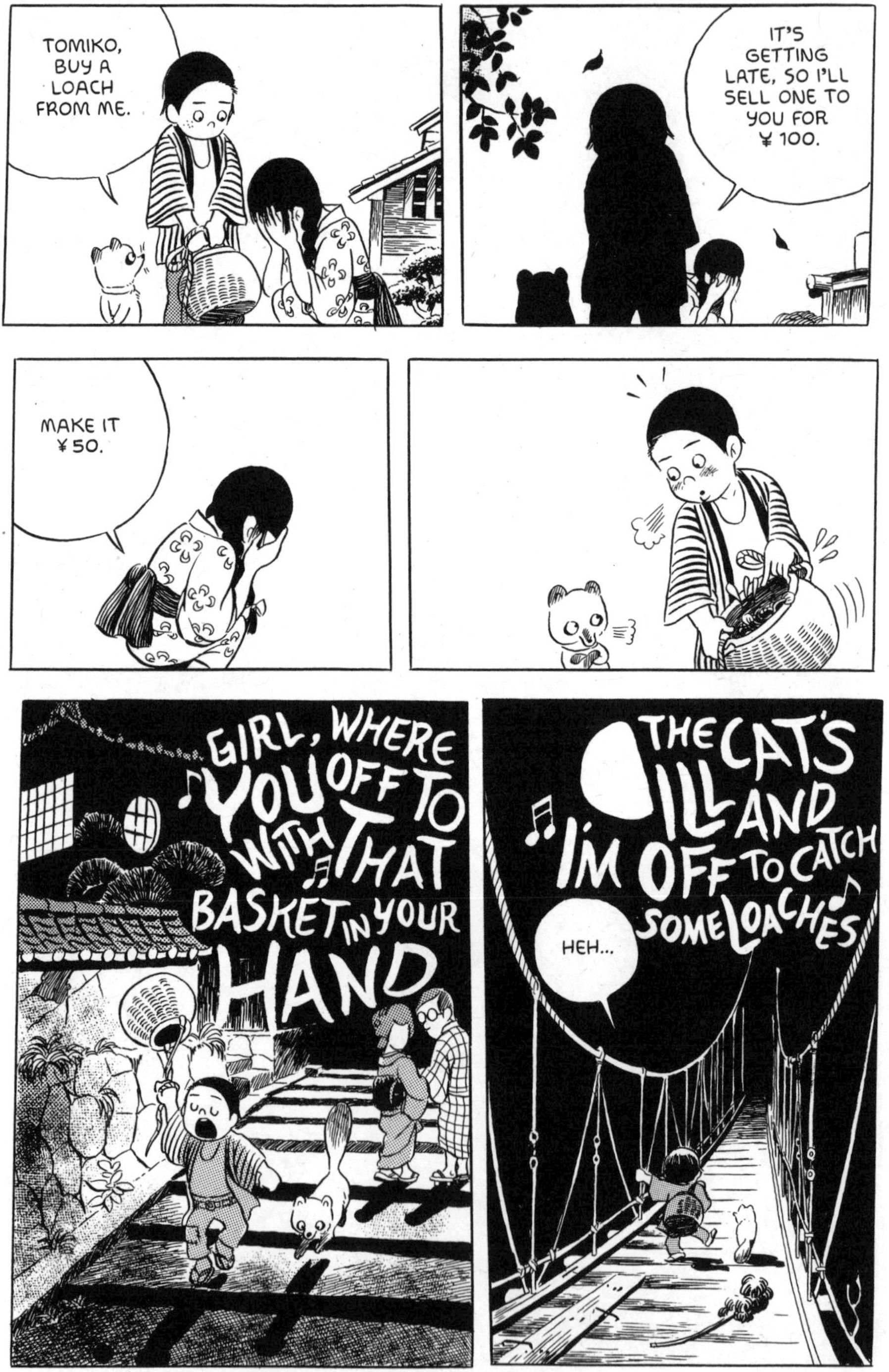
TOMIKO, BUY A LOACH FROM ME.
IT'S GETTING LATE, SO I'LL SELL ONE TO YOU FOR ¥100.
MAKE IT ¥50.
GIRL, WHERE YOU OFF TO WITH THAT BASKET IN YOUR HAND
THE CAT'S ILL AND I'M OFF TO CATCH SOME LOACHES
HEH...

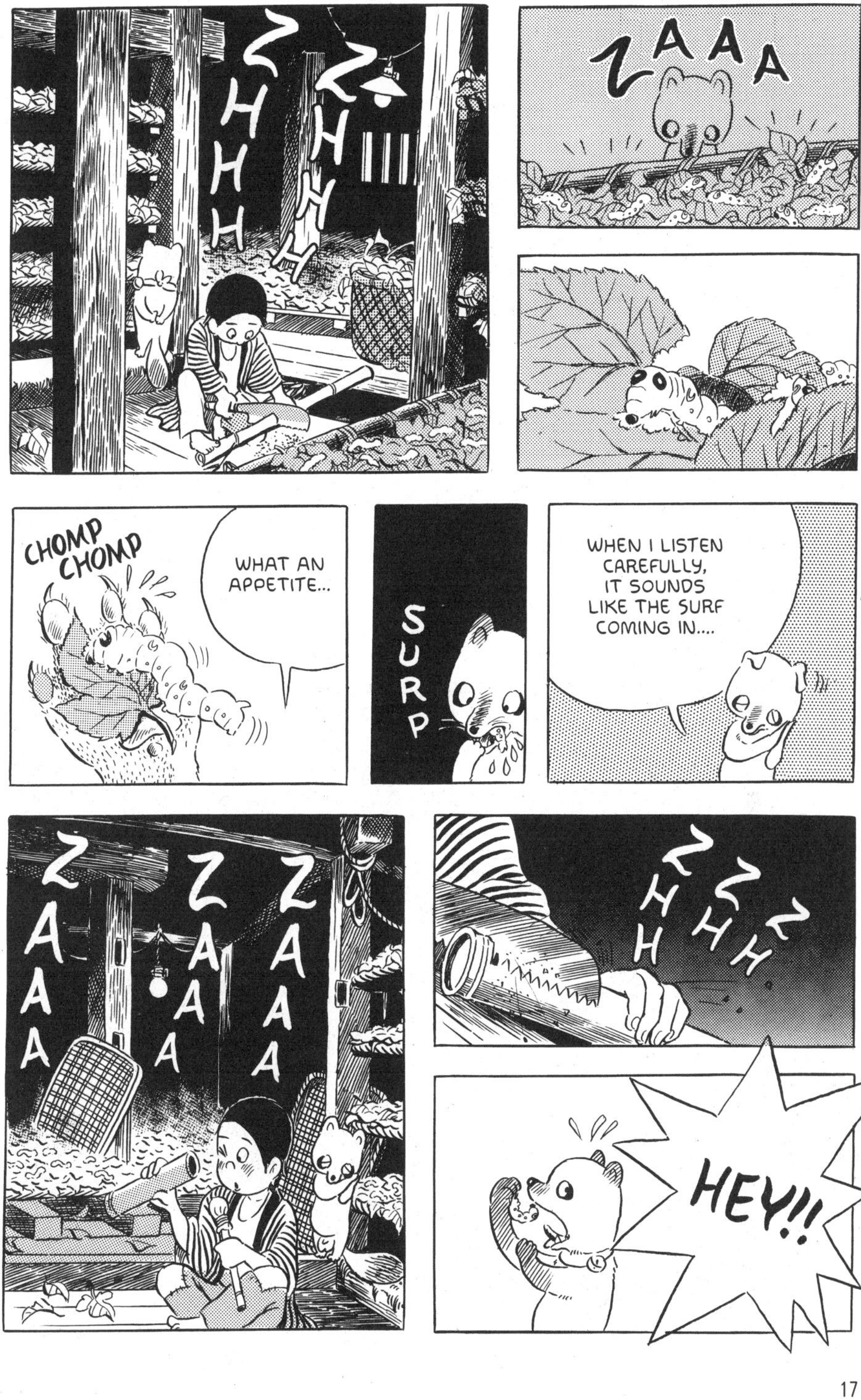
ZHHHH
ZHHHH
ZAAA
CHOMP CHOMP
WHAT AN APPETITE...
SURP
WHEN I LISTEN CAREFULLY, IT SOUNDS LIKE THE SURF COMING IN....
ZAAA
ZAAA
ZAAA
ZHH
ZHH
ZHH
HEY!!

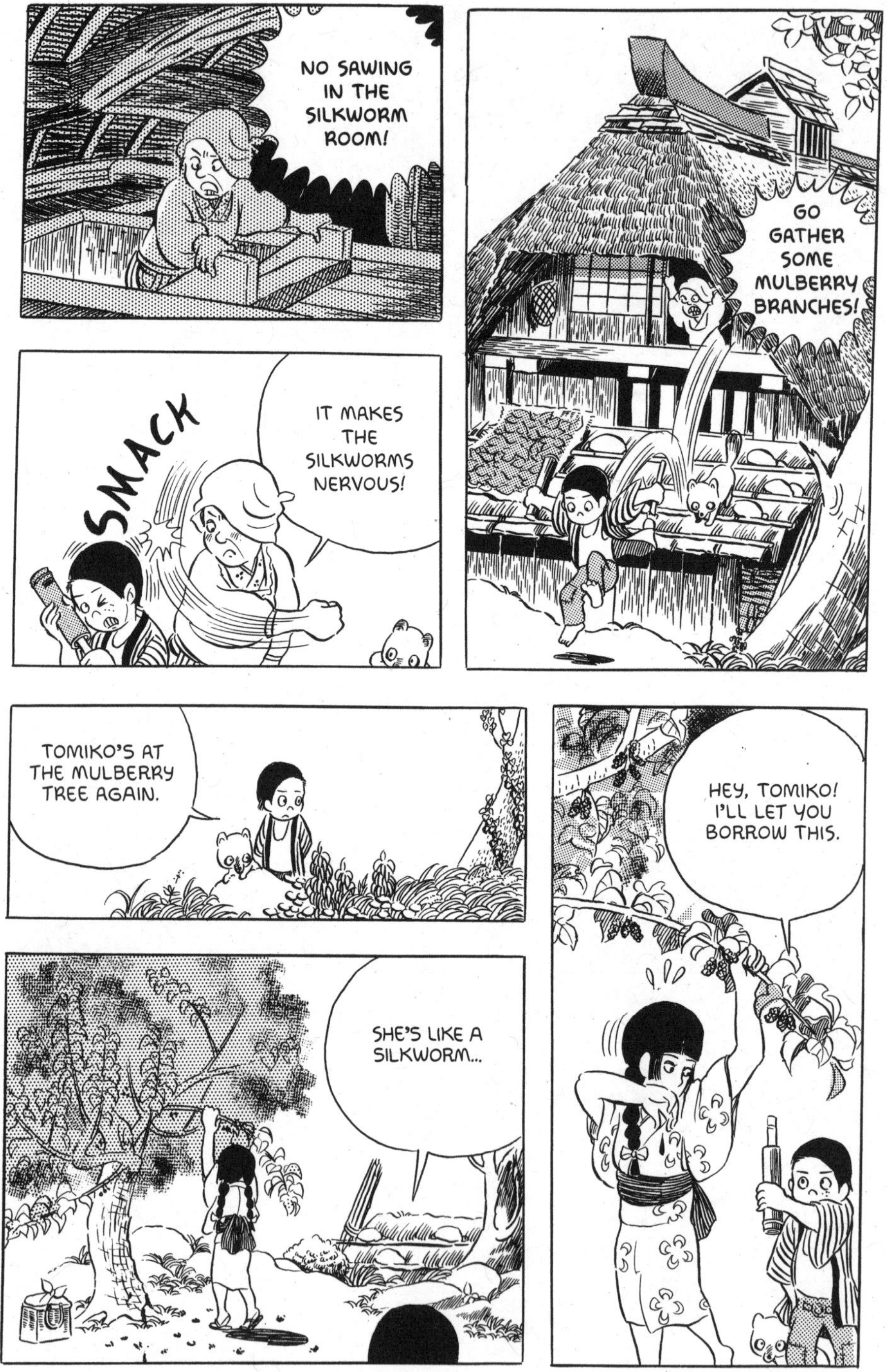
NO SAWING IN THE SILKWORM ROOM!
SMACK
IT MAKES THE SILKWORMS NERVOUS!
GO GATHER SOME MULBERRY BRANCHES!
TOMIKO'S AT THE MULBERRY TREE AGAIN.
SHE'S LIKE A SILKWORM...
HEY, TOMIKO! I'LL LET YOU BORROW THIS.

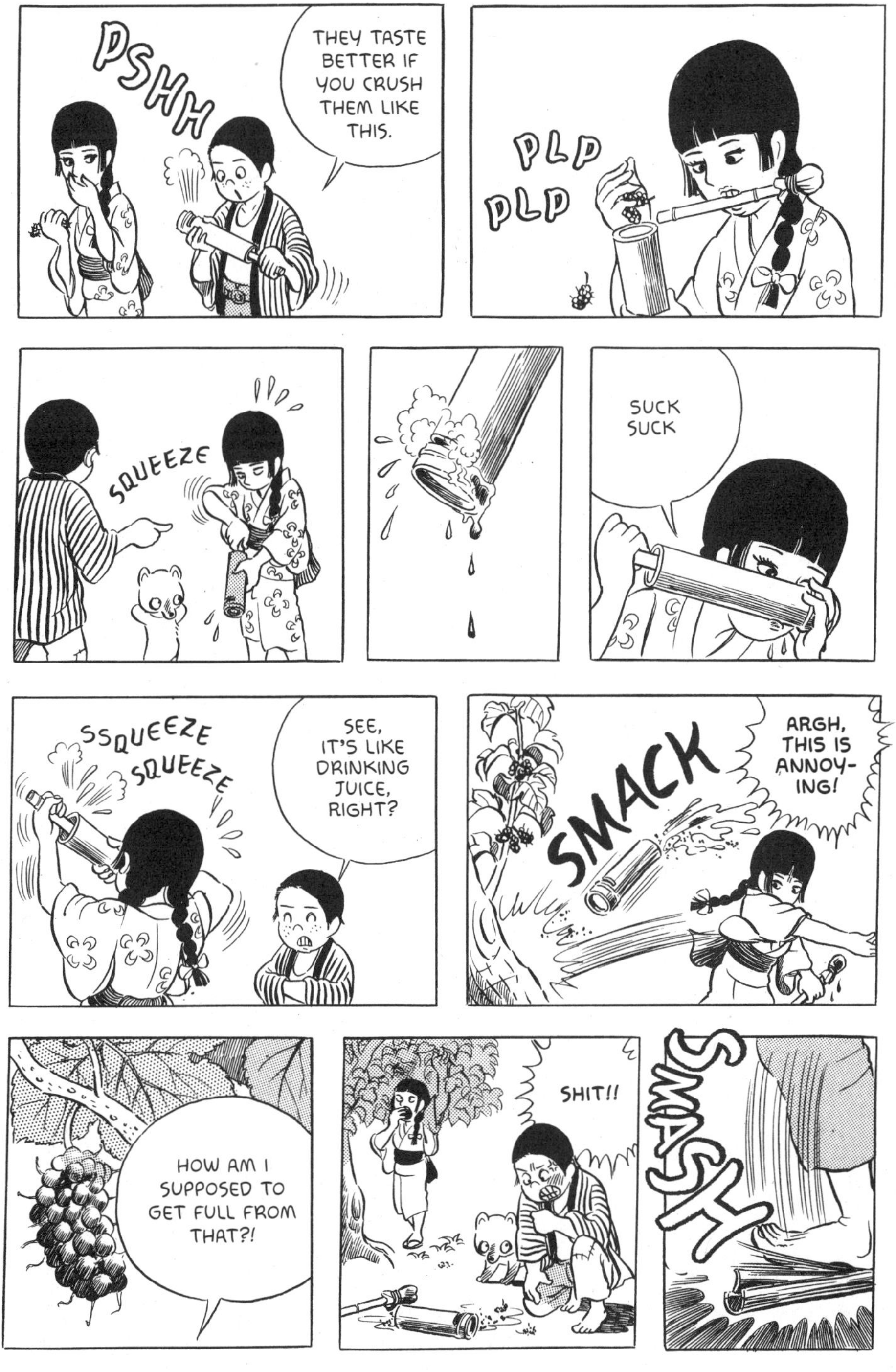
PSHH
THEY TASTE BETTER IF YOU CRUSH THEM LIKE THIS.
PLP PLP
SQUEEZE
SUCK SUCK
SSQUEEZE SQUEEZE
SEE, IT'S LIKE DRINKING JUICE, RIGHT?
SMACK
ARGH, THIS IS ANNOY-ING!
HOW AM I SUPPOSED TO GET FULL FROM THAT?!
SHIT!!
SMASH

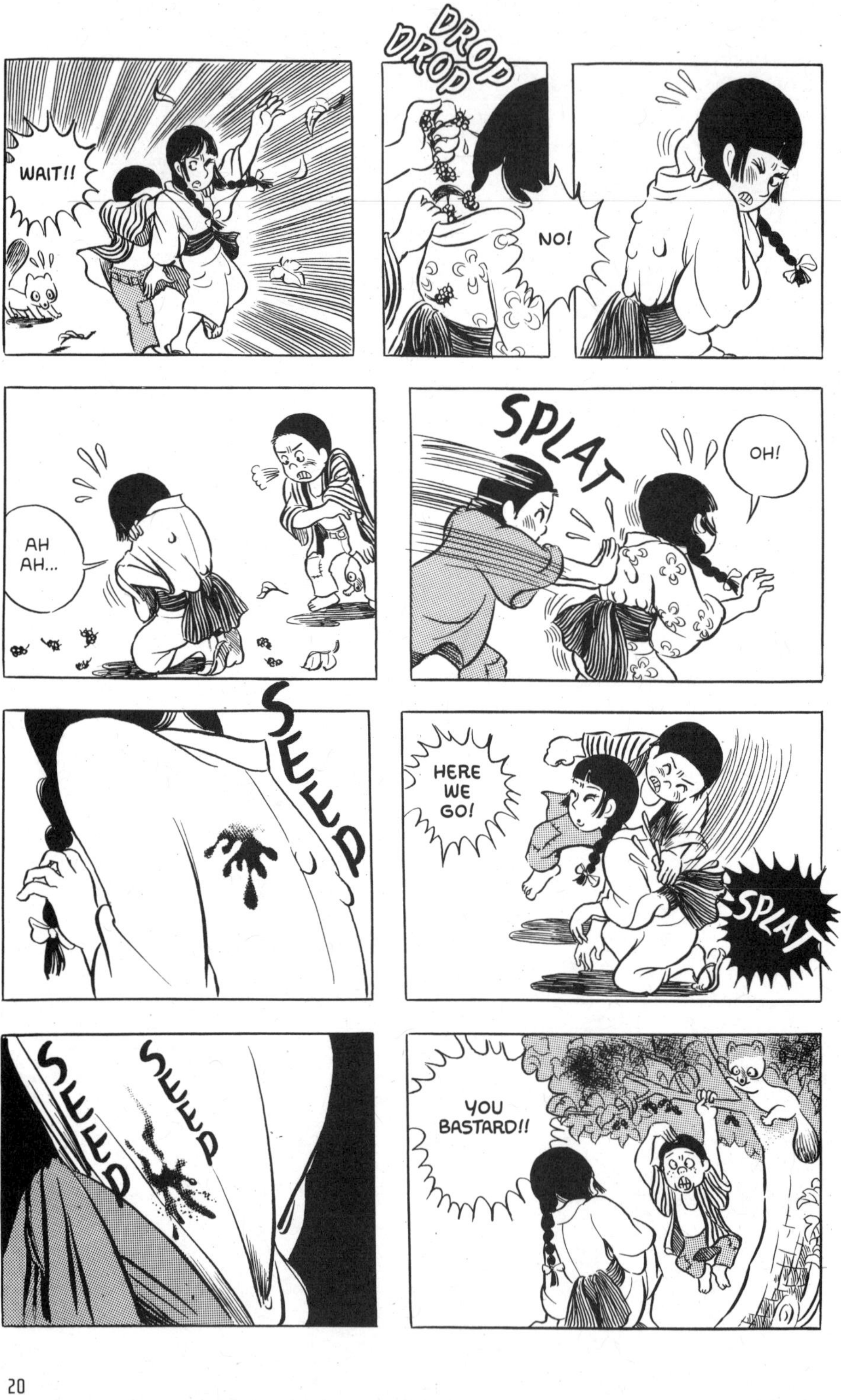
WAIT!!
DROP DROP
NO!
AH AH...
SPLAT
OH!
SEEEP
HERE WE GO!
SPLAT
SEEEP
SEEP
YOU BASTARD!!

SHAKE
SHAKE

AH...

SPLAT!

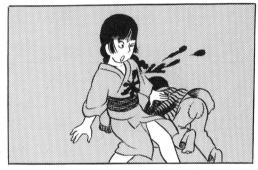

NOOO!!

THAT'S PAYBACK FOR THE OTHER DAY.

THAT'LL TEACH YOU TO MESS WITH ME.

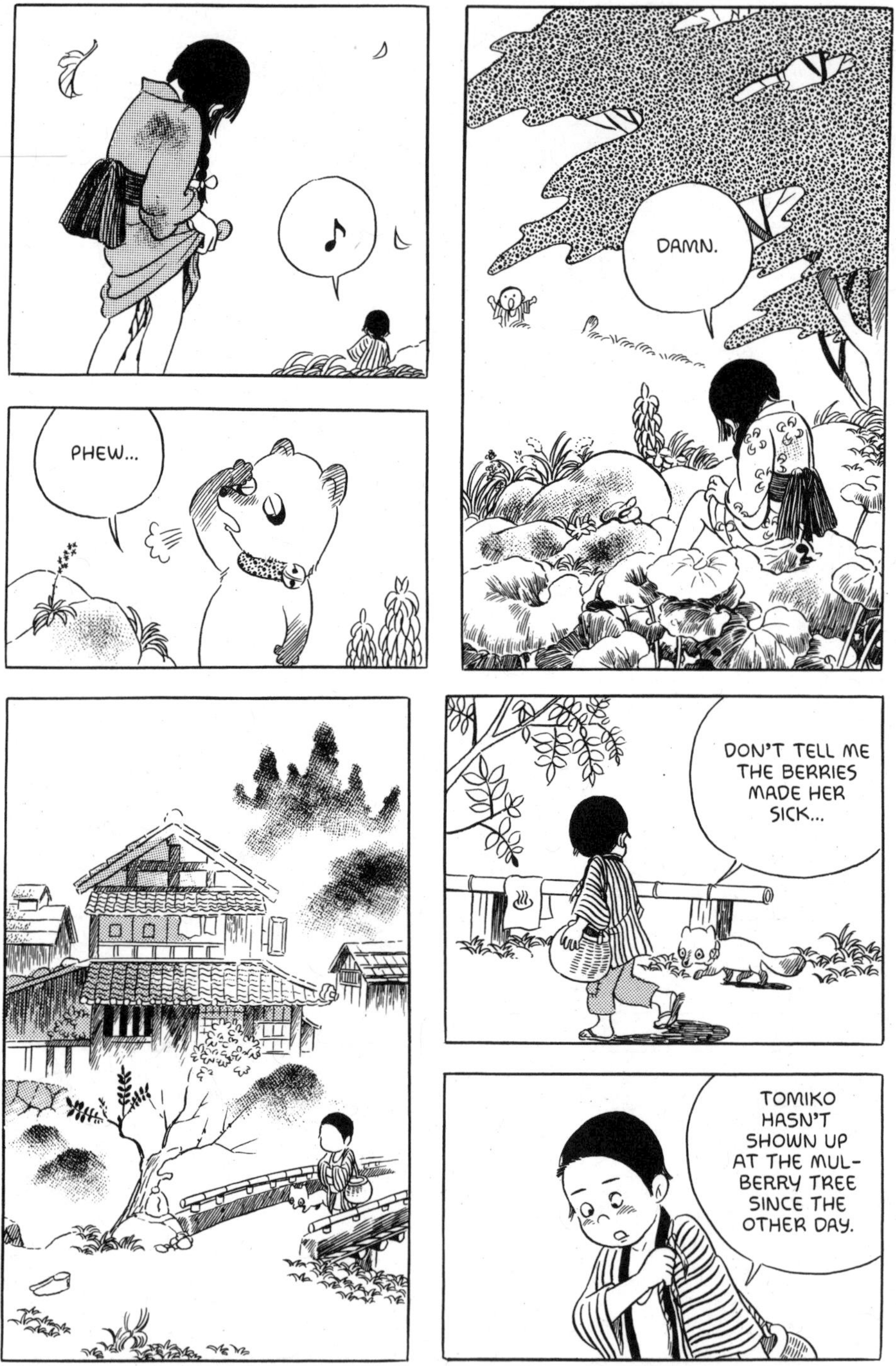
♪
PHEW...
DAMN.
DON'T TELL ME THE BERRIES MADE HER SICK...
TOMIKO HASN'T SHOWN UP AT THE MUL-BERRY TREE SINCE THE OTHER DAY.

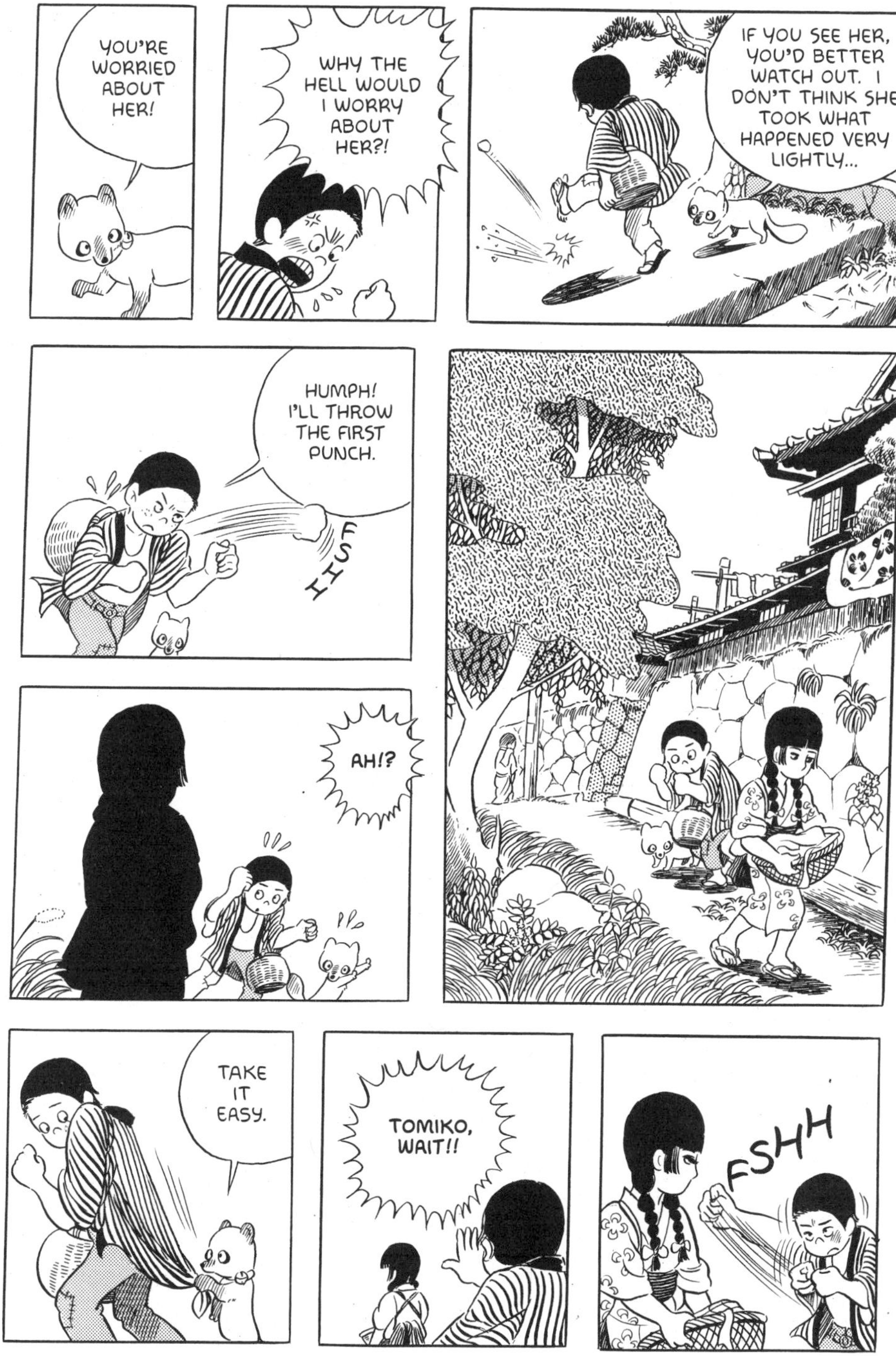
YOU'RE WORRIED ABOUT HER!
WHY THE HELL WOULD I WORRY ABOUT HER?!
IF YOU SEE HER, YOU'D BETTER WATCH OUT. I DON'T THINK SHE TOOK WHAT HAPPENED VERY LIGHTLY...
HUMPH! I'LL THROW THE FIRST PUNCH.
FSHH
AH!?
TAKE IT EASY.
TOMIKO, WAIT!!
FSHH

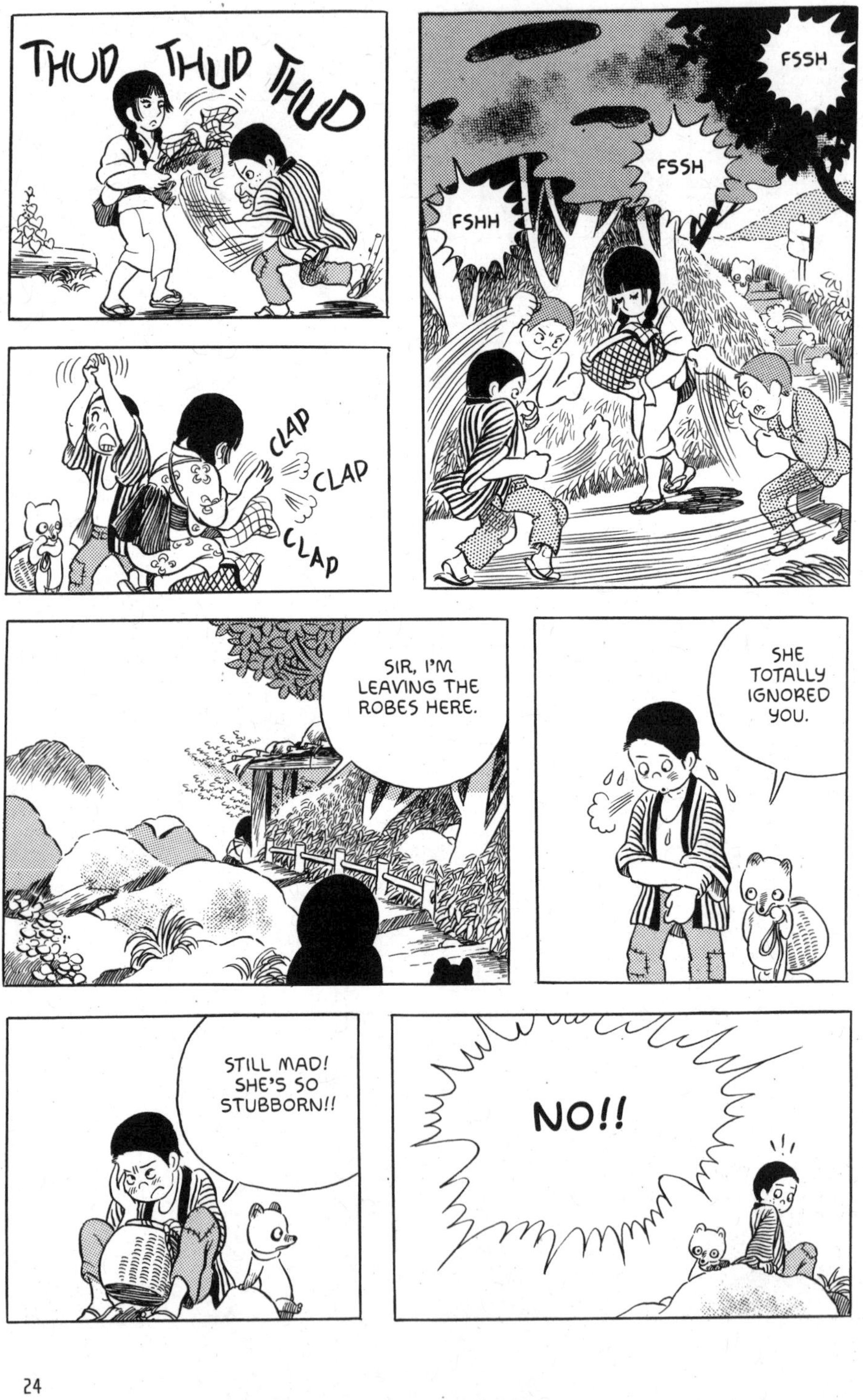
THUD THUD THUD
FSSH
FSSH
FSHH
CLAP CLAP CLAP
SIR, I'M LEAVING THE ROBES HERE.
SHE TOTALLY IGNORED YOU.
STILL MAD! SHE'S SO STUBBORN!!
NO!!

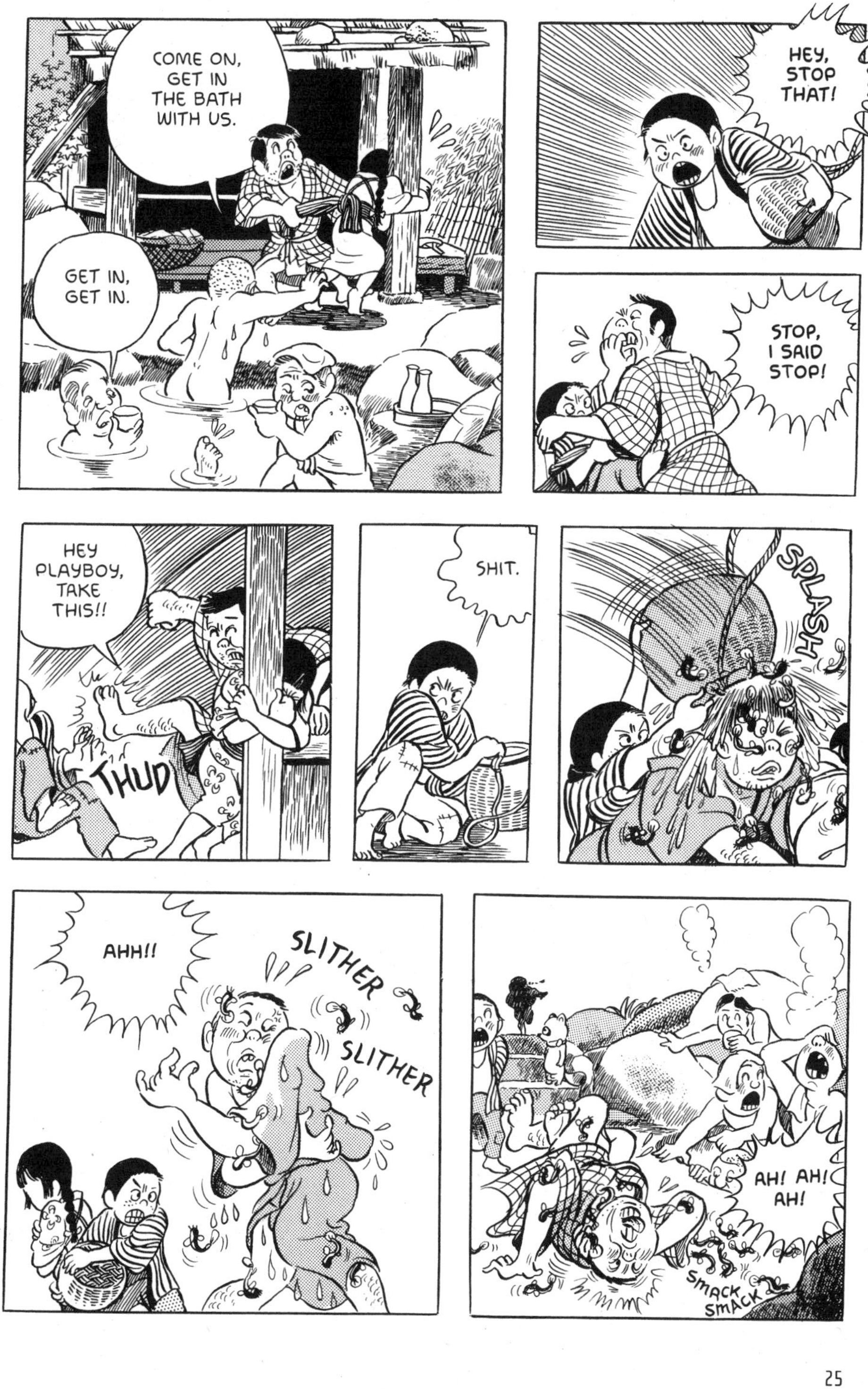
COME ON, GET IN THE BATH WITH US.
GET IN, GET IN.
HEY, STOP THAT!
STOP, I SAID STOP!
HEY PLAYBOY, TAKE THIS!!
THUD
SHIT.
SPLASH
AHH!!
SLITHER
SLITHER
AH! AH! AH!
SMACK SMACK

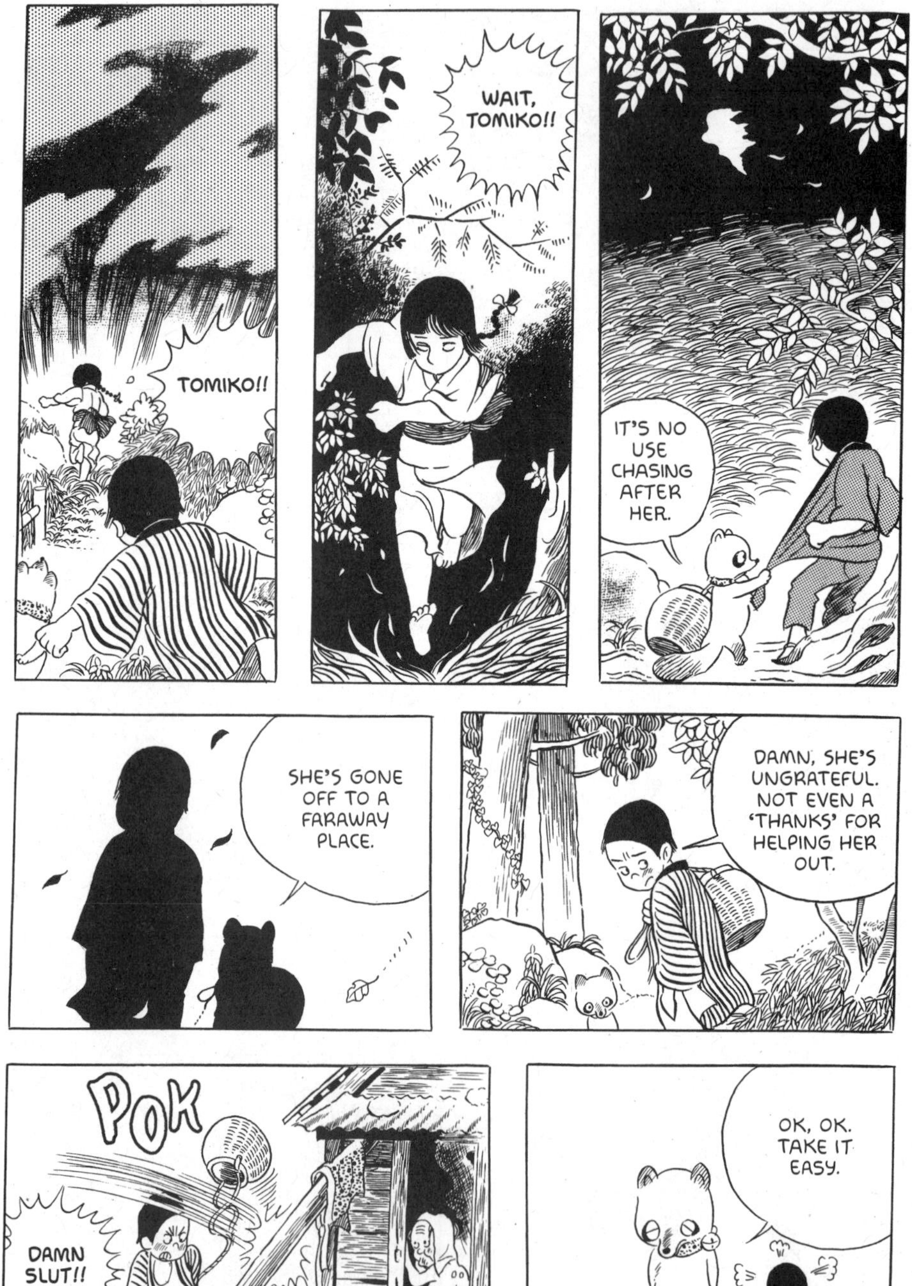
TOMIKO!!
WAIT, TOMIKO!!
IT'S NO USE CHASING AFTER HER.
SHE'S GONE OFF TO A FARAWAY PLACE.
DAMN, SHE'S UNGRATEFUL. NOT EVEN A 'THANKS' FOR HELPING HER OUT.
POK
DAMN SLUT!!
OK, OK. TAKE IT EASY.

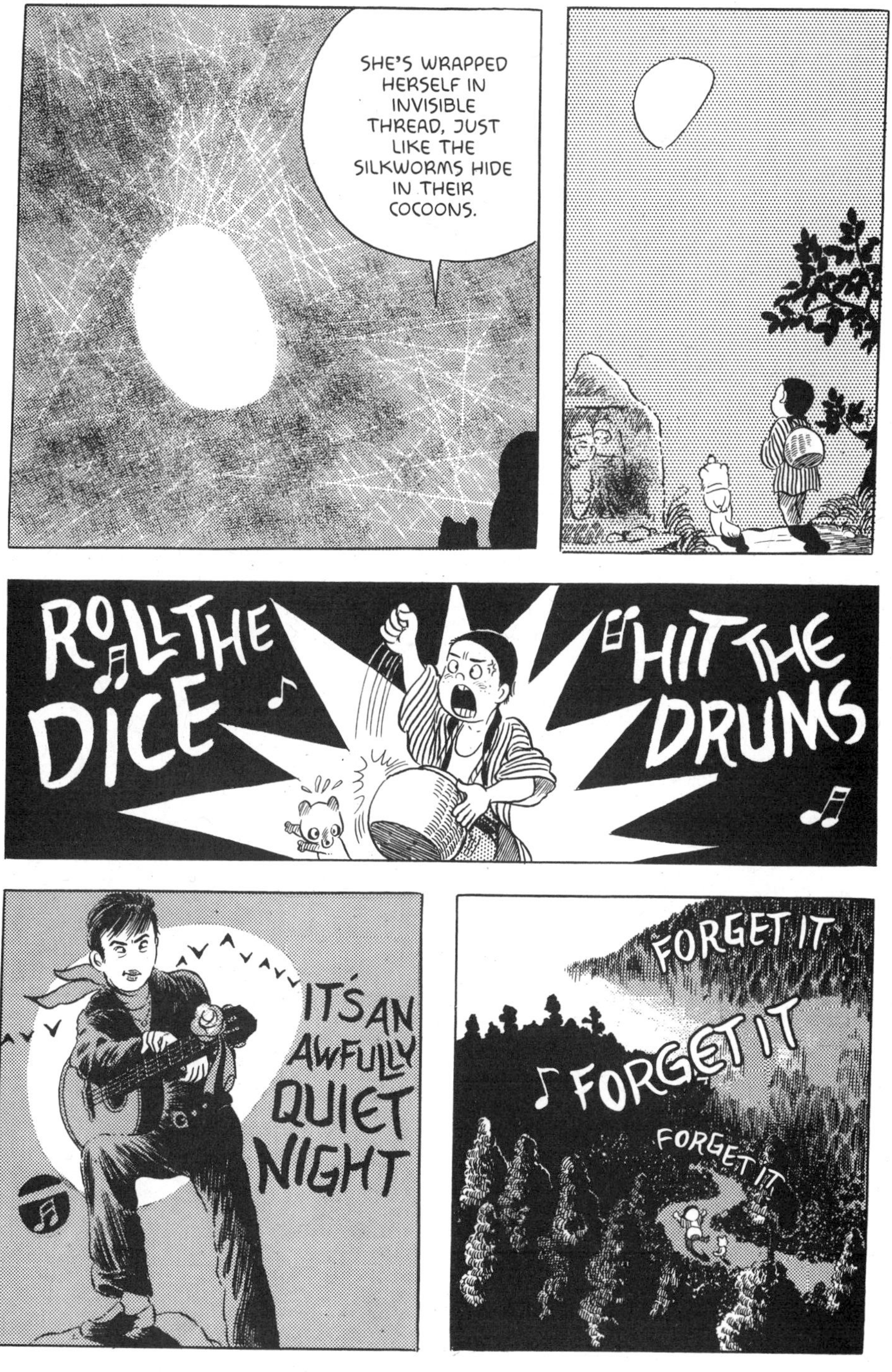
SHE'S WRAPPED HERSELF IN INVISIBLE THREAD, JUST LIKE THE SILKWORMS HIDE IN THEIR COCOONS.
ROLL THE DICE
HIT THE DRUMS
IT'S AN AWFULLY QUIET NIGHT
FORGET IT
FORGET IT
FORGET IT

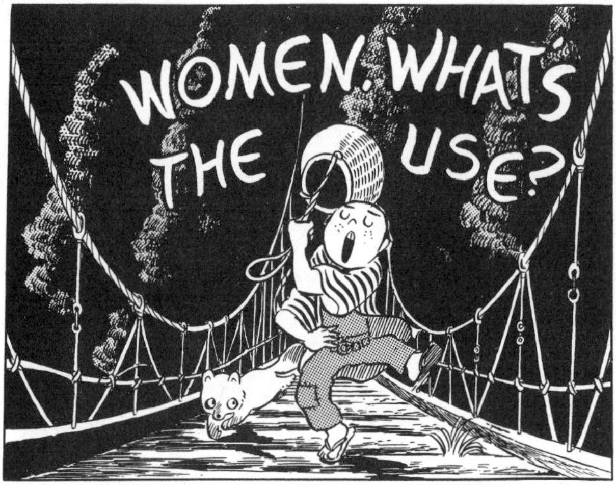
WOMEN, WHAT'S THE USE?

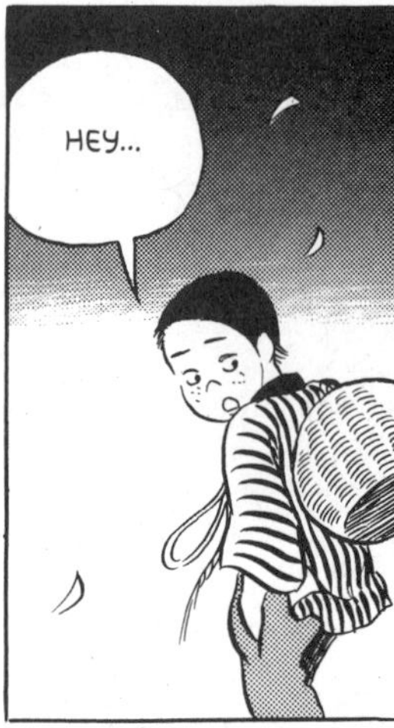
HEY...

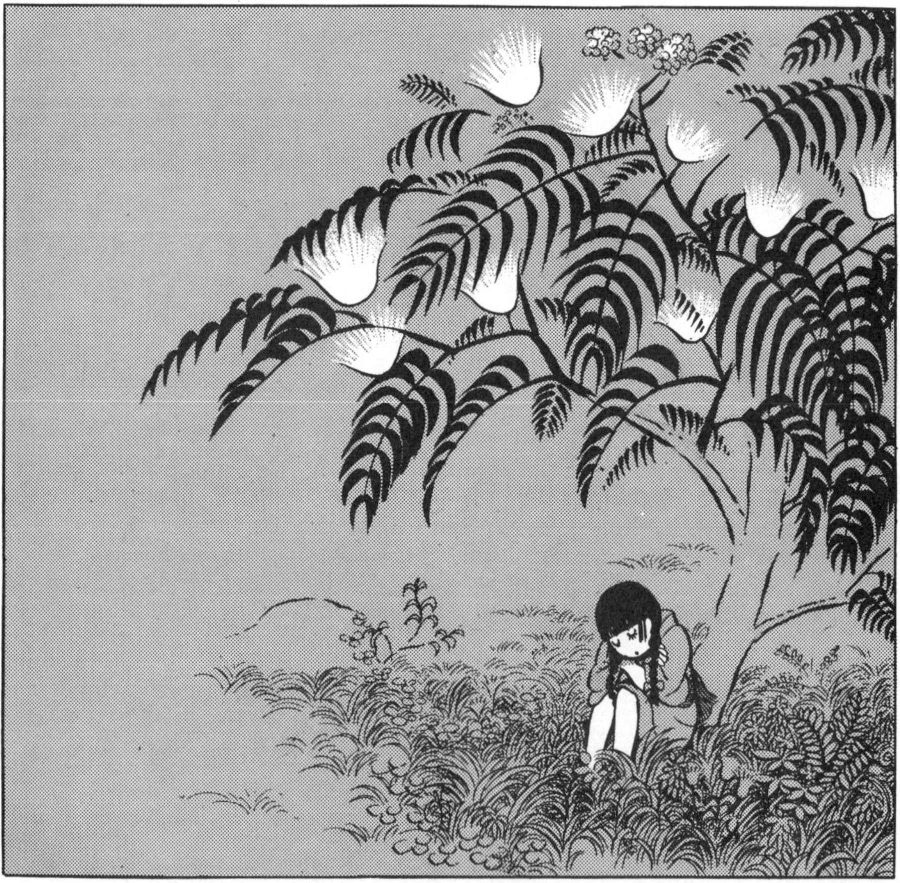

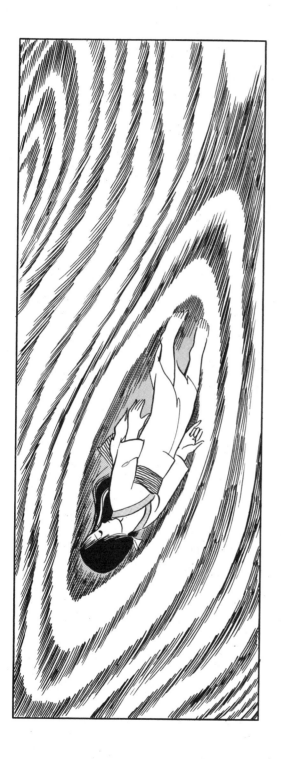

ECHO

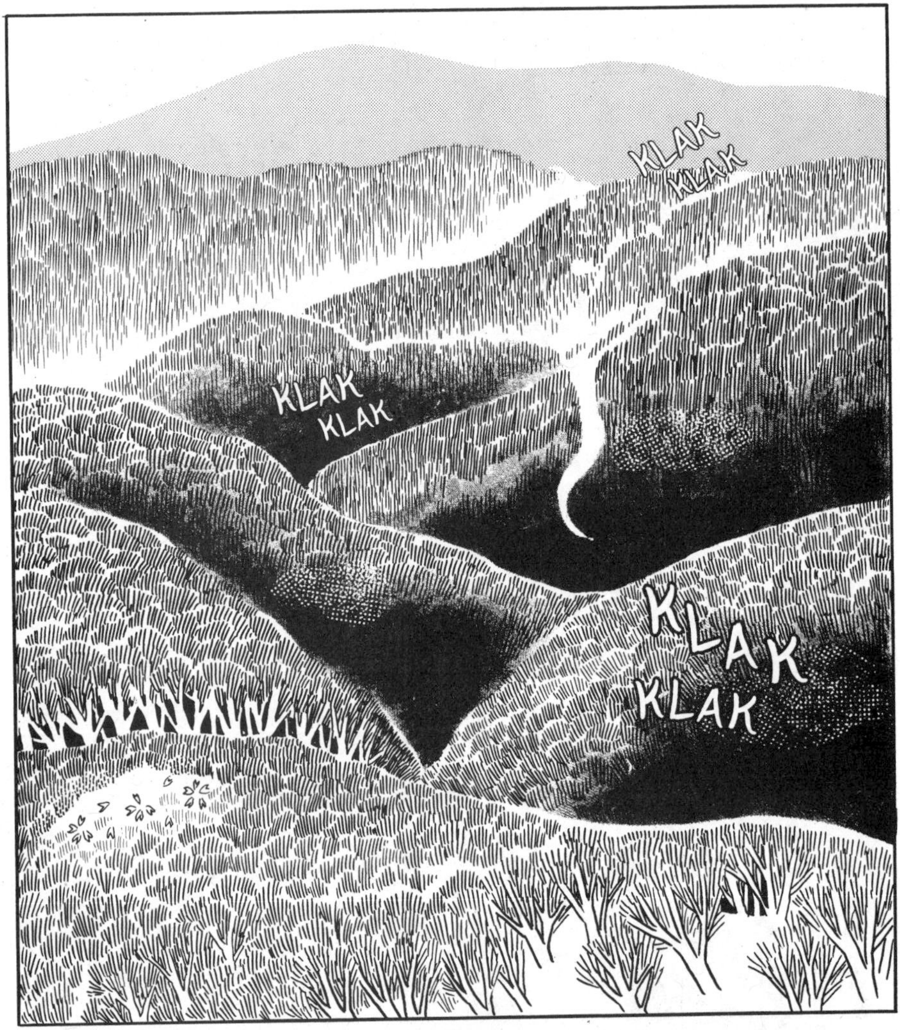
KLAK
KLAK
KLAK
KLAK
KLAK
KLAK

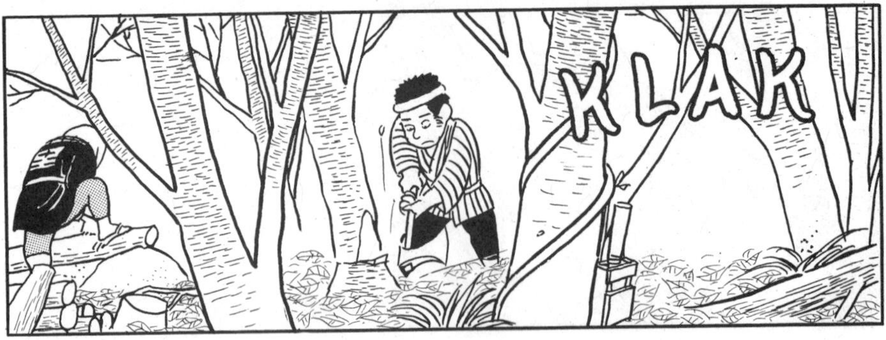
KLAK

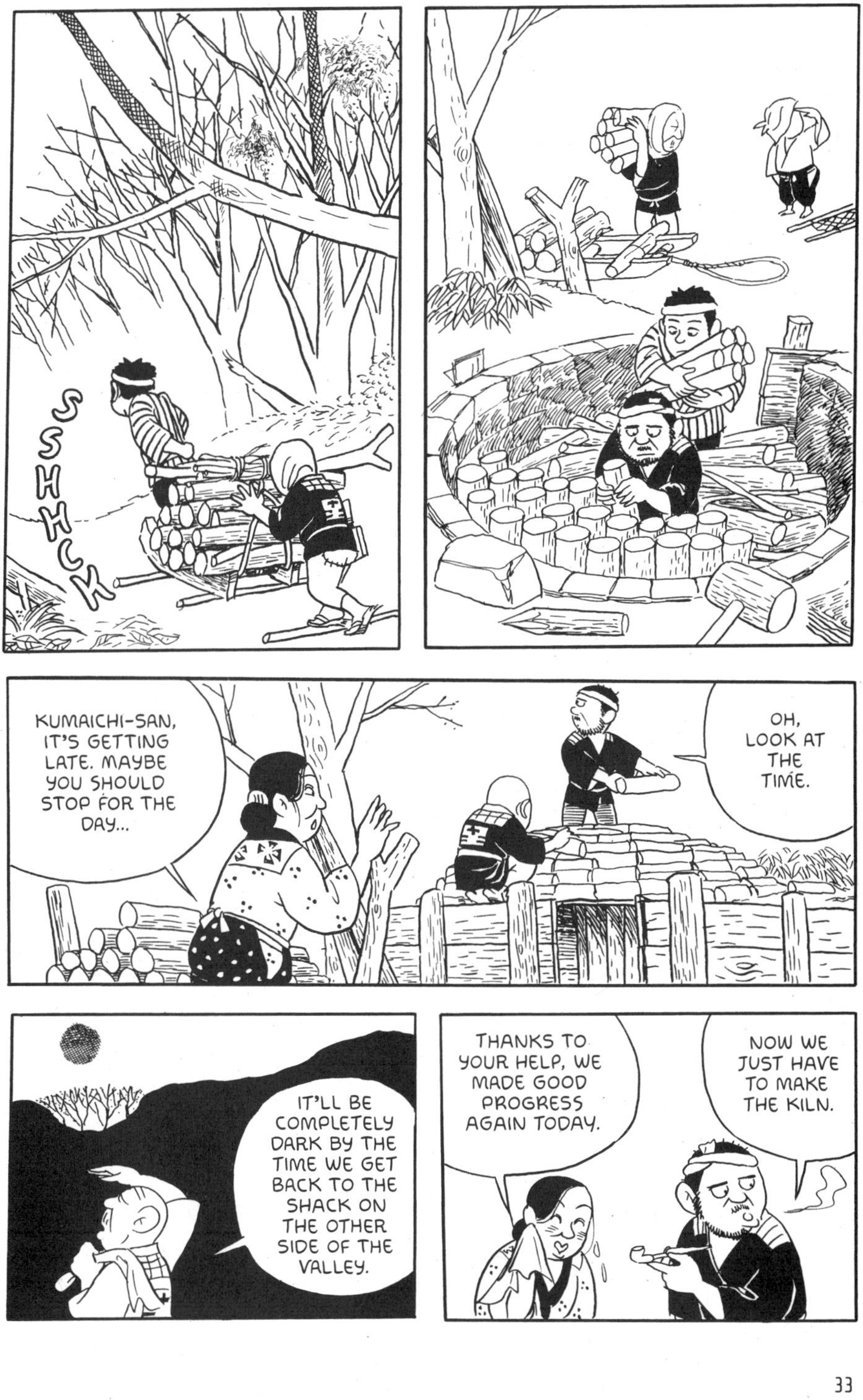
SSHCK
KUMAICHI-SAN, IT'S GETTING LATE. MAYBE YOU SHOULD STOP FOR THE DAY...
OH, LOOK AT THE TIME.
IT'LL BE COMPLETELY DARK BY THE TIME WE GET BACK TO THE SHACK ON THE OTHER SIDE OF THE VALLEY.
THANKS TO YOUR HELP, WE MADE GOOD PROGRESS AGAIN TODAY.
NOW WE JUST HAVE TO MAKE THE KILN.

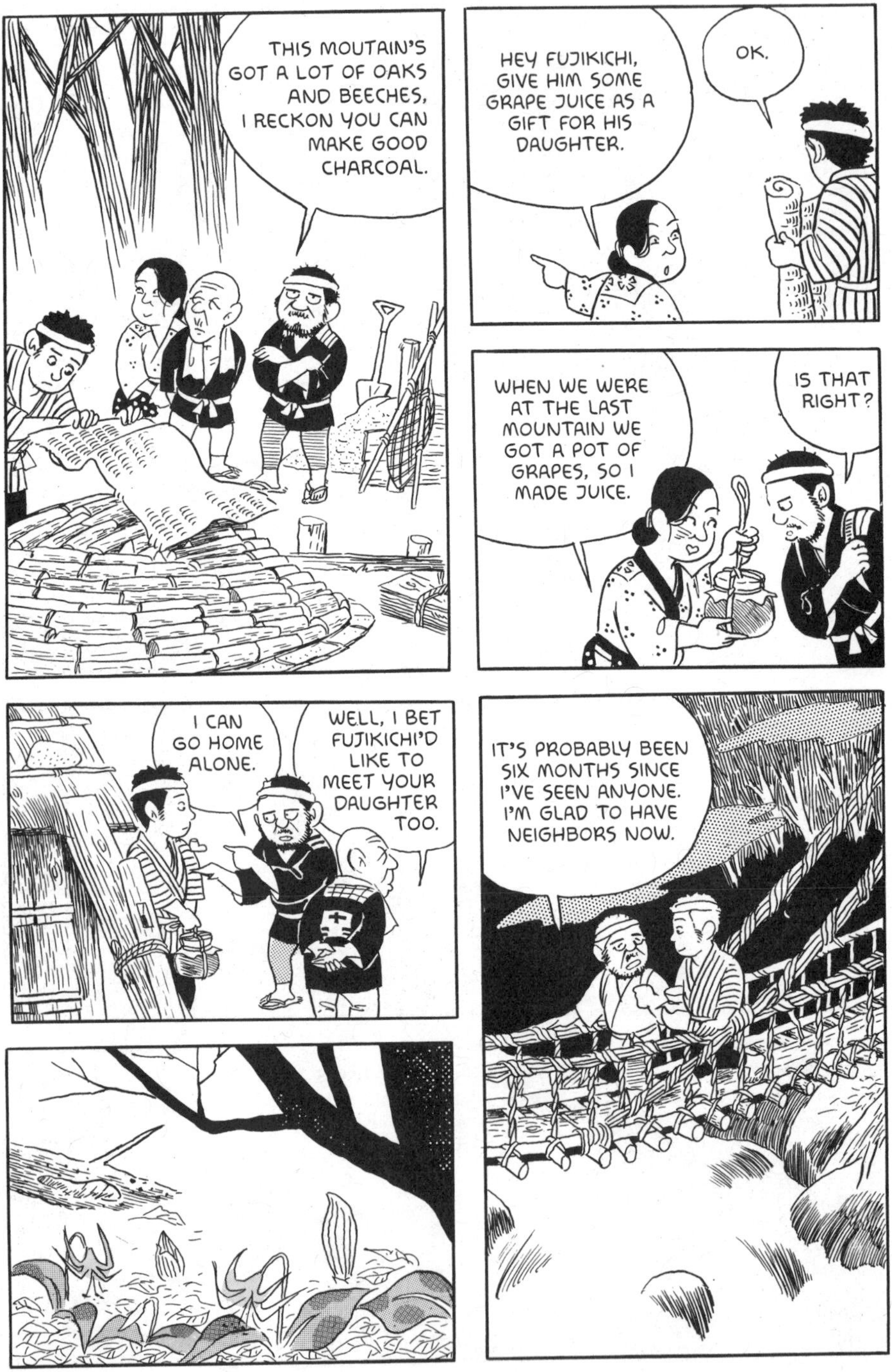
THIS MOUTAIN'S GOT A LOT OF OAKS AND BEECHES, I RECKON YOU CAN MAKE GOOD CHARCOAL.
HEY FUJIKICHI, GIVE HIM SOME GRAPE JUICE AS A GIFT FOR HIS DAUGHTER.
OK.
WHEN WE WERE AT THE LAST MOUNTAIN WE GOT A POT OF GRAPES, SO I MADE JUICE.
IS THAT RIGHT?
I CAN GO HOME ALONE.
WELL, I BET FUJIKICHI'D LIKE TO MEET YOUR DAUGHTER TOO.
IT'S PROBABLY BEEN SIX MONTHS SINCE I'VE SEEN ANYONE. I'M GLAD TO HAVE NEIGHBORS NOW.

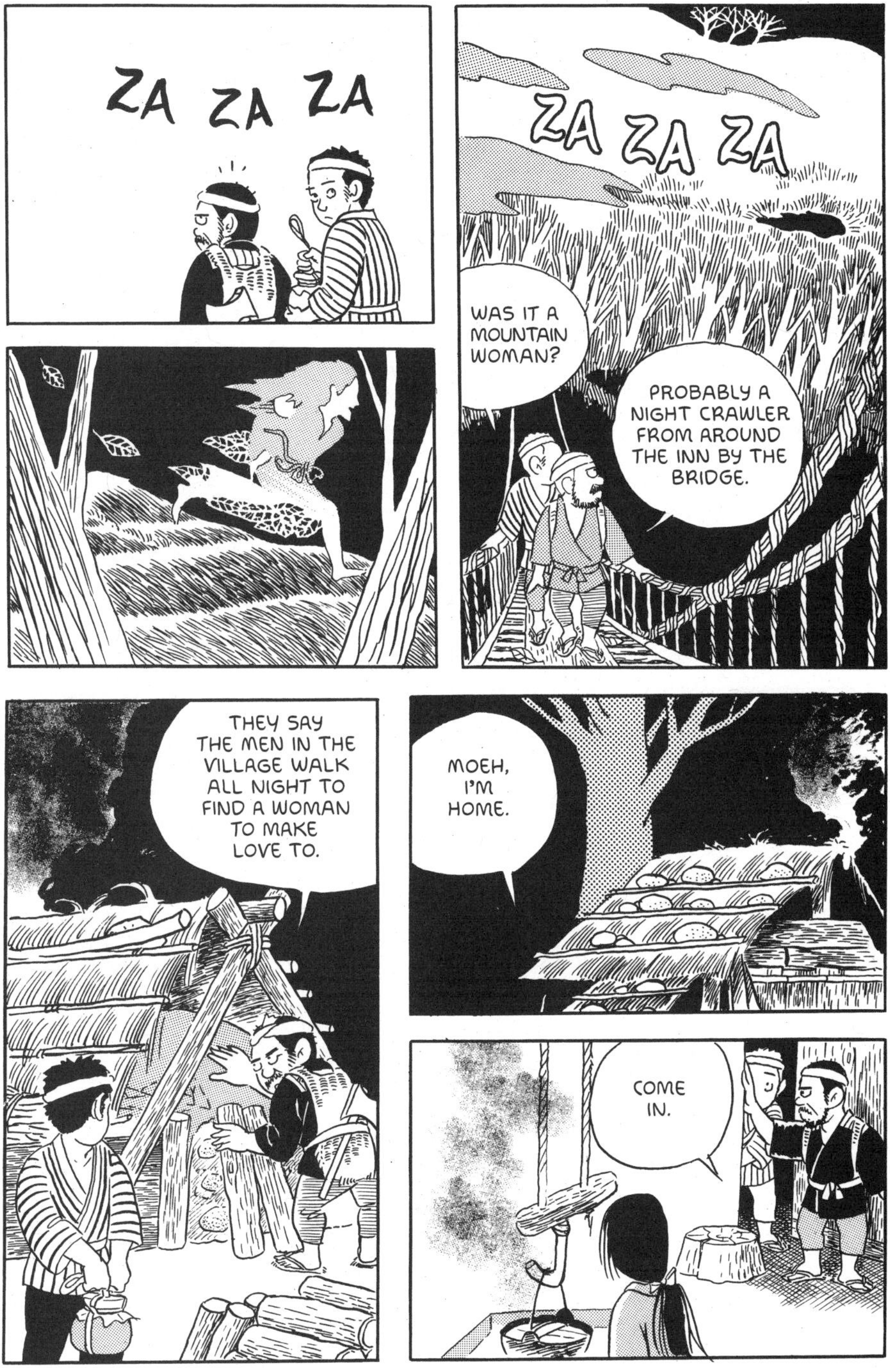
ZA ZA ZA
ZA ZA ZA
WAS IT A MOUNTAIN WOMAN?
PROBABLY A NIGHT CRAWLER FROM AROUND THE INN BY THE BRIDGE.
THEY SAY THE MEN IN THE VILLAGE WALK ALL NIGHT TO FIND A WOMAN TO MAKE LOVE TO.
MOEH, I'M HOME.
COME IN.

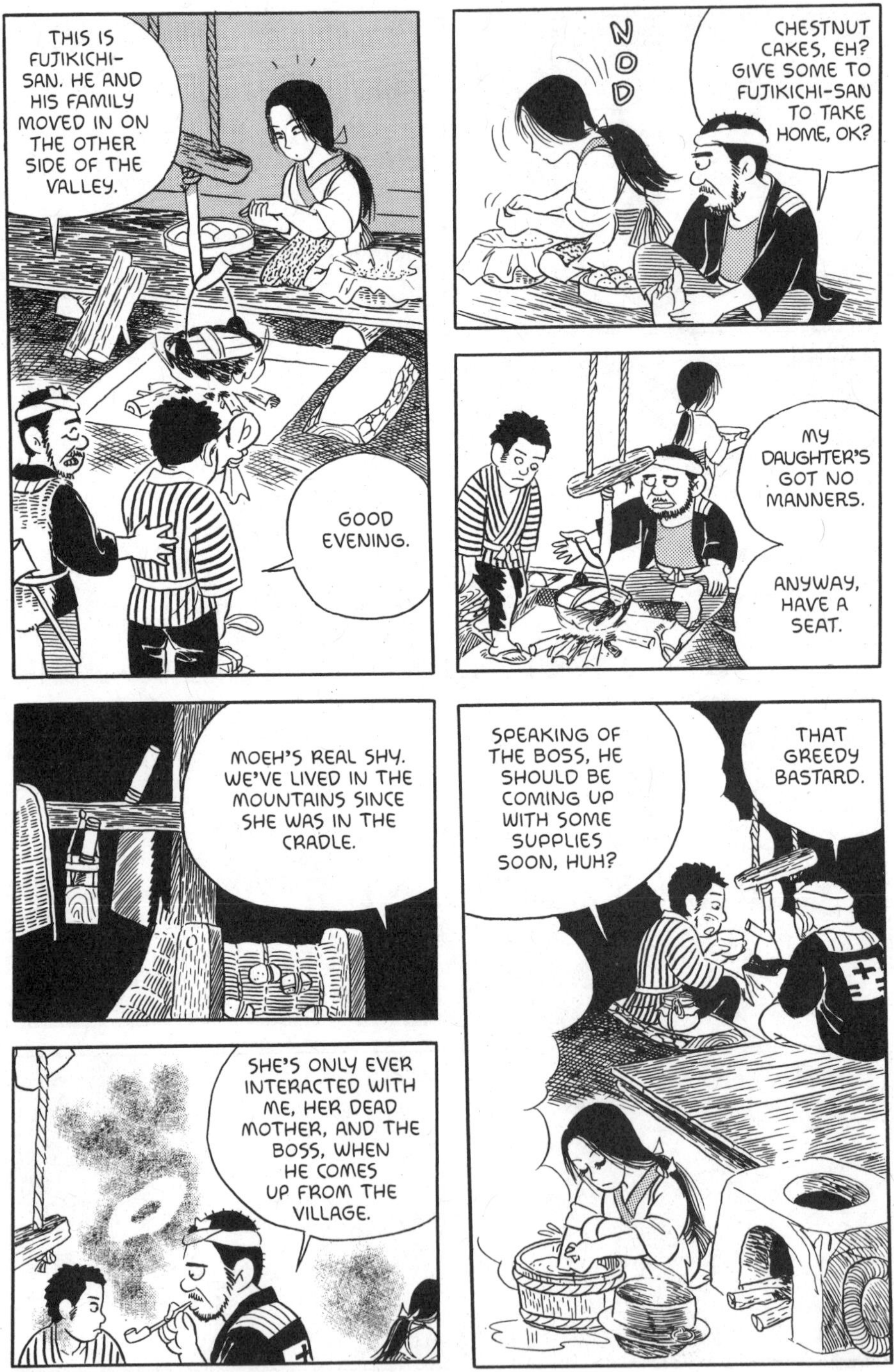
THIS IS FUJIKICHI-SAN. HE AND HIS FAMILY MOVED IN ON THE OTHER SIDE OF THE VALLEY.
GOOD EVENING.
NOD
CHESTNUT CAKES, EH? GIVE SOME TO FUJIKICHI-SAN TO TAKE HOME, OK?
MY DAUGHTER'S GOT NO MANNERS.
ANYWAY, HAVE A SEAT.
MOEH'S REAL SHY. WE'VE LIVED IN THE MOUNTAINS SINCE SHE WAS IN THE CRADLE.
SHE'S ONLY EVER INTERACTED WITH ME, HER DEAD MOTHER, AND THE BOSS, WHEN HE COMES UP FROM THE VILLAGE.
SPEAKING OF THE BOSS, HE SHOULD BE COMING UP WITH SOME SUPPLIES SOON, HUH?
THAT GREEDY BASTARD.

HAVEN'T HEARD A PEEP FROM HIM SINCE LAST FALL WHEN HE DROPPED OFF SOME MILLET AND MISO.

WE WOULD'VE STARVED LONG AGO IF IT WEREN'T FOR THE CHESTNUT TREE.

THAT BOSS IS A REAL MISER...

MOEH, WHAT'RE YOU FUSSING WITH OVER THERE? COME SIT WITH US.

I'M PREPARING CHESTNUT POWDER FOR TOMORROW.

HERE, GRAPE JUICE. IT'S FOR YOU.

THANK YOU...

YOU'RE WELCOME!!

SHE'S EMBARRASSED BECAUSE YOU'RE THE FIRST YOUNG MAN SHE'S EVER MET.

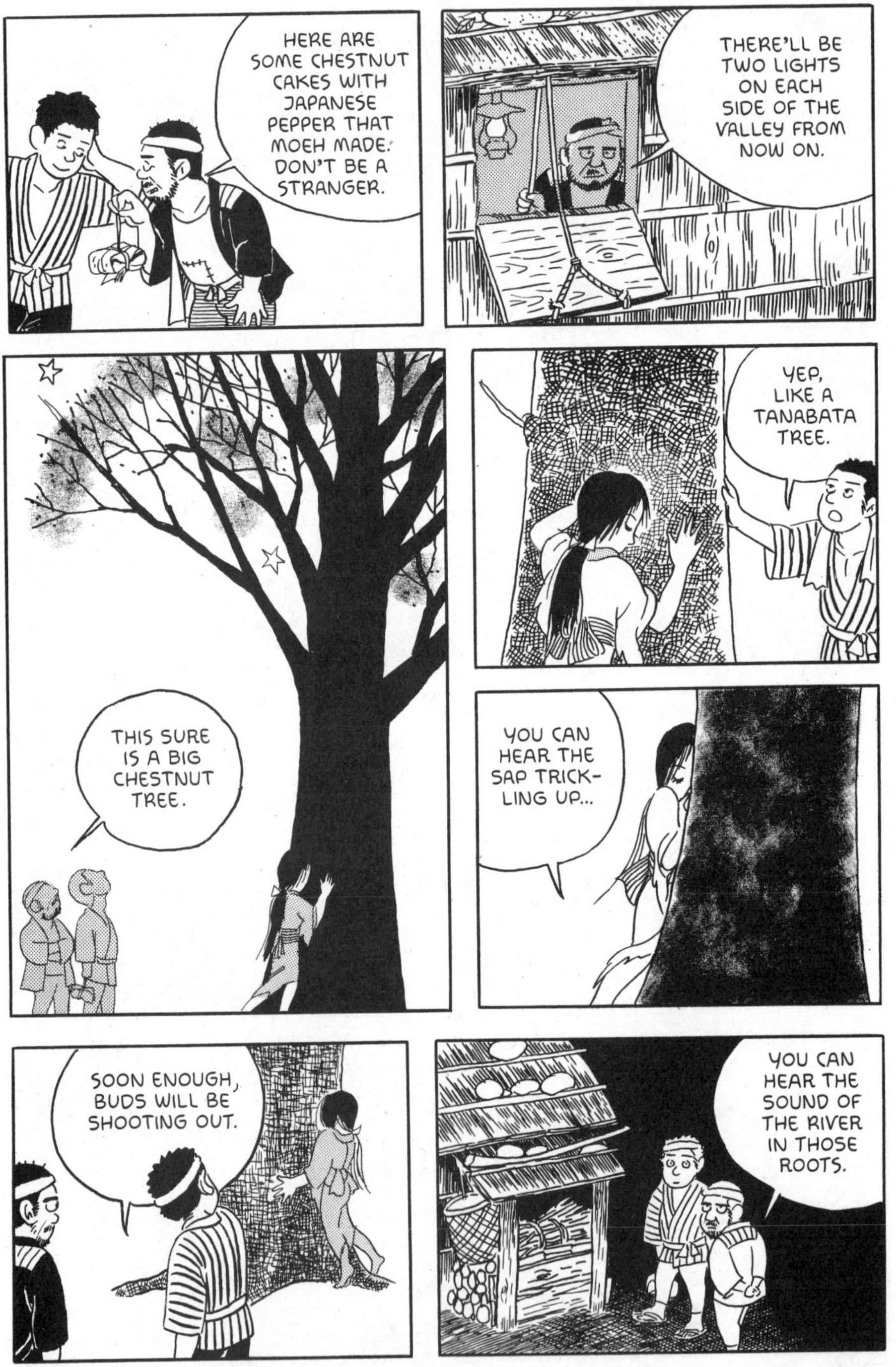
HERE ARE SOME CHESTNUT CAKES WITH JAPANESE PEPPER THAT MOEH MADE. DON'T BE A STRANGER.
THERE'LL BE TWO LIGHTS ON EACH SIDE OF THE VALLEY FROM NOW ON.
THIS SURE IS A BIG CHESTNUT TREE.
YEP, LIKE A TANABATA TREE.
YOU CAN HEAR THE SAP TRICK-LING UP...
SOON ENOUGH, BUDS WILL BE SHOOTING OUT.
YOU CAN HEAR THE SOUND OF THE RIVER IN THOSE ROOTS.

ZZz
TRICKLE
TRICKLE
SSZZ

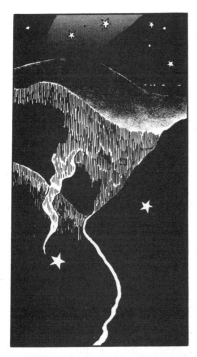

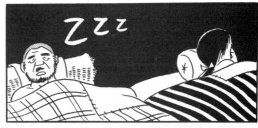

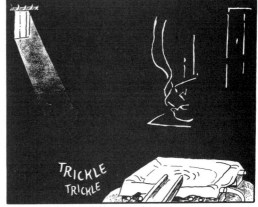

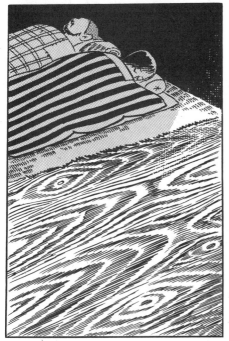

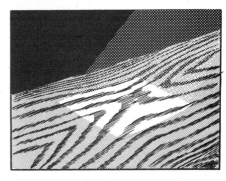

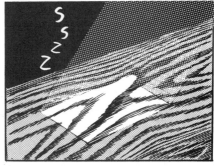

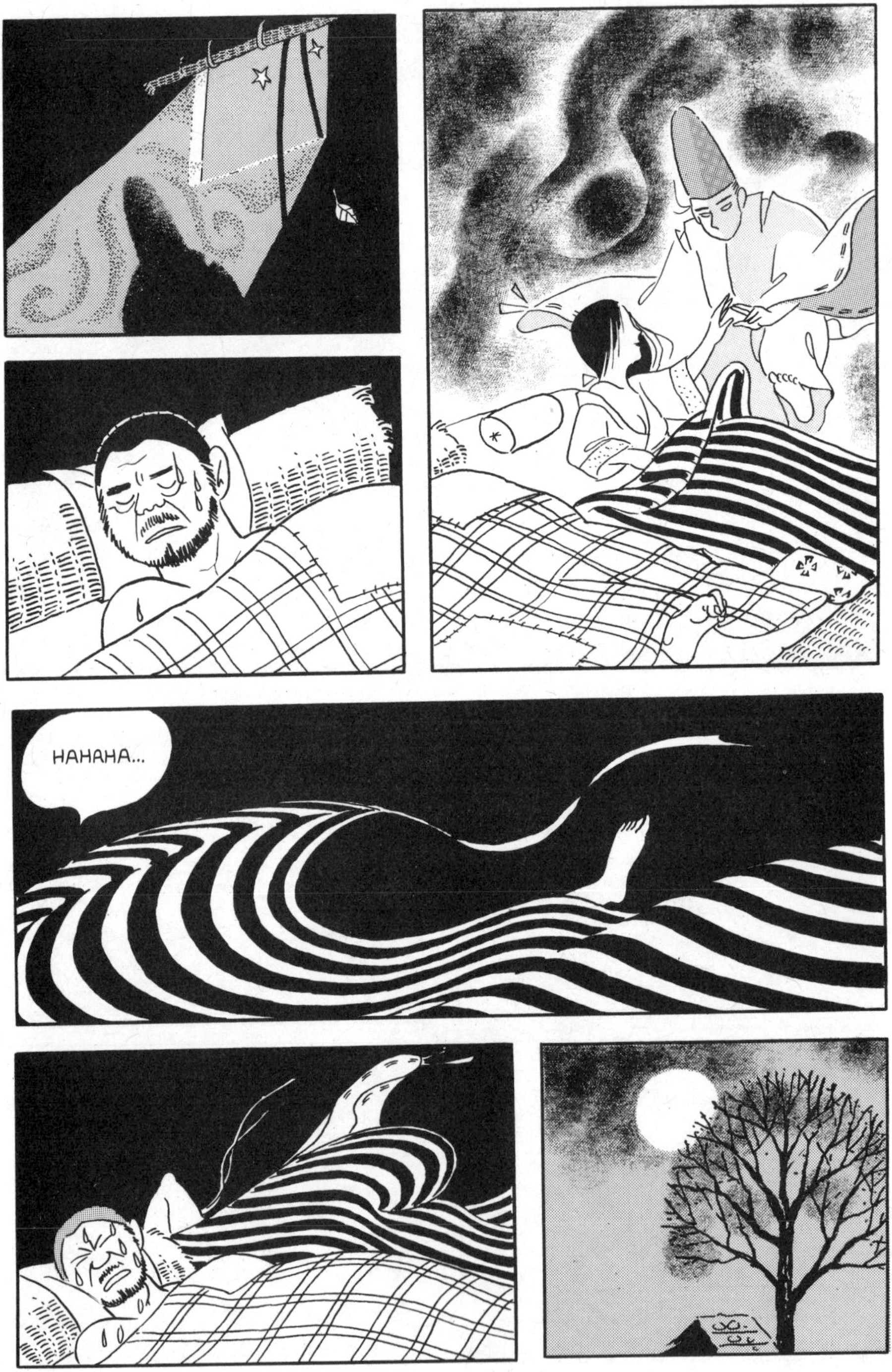
HAHAHA...

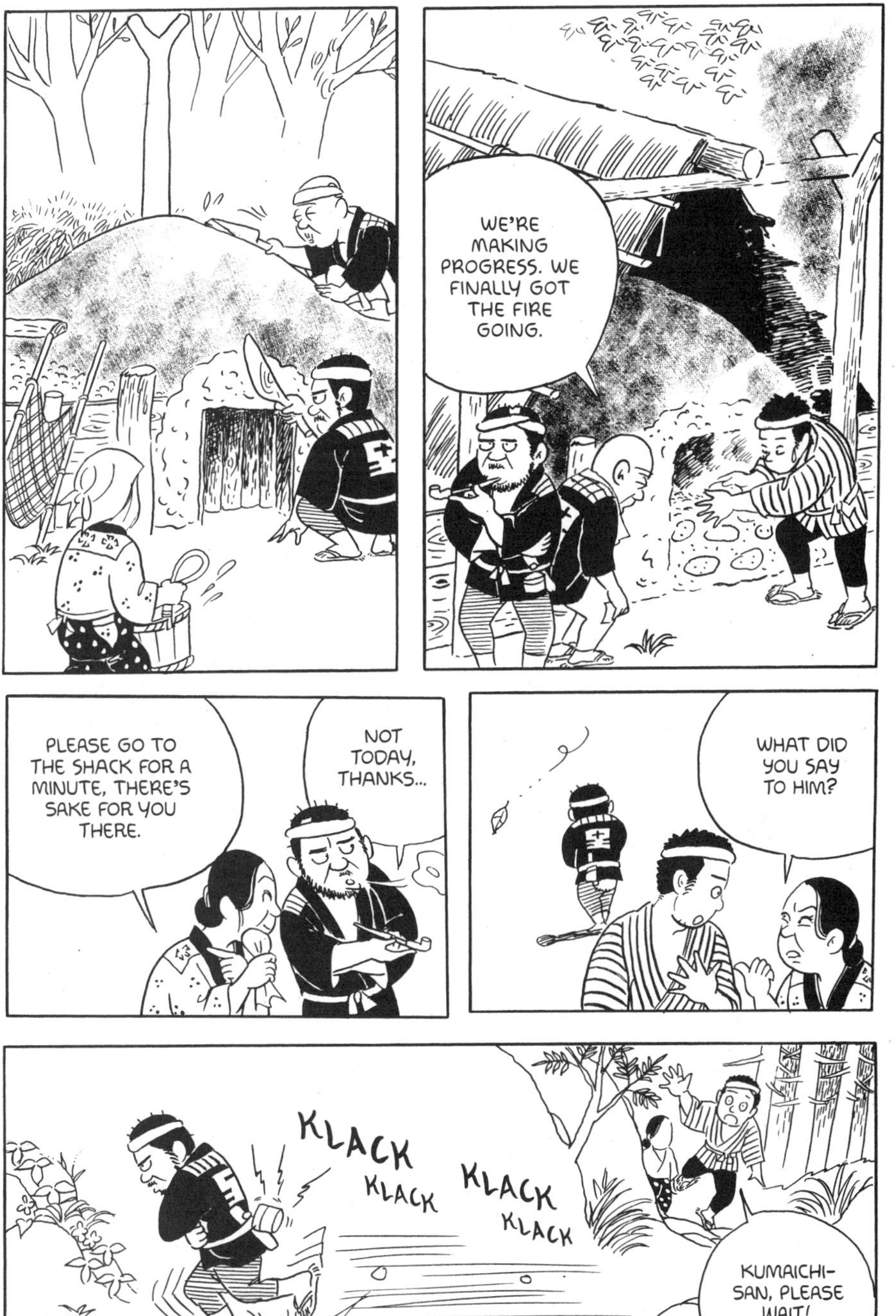
WE'RE MAKING PROGRESS. WE FINALLY GOT THE FIRE GOING.
PLEASE GO TO THE SHACK FOR A MINUTE, THERE'S SAKE FOR YOU THERE.
NOT TODAY, THANKS...
WHAT DID YOU SAY TO HIM?
KLACK KLACK KLACK KLACK
KUMAICHI-SAN, PLEASE WAIT!

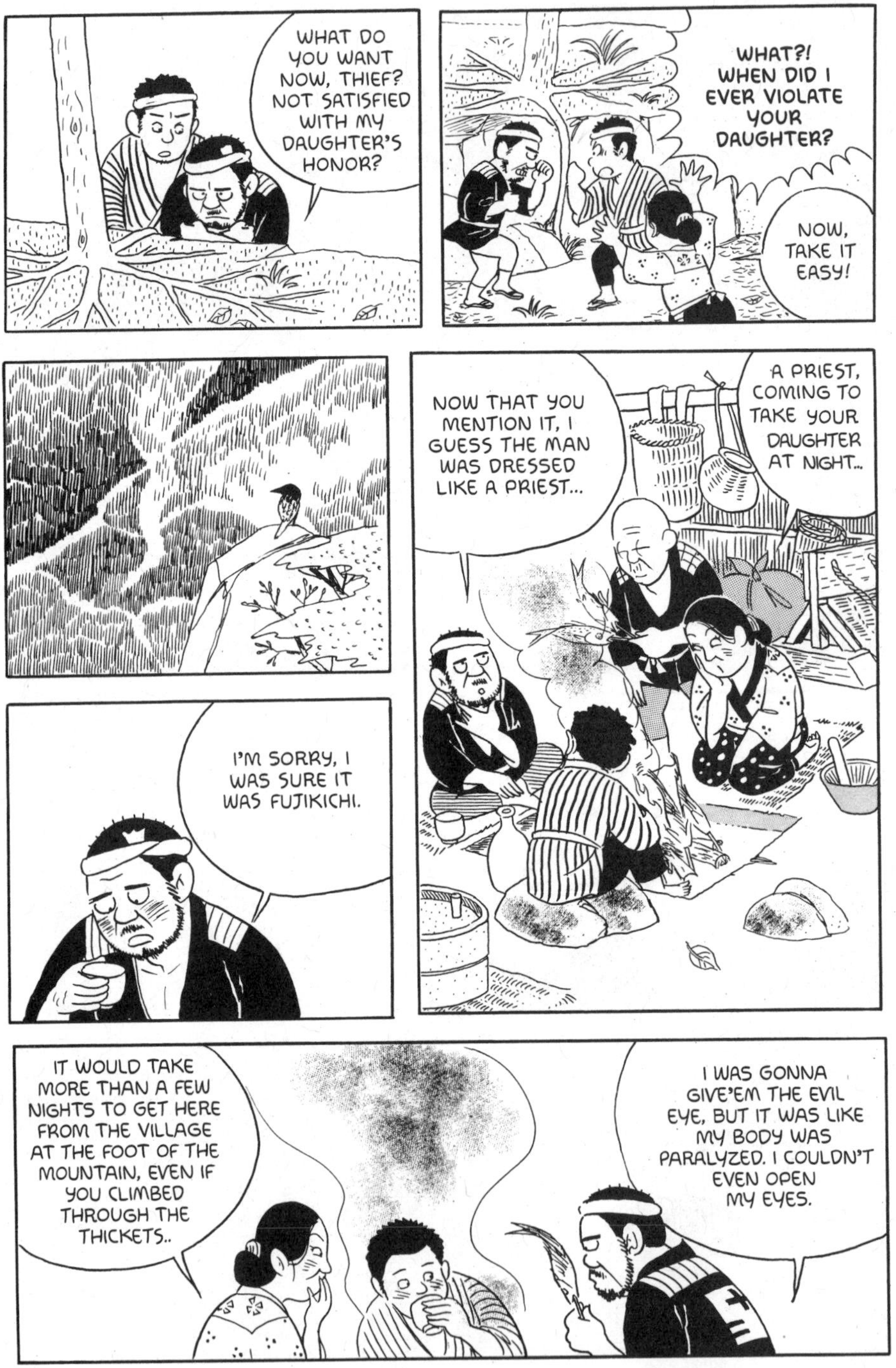
WHAT DO YOU WANT NOW, THIEF? NOT SATISFIED WITH MY DAUGHTER'S HONOR?
WHAT?! WHEN DID I EVER VIOLATE YOUR DAUGHTER?
NOW, TAKE IT EASY!
NOW THAT YOU MENTION IT, I GUESS THE MAN WAS DRESSED LIKE A PRIEST...
A PRIEST, COMING TO TAKE YOUR DAUGHTER AT NIGHT...
I'M SORRY, I WAS SURE IT WAS FUJIKICHI.
IT WOULD TAKE MORE THAN A FEW NIGHTS TO GET HERE FROM THE VILLAGE AT THE FOOT OF THE MOUNTAIN, EVEN IF YOU CLIMBED THROUGH THE THICKETS..
I WAS GONNA GIVE'EM THE EVIL EYE, BUT IT WAS LIKE MY BODY WAS PARALYZED. I COULDN'T EVEN OPEN MY EYES.

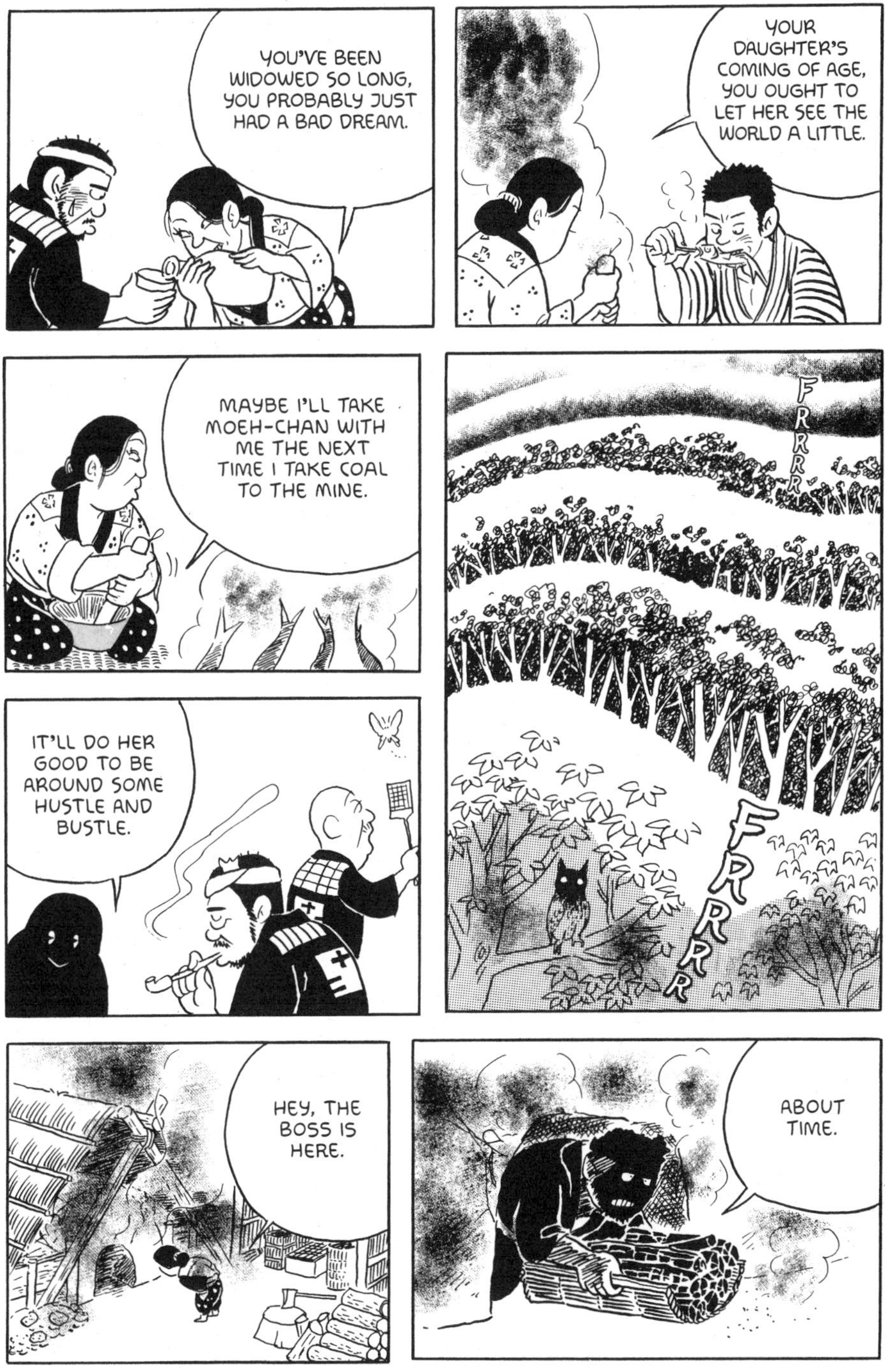
YOU'VE BEEN WIDOWED SO LONG, YOU PROBABLY JUST HAD A BAD DREAM.
YOUR DAUGHTER'S COMING OF AGE, YOU OUGHT TO LET HER SEE THE WORLD A LITTLE.
MAYBE I'LL TAKE MOEH-CHAN WITH ME THE NEXT TIME I TAKE COAL TO THE MINE.
IT'LL DO HER GOOD TO BE AROUND SOME HUSTLE AND BUSTLE.
FRRRR
FRRRR
HEY, THE BOSS IS HERE.
ABOUT TIME.

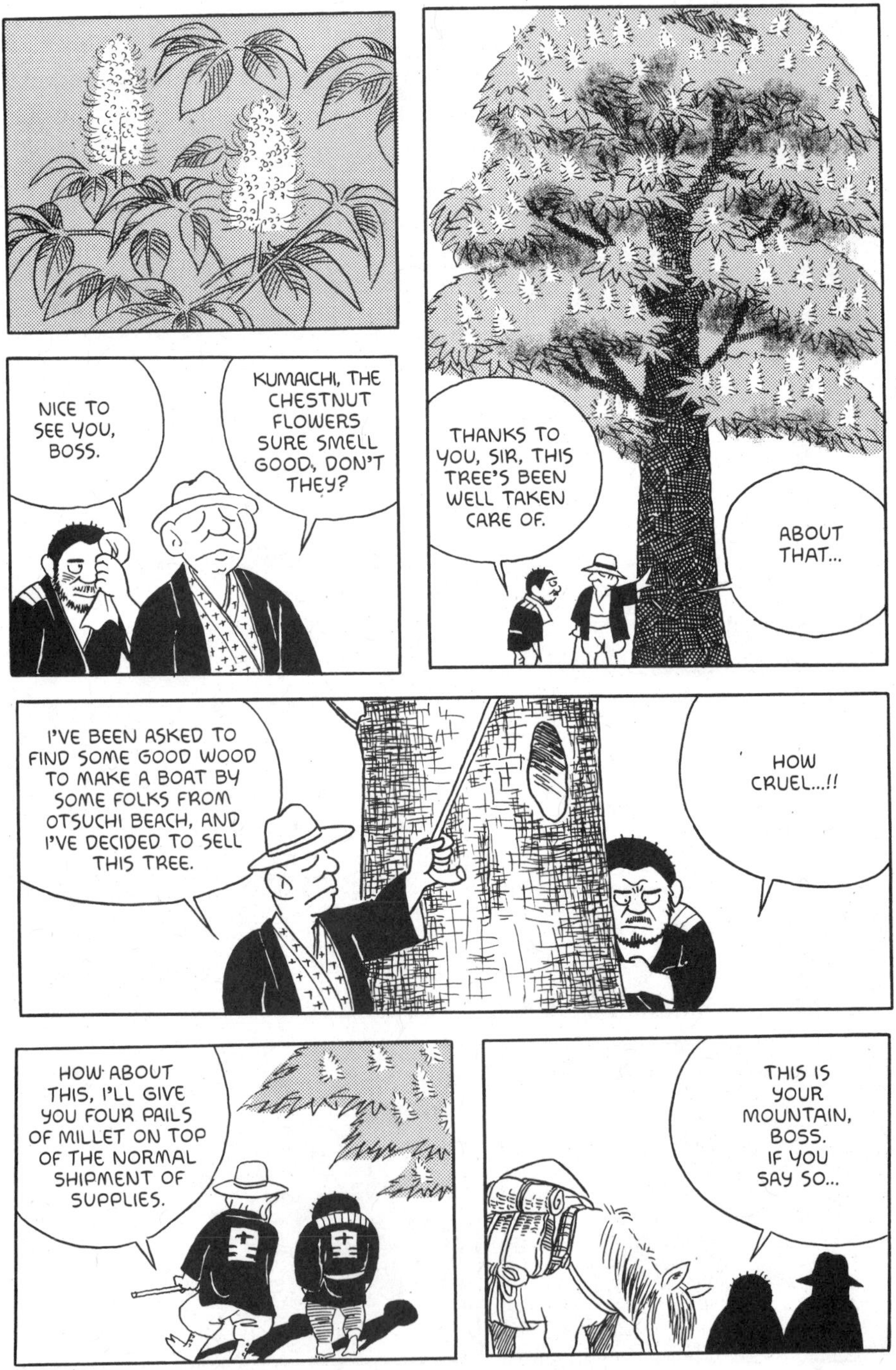
NICE TO SEE YOU, BOSS.
KUMAICHI, THE CHESTNUT FLOWERS SURE SMELL GOOD, DON'T THEY?
THANKS TO YOU, SIR, THIS TREE'S BEEN WELL TAKEN CARE OF.
ABOUT THAT...
I'VE BEEN ASKED TO FIND SOME GOOD WOOD TO MAKE A BOAT BY SOME FOLKS FROM OTSUCHI BEACH, AND I'VE DECIDED TO SELL THIS TREE.
HOW CRUEL...!!
HOW ABOUT THIS, I'LL GIVE YOU FOUR PAILS OF MILLET ON TOP OF THE NORMAL SHIPMENT OF SUPPLIES.
THIS IS YOUR MOUNTAIN, BOSS. IF YOU SAY SO...

LET'S GET TO WORK WHILE THE SUN IS STILL HIGH...

HAVEN'T SEEN YOUR DAUGHTER AROUND.

I'M HAVING HER TAKEN TO THE MINES TOMORROW TO PICK FLOWERS...

THEY SAY THE MINE'S DOING SO WELL PEOPLE BUY FLOWERS THERE.

ZSH ZSH ZSH

IF MOEH KNEW ABOUT THIS SHE'D BE IN TEARS...:

ZSH ZSH

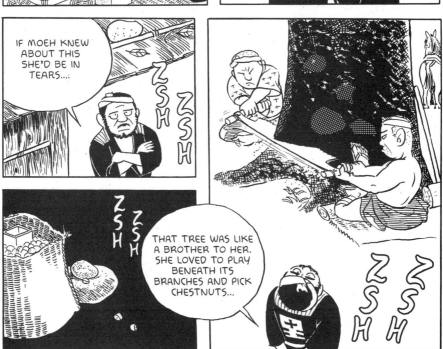

ZSH ZSH

THAT TREE WAS LIKE A BROTHER TO HER. SHE LOVED TO PLAY BENEATH ITS BRANCHES AND PICK CHESTNUTS...

ZSH ZSH

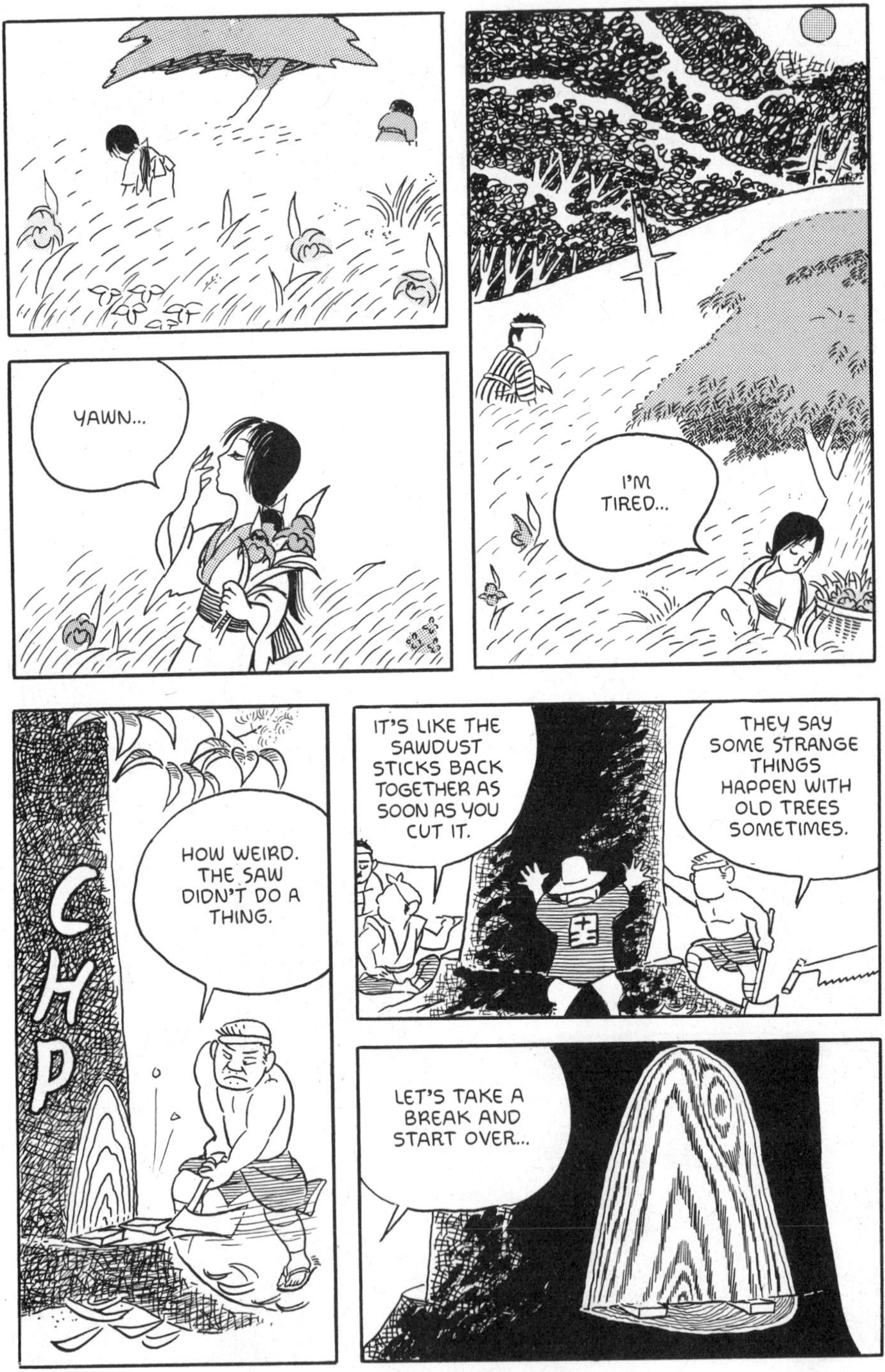
YAWN...
I'M TIRED...
CHP
HOW WEIRD. THE SAW DIDN'T DO A THING.
IT'S LIKE THE SAWDUST STICKS BACK TOGETHER AS SOON AS YOU CUT IT.
THEY SAY SOME STRANGE THINGS HAPPEN WITH OLD TREES SOMETIMES.
LET'S TAKE A BREAK AND START OVER...

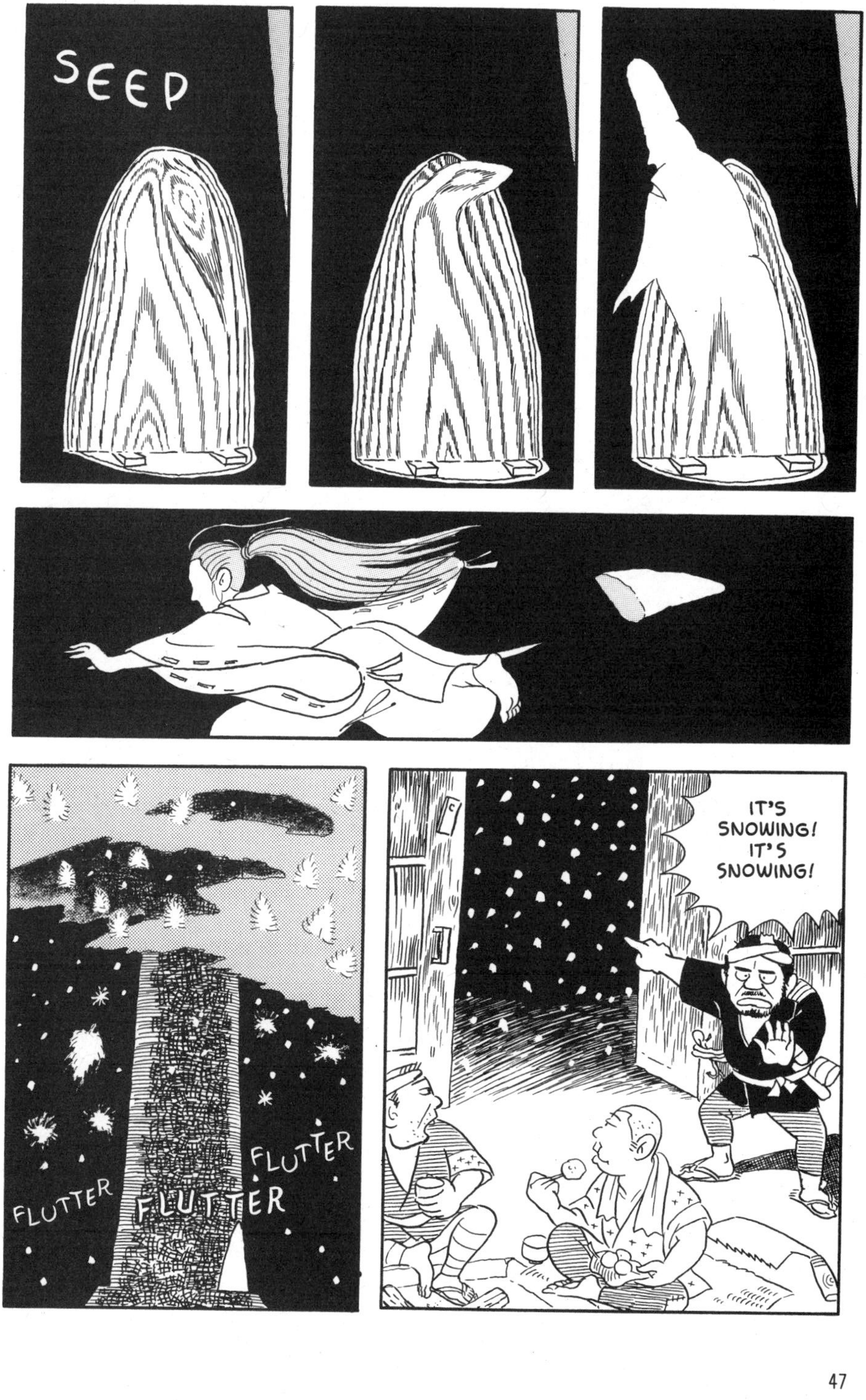
SEEP
FLUTTER
FLUTTER
FLUTTER
IT'S SNOWING! IT'S SNOWING!

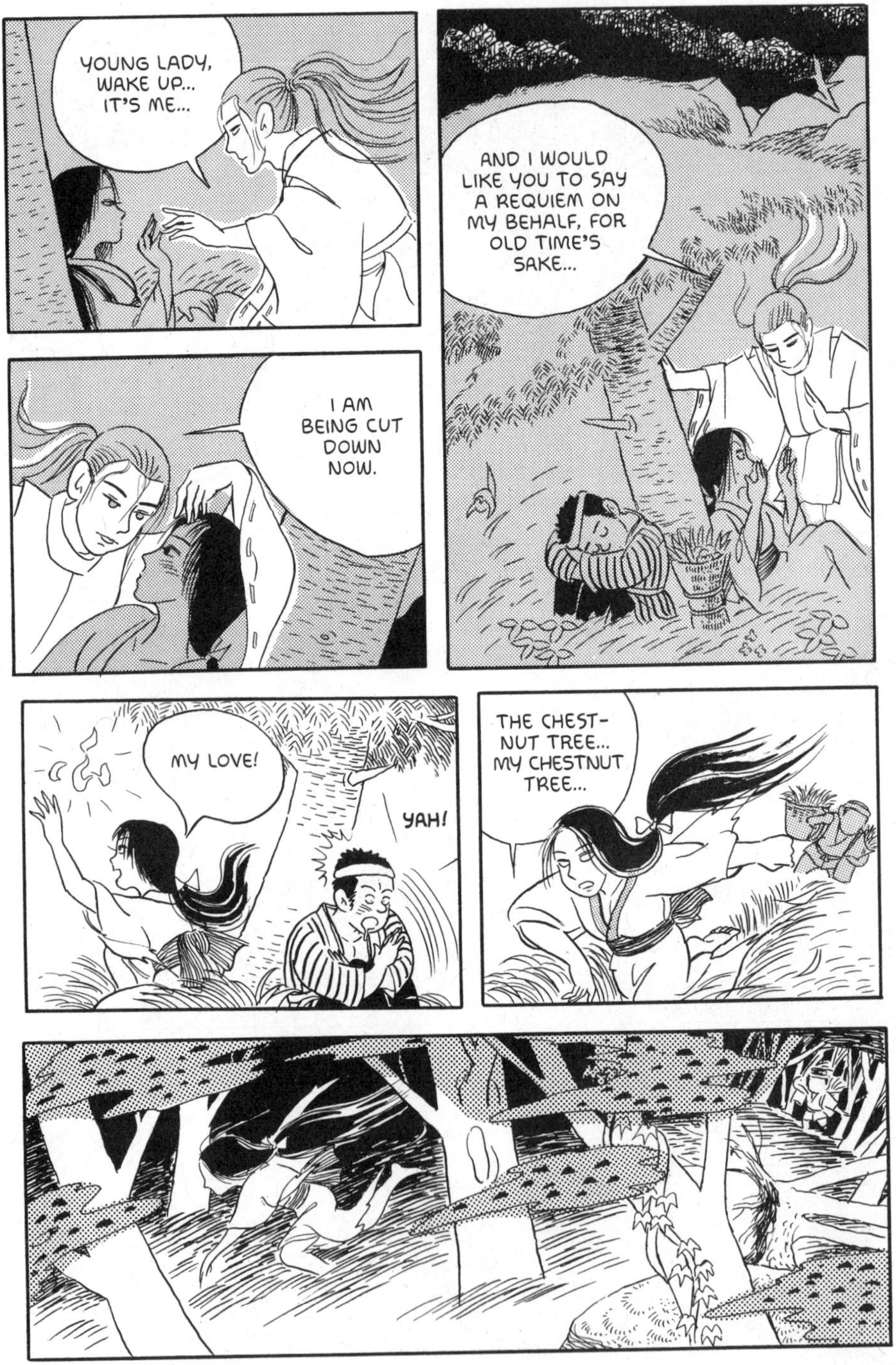
YOUNG LADY, WAKE UP... IT'S ME...
AND I WOULD LIKE YOU TO SAY A REQUIEM ON MY BEHALF, FOR OLD TIME'S SAKE...
I AM BEING CUT DOWN NOW.
MY LOVE!
YAH!
THE CHEST-NUT TREE... MY CHESTNUT TREE...

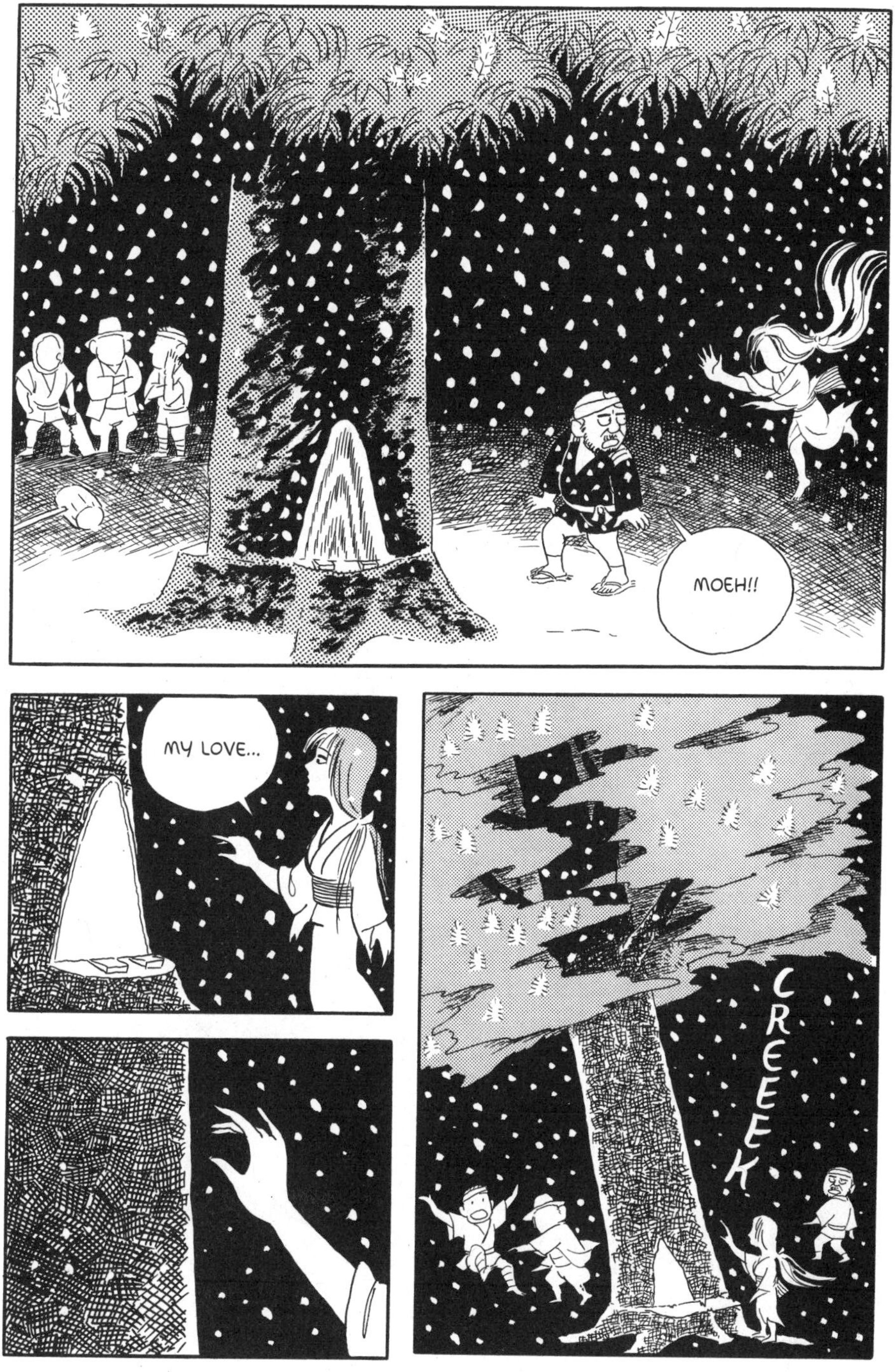
MOEH!!
MY LOVE...
CREEEK

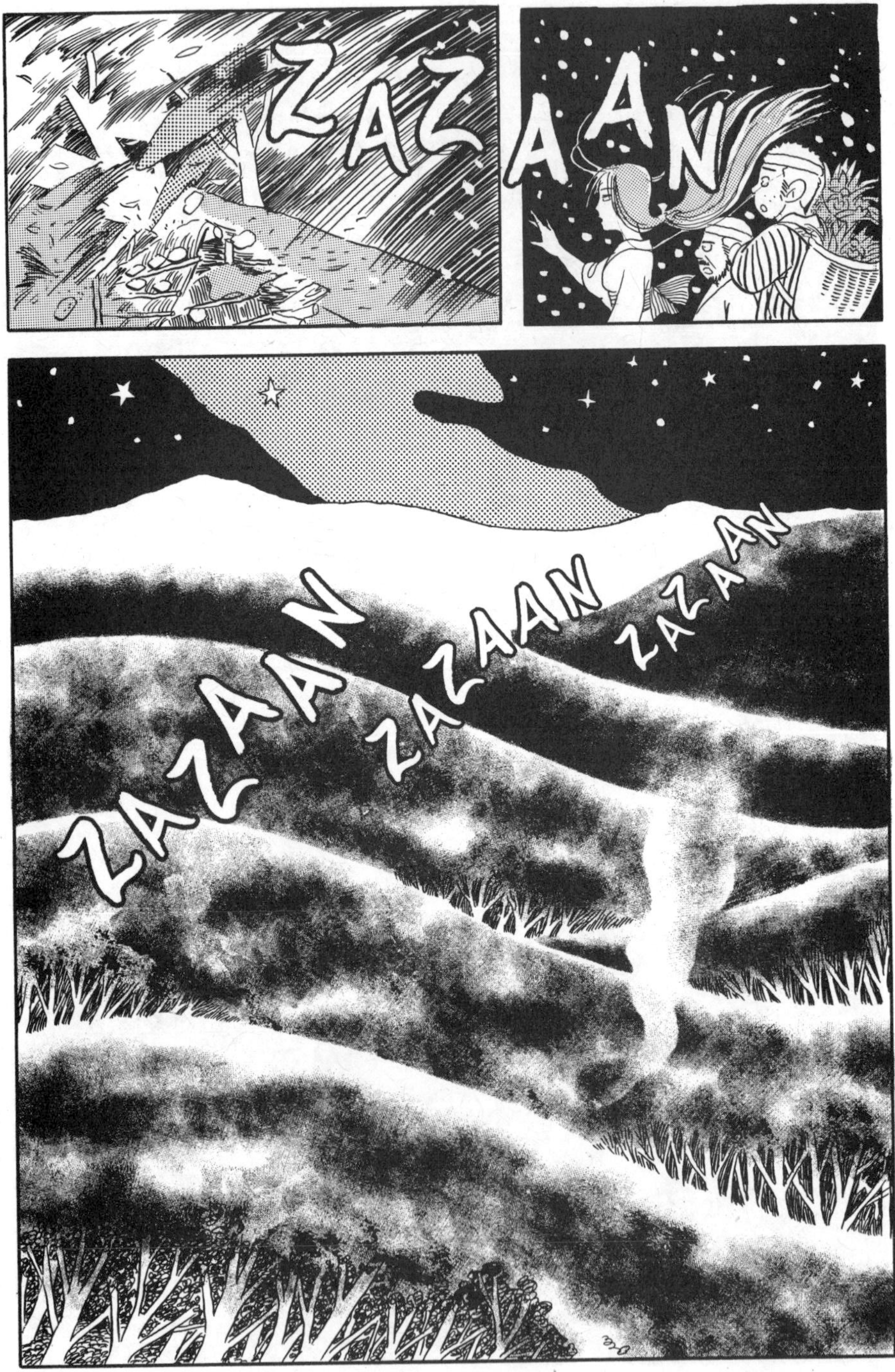
ZAZAAN
ZAZAAN
ZAZAAN
ZAZAAN

CRICKET HILL

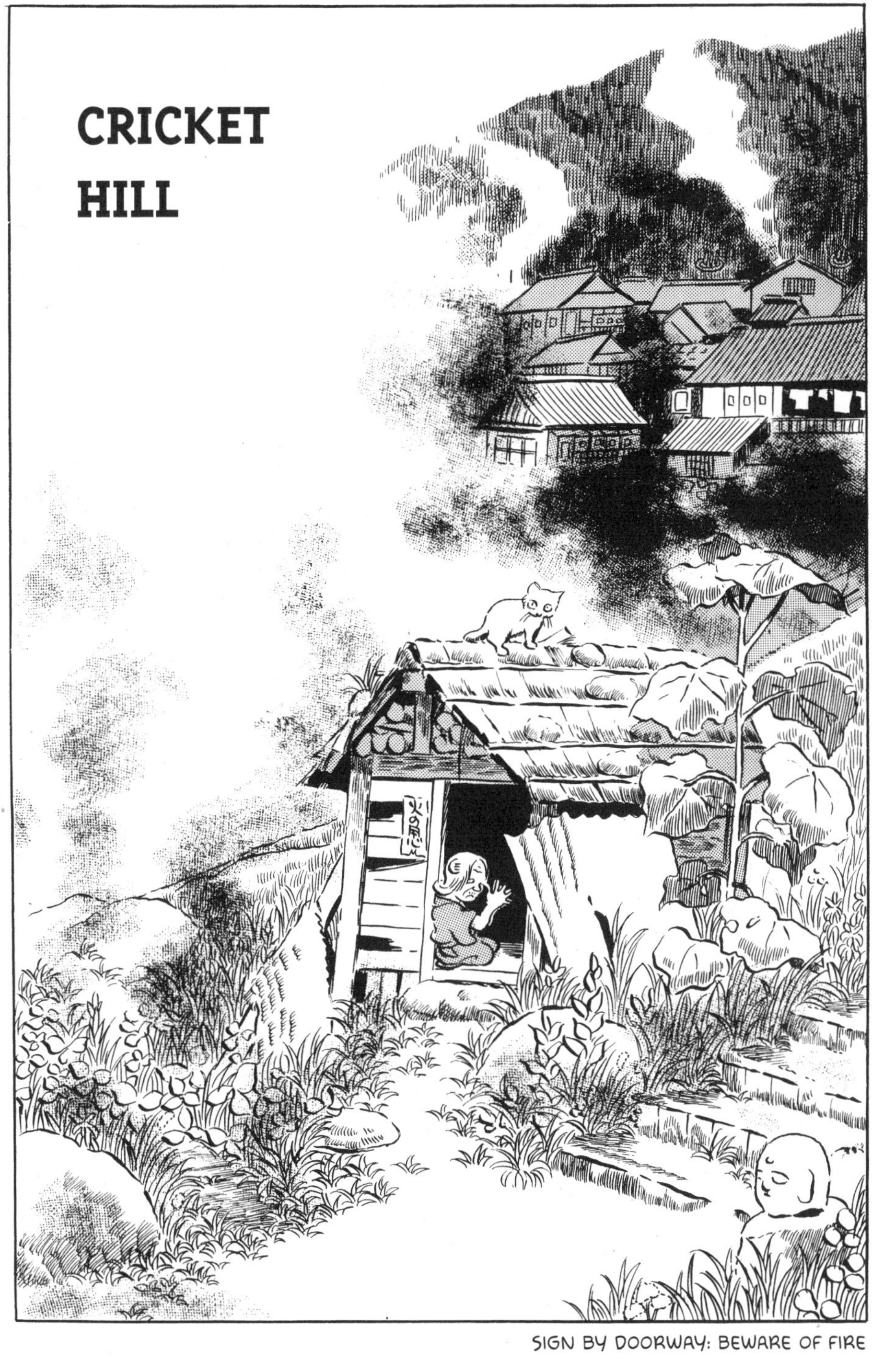
火の用心

SIGN BY DOORWAY: BEWARE OF FIRE

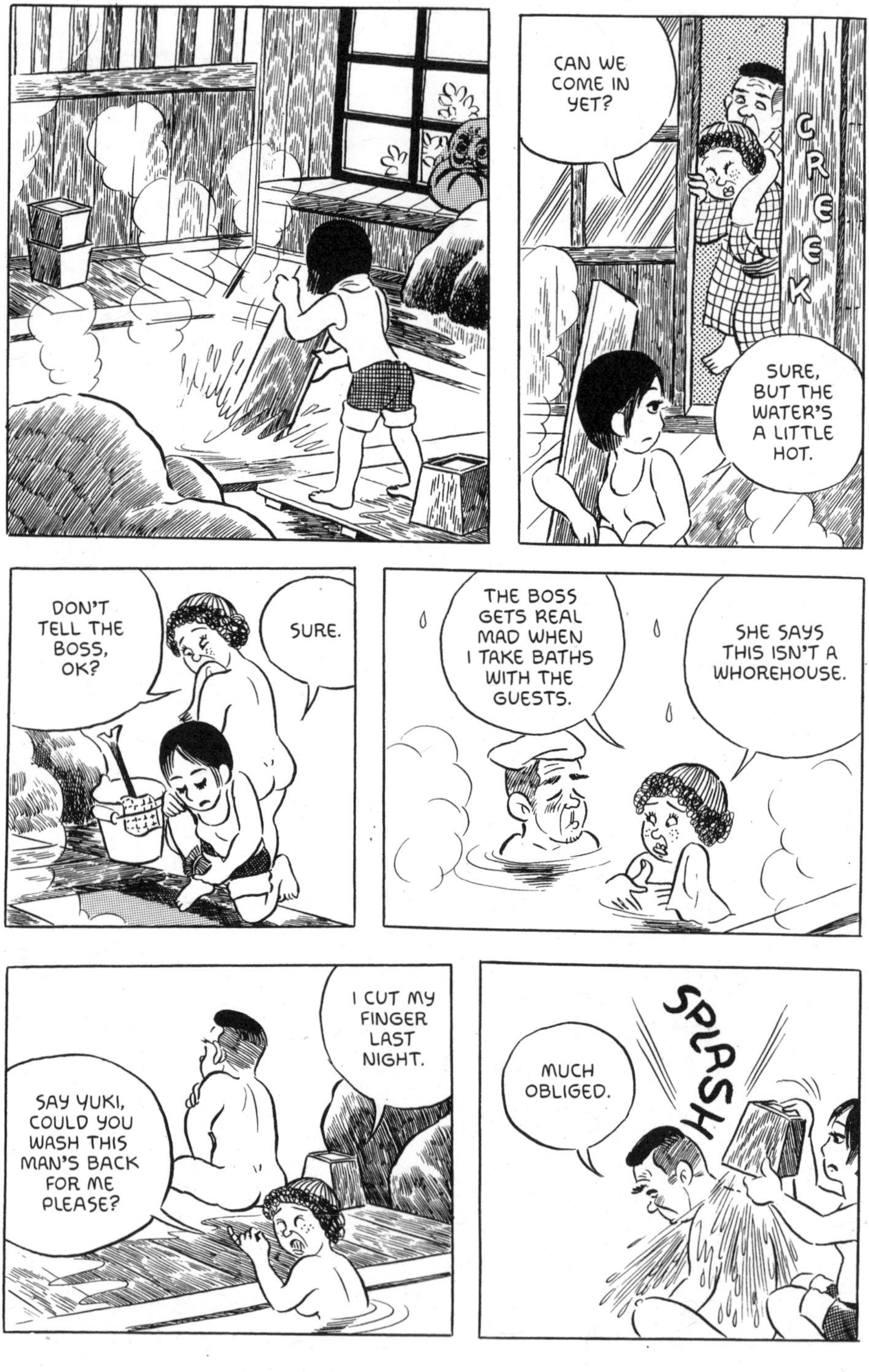
CAN WE COME IN YET?
CREEK
SURE, BUT THE WATER'S A LITTLE HOT.
DON'T TELL THE BOSS, OK?
SURE.
THE BOSS GETS REAL MAD WHEN I TAKE BATHS WITH THE GUESTS.
SHE SAYS THIS ISN'T A WHOREHOUSE.
SAY YUKI, COULD YOU WASH THIS MAN'S BACK FOR ME PLEASE?
I CUT MY FINGER LAST NIGHT.
MUCH OBLIGED.
SPLASH

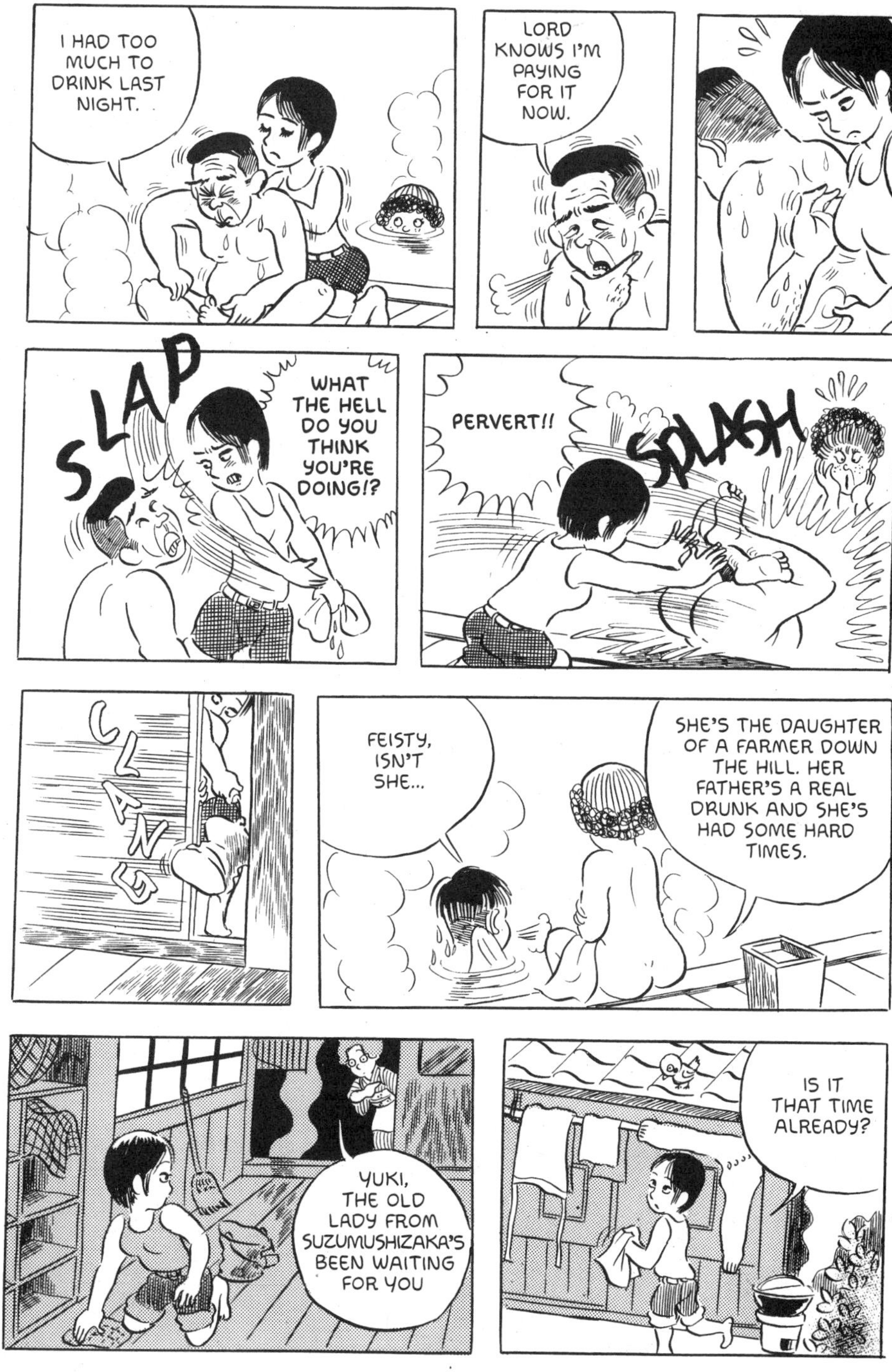
I HAD TOO MUCH TO DRINK LAST NIGHT.
LORD KNOWS I'M PAYING FOR IT NOW.
SLAP
WHAT THE HELL DO YOU THINK YOU'RE DOING!?
PERVERT!!
SPLASH
CLANG
FEISTY, ISN'T SHE...
SHE'S THE DAUGHTER OF A FARMER DOWN THE HILL. HER FATHER'S A REAL DRUNK AND SHE'S HAD SOME HARD TIMES.
YUKI, THE OLD LADY FROM SUZUMUSHIZAKA'S BEEN WAITING FOR YOU
IS IT THAT TIME ALREADY?

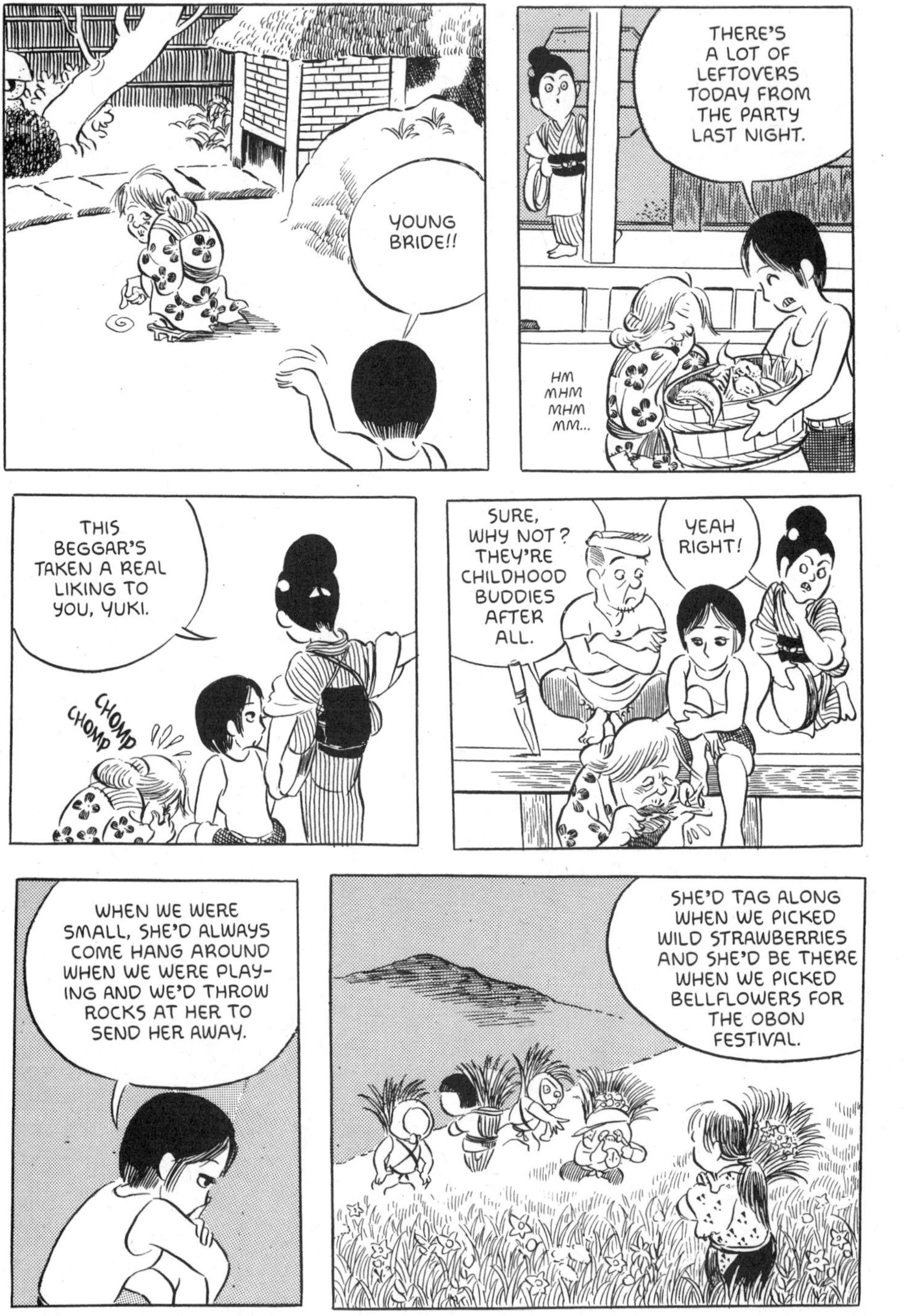
YOUNG BRIDE!!
THERE'S A LOT OF LEFTOVERS TODAY FROM THE PARTY LAST NIGHT.
HM MHM MHM MM...
THIS BEGGAR'S TAKEN A REAL LIKING TO YOU, YUKI.
CHOMP CHOMP
SURE, WHY NOT? THEY'RE CHILDHOOD BUDDIES AFTER ALL.
YEAH RIGHT!
WHEN WE WERE SMALL, SHE'D ALWAYS COME HANG AROUND WHEN WE WERE PLAY-ING AND WE'D THROW ROCKS AT HER TO SEND HER AWAY.
SHE'D TAG ALONG WHEN WE PICKED WILD STRAWBERRIES AND SHE'D BE THERE WHEN WE PICKED BELLFLOWERS FOR THE OBON FESTIVAL.

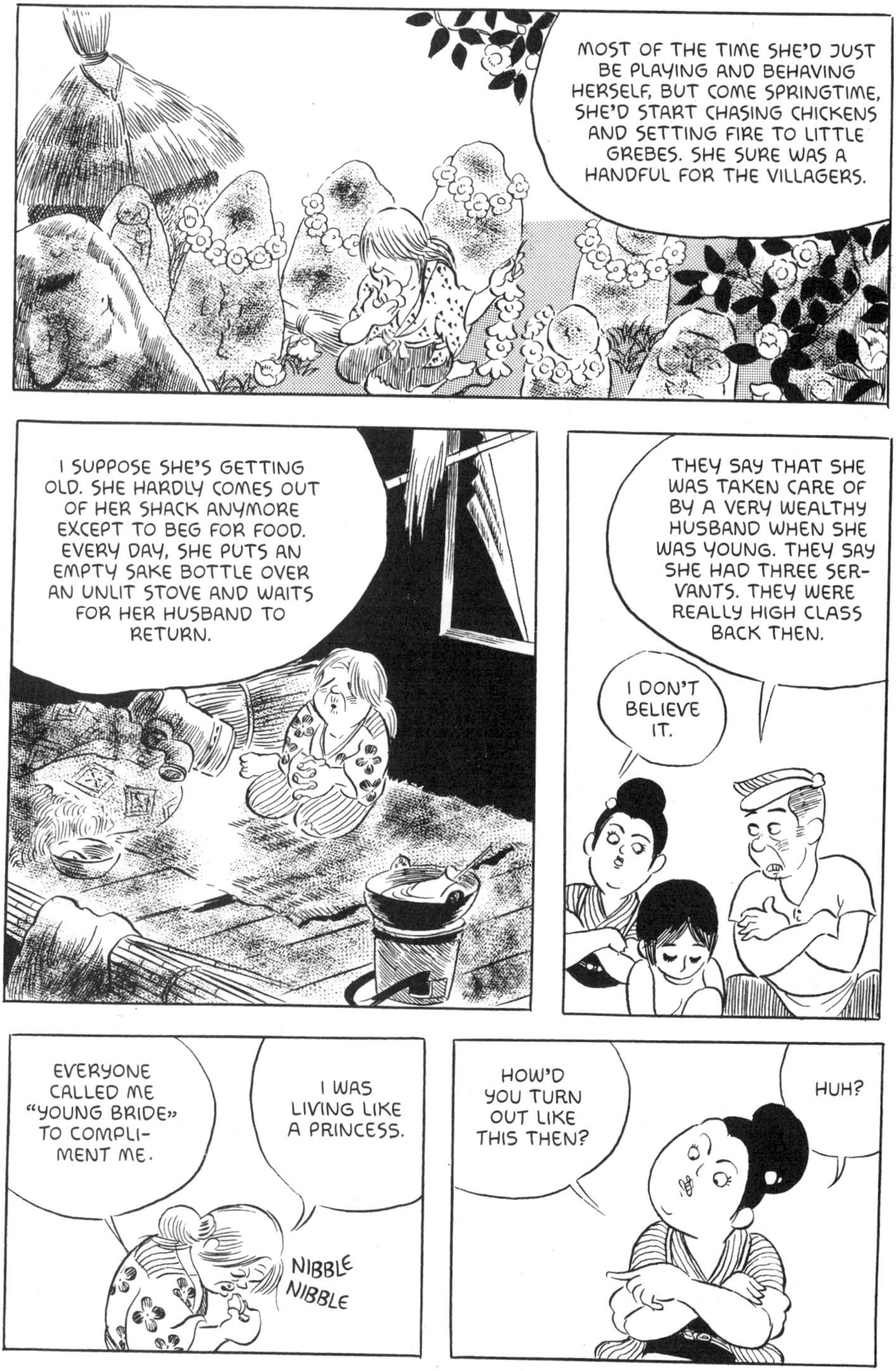
MOST OF THE TIME SHE'D JUST BE PLAYING AND BEHAVING HERSELF, BUT COME SPRINGTIME, SHE'D START CHASING CHICKENS AND SETTING FIRE TO LITTLE GREBES. SHE SURE WAS A HANDFUL FOR THE VILLAGERS.
I SUPPOSE SHE'S GETTING OLD. SHE HARDLY COMES OUT OF HER SHACK ANYMORE EXCEPT TO BEG FOR FOOD. EVERY DAY, SHE PUTS AN EMPTY SAKE BOTTLE OVER AN UNLIT STOVE AND WAITS FOR HER HUSBAND TO RETURN.
THEY SAY THAT SHE WAS TAKEN CARE OF BY A VERY WEALTHY HUSBAND WHEN SHE WAS YOUNG. THEY SAY SHE HAD THREE SERVANTS. THEY WERE REALLY HIGH CLASS BACK THEN.
I DON'T BELIEVE IT.
EVERYONE CALLED ME "YOUNG BRIDE" TO COMPLIMENT ME.
I WAS LIVING LIKE A PRINCESS.
NIBBLE NIBBLE
HOW'D YOU TURN OUT LIKE THIS THEN?
HUH?

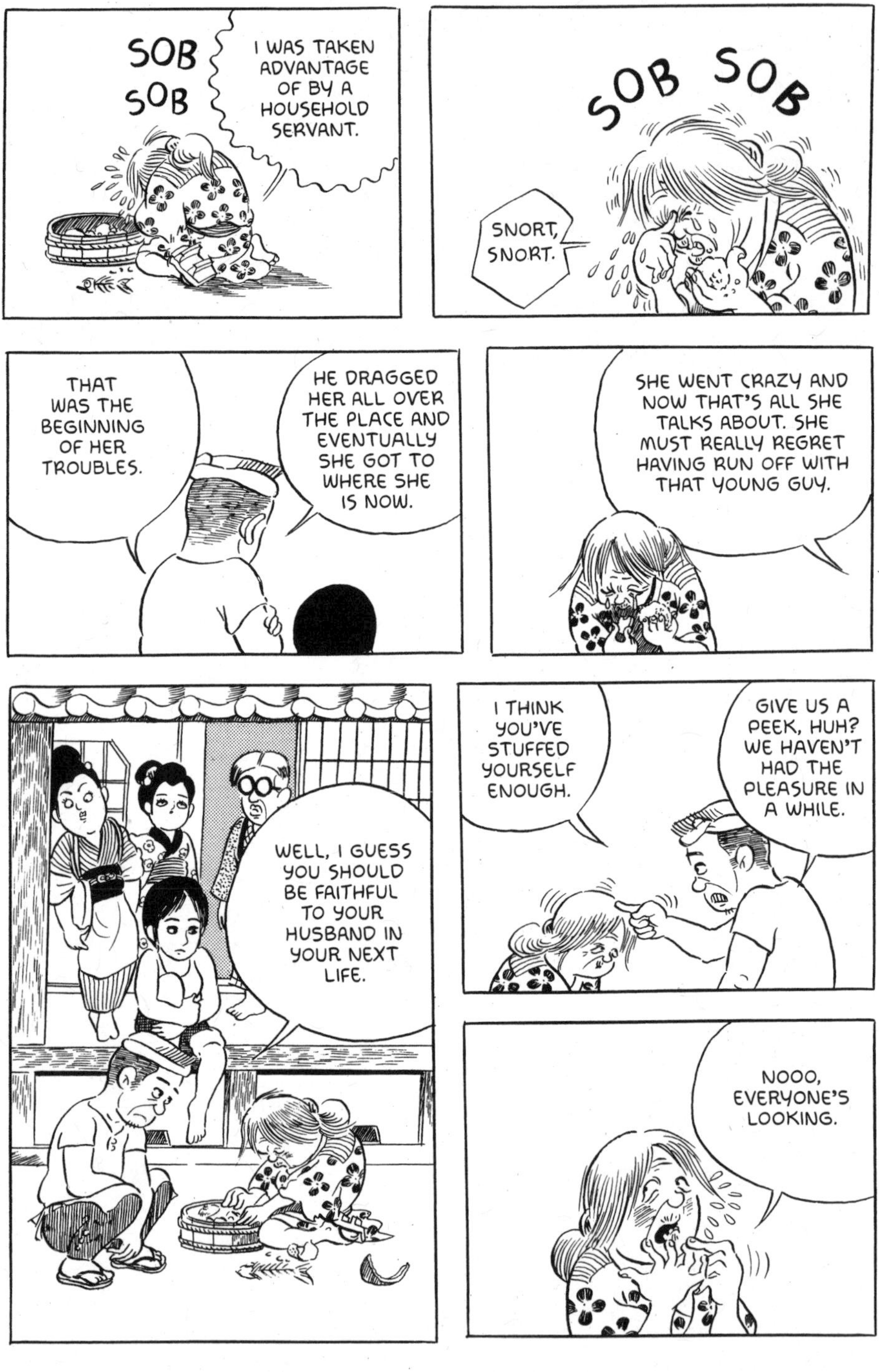
SOB SOB
I WAS TAKEN ADVANTAGE OF BY A HOUSEHOLD SERVANT.
SOB SOB
SNORT, SNORT.
THAT WAS THE BEGINNING OF HER TROUBLES.
HE DRAGGED HER ALL OVER THE PLACE AND EVENTUALLY SHE GOT TO WHERE SHE IS NOW.
SHE WENT CRAZY AND NOW THAT'S ALL SHE TALKS ABOUT. SHE MUST REALLY REGRET HAVING RUN OFF WITH THAT YOUNG GUY.
WELL, I GUESS YOU SHOULD BE FAITHFUL TO YOUR HUSBAND IN YOUR NEXT LIFE.
I THINK YOU'VE STUFFED YOURSELF ENOUGH.
GIVE US A PEEK, HUH? WE HAVEN'T HAD THE PLEASURE IN A WHILE.
NOOO, EVERYONE'S LOOKING.

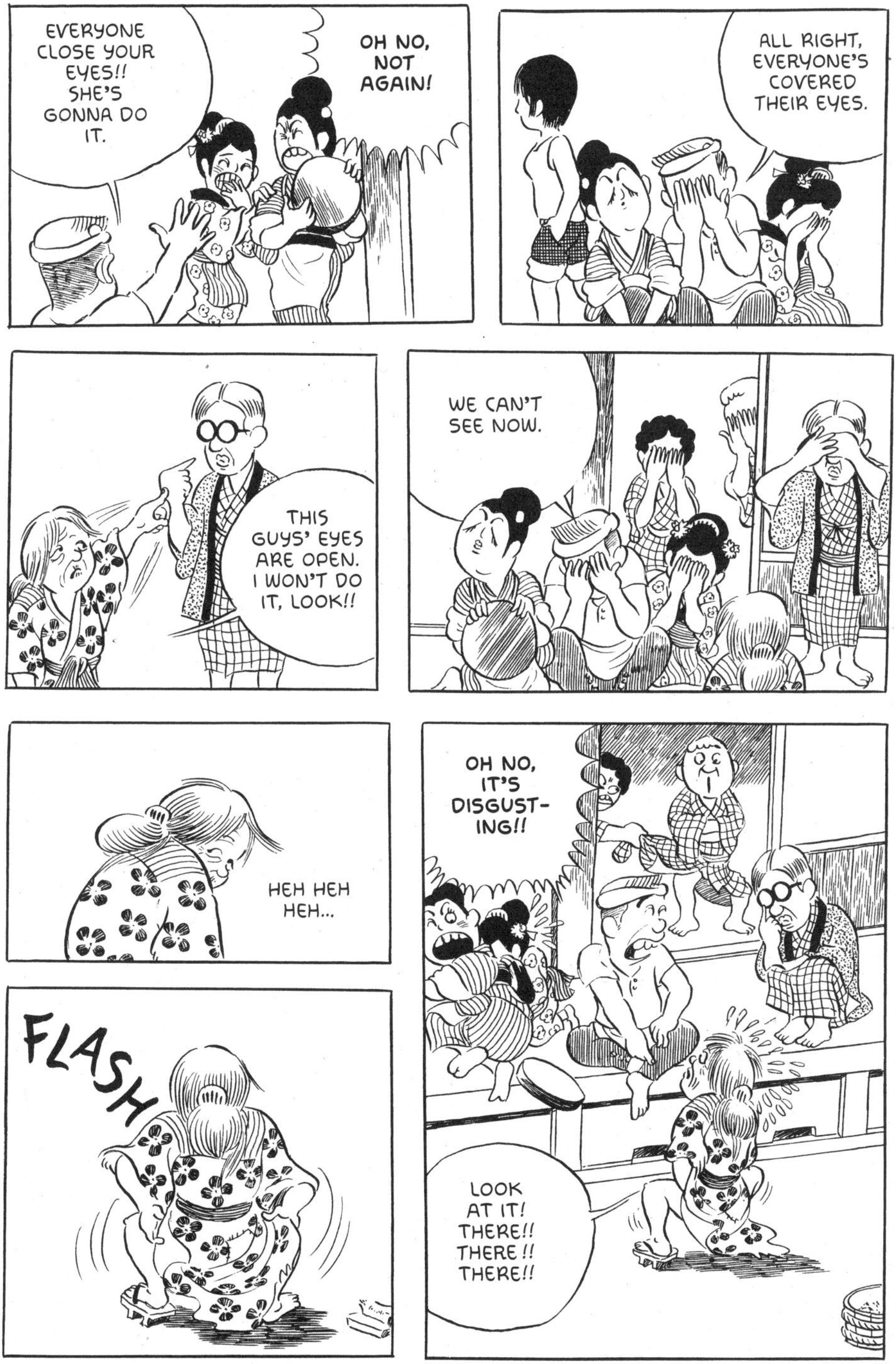
EVERYONE CLOSE YOUR EYES!! SHE'S GONNA DO IT.
OH NO, NOT AGAIN!
ALL RIGHT, EVERYONE'S COVERED THEIR EYES.
THIS GUYS' EYES ARE OPEN. I WON'T DO IT, LOOK!!
WE CAN'T SEE NOW.
HEH HEH HEH...
FLASH
OH NO, IT'S DISGUSTING!!
LOOK AT IT! THERE!! THERE!! THERE!!

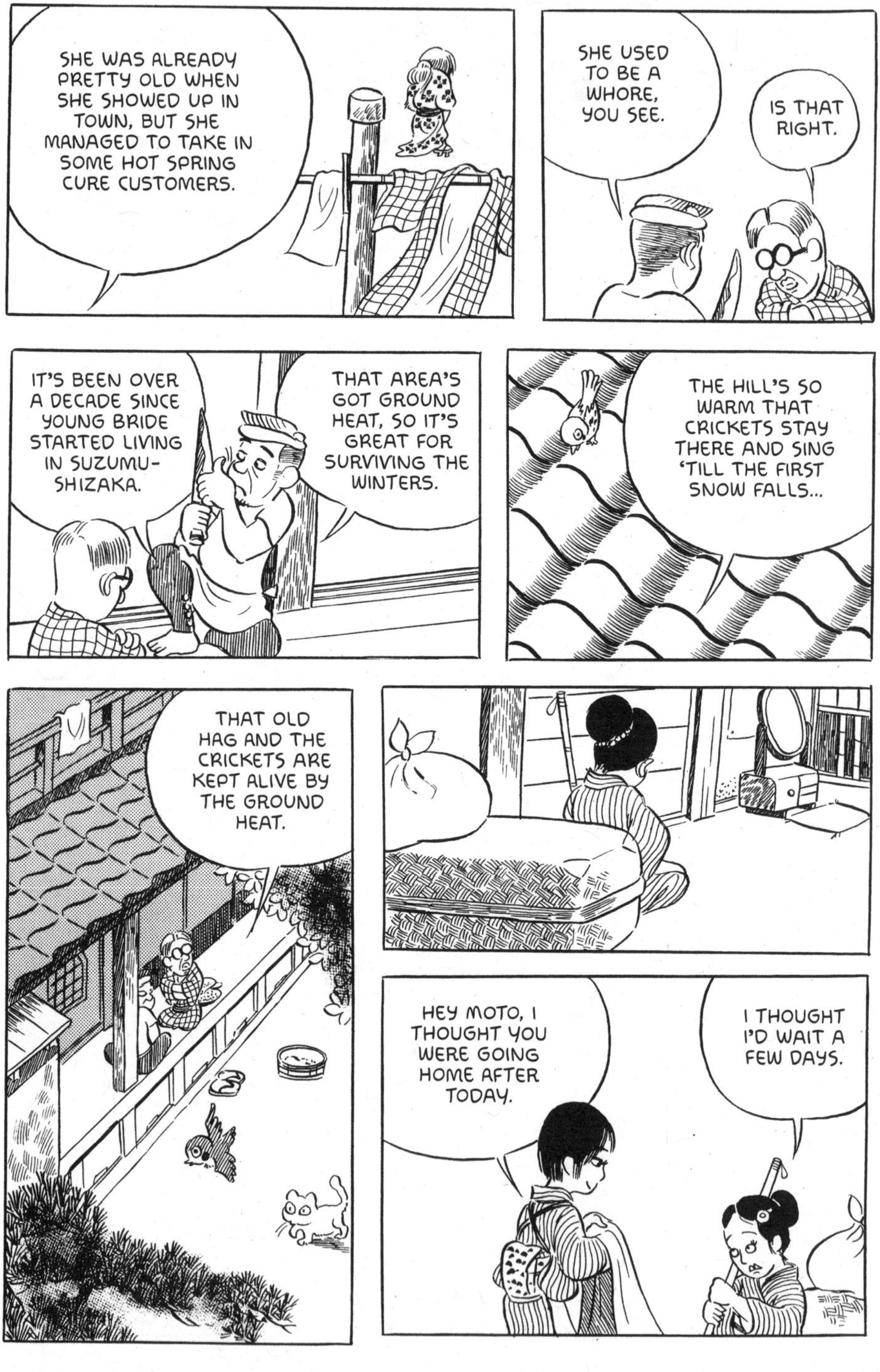
SHE WAS ALREADY PRETTY OLD WHEN SHE SHOWED UP IN TOWN, BUT SHE MANAGED TO TAKE IN SOME HOT SPRING CURE CUSTOMERS.
SHE USED TO BE A WHORE, YOU SEE.
IS THAT RIGHT.
IT'S BEEN OVER A DECADE SINCE YOUNG BRIDE STARTED LIVING IN SUZUMU-SHIZAKA.
THAT AREA'S GOT GROUND HEAT, SO IT'S GREAT FOR SURVIVING THE WINTERS.
THE HILL'S SO WARM THAT CRICKETS STAY THERE AND SING 'TILL THE FIRST SNOW FALLS...
THAT OLD HAG AND THE CRICKETS ARE KEPT ALIVE BY THE GROUND HEAT.
HEY MOTO, I THOUGHT YOU WERE GOING HOME AFTER TODAY.
I THOUGHT I'D WAIT A FEW DAYS.

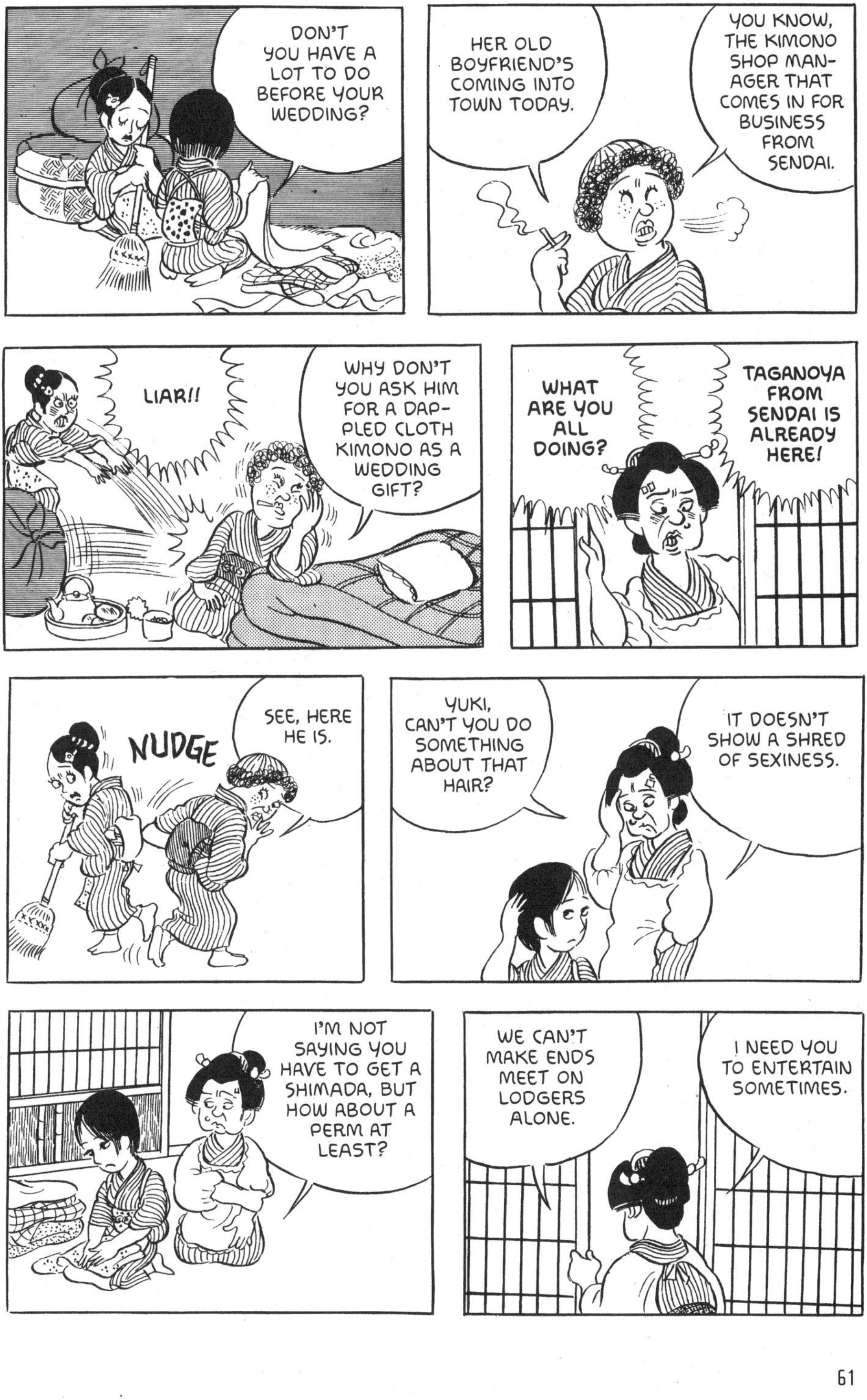
DON'T YOU HAVE A LOT TO DO BEFORE YOUR WEDDING?
HER OLD BOYFRIEND'S COMING INTO TOWN TODAY.
YOU KNOW, THE KIMONO SHOP MAN-AGER THAT COMES IN FOR BUSINESS FROM SENDAI.
LIAR!!
WHY DON'T YOU ASK HIM FOR A DAP-PLED CLOTH KIMONO AS A WEDDING GIFT?
WHAT ARE YOU ALL DOING?
TAGANOYA FROM SENDAI IS ALREADY HERE!
NUDGE
SEE, HERE HE IS.
YUKI, CAN'T YOU DO SOMETHING ABOUT THAT HAIR?
IT DOESN'T SHOW A SHRED OF SEXINESS.
I'M NOT SAYING YOU HAVE TO GET A SHIMADA, BUT HOW ABOUT A PERM AT LEAST?
WE CAN'T MAKE ENDS MEET ON LODGERS ALONE.
I NEED YOU TO ENTERTAIN SOMETIMES.

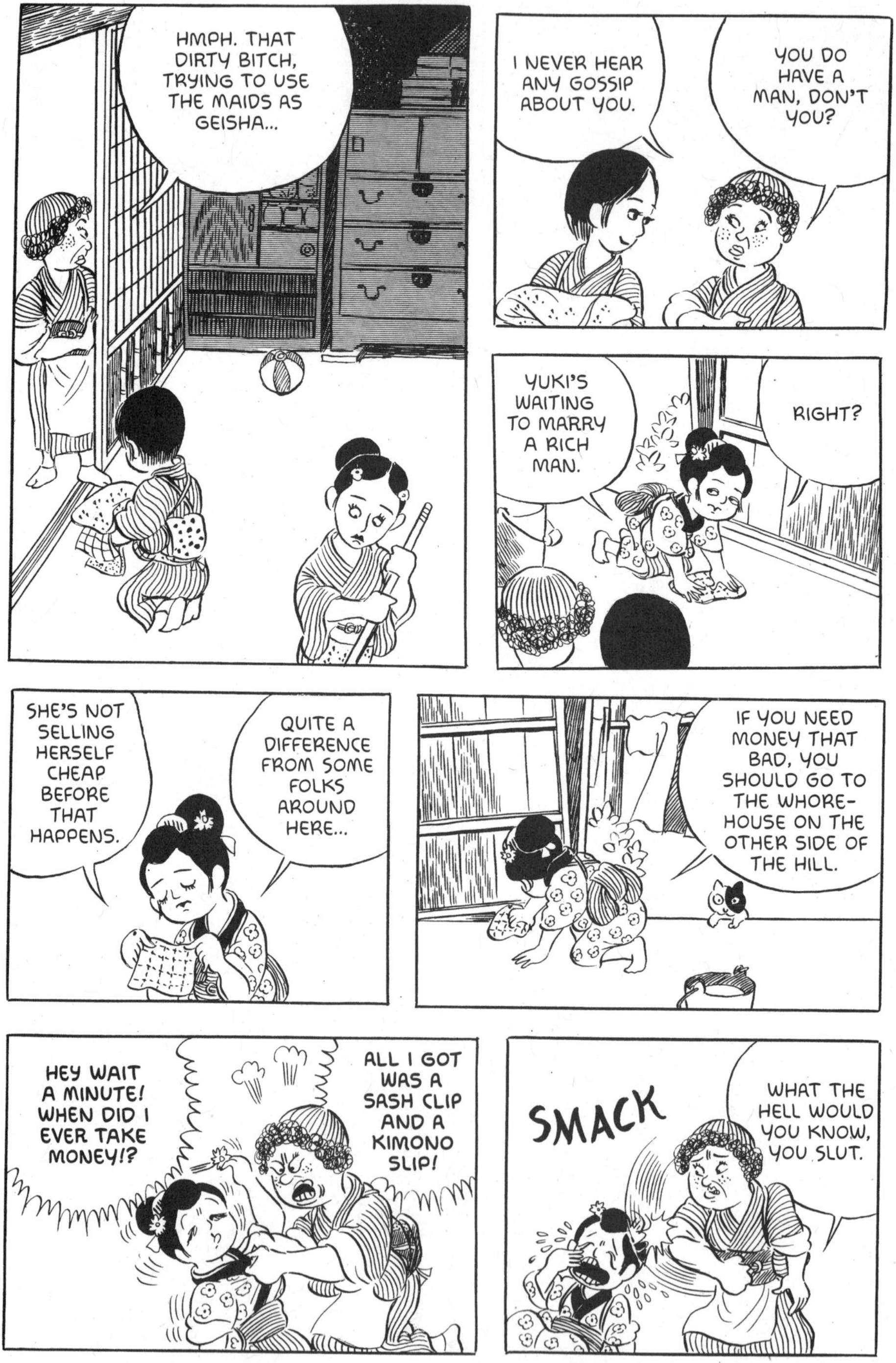
HMPH. THAT DIRTY BITCH, TRYING TO USE THE MAIDS AS GEISHA...
I NEVER HEAR ANY GOSSIP ABOUT YOU.
YOU DO HAVE A MAN, DON'T YOU?
YUKI'S WAITING TO MARRY A RICH MAN.
RIGHT?
SHE'S NOT SELLING HERSELF CHEAP BEFORE THAT HAPPENS.
QUITE A DIFFERENCE FROM SOME FOLKS AROUND HERE...
IF YOU NEED MONEY THAT BAD, YOU SHOULD GO TO THE WHORE-HOUSE ON THE OTHER SIDE OF THE HILL.
HEY WAIT A MINUTE! WHEN DID I EVER TAKE MONEY!?
ALL I GOT WAS A SASH CLIP AND A KIMONO SLIP!
SMACK
WHAT THE HELL WOULD YOU KNOW, YOU SLUT.

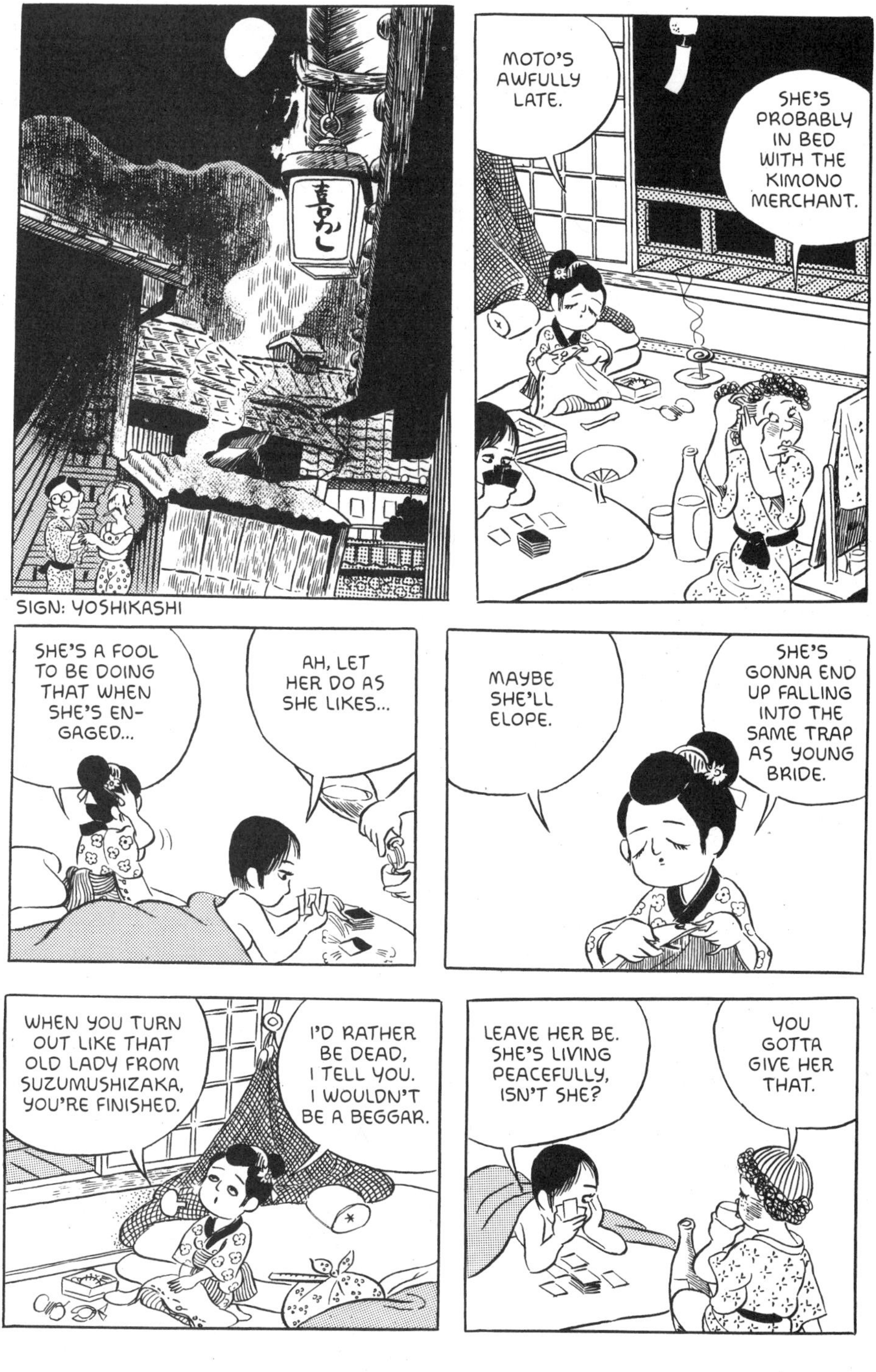
SIGN: YOSHIKASHI
MOTO'S AWFULLY LATE.
SHE'S PROBABLY IN BED WITH THE KIMONO MERCHANT.
SHE'S A FOOL TO BE DOING THAT WHEN SHE'S EN-GAGED...
AH, LET HER DO AS SHE LIKES...
MAYBE SHE'LL ELOPE.
SHE'S GONNA END UP FALLING INTO THE SAME TRAP AS YOUNG BRIDE.
WHEN YOU TURN OUT LIKE THAT OLD LADY FROM SUZUMUSHIZAKA, YOU'RE FINISHED.
I'D RATHER BE DEAD, I TELL YOU. I WOULDN'T BE A BEGGAR.
LEAVE HER BE. SHE'S LIVING PEACEFULLY, ISN'T SHE?
YOU GOTTA GIVE HER THAT.

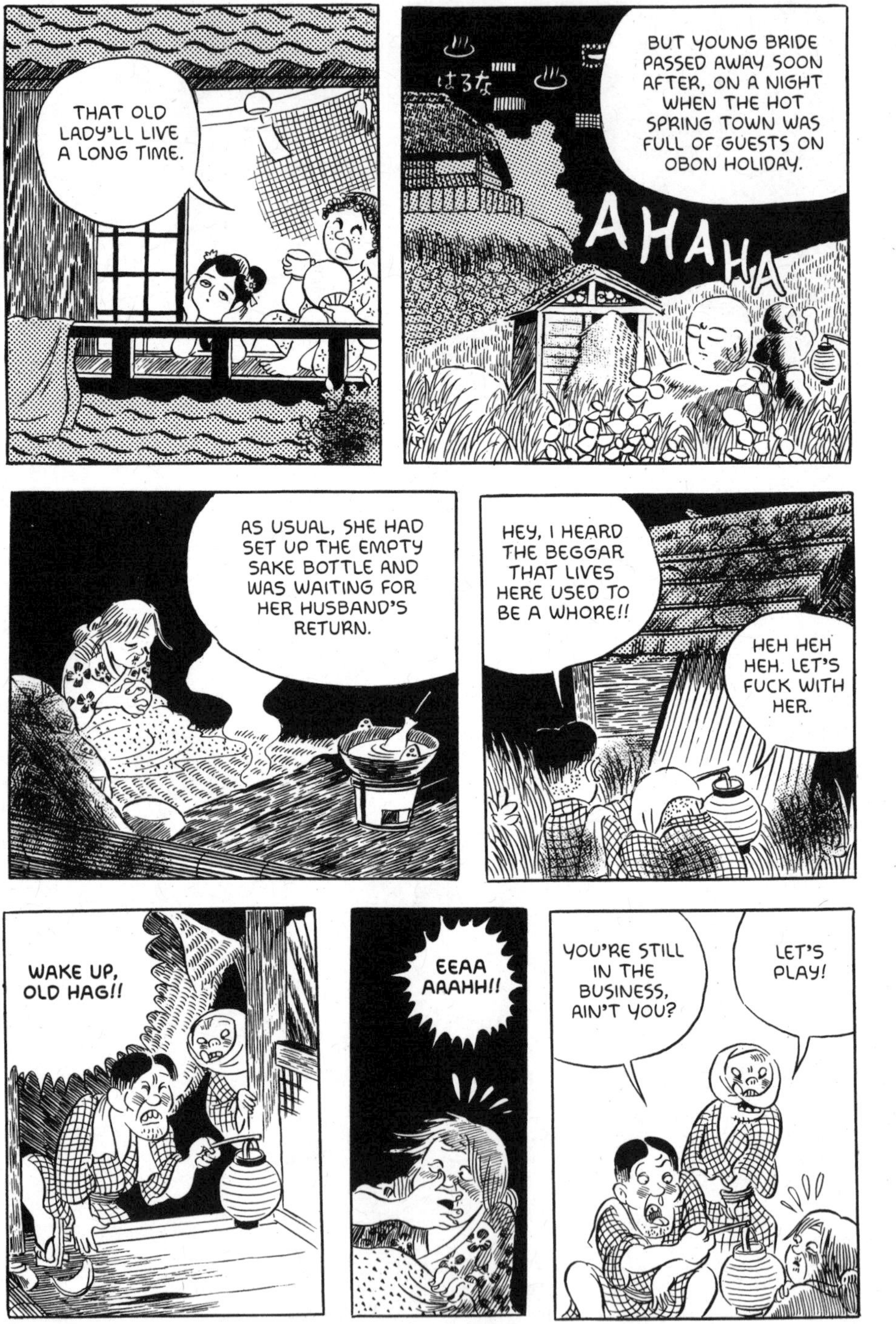
THAT OLD LADY'LL LIVE A LONG TIME.
はるな
BUT YOUNG BRIDE PASSED AWAY SOON AFTER, ON A NIGHT WHEN THE HOT SPRING TOWN WAS FULL OF GUESTS ON OBON HOLIDAY.
AHAHA
AS USUAL, SHE HAD SET UP THE EMPTY SAKE BOTTLE AND WAS WAITING FOR HER HUSBAND'S RETURN.
HEY, I HEARD THE BEGGAR THAT LIVES HERE USED TO BE A WHORE!!
HEH HEH HEH. LET'S FUCK WITH HER.
WAKE UP, OLD HAG!!
EEAA AAAHH!!
YOU'RE STILL IN THE BUSINESS, AIN'T YOU?
LET'S PLAY!

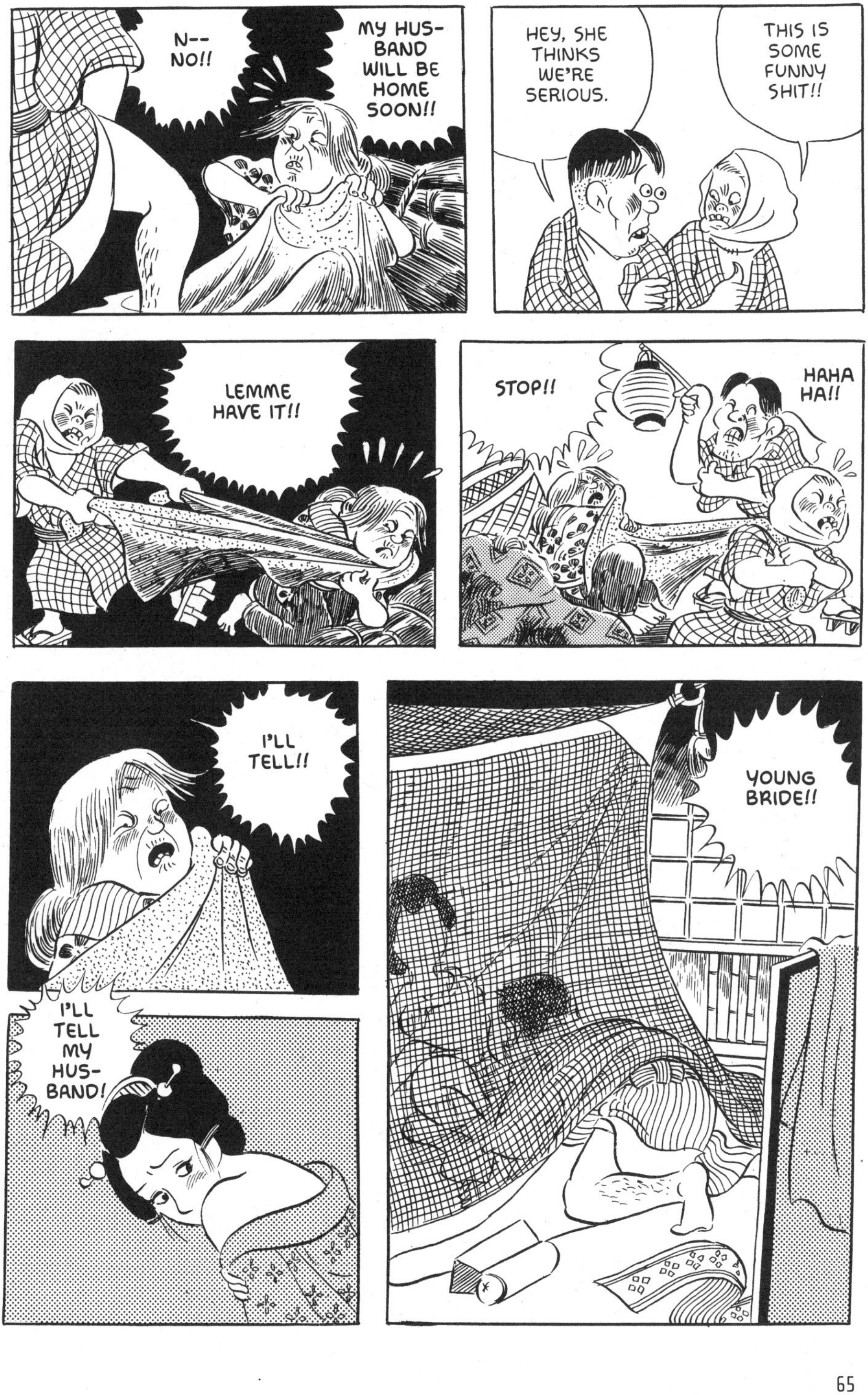
N-- NO!!
MY HUS-BAND WILL BE HOME SOON!!
HEY, SHE THINKS WE'RE SERIOUS.
THIS IS SOME FUNNY SHIT!!
LEMME HAVE IT!!
STOP!!
HAHA HA!!
I'LL TELL!!
I'LL TELL MY HUS-BAND!
YOUNG BRIDE!!

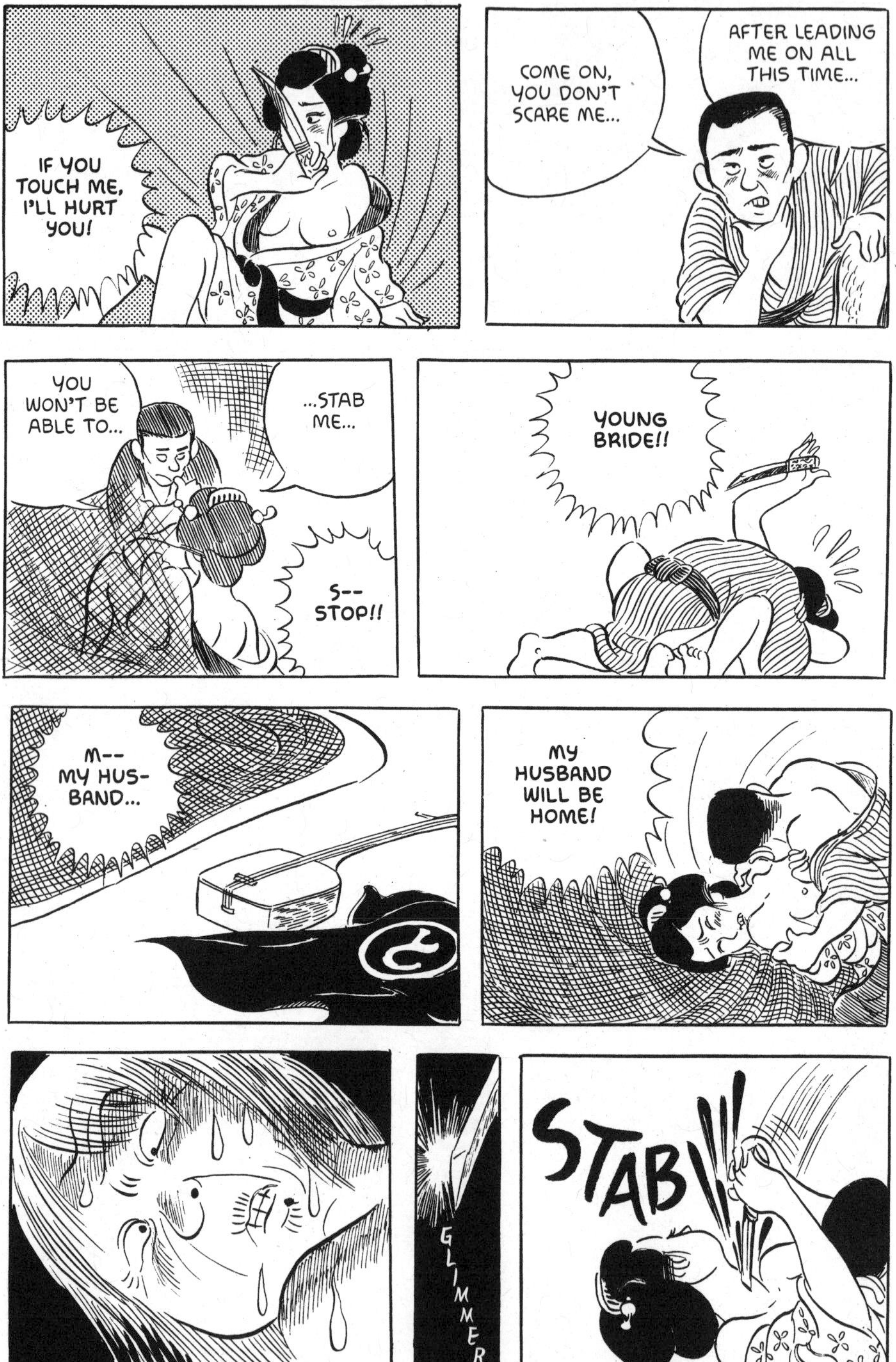
IF YOU TOUCH ME, I'LL HURT YOU!
COME ON, YOU DON'T SCARE ME...
AFTER LEADING ME ON ALL THIS TIME...
YOU WON'T BE ABLE TO...
...STAB ME...
S-- STOP!!
YOUNG BRIDE!!
M-- MY HUS-BAND...
MY HUSBAND WILL BE HOME!
GLIMMER
STAB

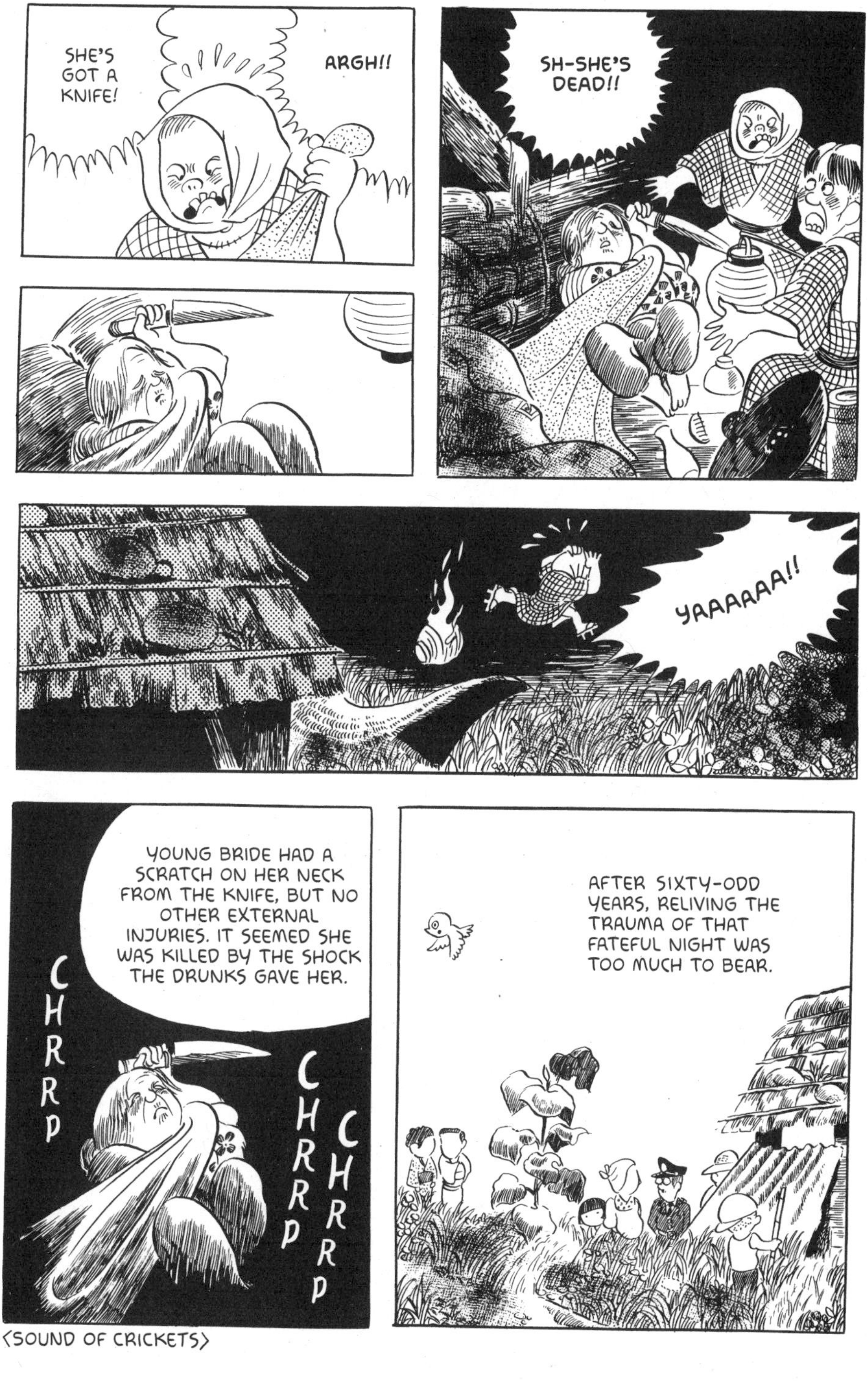
SHE'S GOT A KNIFE!
ARGH!!
SH-SHE'S DEAD!!
YAAAAAA!!
YOUNG BRIDE HAD A SCRATCH ON HER NECK FROM THE KNIFE, BUT NO OTHER EXTERNAL INJURIES. IT SEEMED SHE WAS KILLED BY THE SHOCK THE DRUNKS GAVE HER.
CHRRP
CHRRP
CHRRP
AFTER SIXTY-ODD YEARS, RELIVING THE TRAUMA OF THAT FATEFUL NIGHT WAS TOO MUCH TO BEAR.

<SOUND OF CRICKETS>

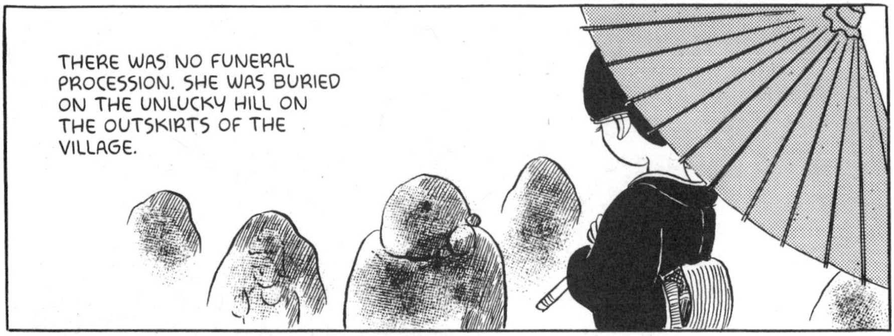
THERE WAS NO FUNERAL PROCESSION. SHE WAS BURIED ON THE UNLUCKY HILL ON THE OUTSKIRTS OF THE VILLAGE.

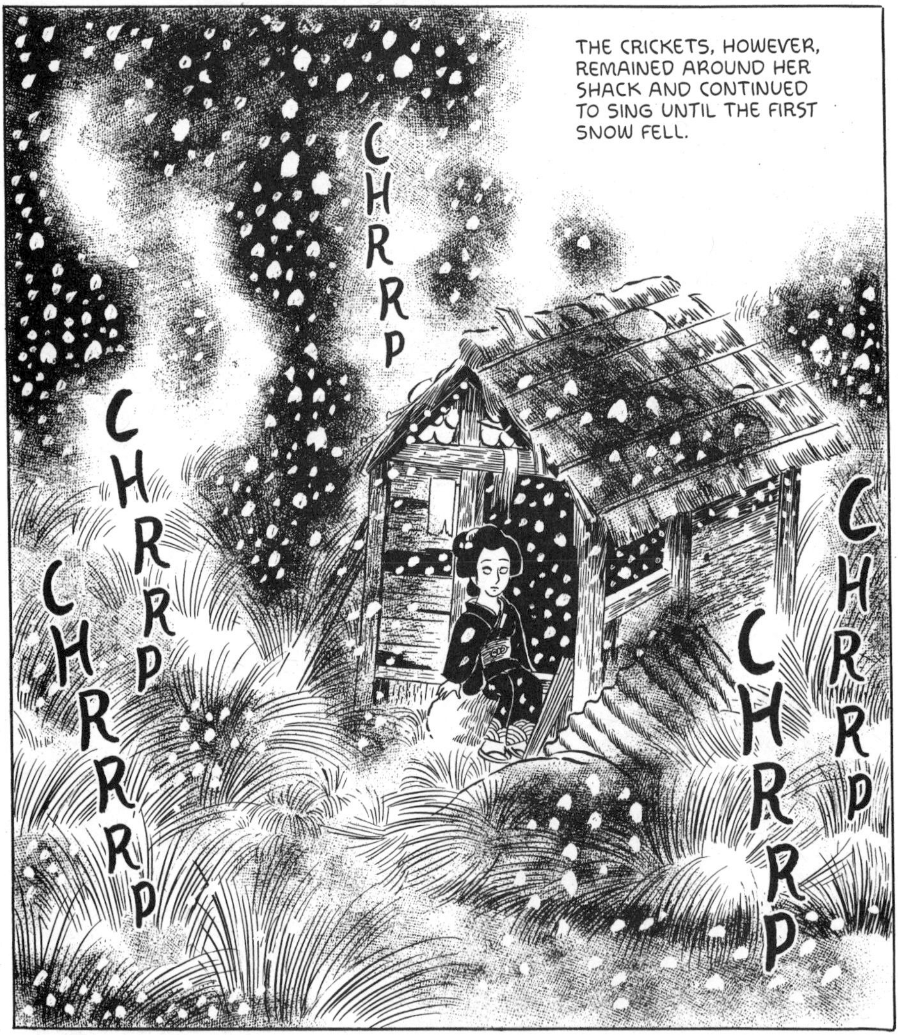
THE CRICKETS, HOWEVER, REMAINED AROUND HER SHACK AND CONTINUED TO SING UNTIL THE FIRST SNOW FELL.
CHRRP
CHRRRRP
CHRRP
CHRRRP
CHRRP

PULP NOVEL ABOUT A SACK

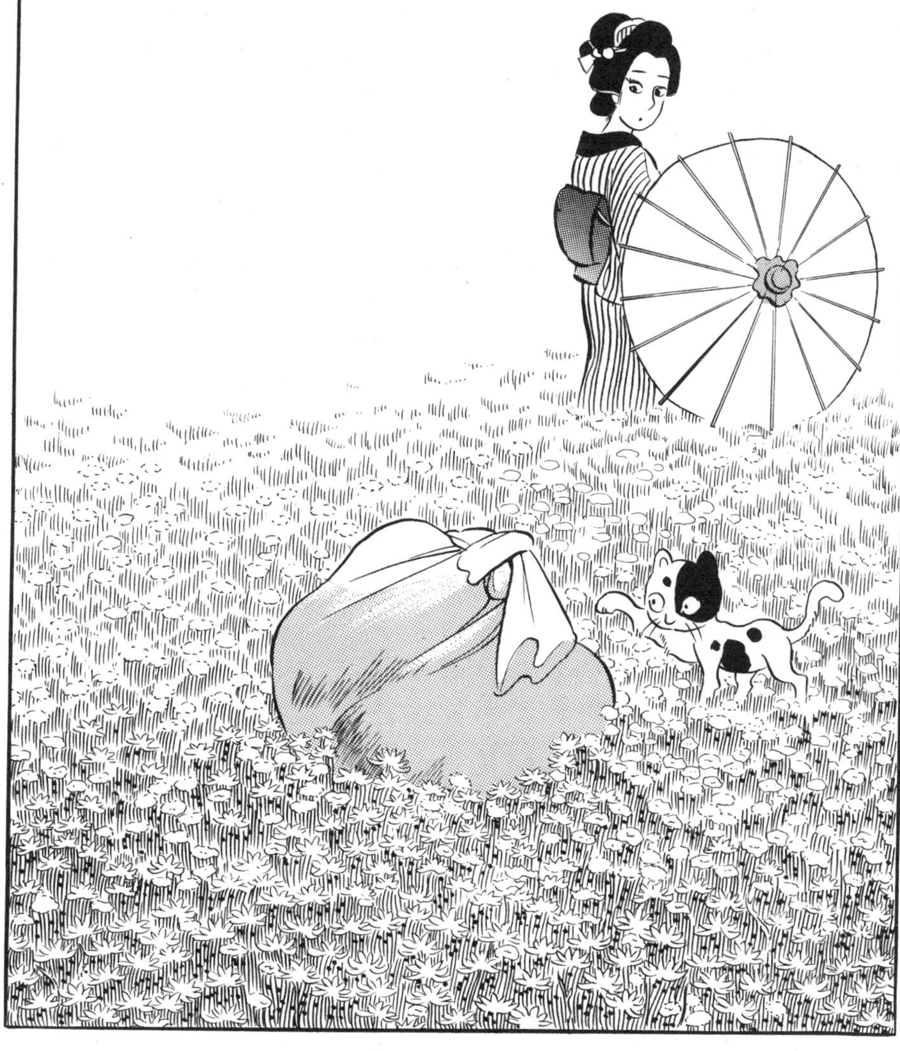

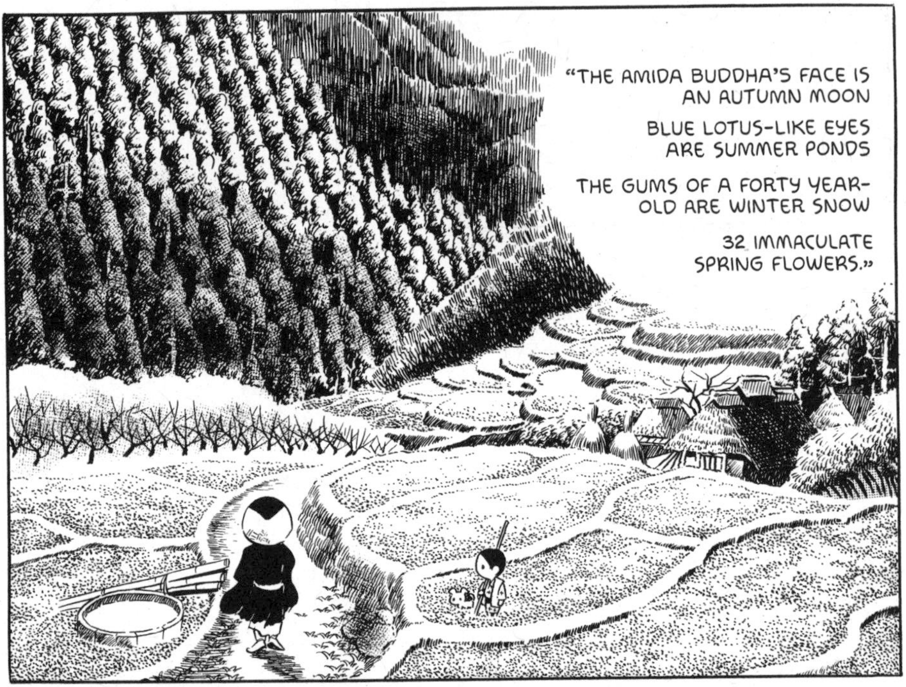
"THE AMIDA BUDDHA'S FACE IS AN AUTUMN MOON
BLUE LOTUS-LIKE EYES ARE SUMMER PONDS
THE GUMS OF A FORTY YEAR-OLD ARE WINTER SNOW
32 IMMACULATE SPRING FLOWERS."

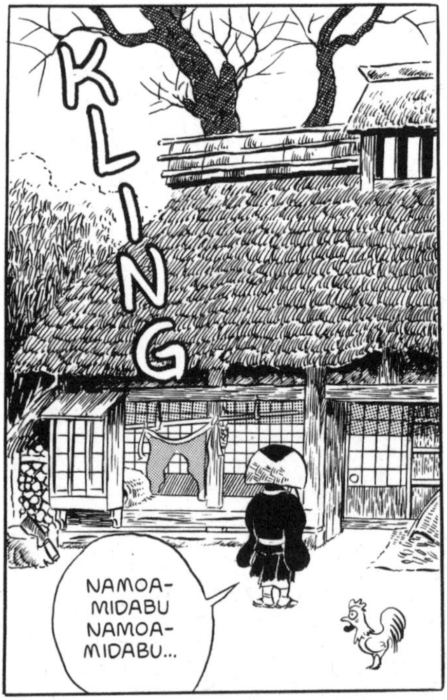
KLING
NAMOA-MIDABU NAMOA-MIDABU...

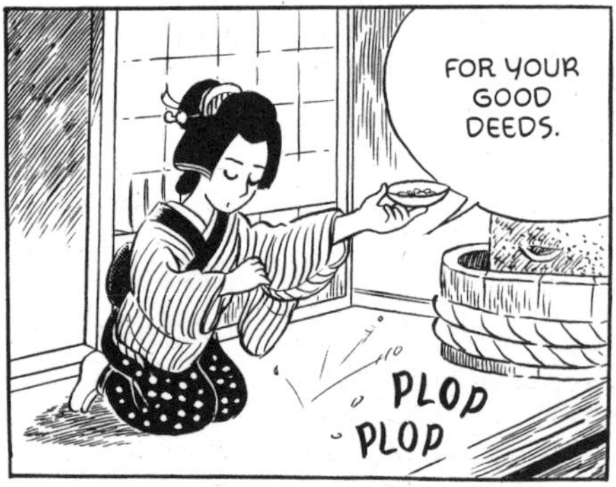
FOR YOUR GOOD DEEDS.
PLOP PLOP

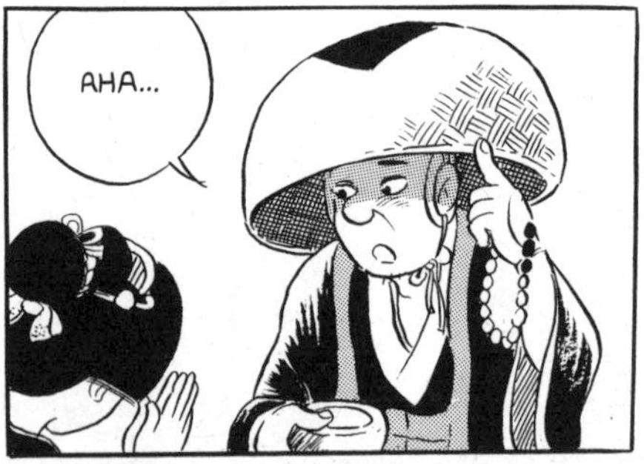
AHA...

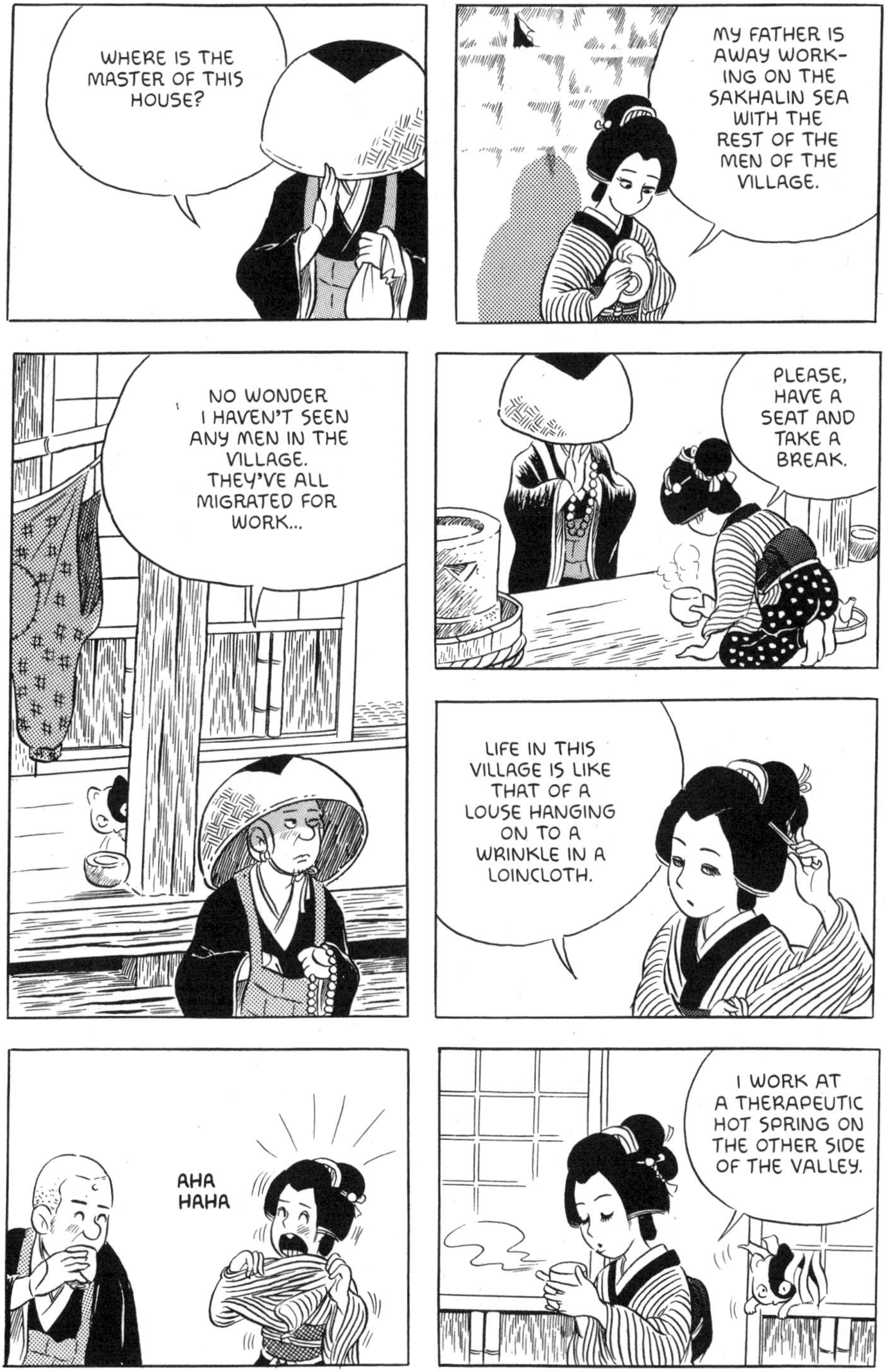
WHERE IS THE MASTER OF THIS HOUSE?
MY FATHER IS AWAY WORKING ON THE SAKHALIN SEA WITH THE REST OF THE MEN OF THE VILLAGE.
NO WONDER I HAVEN'T SEEN ANY MEN IN THE VILLAGE. THEY'VE ALL MIGRATED FOR WORK...
PLEASE, HAVE A SEAT AND TAKE A BREAK.
LIFE IN THIS VILLAGE IS LIKE THAT OF A LOUSE HANGING ON TO A WRINKLE IN A LOINCLOTH.
AHA HAHA
I WORK AT A THERAPEUTIC HOT SPRING ON THE OTHER SIDE OF THE VALLEY.

I'VE COME TO TAKE CARE OF THE CATTLE, SINCE MY MOTHER IS WITH THE OTHER WOMEN OF THE VILLAGE CHANTING THE PRAISES OF BUDDHA.

SO TODAY IS A DAY FOR PRAISING BUDDHA HERE...

THEY MUST BE CHANTING FOR THE SAFE RETURN OF THE MEN OF THE VILLAGE...

I DON'T KNOW ABOUT THAT...

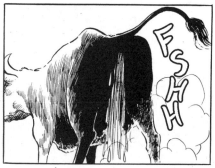

THEY'RE PROBABLY GETTING DRUNK ON UNFILTERED SAKE INSTEAD.

YOU SHOULD VISIT THEM AT THE INN. THE WOMEN'LL BE PLEASED.

FSHH

FSHH

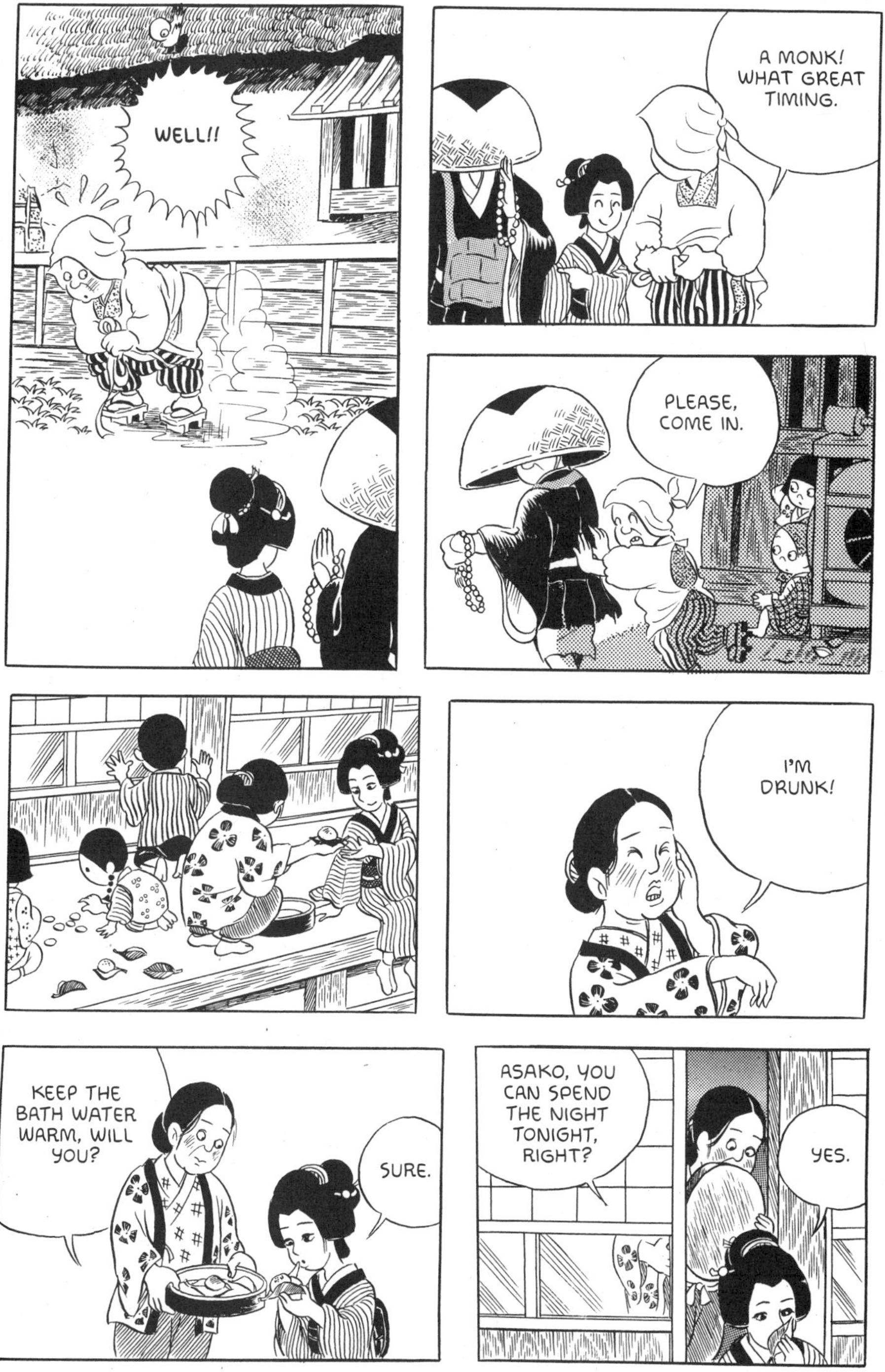
WELL!!
A MONK! WHAT GREAT TIMING.
PLEASE, COME IN.
I'M DRUNK!
KEEP THE BATH WATER WARM, WILL YOU?
SURE.
ASAKO, YOU CAN SPEND THE NIGHT TONIGHT, RIGHT?
YES.

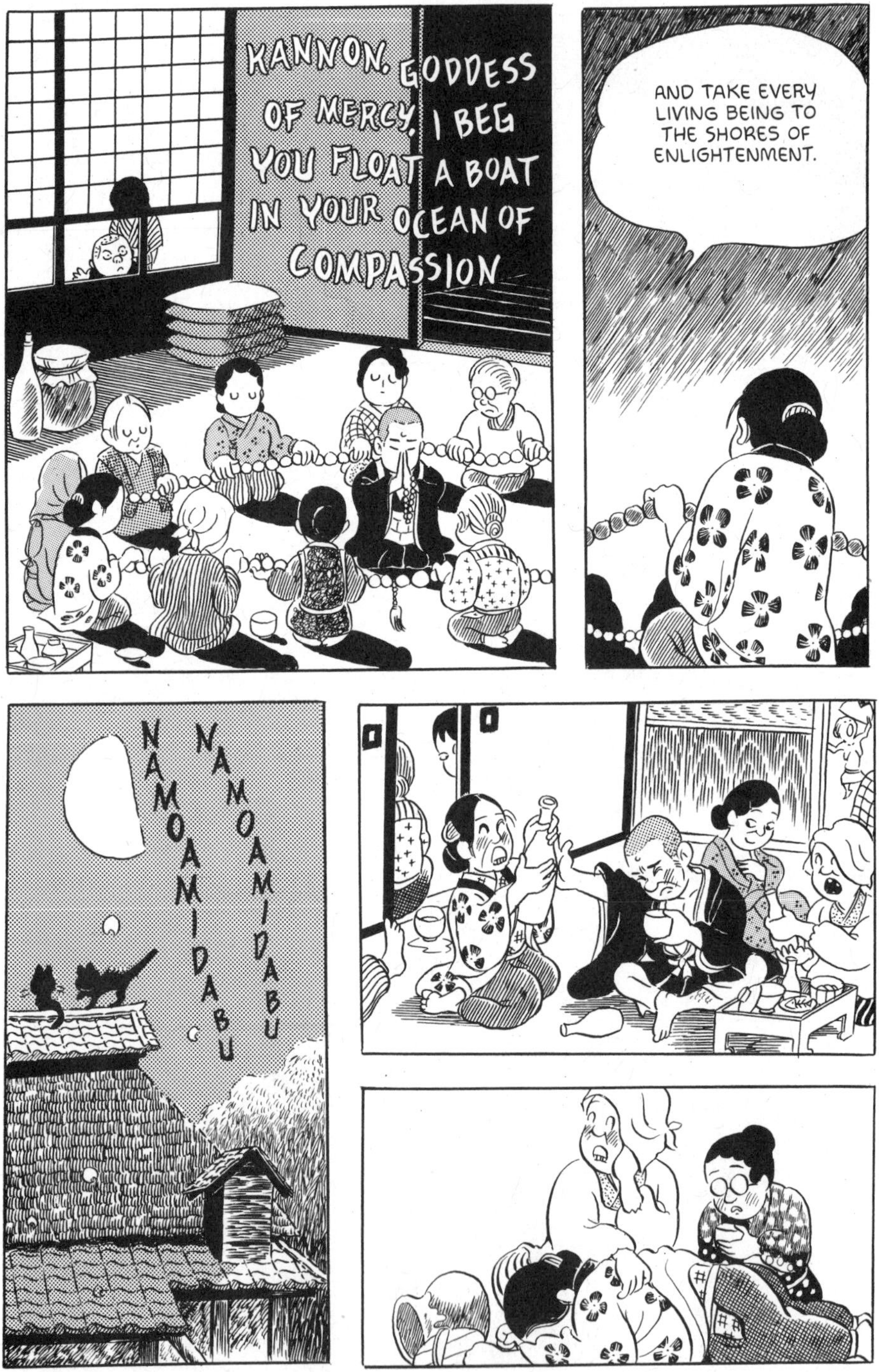
KANNON, GODDESS OF MERCY, I BEG YOU FLOAT A BOAT IN YOUR OCEAN OF COMPASSION
AND TAKE EVERY LIVING BEING TO THE SHORES OF ENLIGHTENMENT.
NAMOAMIDABU
NAMOAMIDABU

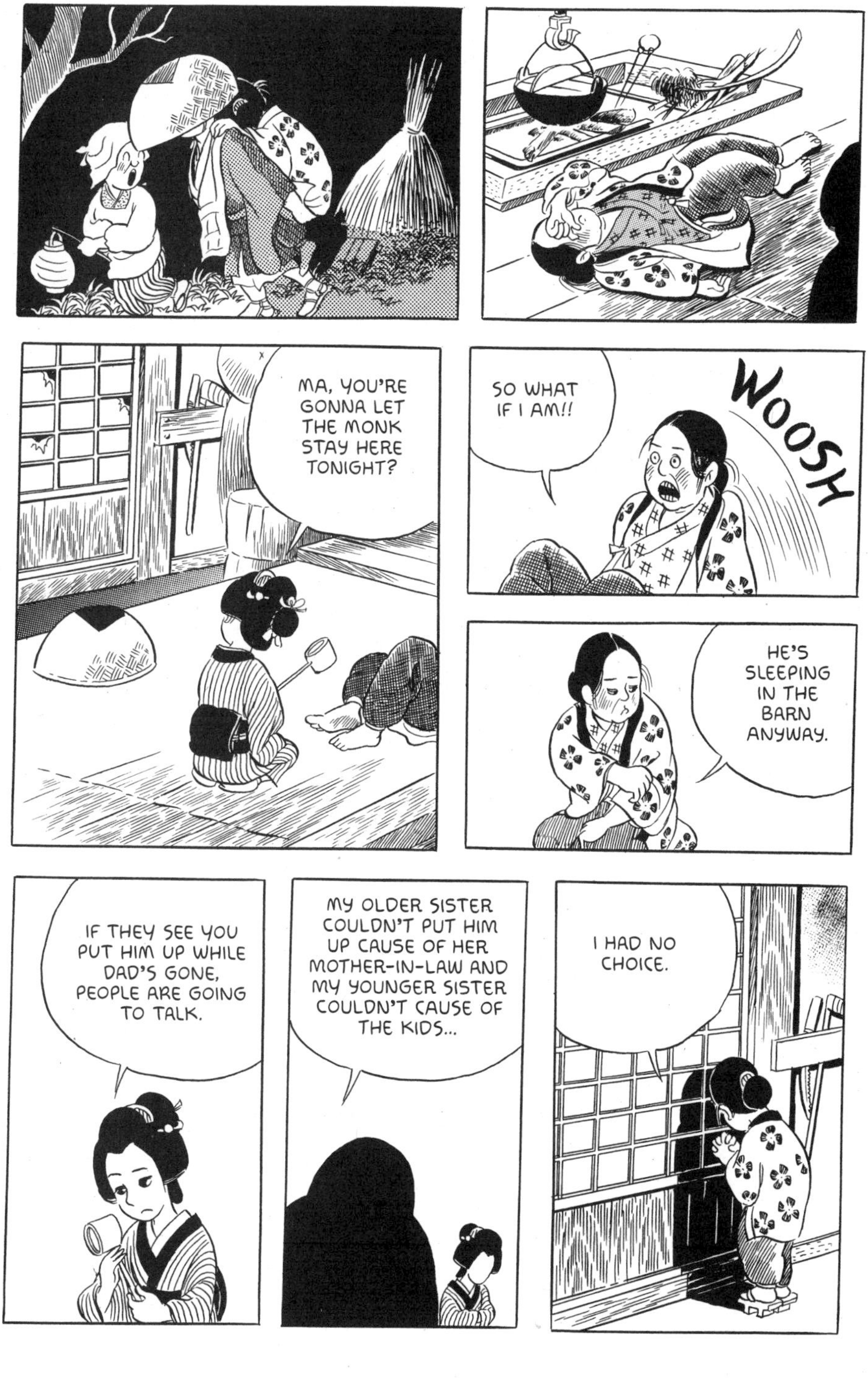
MA, YOU'RE GONNA LET THE MONK STAY HERE TONIGHT?
SO WHAT IF I AM!!
WOOSH
HE'S SLEEPING IN THE BARN ANYWAY.
IF THEY SEE YOU PUT HIM UP WHILE DAD'S GONE, PEOPLE ARE GOING TO TALK.
MY OLDER SISTER COULDN'T PUT HIM UP CAUSE OF HER MOTHER-IN-LAW AND MY YOUNGER SISTER COULDN'T CAUSE OF THE KIDS...
I HAD NO CHOICE.

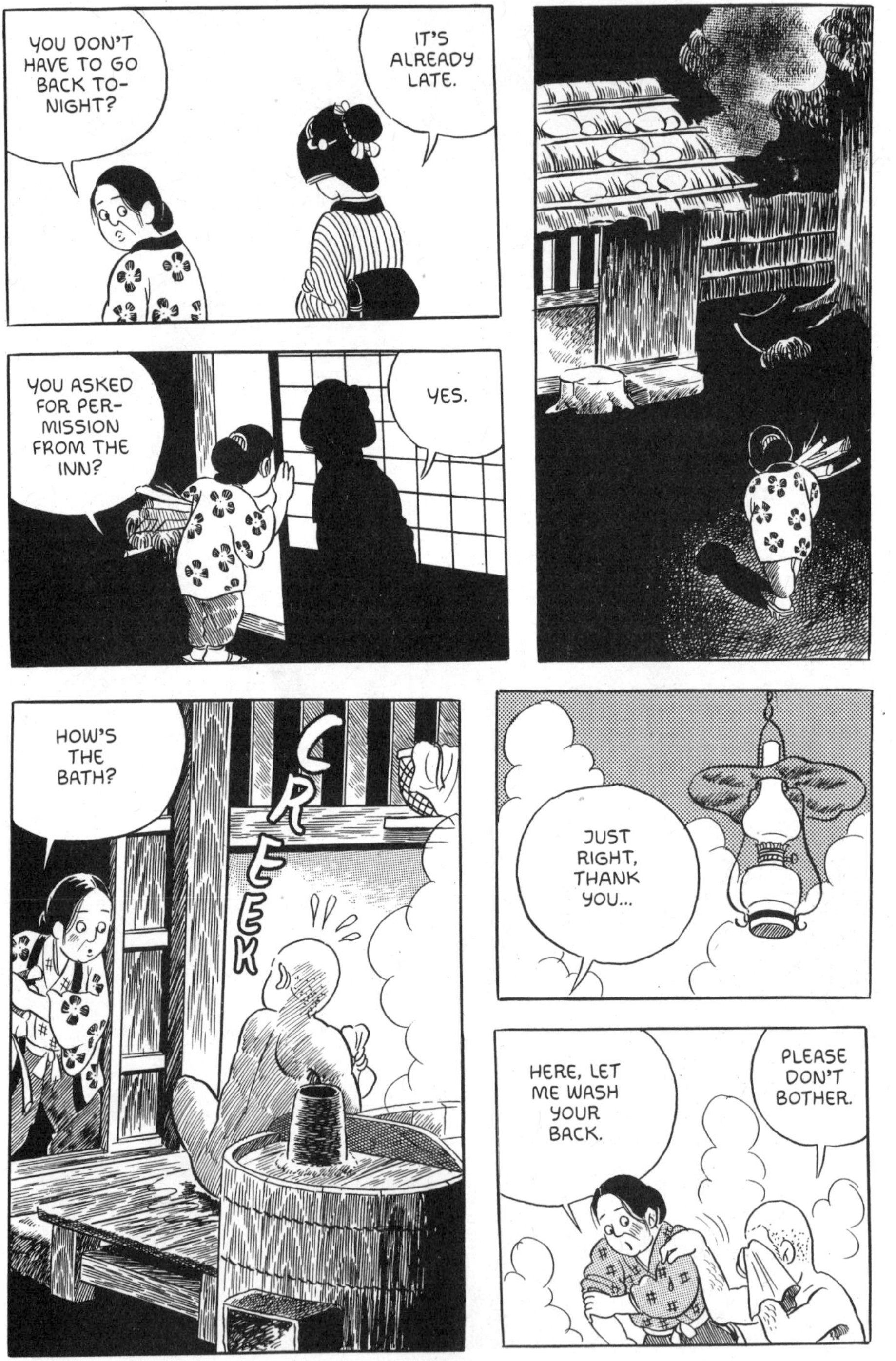
YOU DON'T HAVE TO GO BACK TO-NIGHT?
IT'S ALREADY LATE.
YOU ASKED FOR PER-MISSION FROM THE INN?
YES.
HOW'S THE BATH?
CREEK
JUST RIGHT, THANK YOU...
HERE, LET ME WASH YOUR BACK.
PLEASE DON'T BOTHER.

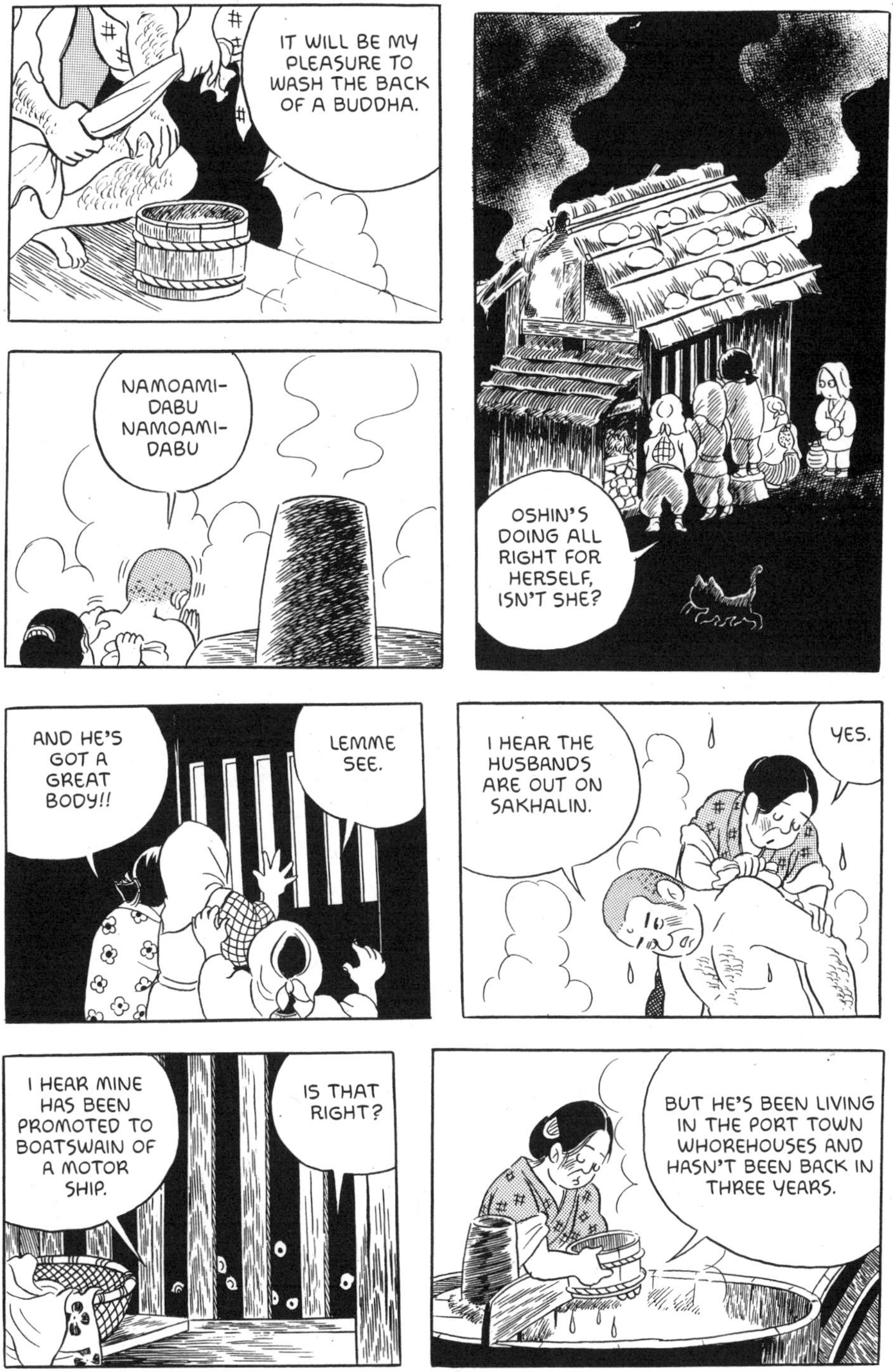
IT WILL BE MY PLEASURE TO WASH THE BACK OF A BUDDHA.
NAMOAMI-DABU NAMOAMI-DABU
OSHIN'S DOING ALL RIGHT FOR HERSELF, ISN'T SHE?
AND HE'S GOT A GREAT BODY!!
LEMME SEE.
I HEAR THE HUSBANDS ARE OUT ON SAKHALIN.
YES.
I HEAR MINE HAS BEEN PROMOTED TO BOATSWAIN OF A MOTOR SHIP.
IS THAT RIGHT?
BUT HE'S BEEN LIVING IN THE PORT TOWN WHOREHOUSES AND HASN'T BEEN BACK IN THREE YEARS.

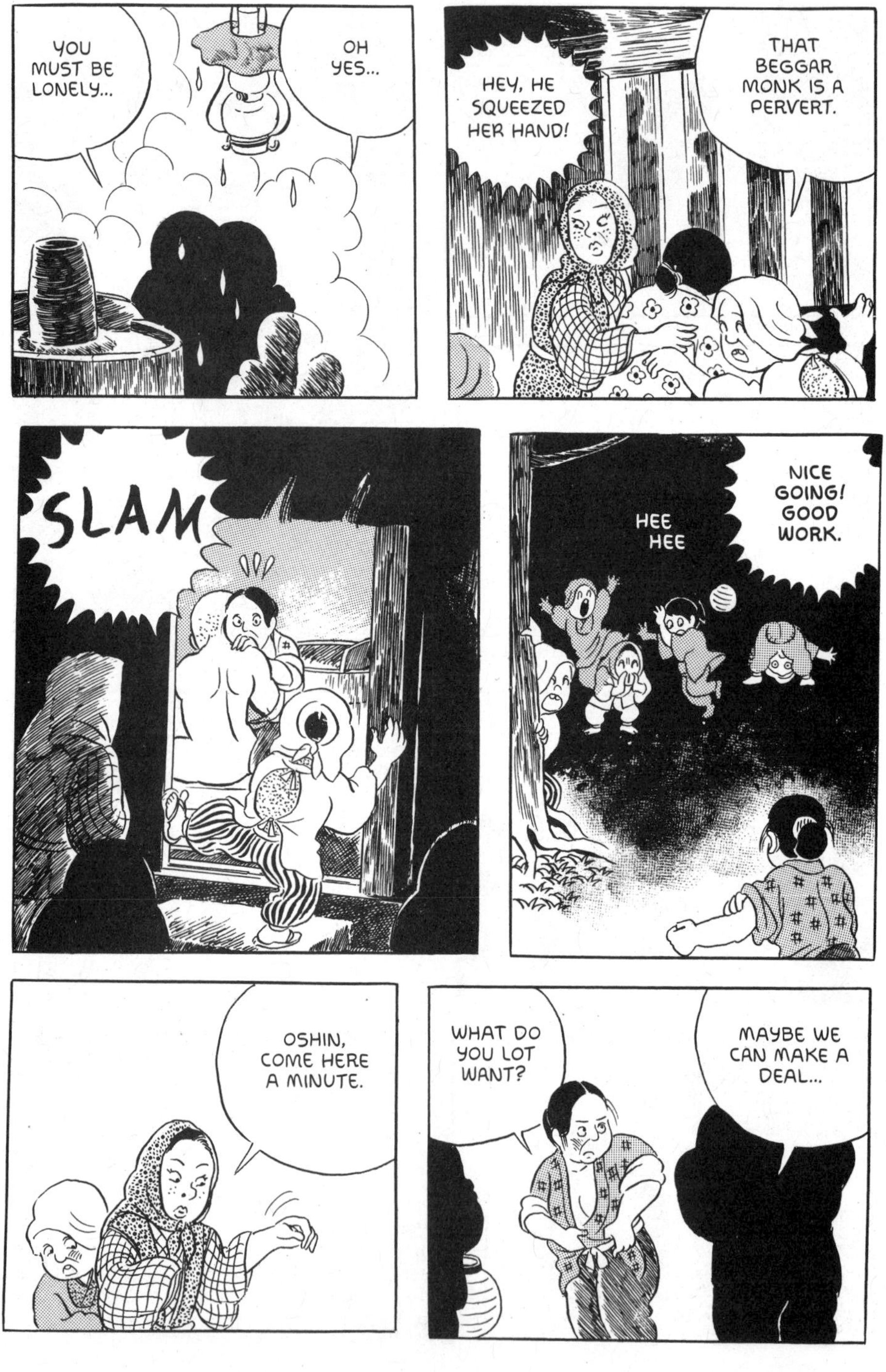
YOU MUST BE LONELY...
OH YES...
HEY, HE SQUEEZED HER HAND!
THAT BEGGAR MONK IS A PERVERT.
SLAM
HEE HEE
NICE GOING! GOOD WORK.
OSHIN, COME HERE A MINUTE.
WHAT DO YOU LOT WANT?
MAYBE WE CAN MAKE A DEAL...

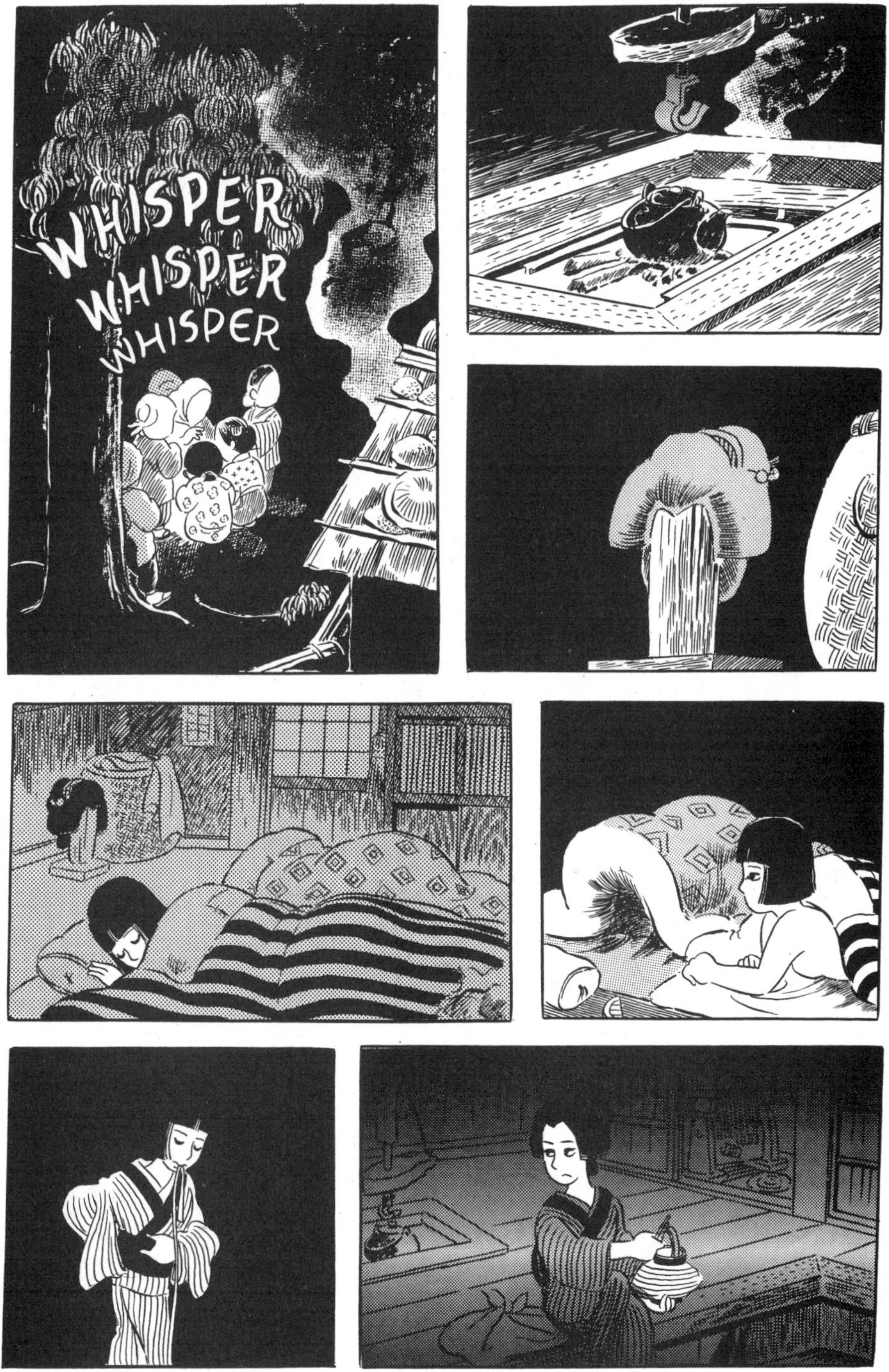
WHISPER
WHISPER
WHISPER

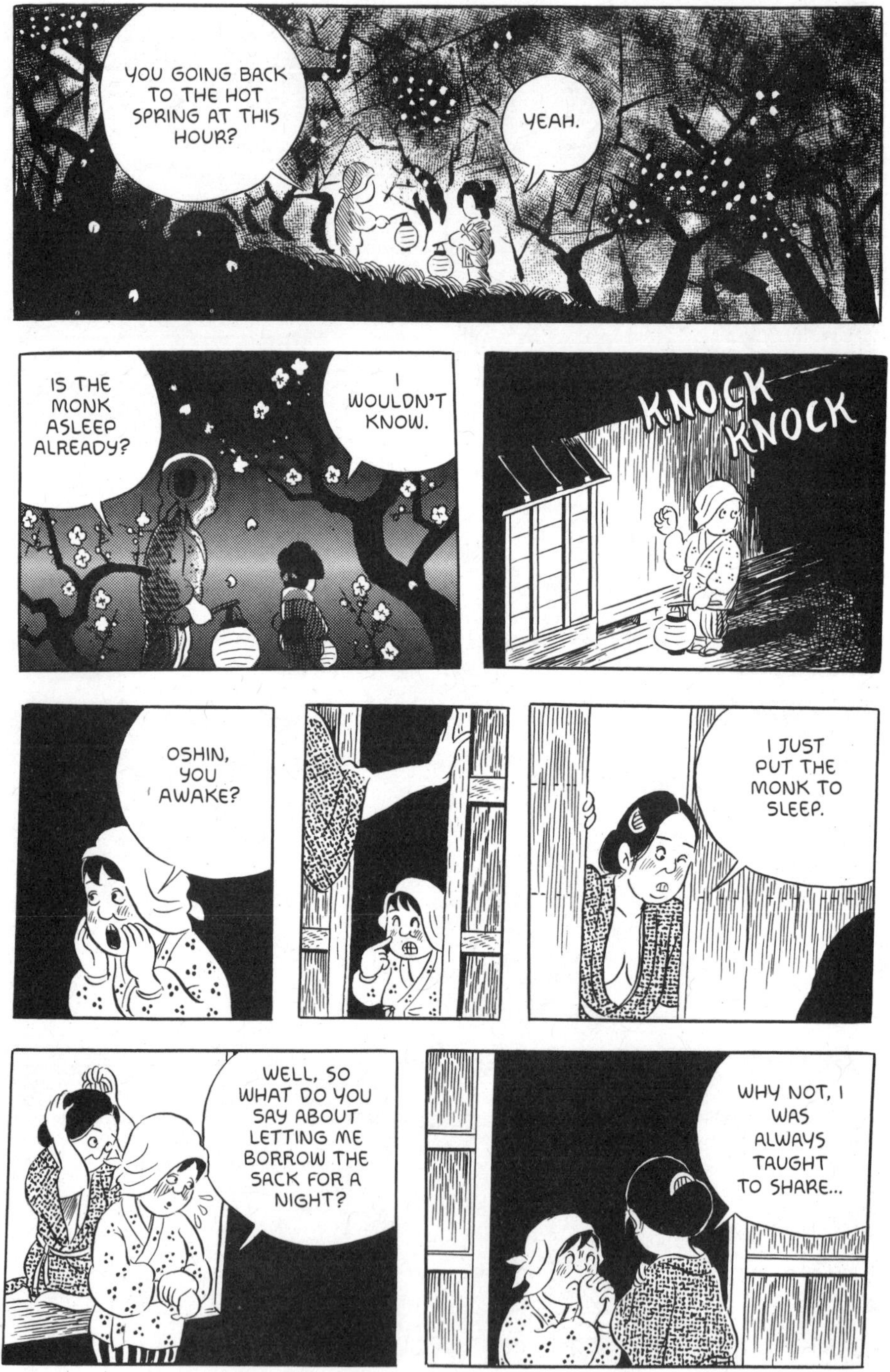
YOU GOING BACK TO THE HOT SPRING AT THIS HOUR?
YEAH.
IS THE MONK ASLEEP ALREADY?
I WOULDN'T KNOW.
KNOCK KNOCK
OSHIN, YOU AWAKE?
I JUST PUT THE MONK TO SLEEP.
WELL, SO WHAT DO YOU SAY ABOUT LETTING ME BORROW THE SACK FOR A NIGHT?
WHY NOT, I WAS ALWAYS TAUGHT TO SHARE...

GIMME A HAND, WILL YOU?

HUR-RUMPH...

THUD

...

IT'S A LIVELY BAG FOR SURE.

NOBODY WILL PAY YOU ANY MIND.

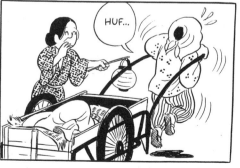

HUF...

HUMPH...

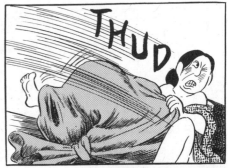

THUD

BRING HIM BACK TO THE BARN BY MORNING, ALL RIGHT?

UH HUH.

FROM THAT DAY ON, A MYSTERIOUS BAG WAS CARRIED OUT FROM OSHIN'S BARN NIGHT AFTER NIGHT.

THE SACK WAS PASSED ALONG FROM ONE WOMAN TO THE NEXT LIKE A ROSARY BEAD.

HEY, KID!!

IF YOU FEED HIM TOO MUCH BLUE LOTUS, YOU'LL GIVE HIM DIARRHEA.

SAY, WHAT'S IN THE BAG?

IT'S CALCIUM SUPER-PHOSPHATE.

GET AWAY FROM IT, KID!

CRACK

MOO

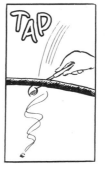

TAP

SPIT SPIT

THUD

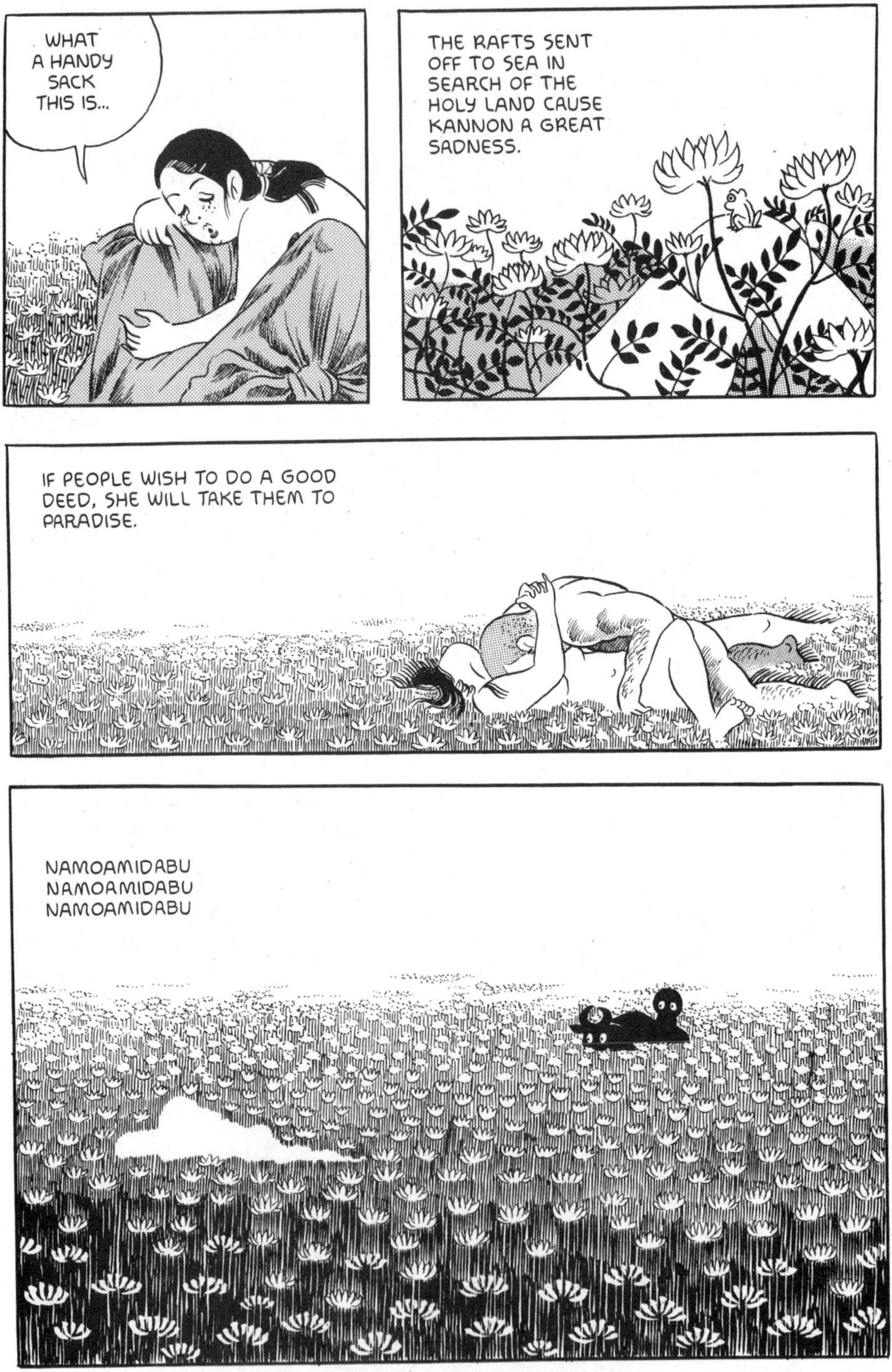
WHAT A HANDY SACK THIS IS...
THE RAFTS SENT OFF TO SEA IN SEARCH OF THE HOLY LAND CAUSE KANNON A GREAT SADNESS.
IF PEOPLE WISH TO DO A GOOD DEED, SHE WILL TAKE THEM TO PARADISE.
NAMOAMIDABU
NAMOAMIDABU
NAMOAMIDABU

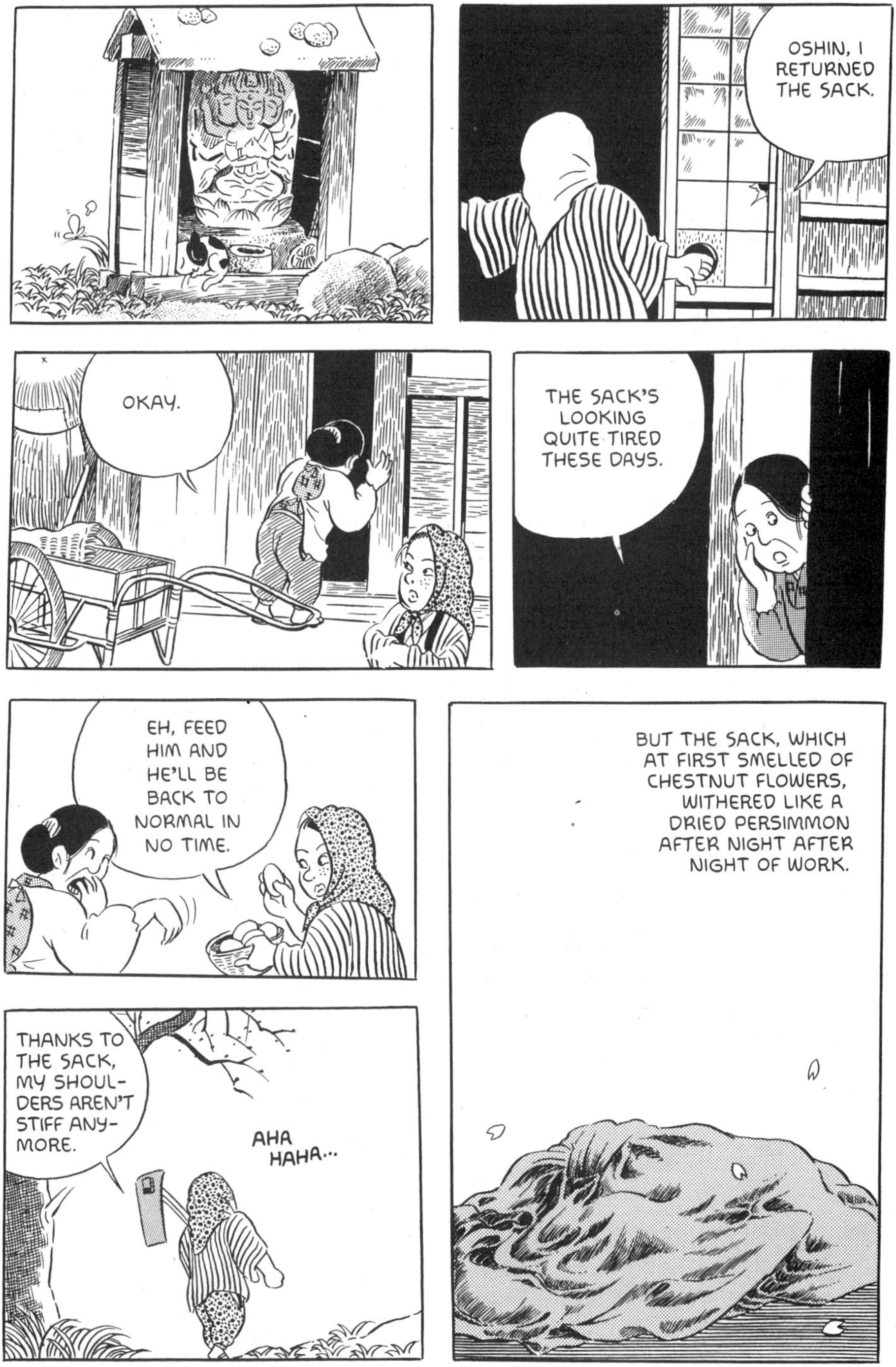
OSHIN, I RETURNED THE SACK.
OKAY.
THE SACK'S LOOKING QUITE TIRED THESE DAYS.
EH, FEED HIM AND HE'LL BE BACK TO NORMAL IN NO TIME.
THANKS TO THE SACK, MY SHOULDERS AREN'T STIFF ANYMORE.
AHA HAHA...
BUT THE SACK, WHICH AT FIRST SMELLED OF CHESTNUT FLOWERS, WITHERED LIKE A DRIED PERSIMMON AFTER NIGHT AFTER NIGHT OF WORK.

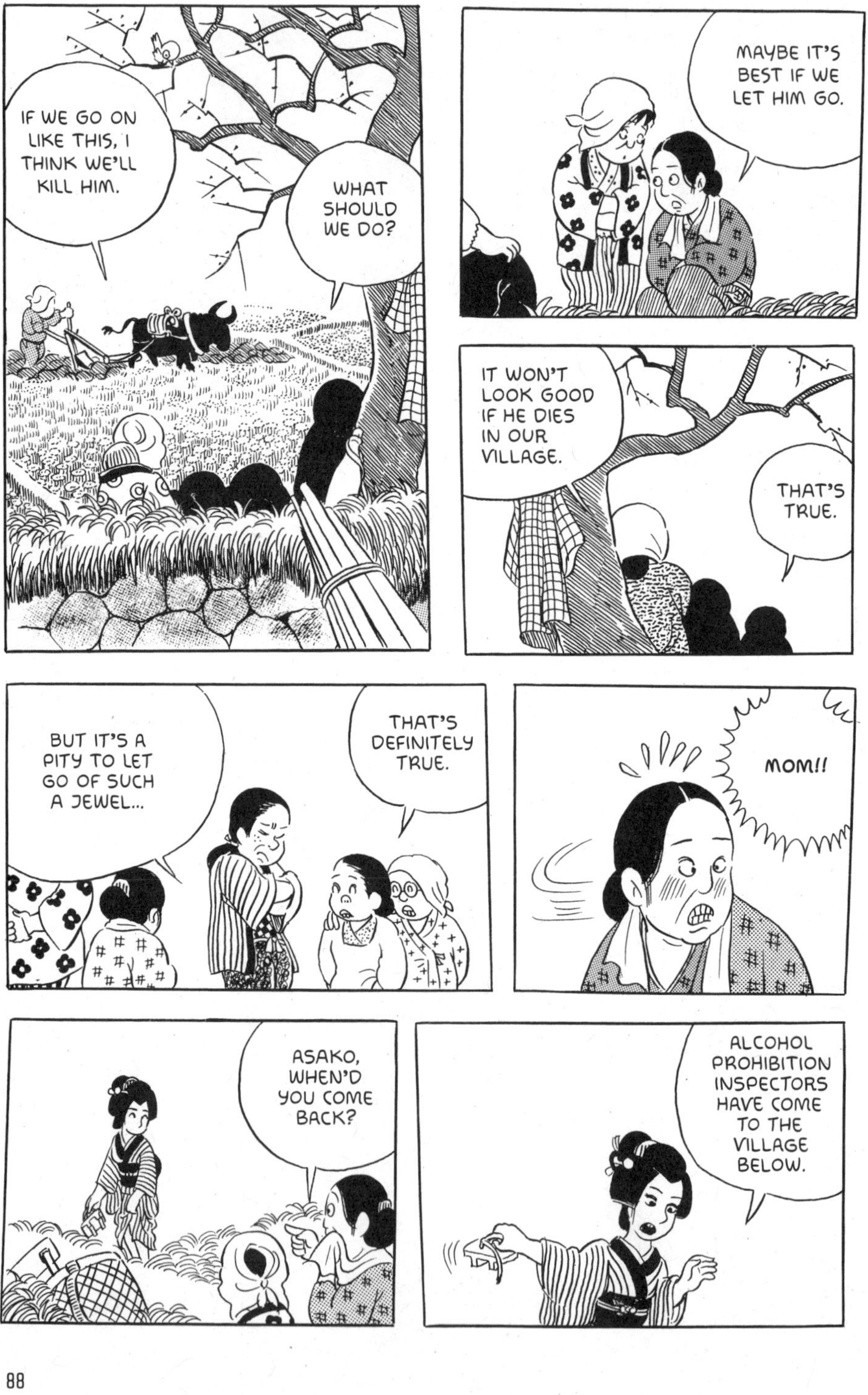
IF WE GO ON LIKE THIS, I THINK WE'LL KILL HIM.
WHAT SHOULD WE DO?
MAYBE IT'S BEST IF WE LET HIM GO.
IT WON'T LOOK GOOD IF HE DIES IN OUR VILLAGE.
THAT'S TRUE.
BUT IT'S A PITY TO LET GO OF SUCH A JEWEL...
THAT'S DEFINITELY TRUE.
MOM!!
ASAKO, WHEN'D YOU COME BACK?
ALCOHOL PROHIBITION INSPECTORS HAVE COME TO THE VILLAGE BELOW.

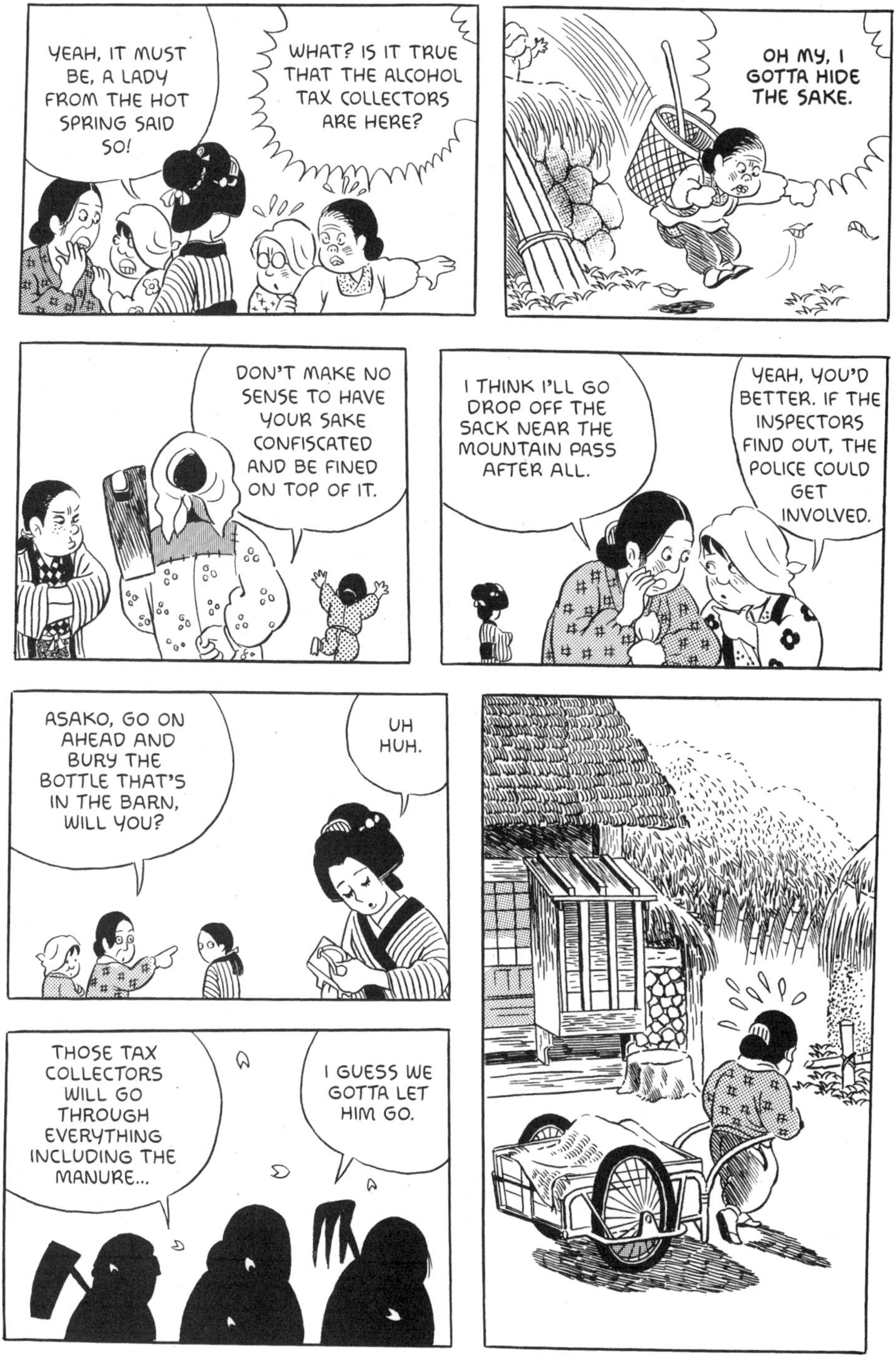
YEAH, IT MUST BE, A LADY FROM THE HOT SPRING SAID SO!
WHAT? IS IT TRUE THAT THE ALCOHOL TAX COLLECTORS ARE HERE?
OH MY, I GOTTA HIDE THE SAKE.
DON'T MAKE NO SENSE TO HAVE YOUR SAKE CONFISCATED AND BE FINED ON TOP OF IT.
I THINK I'LL GO DROP OFF THE SACK NEAR THE MOUNTAIN PASS AFTER ALL.
YEAH, YOU'D BETTER. IF THE INSPECTORS FIND OUT, THE POLICE COULD GET INVOLVED.
ASAKO, GO ON AHEAD AND BURY THE BOTTLE THAT'S IN THE BARN, WILL YOU?
UH HUH.
THOSE TAX COLLECTORS WILL GO THROUGH EVERYTHING INCLUDING THE MANURE...
I GUESS WE GOTTA LET HIM GO.

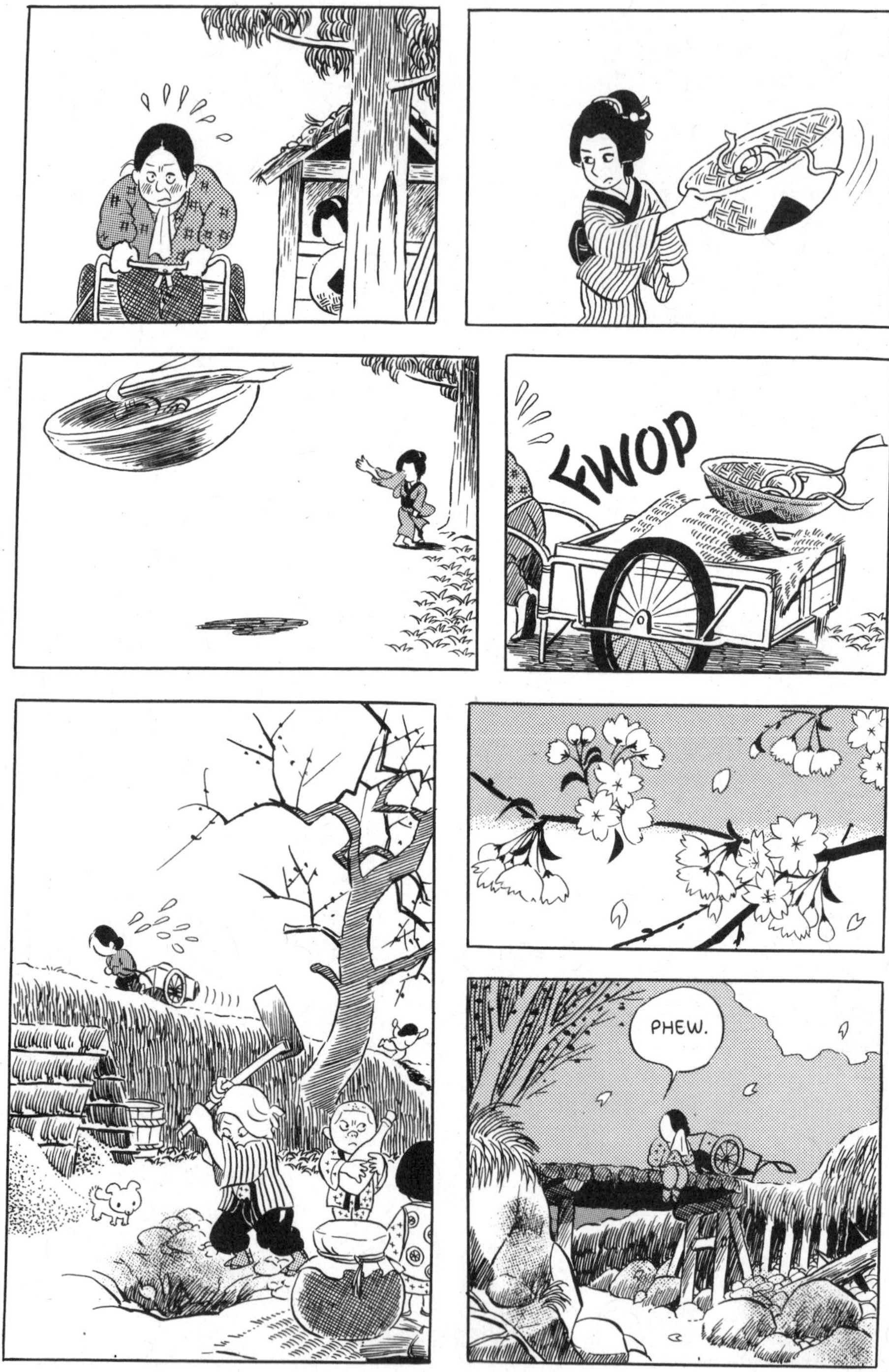
FWOP
PHEW.

THE WEIGHT'S FINALLY OFF MY SHOULDERS.

WOOSH

COME AT ME, TAXMAN, SEE IF I CARE!!

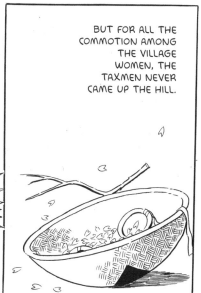

BUT FOR ALL THE COMMOTION AMONG THE VILLAGE WOMEN, THE TAXMEN NEVER CAME UP THE HILL.

AND A WRINKLED MONK LEFT HIS SACK TO CRAWL OVER THE MOUNTAIN PASS.

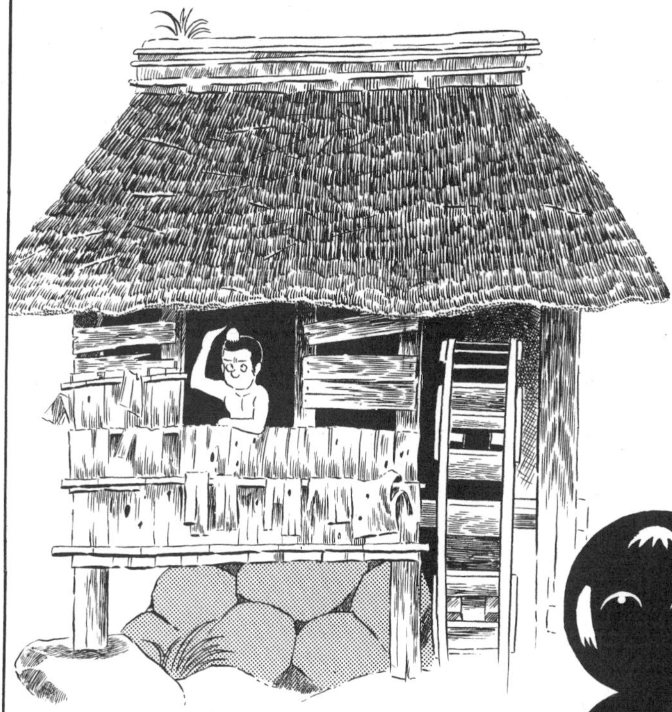

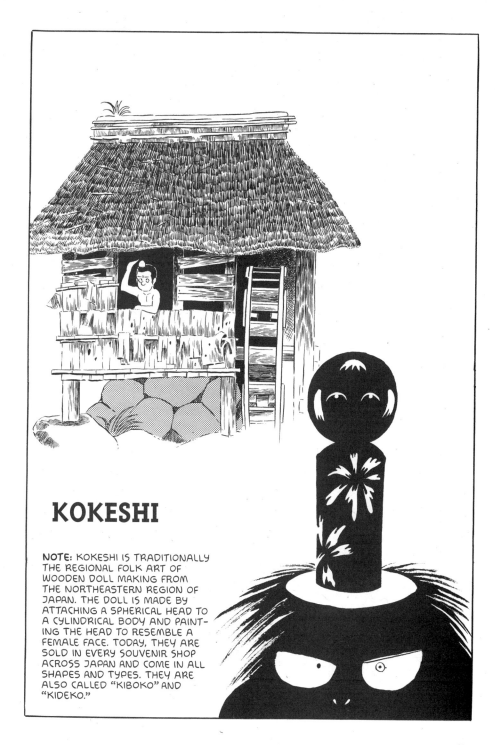

KOKESHI

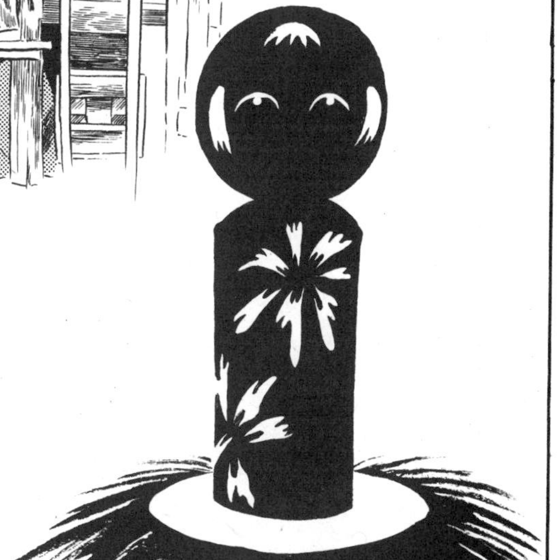

NOTE: KOKESHI IS TRADITIONALLY THE REGIONAL FOLK ART OF WOODEN DOLL MAKING FROM THE NORTHEASTERN REGION OF JAPAN. THE DOLL IS MADE BY ATTACHING A SPHERICAL HEAD TO A CYLINDRICAL BODY AND PAINTING THE HEAD TO RESEMBLE A FEMALE FACE. TODAY, THEY ARE SOLD IN EVERY SOUVENIR SHOP ACROSS JAPAN AND COME IN ALL SHAPES AND TYPES. THEY ARE ALSO CALLED "KIBOKO" AND "KIDEKO."

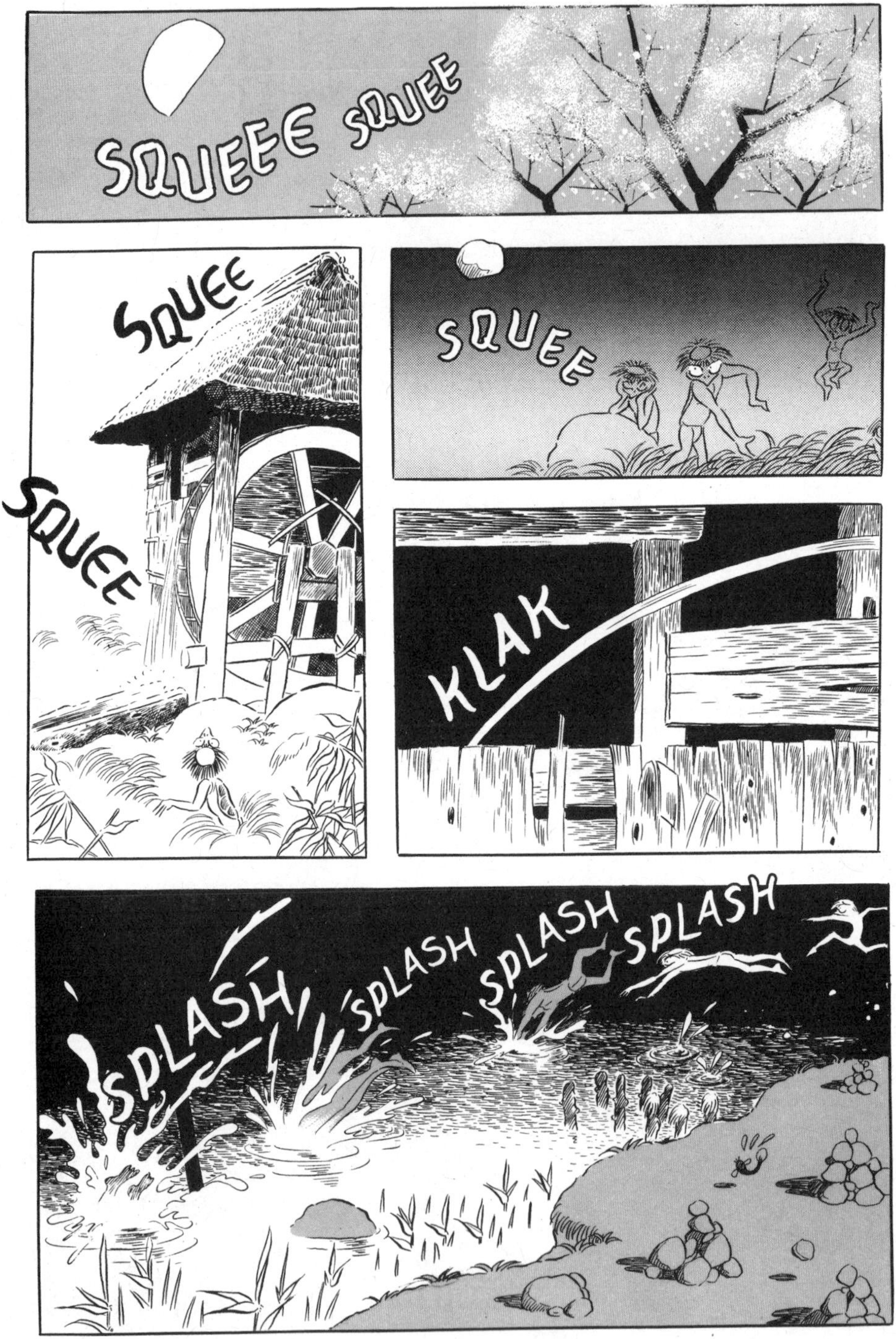
SQUEEE SQUEE
SQUEE
SQUEE
SQUEE
KLAK
SPLASH
SPLASH
SPLASH
SPLASH

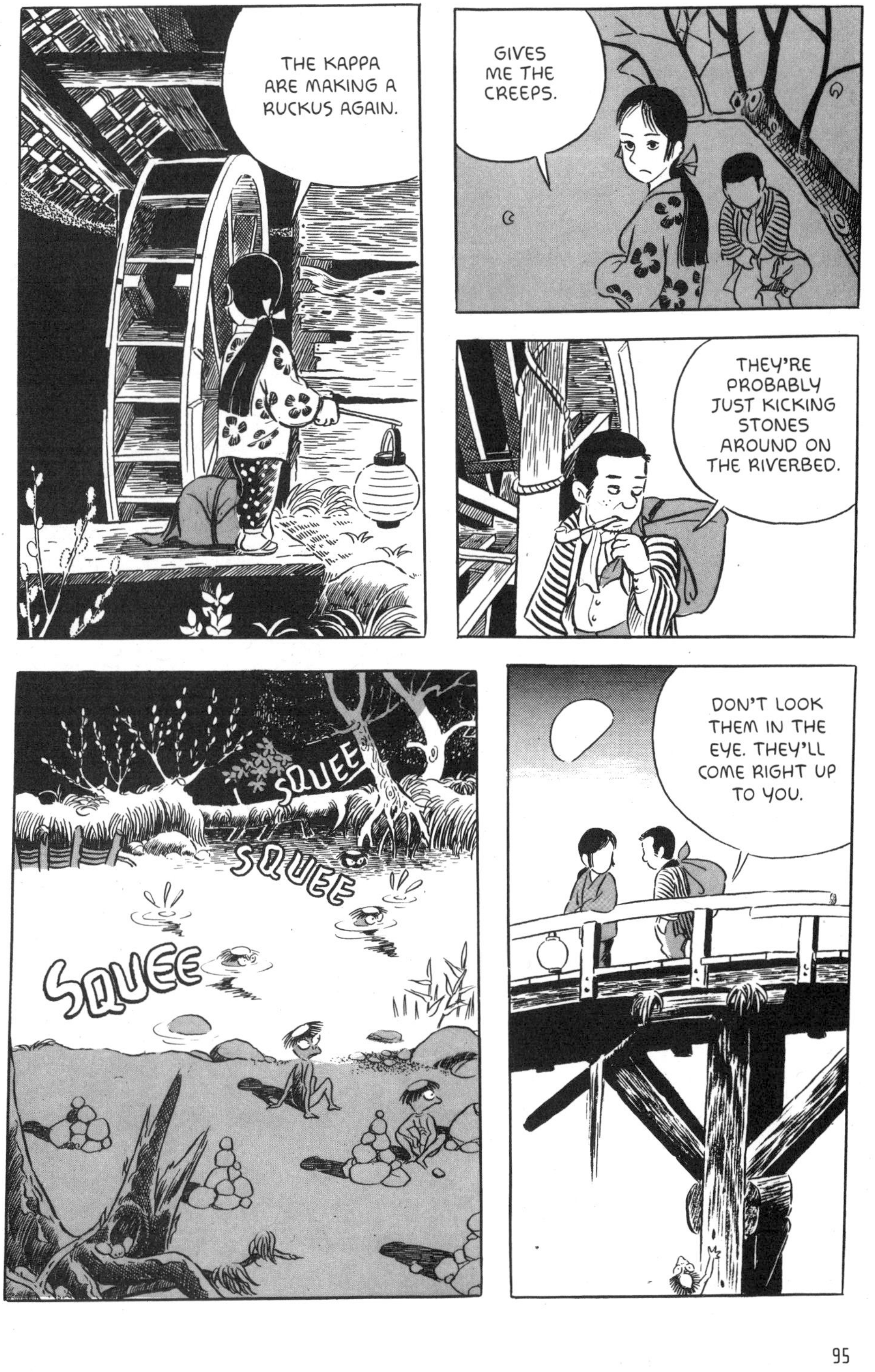
THE KAPPA ARE MAKING A RUCKUS AGAIN.
GIVES ME THE CREEPS.
THEY'RE PROBABLY JUST KICKING STONES AROUND ON THE RIVERBED.
SQUEE
SQUEE
SQUEE
DON'T LOOK THEM IN THE EYE. THEY'LL COME RIGHT UP TO YOU.

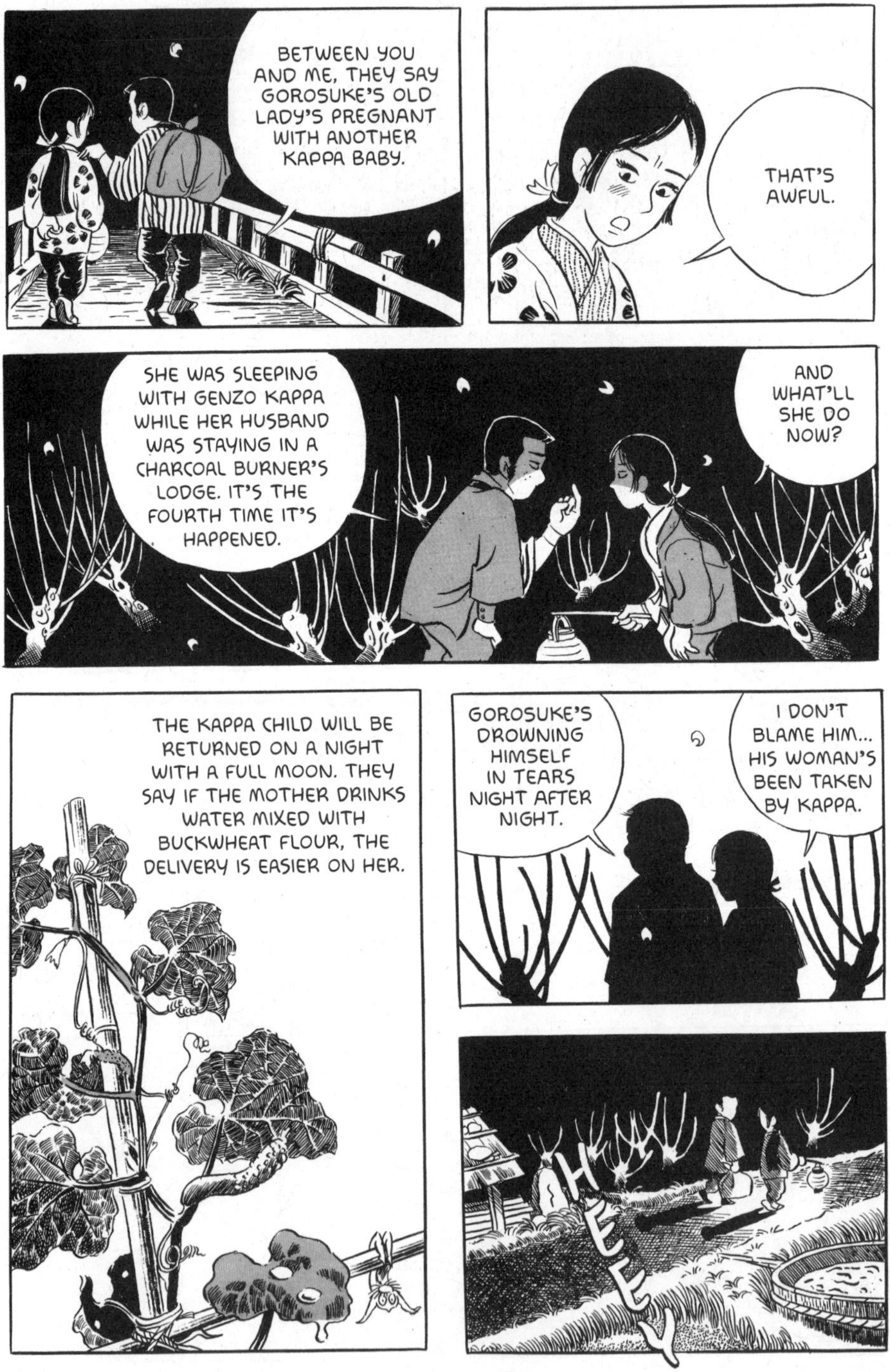
BETWEEN YOU AND ME, THEY SAY GOROSUKE'S OLD LADY'S PREGNANT WITH ANOTHER KAPPA BABY.
THAT'S AWFUL.
SHE WAS SLEEPING WITH GENZO KAPPA WHILE HER HUSBAND WAS STAYING IN A CHARCOAL BURNER'S LODGE. IT'S THE FOURTH TIME IT'S HAPPENED.
AND WHAT'LL SHE DO NOW?
THE KAPPA CHILD WILL BE RETURNED ON A NIGHT WITH A FULL MOON. THEY SAY IF THE MOTHER DRINKS WATER MIXED WITH BUCKWHEAT FLOUR, THE DELIVERY IS EASIER ON HER.
GOROSUKE'S DROWNING HIMSELF IN TEARS NIGHT AFTER NIGHT.
I DON'T BLAME HIM... HIS WOMAN'S BEEN TAKEN BY KAPPA.

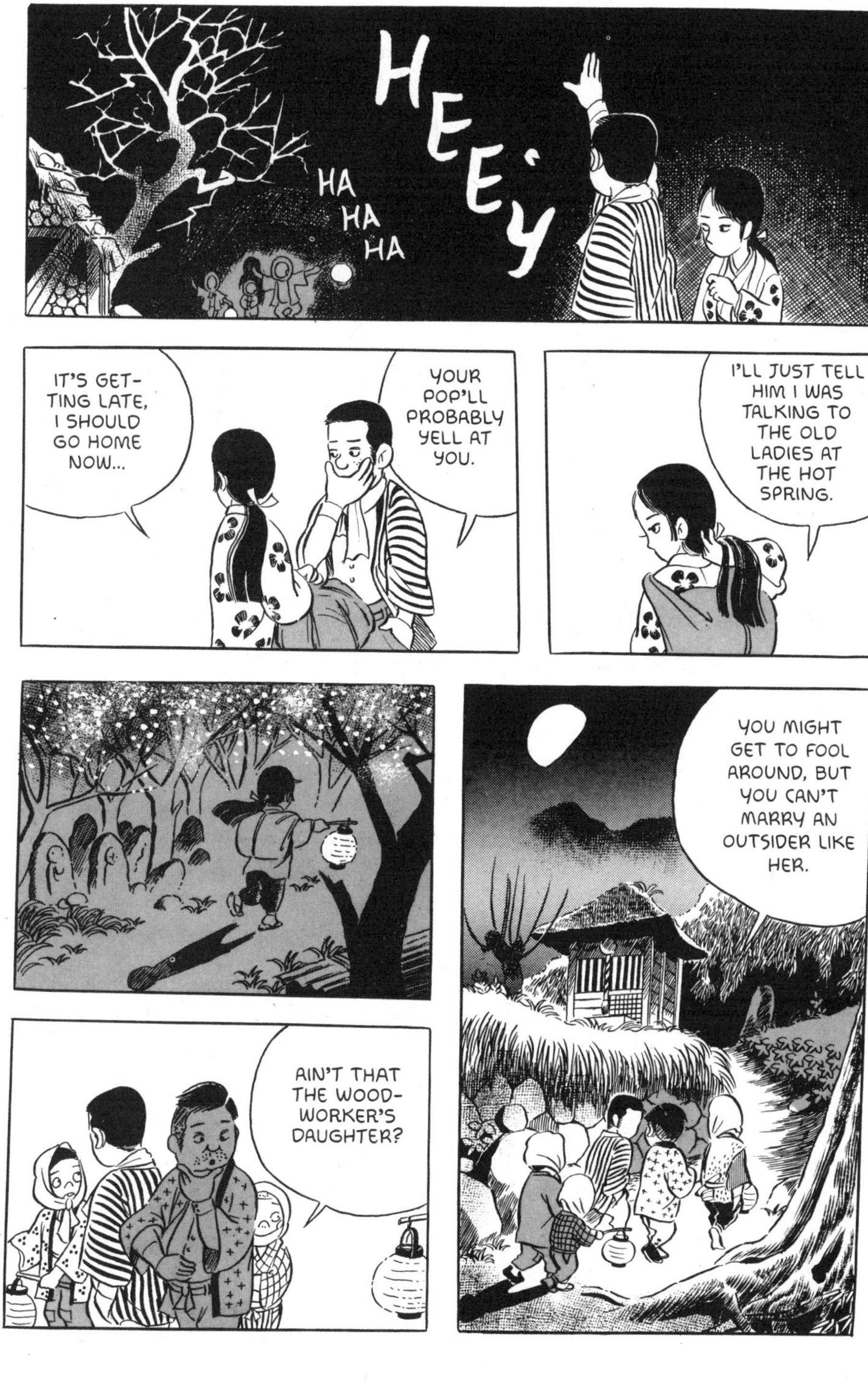
HEEEY
HA HA HA
IT'S GETTING LATE, I SHOULD GO HOME NOW...
YOUR POP'LL PROBABLY YELL AT YOU.
I'LL JUST TELL HIM I WAS TALKING TO THE OLD LADIES AT THE HOT SPRING.
AIN'T THAT THE WOODWORKER'S DAUGHTER?
YOU MIGHT GET TO FOOL AROUND, BUT YOU CAN'T MARRY AN OUTSIDER LIKE HER.

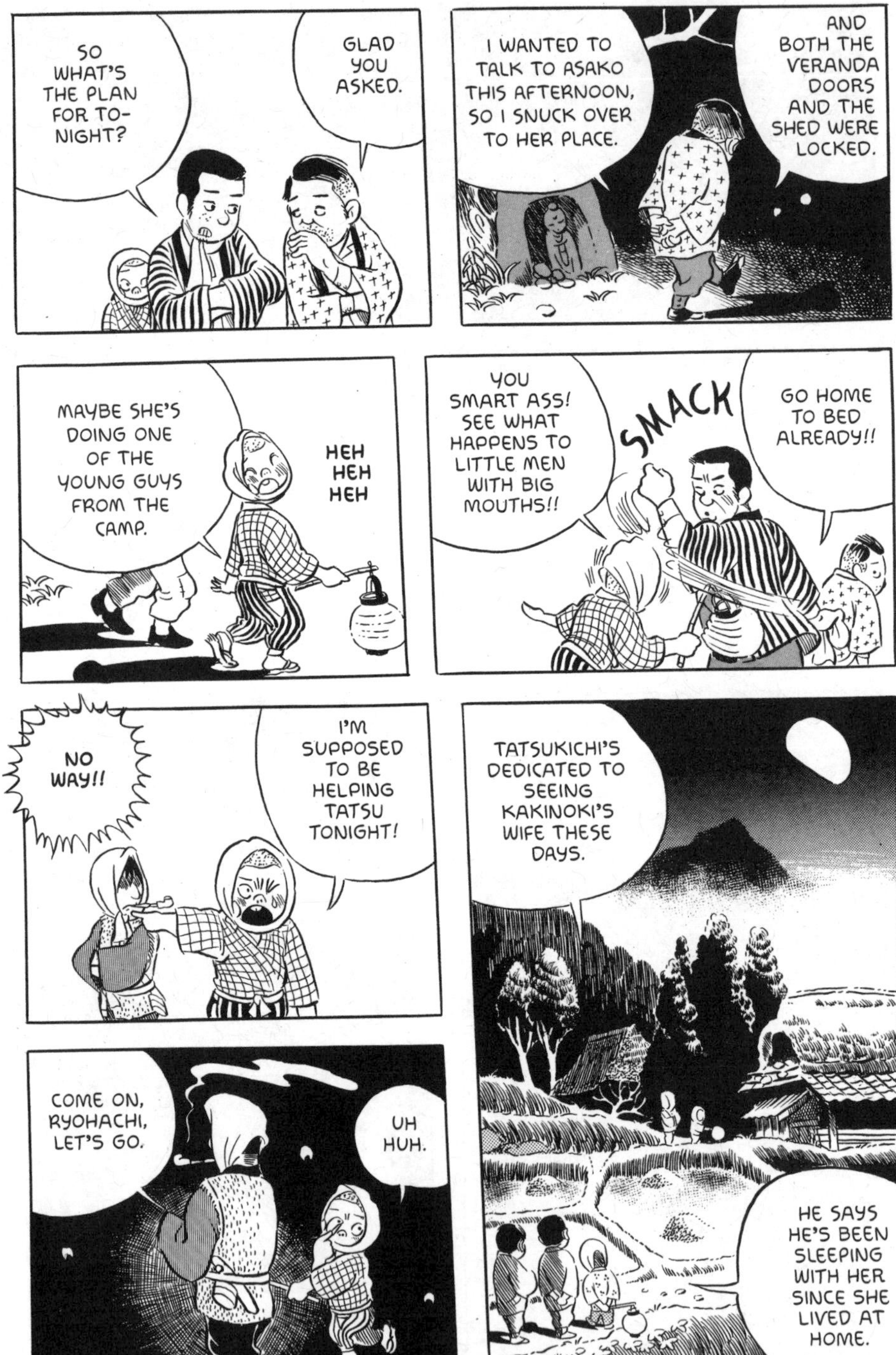
SO WHAT'S THE PLAN FOR TO-NIGHT?
GLAD YOU ASKED.
I WANTED TO TALK TO ASAKO THIS AFTERNOON, SO I SNUCK OVER TO HER PLACE.
AND BOTH THE VERANDA DOORS AND THE SHED WERE LOCKED.
MAYBE SHE'S DOING ONE OF THE YOUNG GUYS FROM THE CAMP.
HEH HEH HEH
YOU SMART ASS! SEE WHAT HAPPENS TO LITTLE MEN WITH BIG MOUTHS!!
SMACK
GO HOME TO BED ALREADY!!
NO WAY!!
I'M SUPPOSED TO BE HELPING TATSU TONIGHT!
COME ON, RYOHACHI, LET'S GO.
UH HUH.
TATSUKICHI'S DEDICATED TO SEEING KAKINOKI'S WIFE THESE DAYS.
HE SAYS HE'S BEEN SLEEPING WITH HER SINCE SHE LIVED AT HOME.

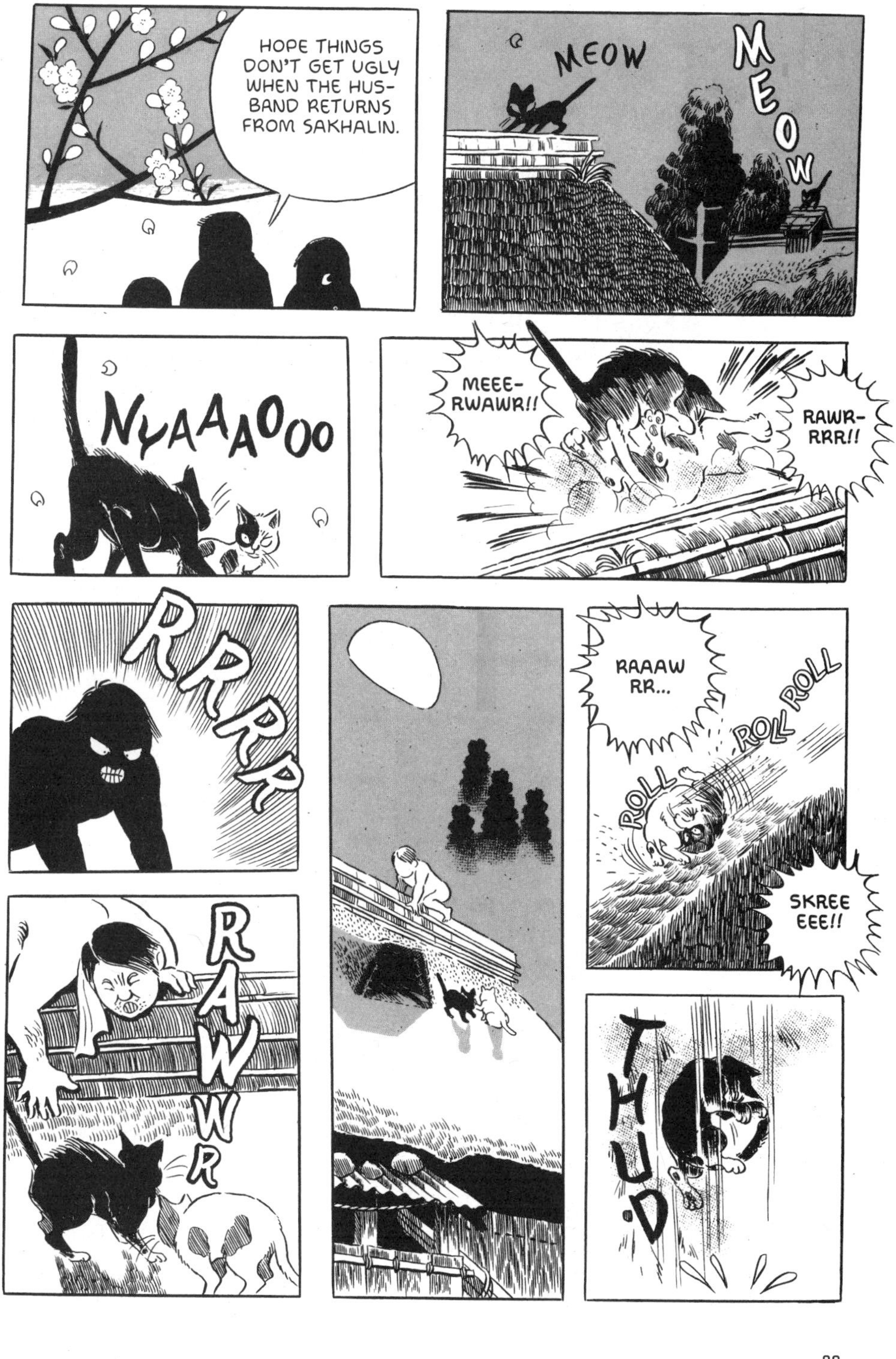

HOPE THINGS DON'T GET UGLY WHEN THE HUS- BAND RETURNS FROM SAKHALIN.
MEOW
MEOW
NYAAAOOO
MEEE- RWAWR!!
RAWR- RRR!!
RRRR
RAAAW RR...
ROLL ROLL ROLL ROLL
SKREE EEE!!
RAWWR
THUD

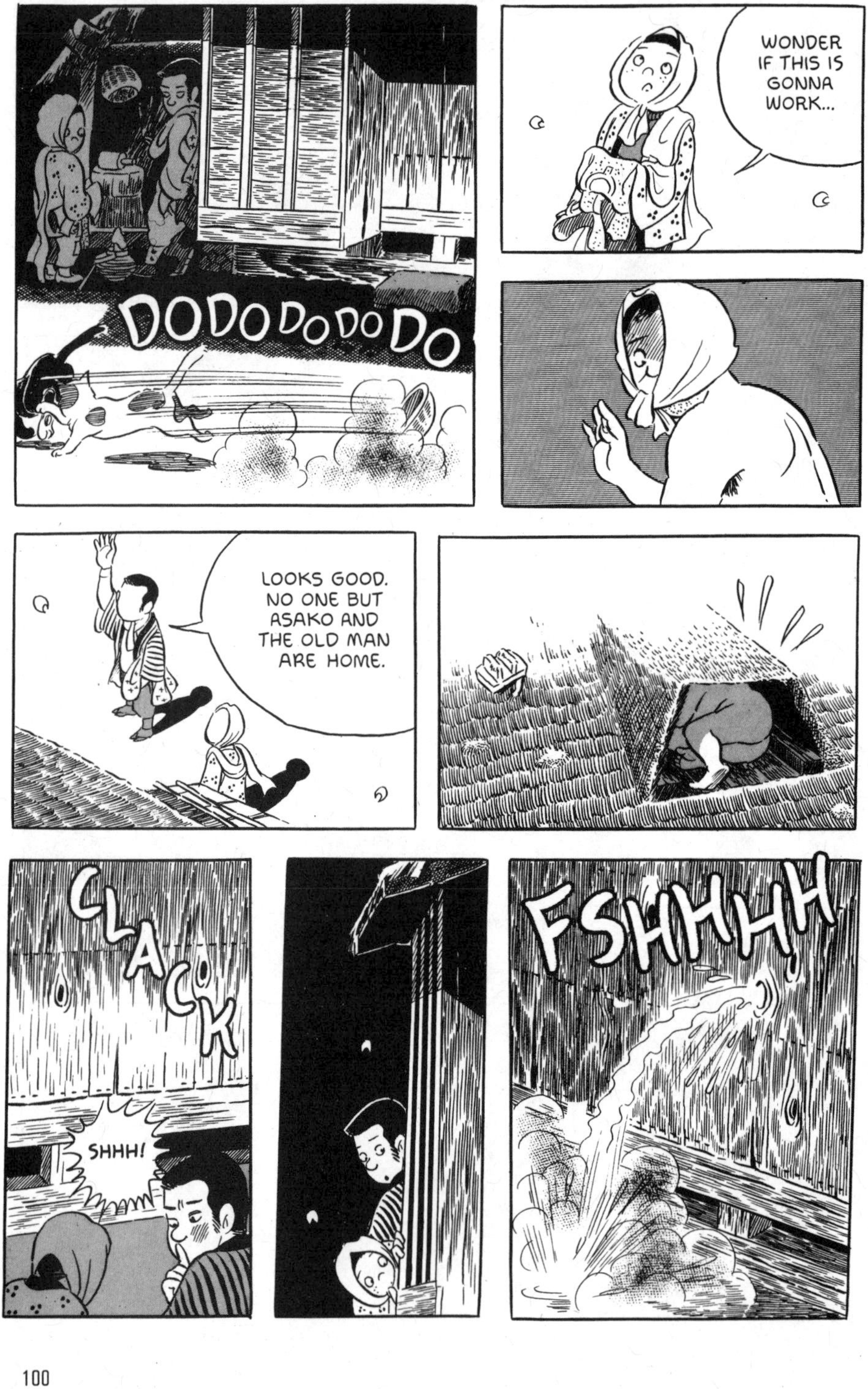
DODODODODO
WONDER IF THIS IS GONNA WORK...
LOOKS GOOD. NO ONE BUT ASAKO AND THE OLD MAN ARE HOME.
CLACK
SHHH!
FSHHHH

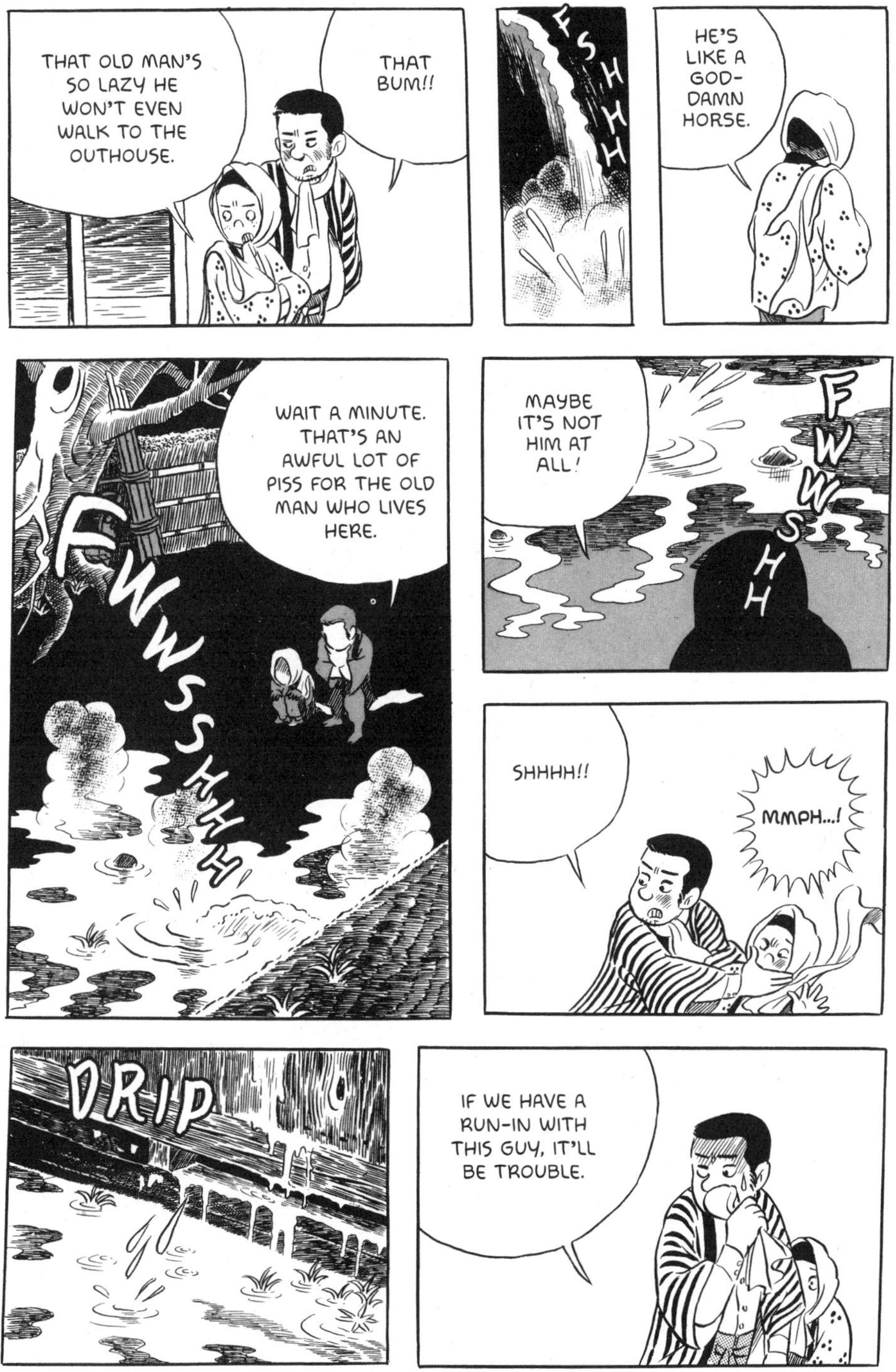
THAT OLD MAN'S SO LAZY HE WON'T EVEN WALK TO THE OUTHOUSE.
THAT BUM!!
FSHHH
HE'S LIKE A GOD-DAMN HORSE.
FWWSSHHH
WAIT A MINUTE. THAT'S AN AWFUL LOT OF PISS FOR THE OLD MAN WHO LIVES HERE.
MAYBE IT'S NOT HIM AT ALL!
FWWSHH
SHHHH!!
MMPH...!
DRIP
IF WE HAVE A RUN-IN WITH THIS GUY, IT'LL BE TROUBLE.

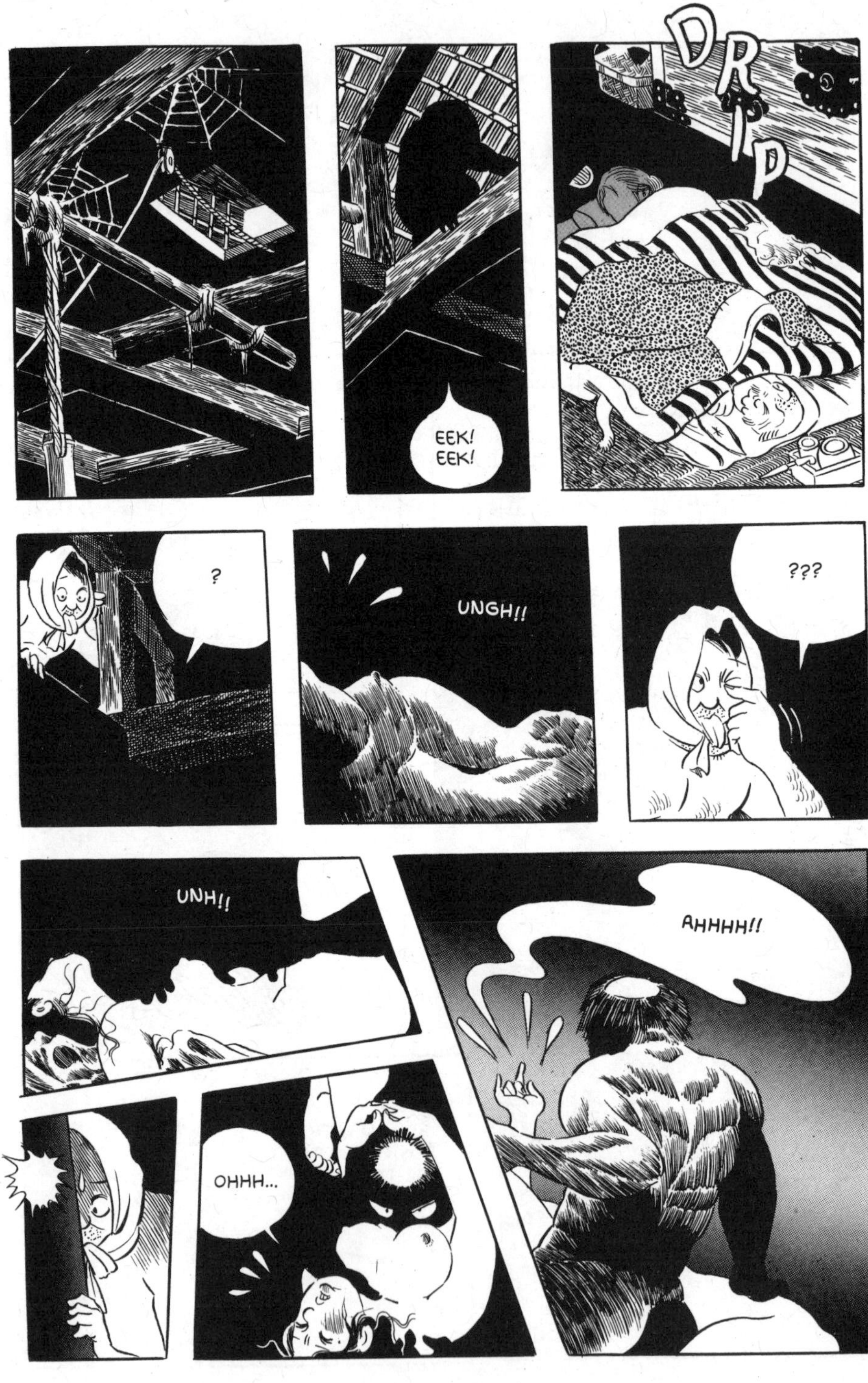
EEK!
EEK!
DRIP
?
UNGH!!
???
UNH!!
OHHH...
AHHHH!!

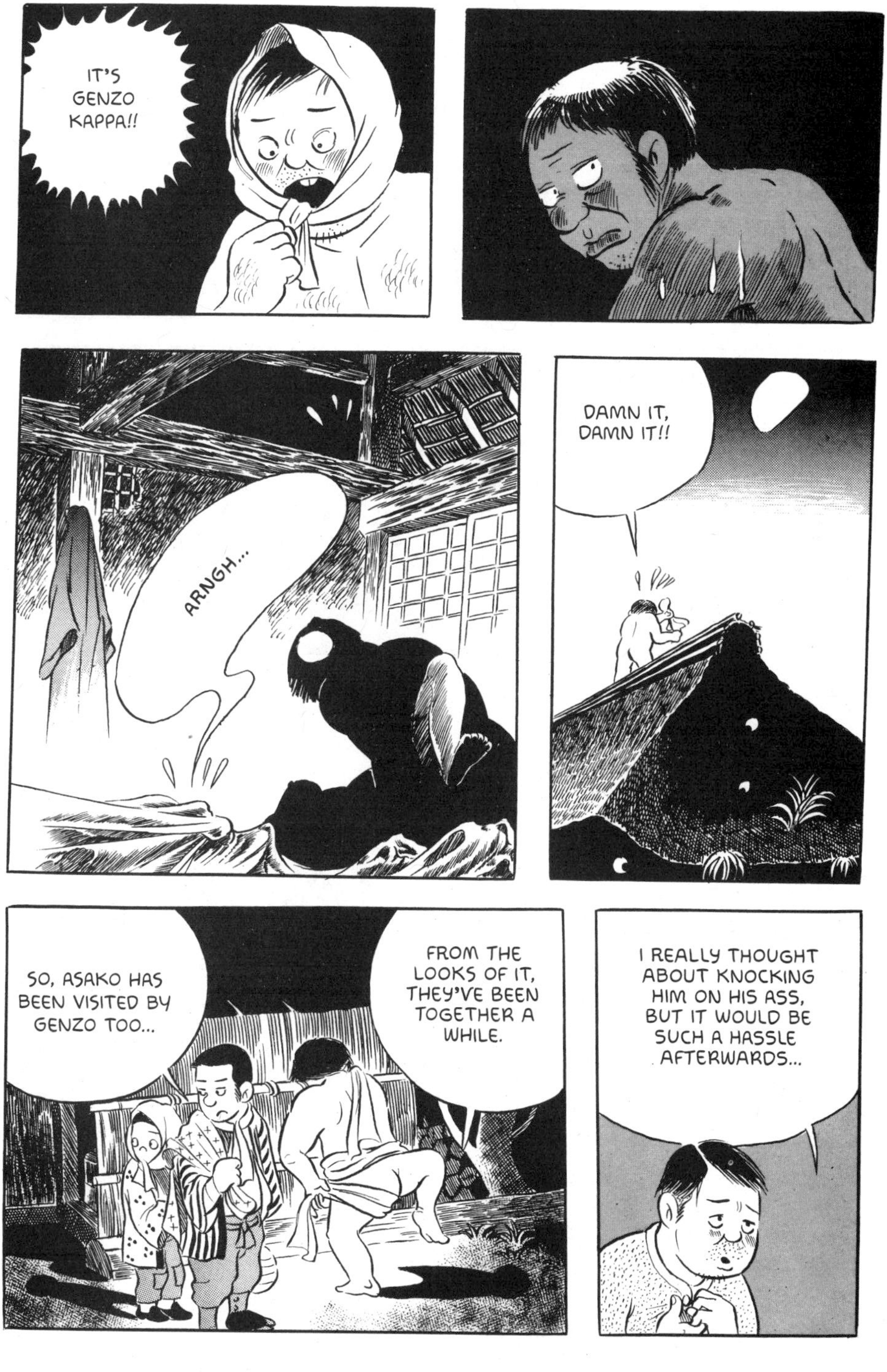
IT'S GENZO KAPPA!!
ARNGH...
DAMN IT, DAMN IT!!
SO, ASAKO HAS BEEN VISITED BY GENZO TOO...
FROM THE LOOKS OF IT, THEY'VE BEEN TOGETHER A WHILE.
I REALLY THOUGHT ABOUT KNOCKING HIM ON HIS ASS, BUT IT WOULD BE SUCH A HASSLE AFTERWARDS...

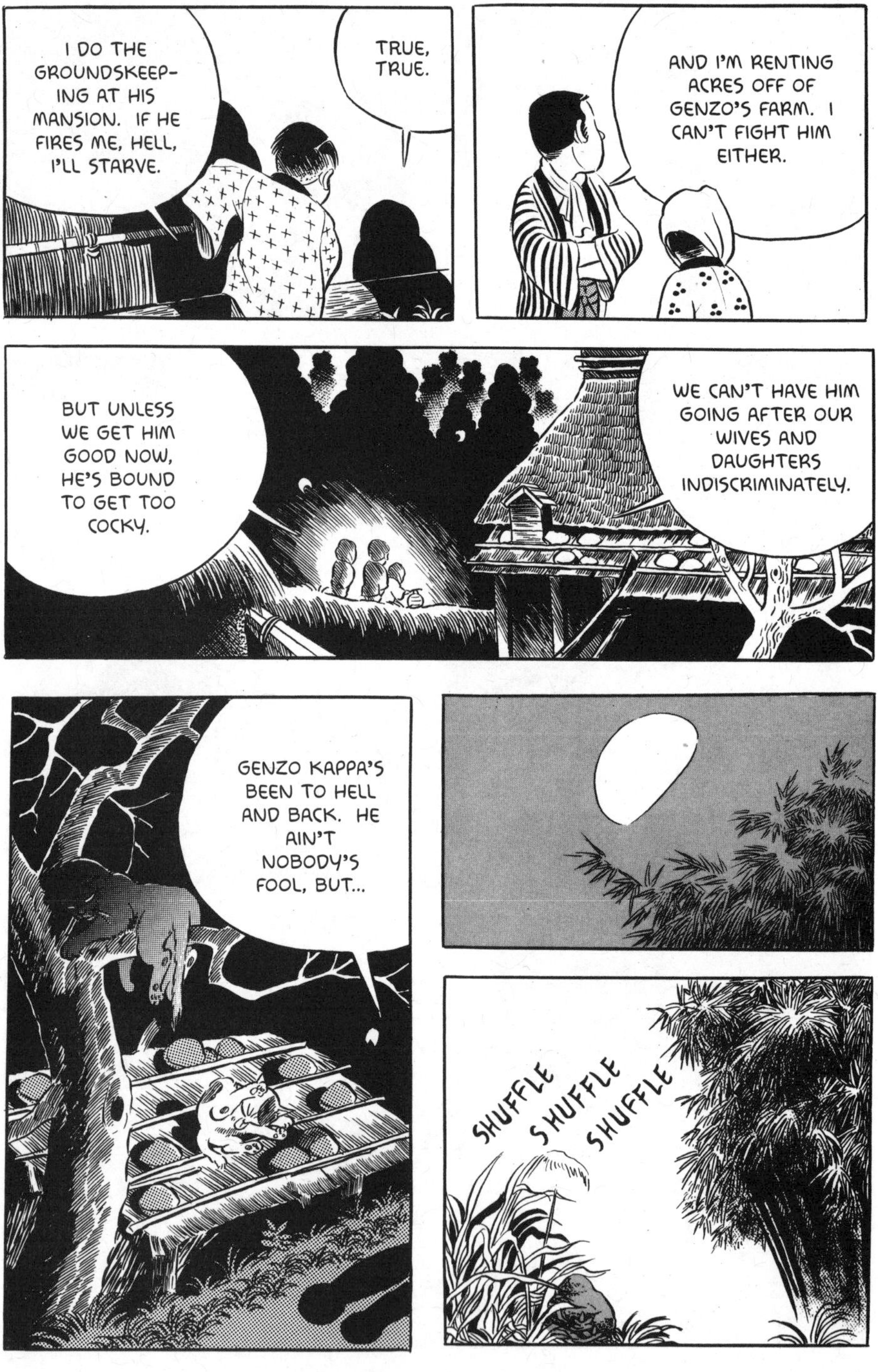
I DO THE GROUNDSKEEPING AT HIS MANSION. IF HE FIRES ME, HELL, I'LL STARVE.
TRUE, TRUE.
AND I'M RENTING ACRES OFF OF GENZO'S FARM. I CAN'T FIGHT HIM EITHER.
BUT UNLESS WE GET HIM GOOD NOW, HE'S BOUND TO GET TOO COCKY.
WE CAN'T HAVE HIM GOING AFTER OUR WIVES AND DAUGHTERS INDISCRIMINATELY.
GENZO KAPPA'S BEEN TO HELL AND BACK. HE AIN'T NOBODY'S FOOL, BUT...
SHUFFLE
SHUFFLE
SHUFFLE

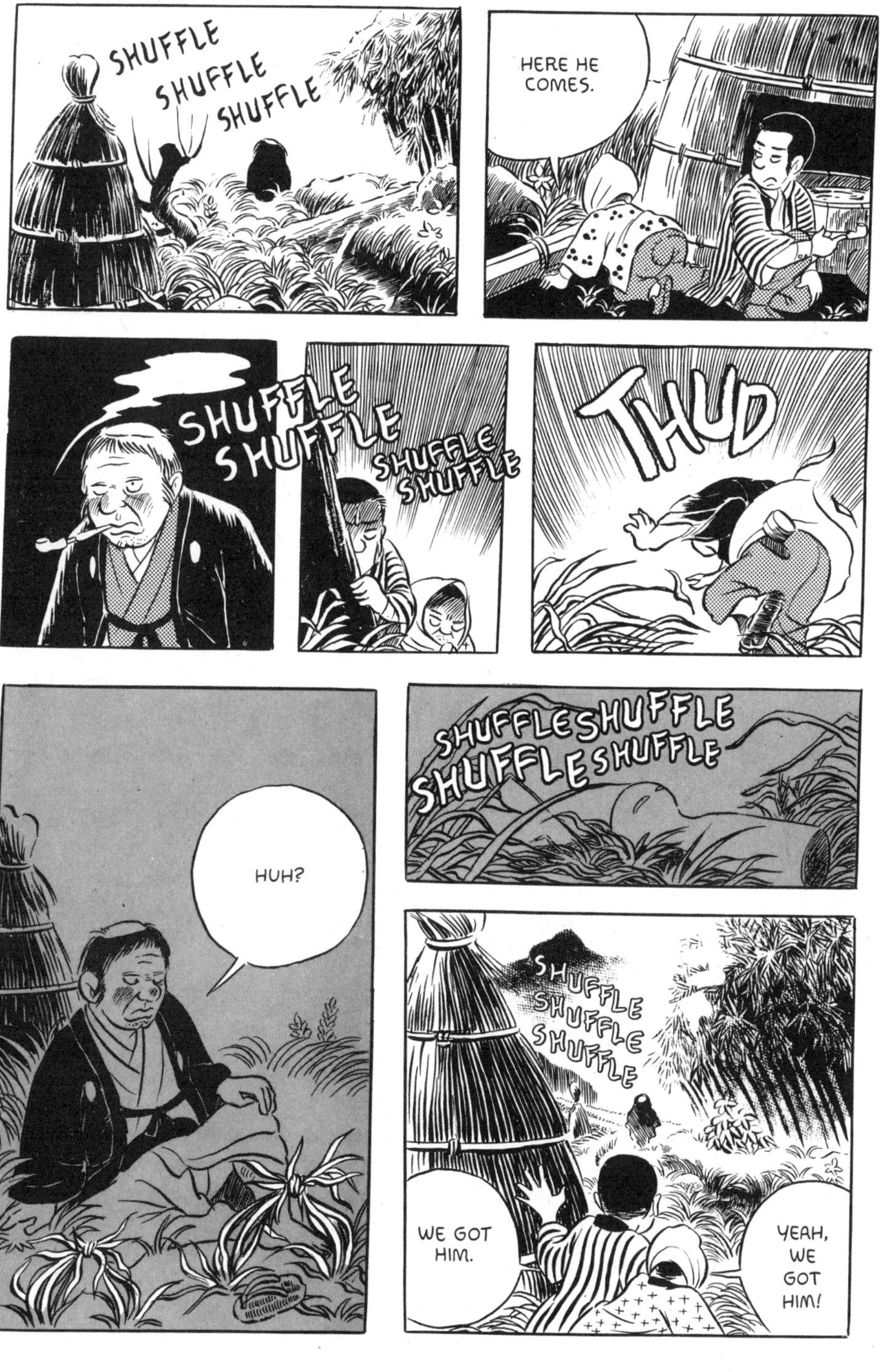
SHUFFLE
SHUFFLE
SHUFFLE
HERE HE COMES.
SHUFFLE
SHUFFLE
SHUFFLE
SHUFFLE
THUD
HUH?
SHUFFLESHUFFLE
SHUFFLESHUFFLE
SHUFFLE
SHUFFLE
SHUFFLE
WE GOT HIM.
YEAH, WE GOT HIM!

LOOK, A WOODEN DOLL.

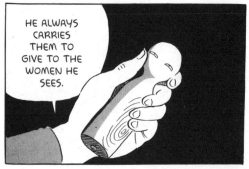

HE ALWAYS CARRIES THEM TO GIVE TO THE WOMEN HE SEES.

WHEN THE BROAD GETS PREGNANT, GENZO STOPS VISITING HER SO MUCH, AND HE GIVES HER ONE OF THESE TO SNUGGLE UP WITH AT NIGHT.

NO WONDER THERE ARE SO MANY KAPPA AROUND.

TOSS

AND AFTER THE BABY'S BORN AND RETURNED TO THE NETHER-WORLD, THIS DOLL WILL BE HER KEEPSAKE.

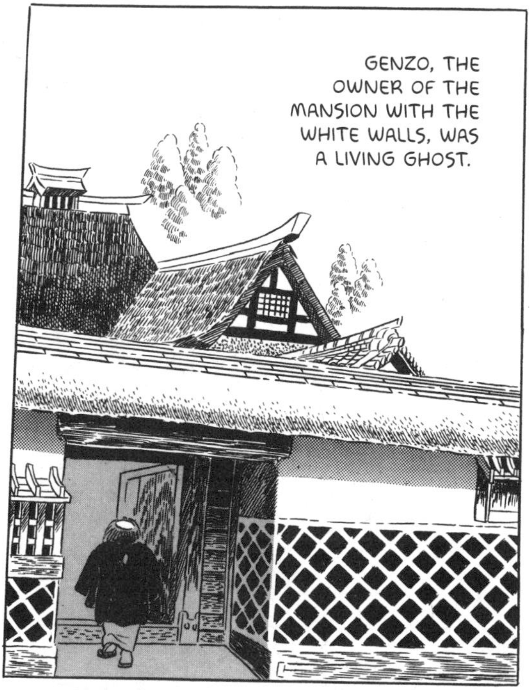
GENZO, THE OWNER OF THE MANSION WITH THE WHITE WALLS, WAS A LIVING GHOST.
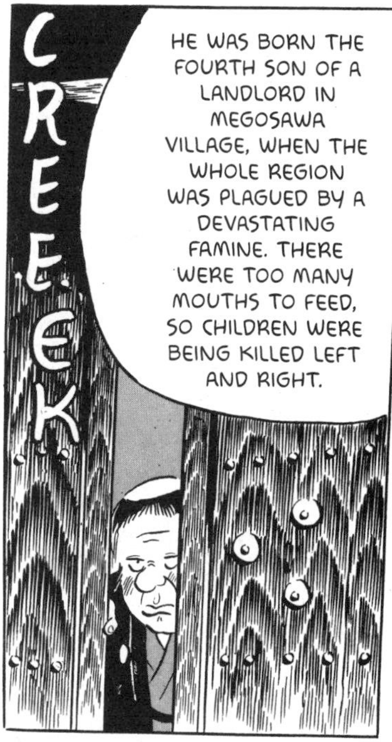
CREEK
HE WAS BORN THE FOURTH SON OF A LANDLORD IN MEGOSAWA VILLAGE, WHEN THE WHOLE REGION WAS PLAGUED BY A DEVASTATING FAMINE. THERE WERE TOO MANY MOUTHS TO FEED, SO CHILDREN WERE BEING KILLED LEFT AND RIGHT.
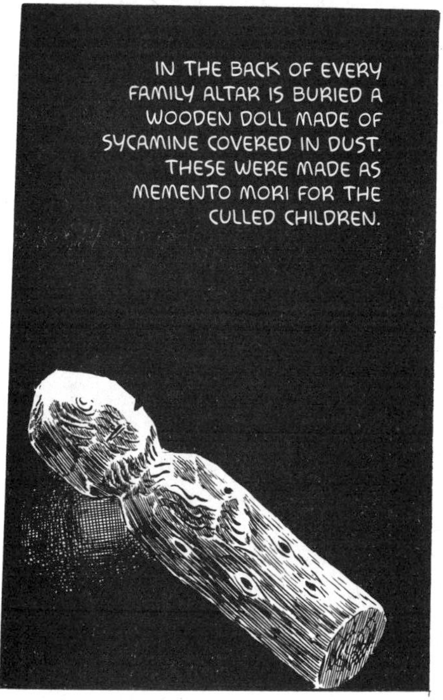
IN THE BACK OF EVERY FAMILY ALTAR IS BURIED A WOODEN DOLL MADE OF SYCAMINE COVERED IN DUST. THESE WERE MADE AS MEMENTO MORI FOR THE CULLED CHILDREN.
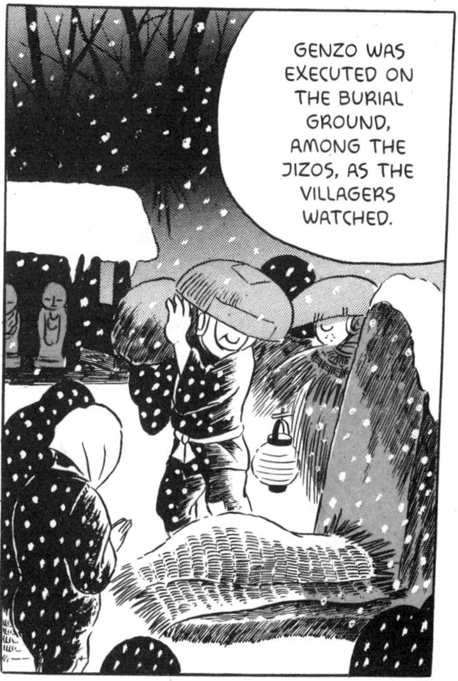
GENZO WAS EXECUTED ON THE BURIAL GROUND, AMONG THE JIZOS, AS THE VILLAGERS WATCHED.

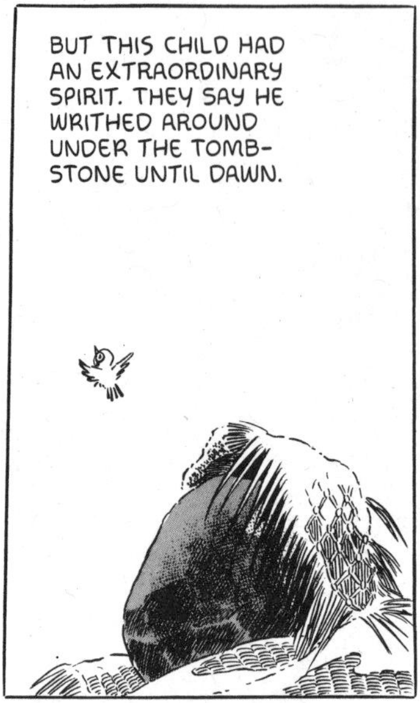
BUT THIS CHILD HAD AN EXTRAORDINARY SPIRIT. THEY SAY HE WRITHED AROUND UNDER THE TOMB- STONE UNTIL DAWN.

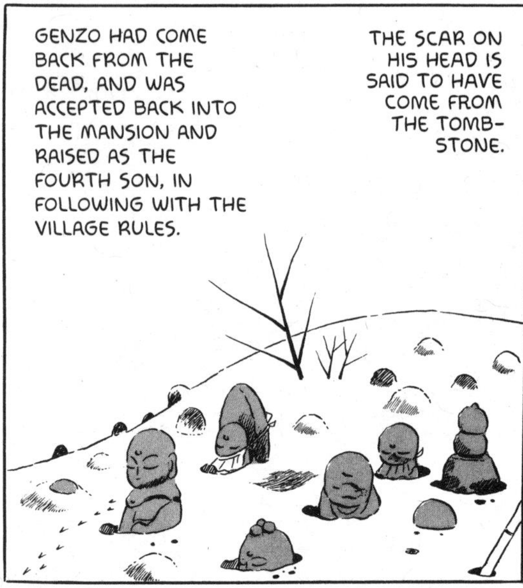
GENZO HAD COME BACK FROM THE DEAD, AND WAS ACCEPTED BACK INTO THE MANSION AND RAISED AS THE FOURTH SON, IN FOLLOWING WITH THE VILLAGE RULES.
THE SCAR ON HIS HEAD IS SAID TO HAVE COME FROM THE TOMB- STONE.

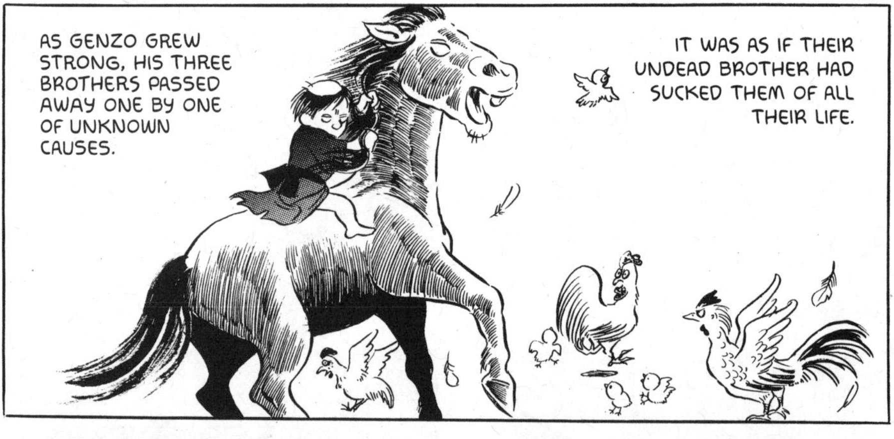
AS GENZO GREW STRONG, HIS THREE BROTHERS PASSED AWAY ONE BY ONE OF UNKNOWN CAUSES.
IT WAS AS IF THEIR UNDEAD BROTHER HAD SUCKED THEM OF ALL THEIR LIFE.

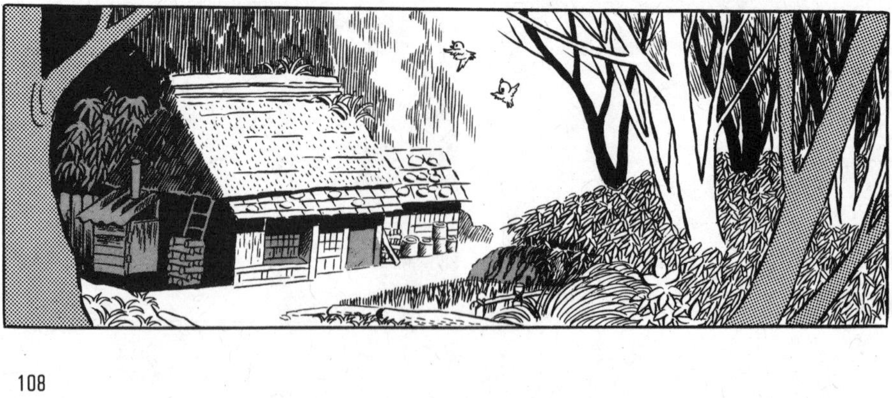

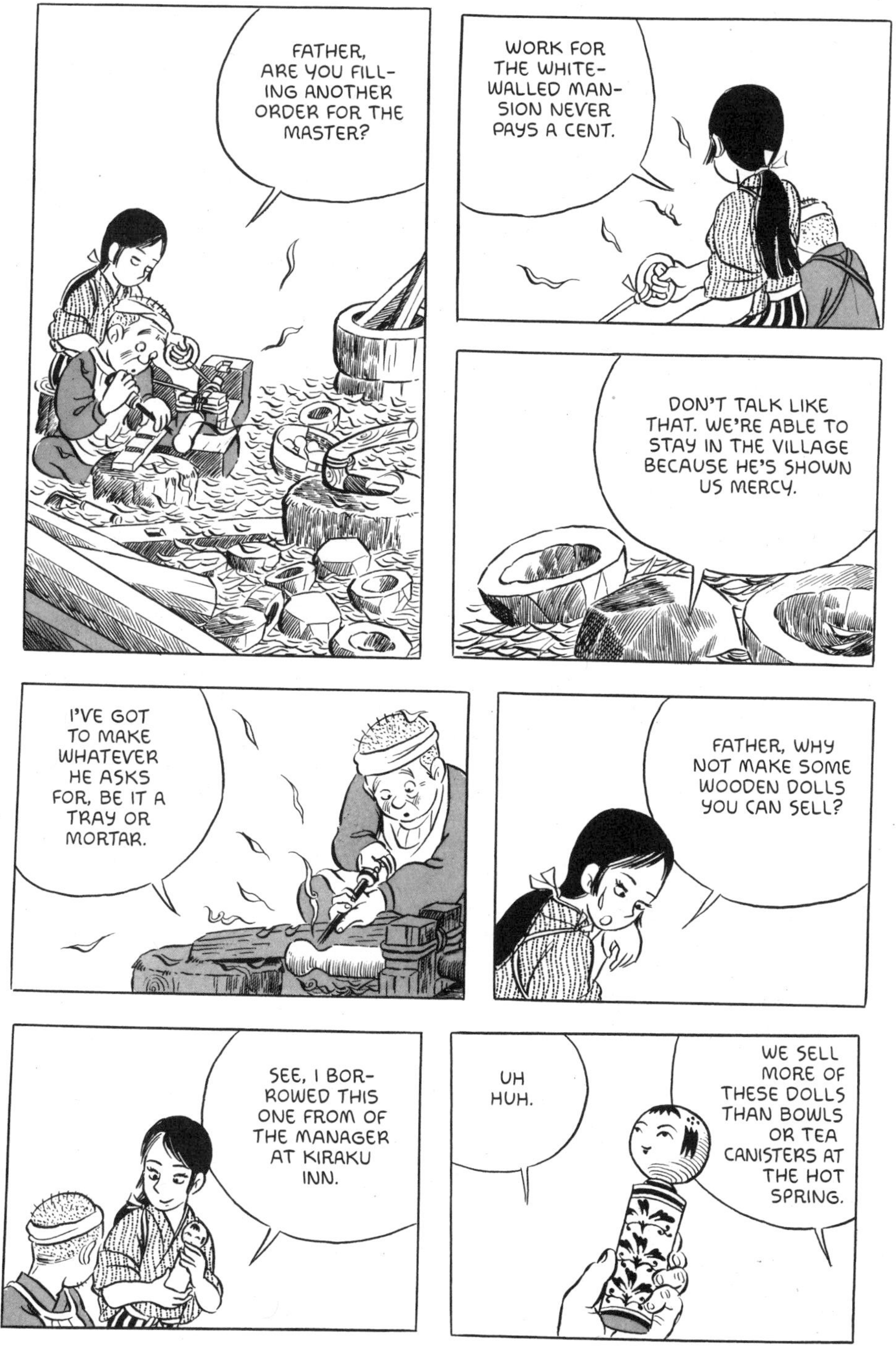
FATHER, ARE YOU FILLING ANOTHER ORDER FOR THE MASTER?
WORK FOR THE WHITE-WALLED MANSION NEVER PAYS A CENT.
DON'T TALK LIKE THAT. WE'RE ABLE TO STAY IN THE VILLAGE BECAUSE HE'S SHOWN US MERCY.
I'VE GOT TO MAKE WHATEVER HE ASKS FOR, BE IT A TRAY OR MORTAR.
FATHER, WHY NOT MAKE SOME WOODEN DOLLS YOU CAN SELL?
SEE, I BORROWED THIS ONE FROM OF THE MANAGER AT KIRAKU INN.
UH HUH.
WE SELL MORE OF THESE DOLLS THAN BOWLS OR TEA CANISTERS AT THE HOT SPRING.

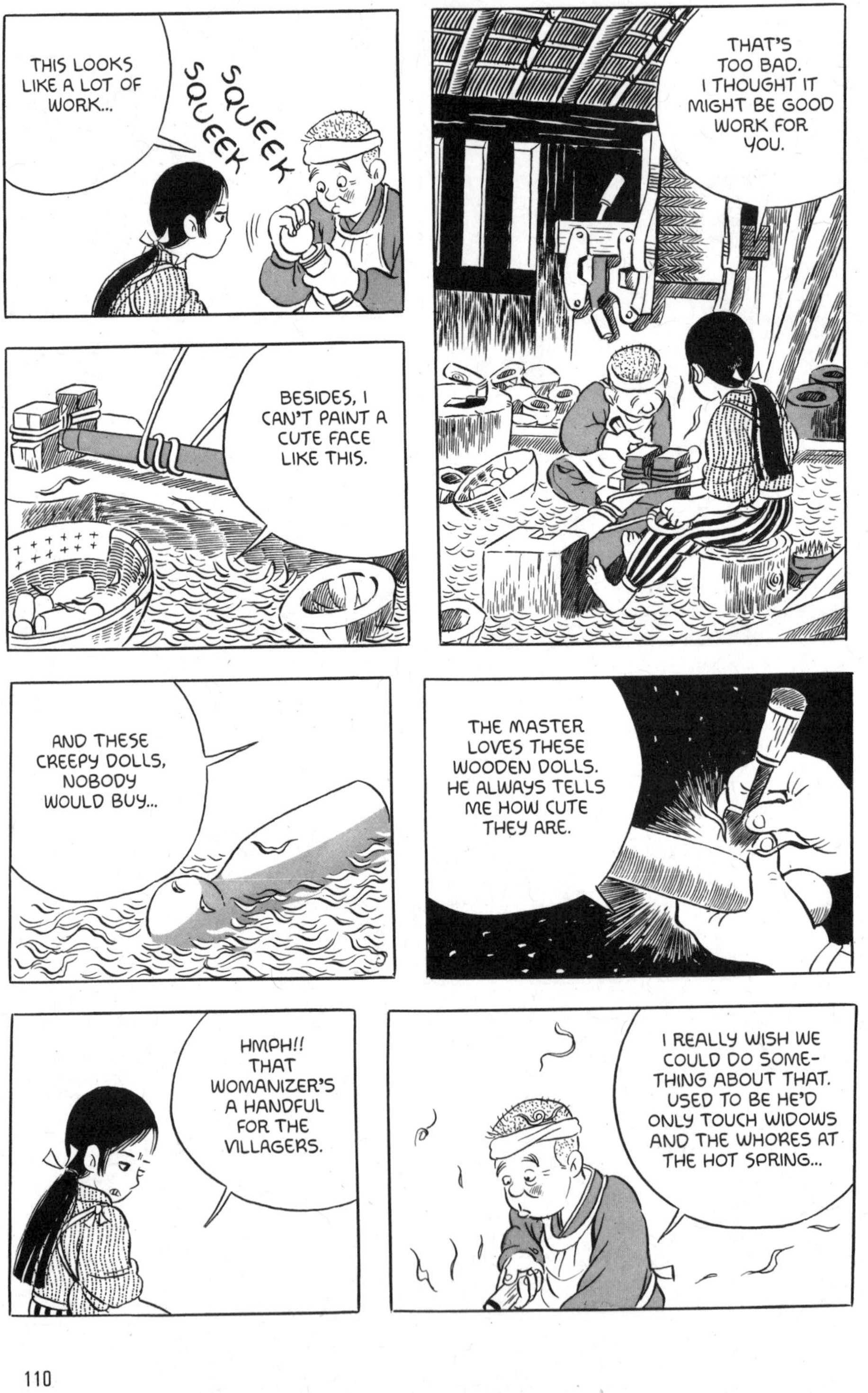
THIS LOOKS LIKE A LOT OF WORK...
SQUEEEK SQUEEEK
BESIDES, I CAN'T PAINT A CUTE FACE LIKE THIS.
THAT'S TOO BAD. I THOUGHT IT MIGHT BE GOOD WORK FOR YOU.
AND THESE CREEPY DOLLS, NOBODY WOULD BUY...
THE MASTER LOVES THESE WOODEN DOLLS. HE ALWAYS TELLS ME HOW CUTE THEY ARE.
HMPH!! THAT WOMANIZER'S A HANDFUL FOR THE VILLAGERS.
I REALLY WISH WE COULD DO SOME-THING ABOUT THAT. USED TO BE HE'D ONLY TOUCH WIDOWS AND THE WHORES AT THE HOT SPRING...

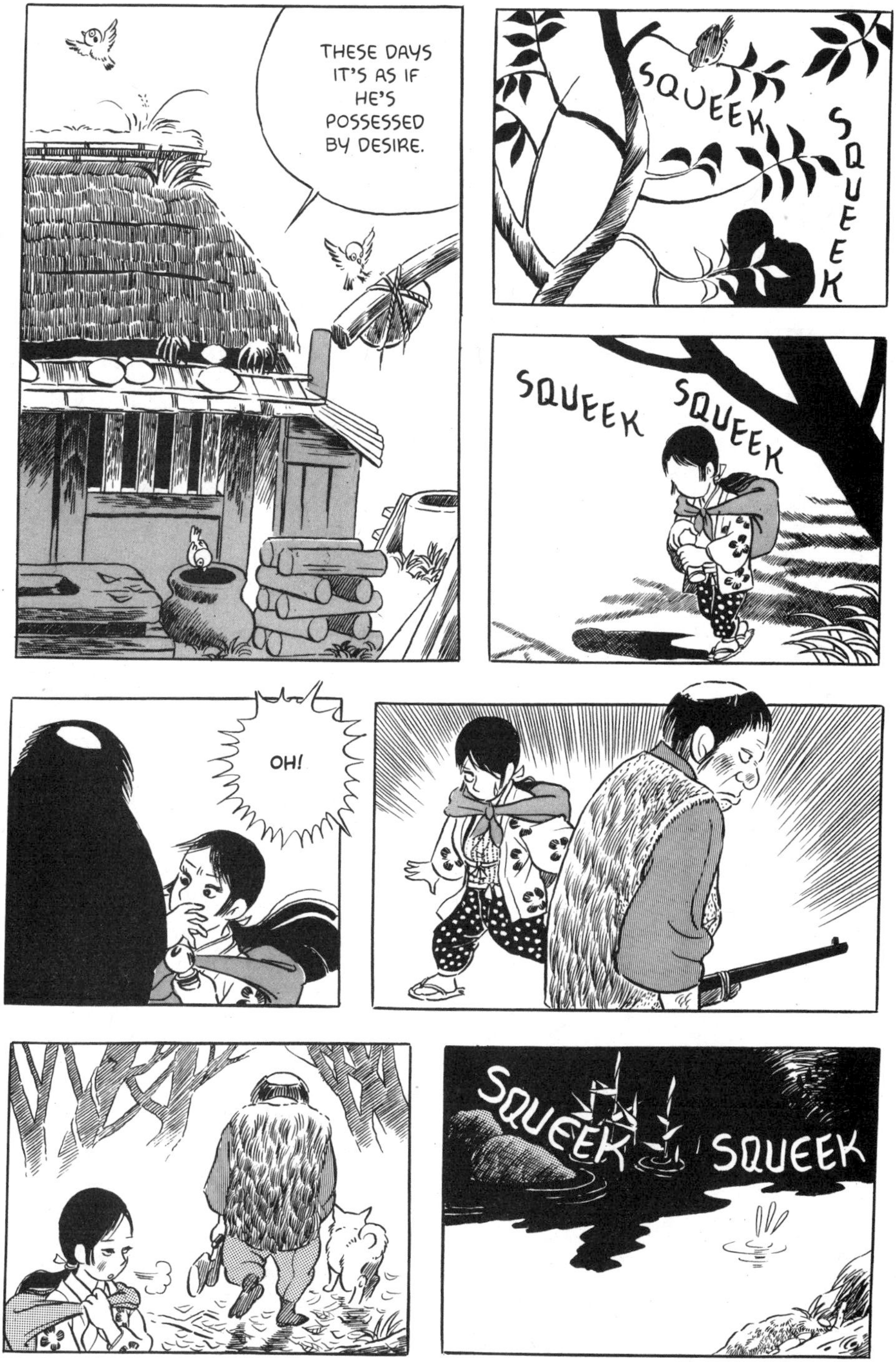
THESE DAYS IT'S AS IF HE'S POSSESSED BY DESIRE.
SQUEEK
SQUEEK
SQUEEK
SQUEEK
OH!
SQUEEK
SQUEEK

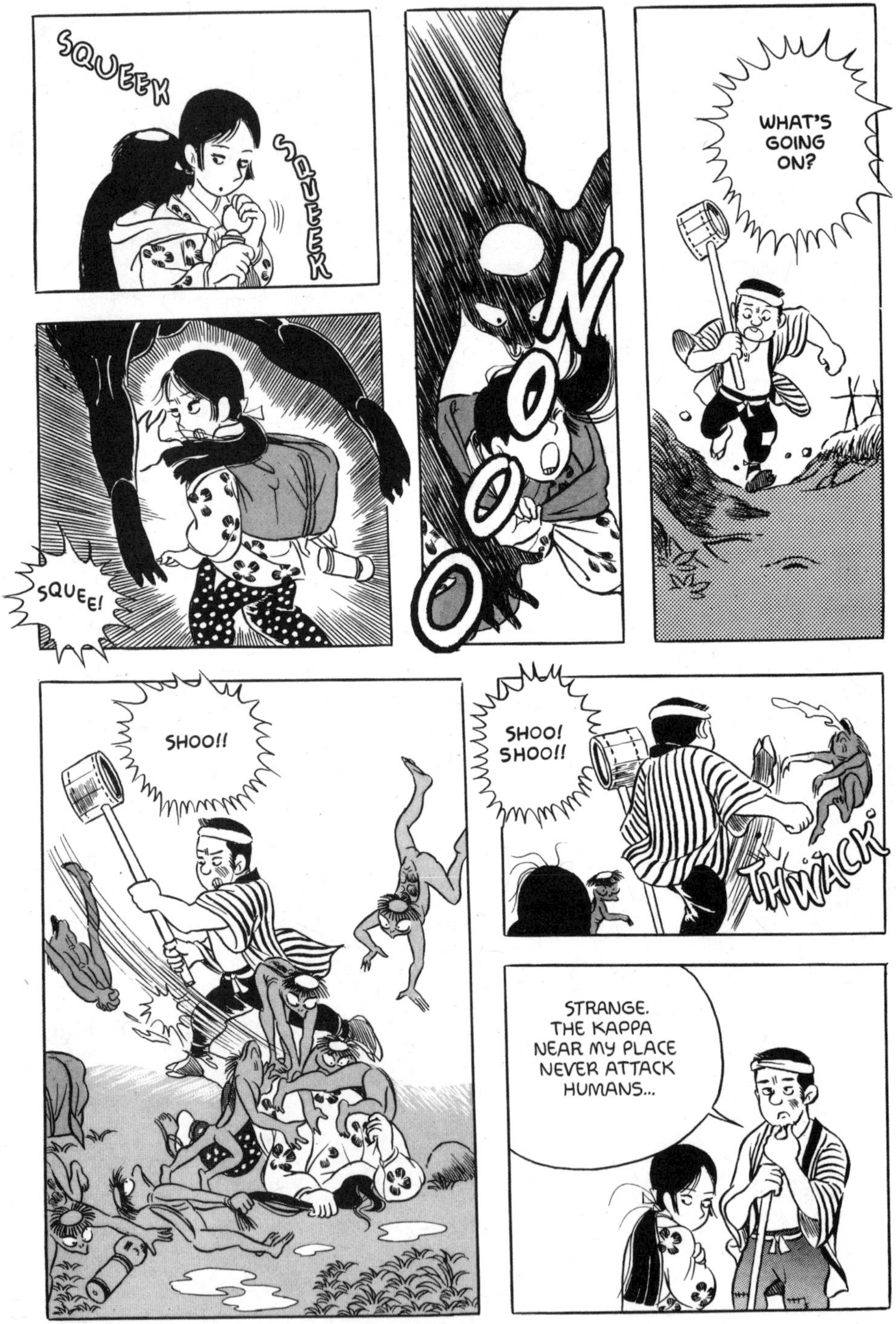
SQUEEEK
SQUEEEK
SQUEE!
OOOOON
WHAT'S GOING ON?
SHOO!!
SHOO! SHOO!!
THWACK
STRANGE. THE KAPPA NEAR MY PLACE NEVER ATTACK HUMANS...

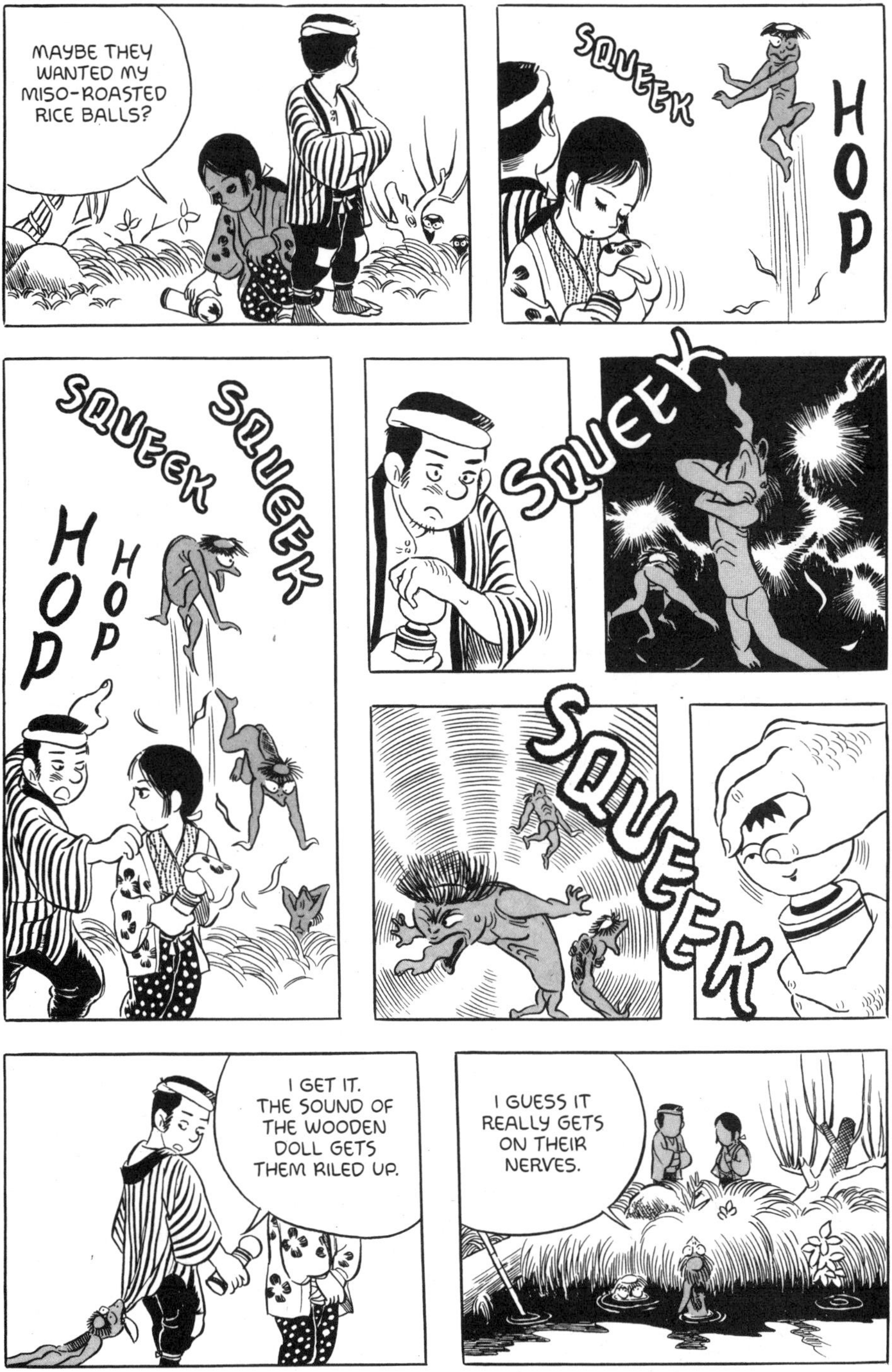
MAYBE THEY WANTED MY MISO-ROASTED RICE BALLS?
SQUEEK
HOP
SQUEEK
SQUEEK
HOP
HOP
SQUEEK
SQUEEK
I GET IT. THE SOUND OF THE WOODEN DOLL GETS THEM RILED UP.
I GUESS IT REALLY GETS ON THEIR NERVES.

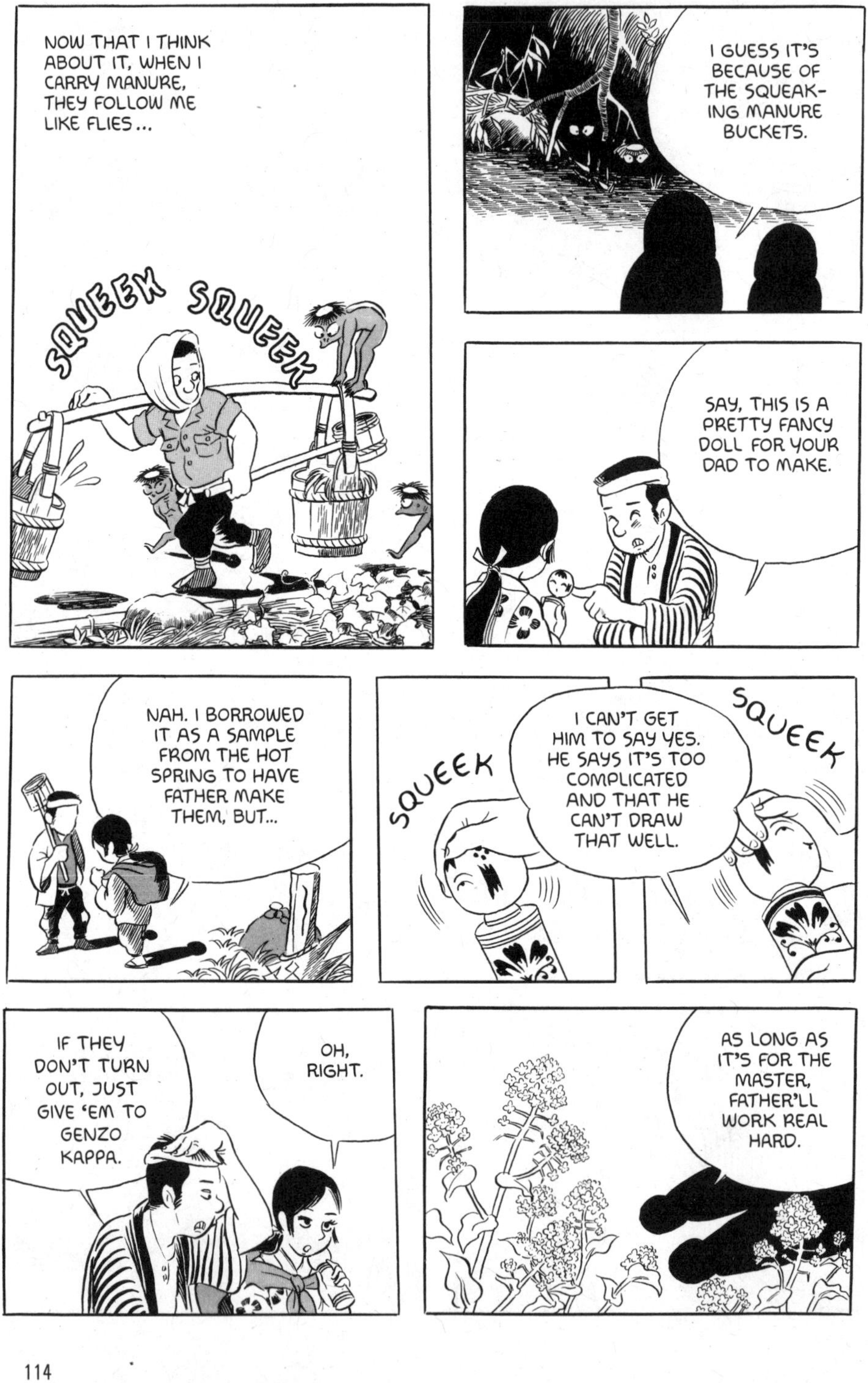
NOW THAT I THINK ABOUT IT, WHEN I CARRY MANURE, THEY FOLLOW ME LIKE FLIES...
SQUEEK SQUEEK
I GUESS IT'S BECAUSE OF THE SQUEAK-ING MANURE BUCKETS.
SAY, THIS IS A PRETTY FANCY DOLL FOR YOUR DAD TO MAKE.
NAH. I BORROWED IT AS A SAMPLE FROM THE HOT SPRING TO HAVE FATHER MAKE THEM, BUT...
SQUEEK
I CAN'T GET HIM TO SAY YES. HE SAYS IT'S TOO COMPLICATED AND THAT HE CAN'T DRAW THAT WELL.
SQUEEK
IF THEY DON'T TURN OUT, JUST GIVE 'EM TO GENZO KAPPA.
OH, RIGHT.
AS LONG AS IT'S FOR THE MASTER, FATHER'LL WORK REAL HARD.

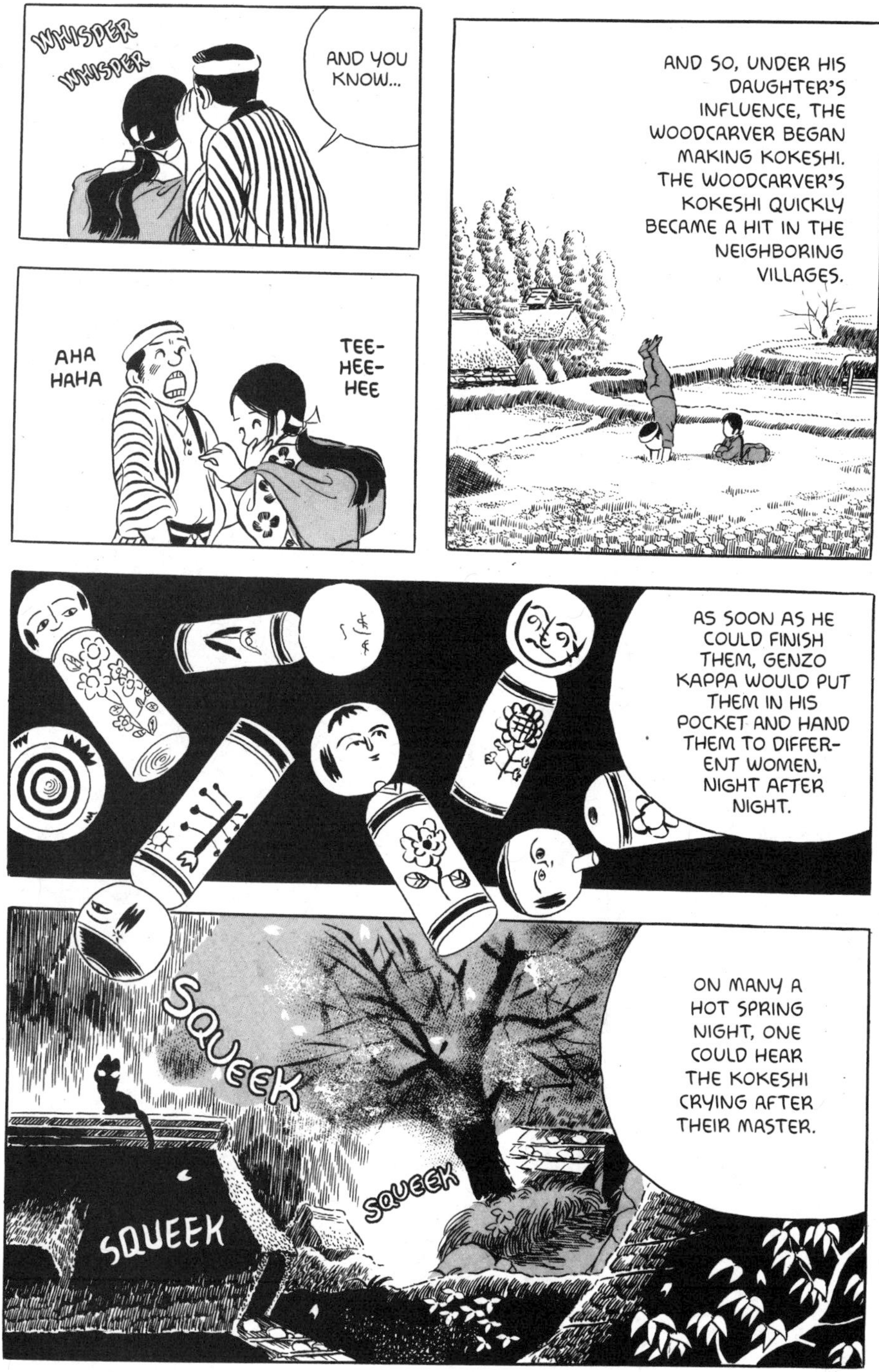
WHISPER
WHISPER
AND YOU KNOW...
AHA HAHA
TEE-HEE-HEE
AND SO, UNDER HIS DAUGHTER'S INFLUENCE, THE WOODCARVER BEGAN MAKING KOKESHI. THE WOODCARVER'S KOKESHI QUICKLY BECAME A HIT IN THE NEIGHBORING VILLAGES.
AS SOON AS HE COULD FINISH THEM, GENZO KAPPA WOULD PUT THEM IN HIS POCKET AND HAND THEM TO DIFFER-ENT WOMEN, NIGHT AFTER NIGHT.
SQUEEK
SQUEEK
SQUEEK
SQUEEK
ON MANY A HOT SPRING NIGHT, ONE COULD HEAR THE KOKESHI CRYING AFTER THEIR MASTER.

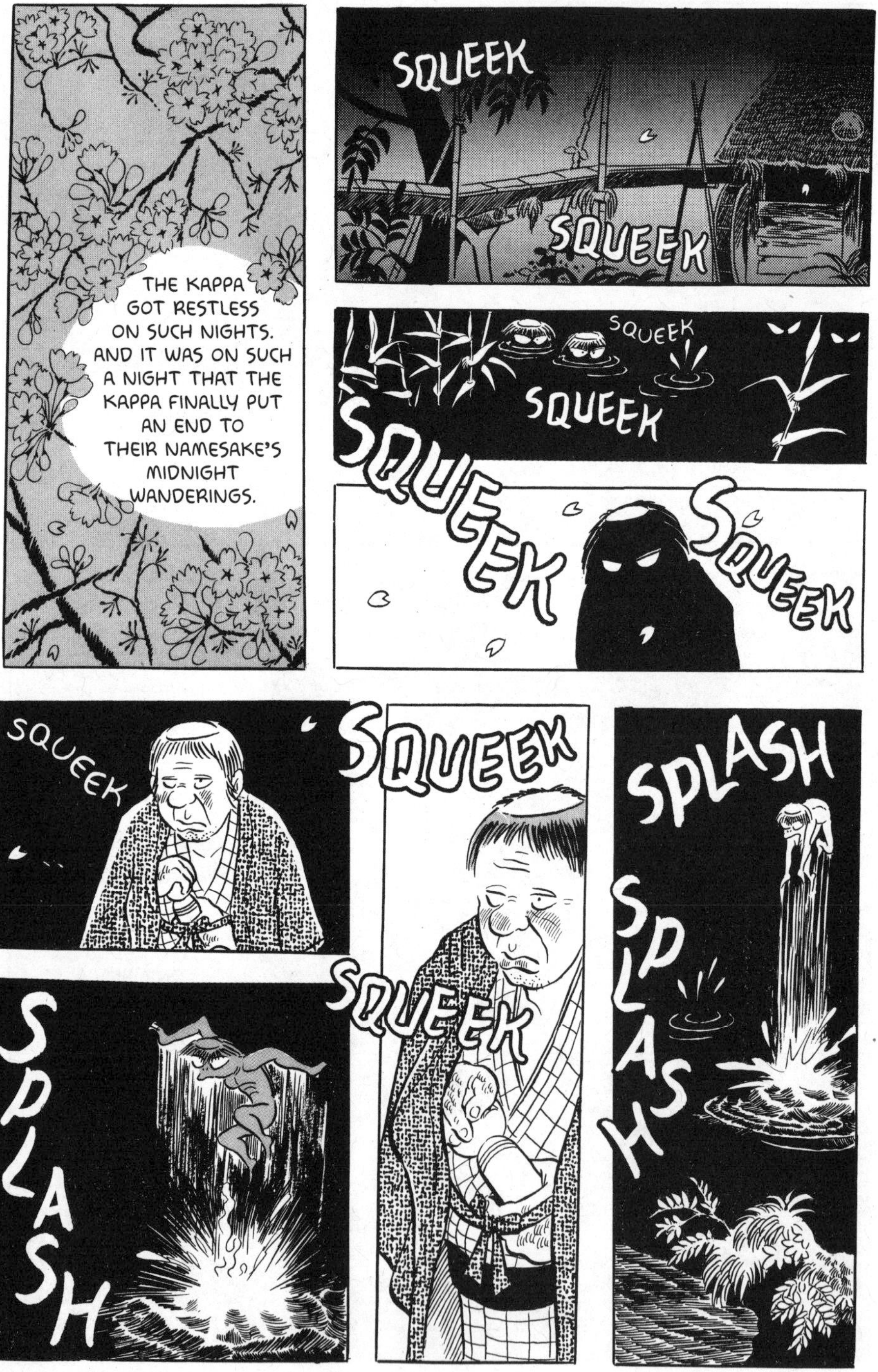
THE KAPPA GOT RESTLESS ON SUCH NIGHTS. AND IT WAS ON SUCH A NIGHT THAT THE KAPPA FINALLY PUT AN END TO THEIR NAMESAKE'S MIDNIGHT WANDERINGS.
SQUEEK
SQUEEK
SQUEEK
SQUEEK
SQUEEK
SQUEEK
SQUEEK
SQUEEK
SQUEEK
SPLASH
SPLASH
SPLASH
SQUEEK

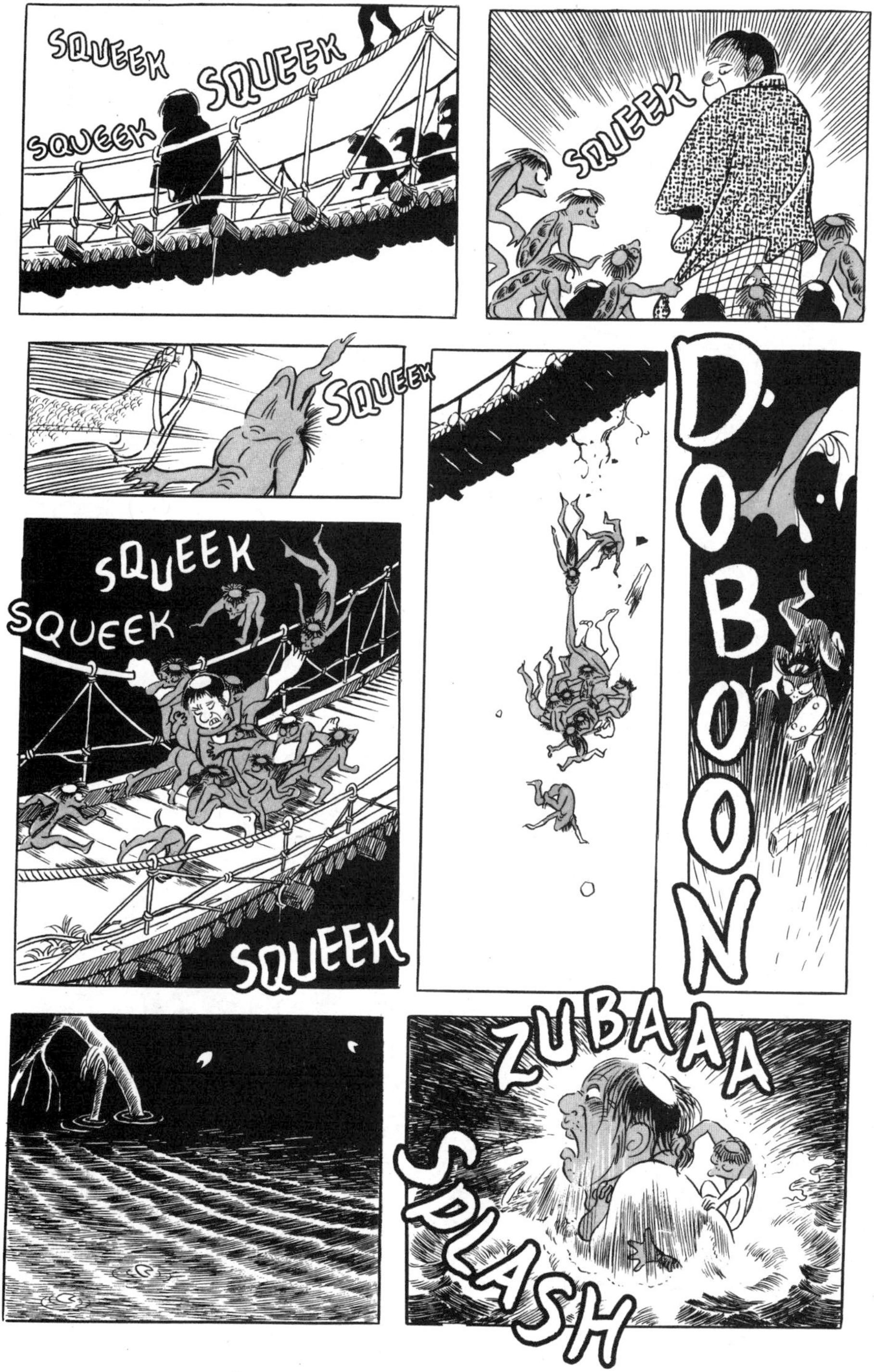
SQUEEK
SQUEEK
SQUEEK
SQUEEK
SQUEEK
SQUEEK
SQUEEK
SQUEEK
DOBOON
ZUBAAA
SPLASH

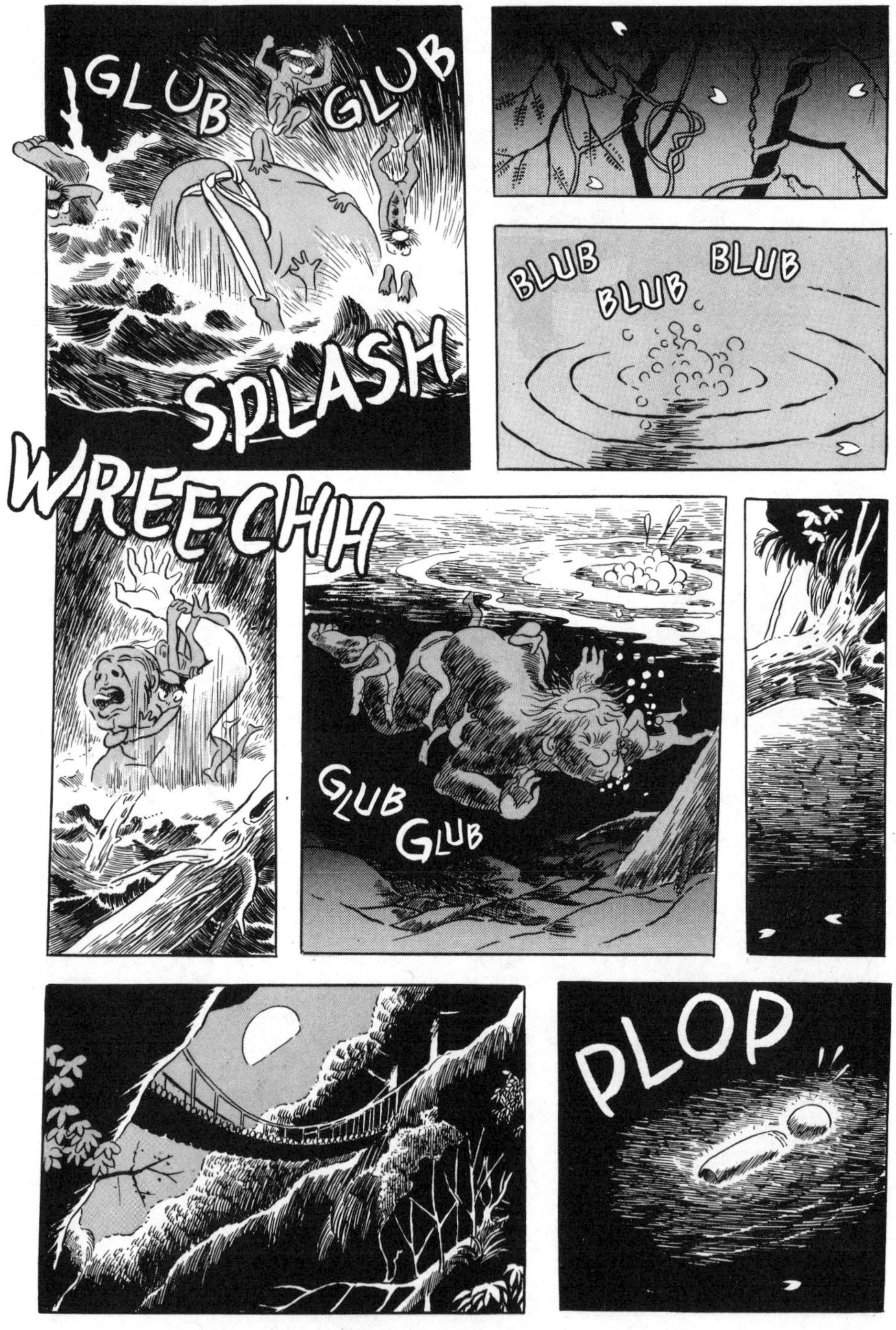
GLUB GLUB
SPLASH
BLUB BLUB BLUB
WREECHH
GLUB GLUB
PLOP

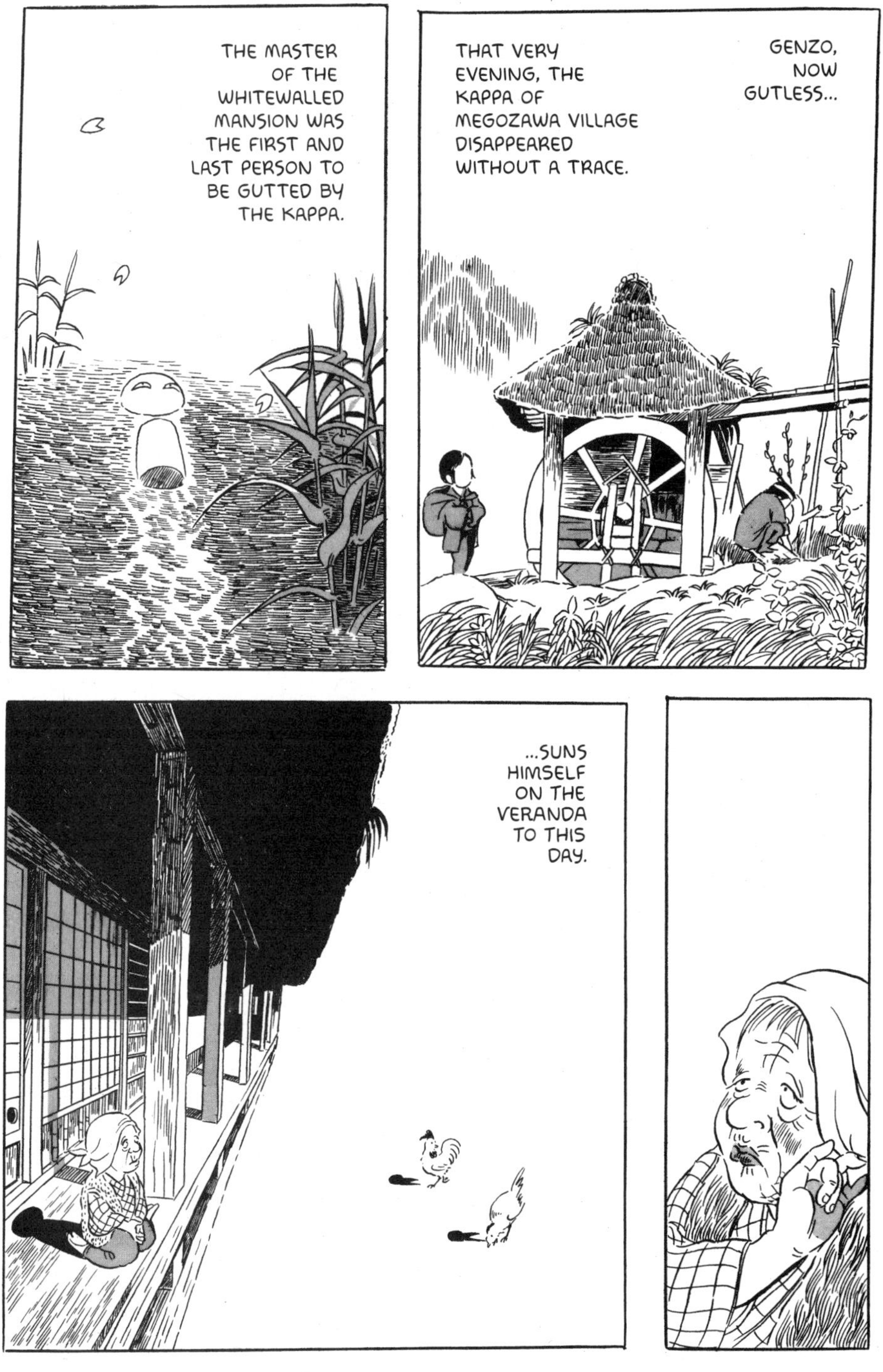
THE MASTER OF THE WHITEWALLED MANSION WAS THE FIRST AND LAST PERSON TO BE GUTTED BY THE KAPPA.
THAT VERY EVENING, THE KAPPA OF MEGOZAWA VILLAGE DISAPPEARED WITHOUT A TRACE.
GENZO, NOW GUTLESS...
...SUNS HIMSELF ON THE VERANDA TO THIS DAY.

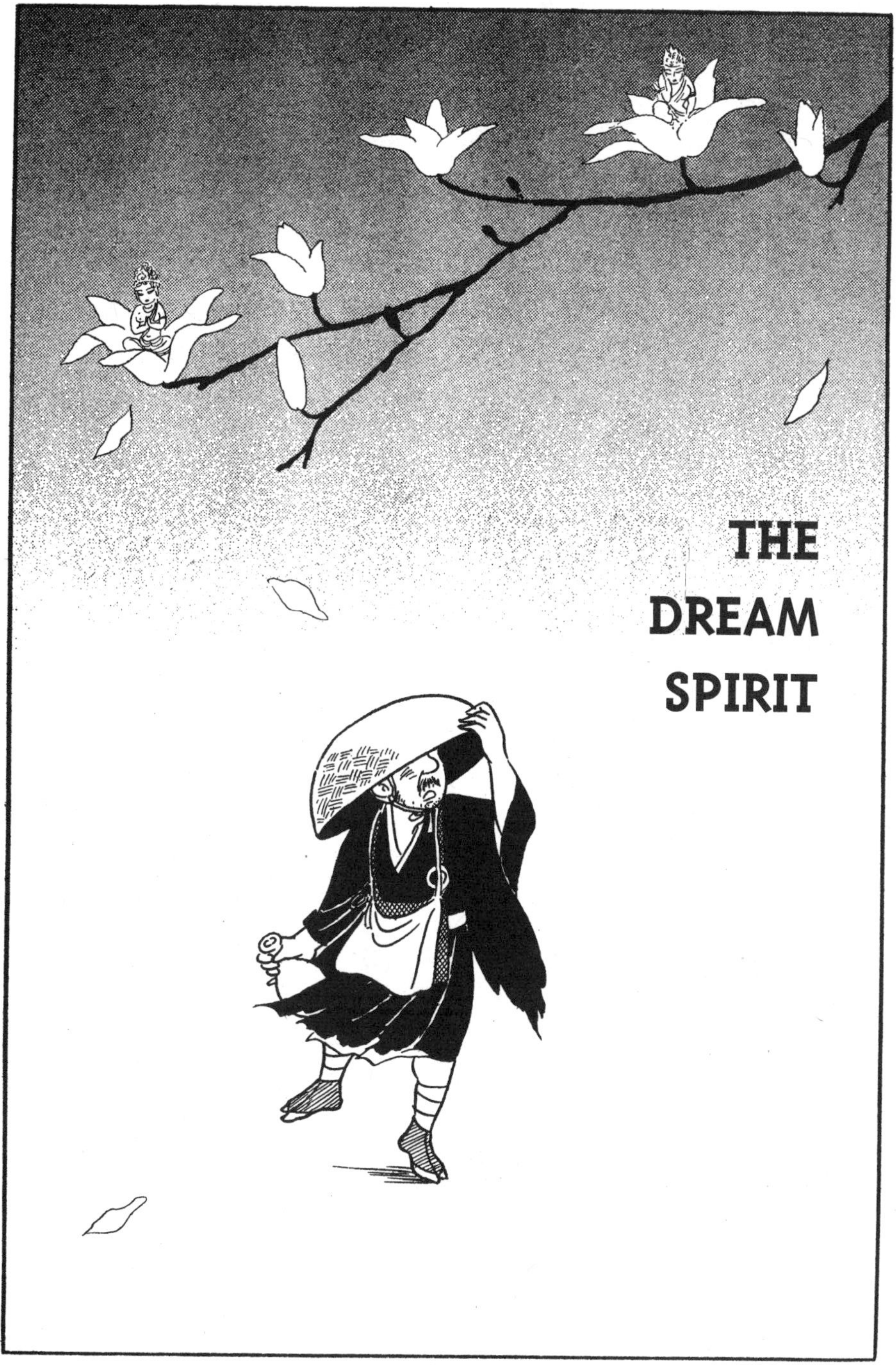
THE DREAM SPIRIT

TO THE MOUNTAIN
AND TO THE SKY.
MAKAHANNYAHARA
MITTASHINGYO

KANJISAI,
BOSATSU,
GYOUJIN,
HANNYAHARA,
MITTAJI

FSH

OH, OH...
OH...

KLUCK

KLUCK

KLUCK

KLUCK

ITCH

ITCH

ITCH

HMM, IT'S ALREADY CHANGING FROM LOUSE TO FLEA SEASON.

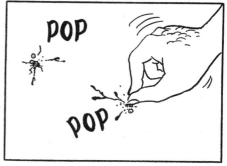

POP

POP

IT'S THE SOUND OF FLEAS BEING KILLED.

POP

POP

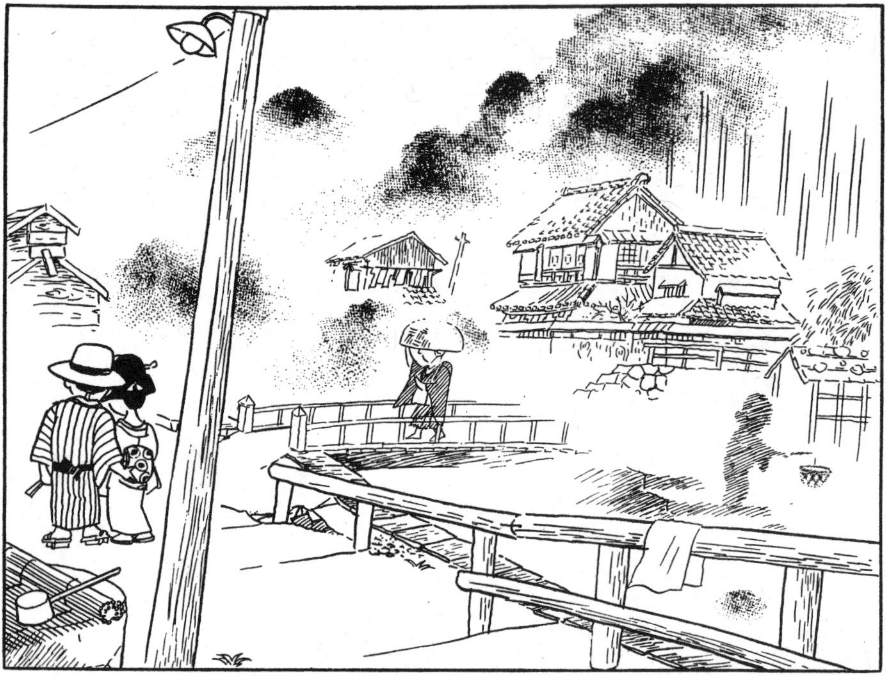

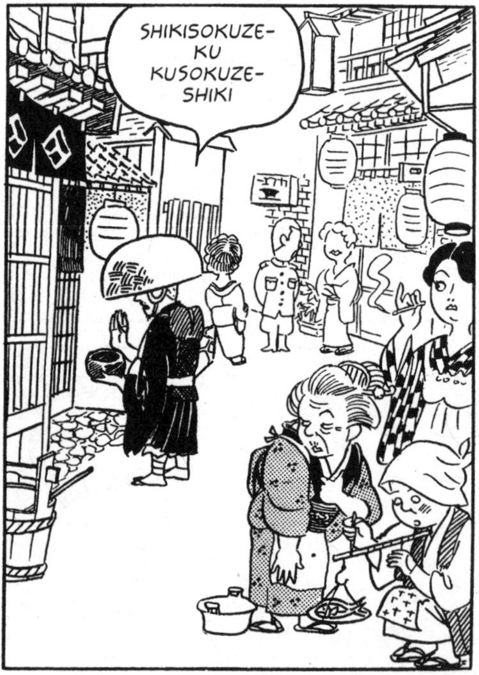
SHIKISOKUZE-
KU
KUSOKUZE-
SHIKI

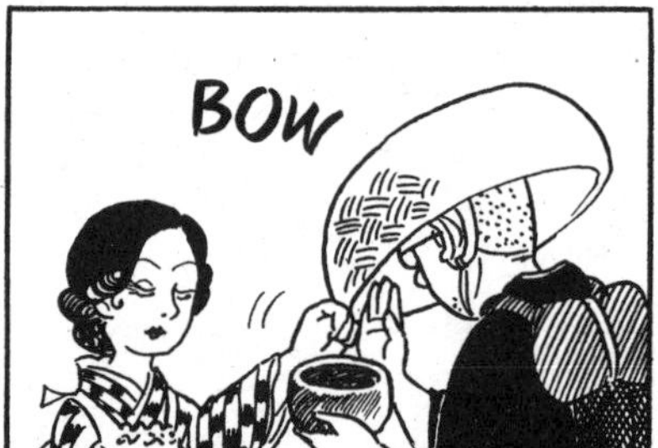
BOW

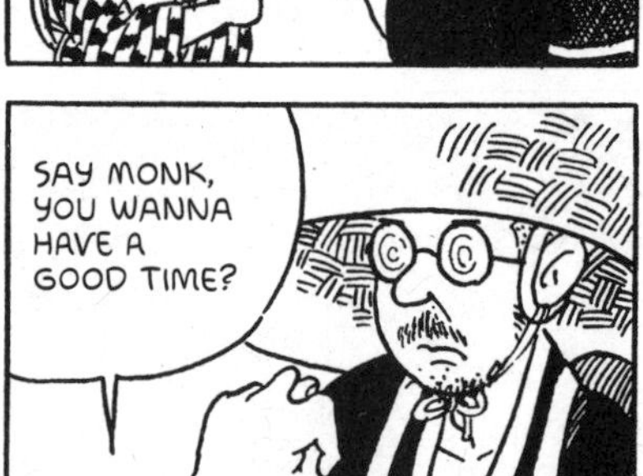
SAY MONK, YOU WANNA HAVE A GOOD TIME?

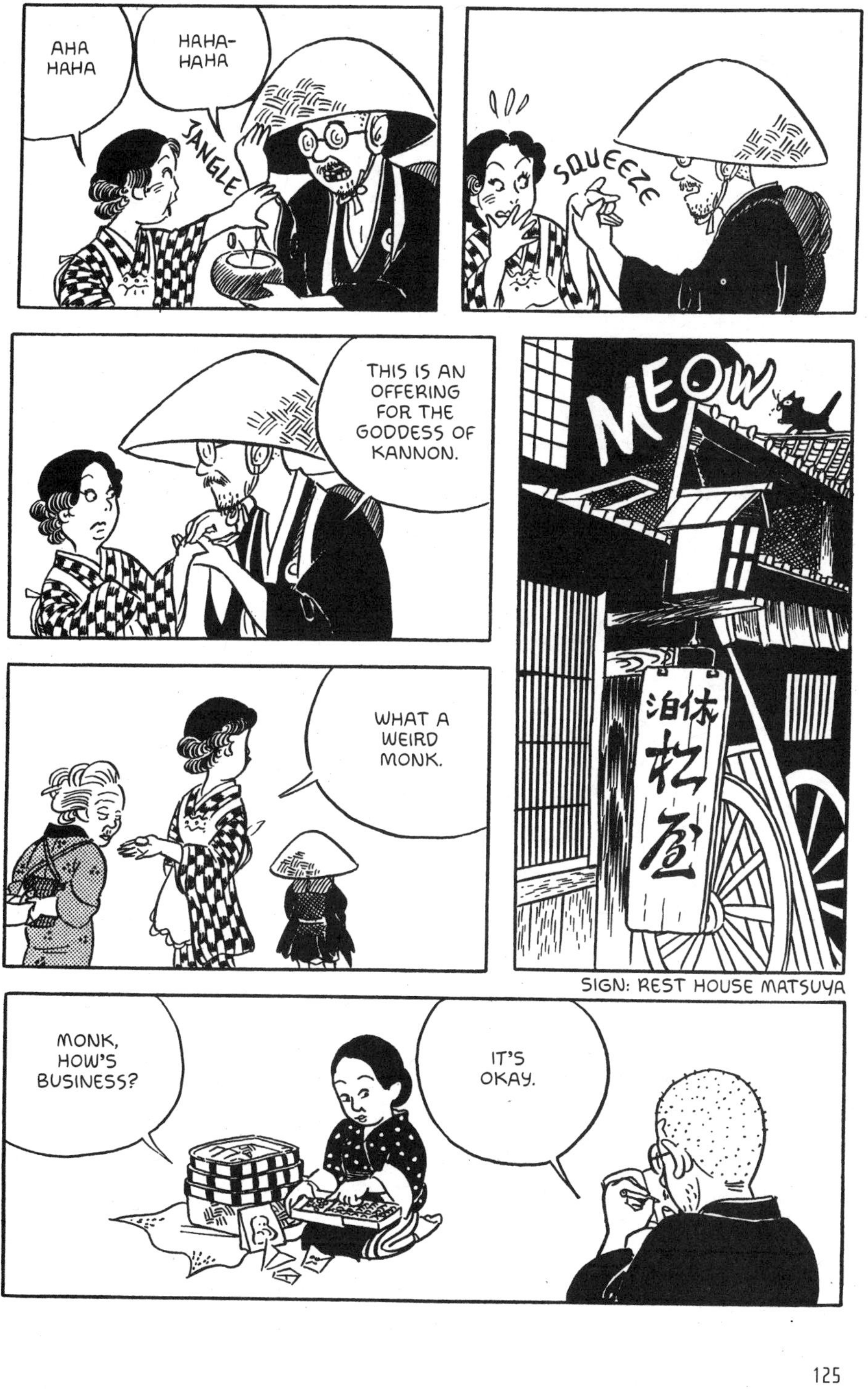
AHA HAHA
HAHA-HAHA
JANGLE
SQUEEZE
THIS IS AN OFFERING FOR THE GODDESS OF KANNON.
WHAT A WEIRD MONK.
MEOW
休泊
松屋
SIGN: REST HOUSE MATSUYA
MONK, HOW'S BUSINESS?
IT'S OKAY.

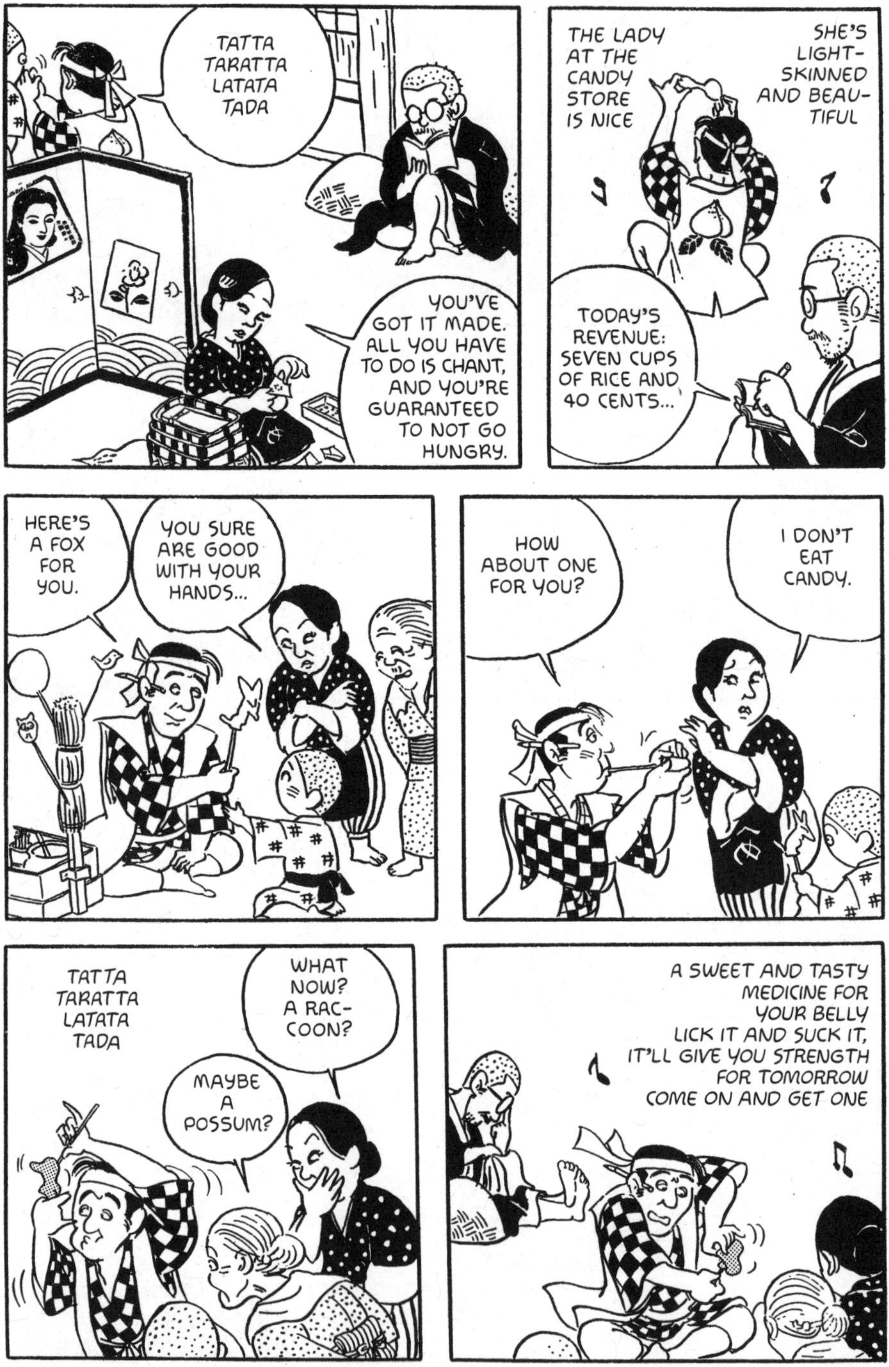
TATTA TARATTA LATATA TADA
YOU'VE GOT IT MADE. ALL YOU HAVE TO DO IS CHANT, AND YOU'RE GUARANTEED TO NOT GO HUNGRY.
THE LADY AT THE CANDY STORE IS NICE
SHE'S LIGHT-SKINNED AND BEAU-TIFUL
TODAY'S REVENUE: SEVEN CUPS OF RICE AND 40 CENTS...
HERE'S A FOX FOR YOU.
YOU SURE ARE GOOD WITH YOUR HANDS...
HOW ABOUT ONE FOR YOU?
I DON'T EAT CANDY.
TATTA TARATTA LATATA TADA
WHAT NOW? A RAC-COON?
MAYBE A POSSUM?
A SWEET AND TASTY MEDICINE FOR YOUR BELLY
LICK IT AND SUCK IT,
IT'LL GIVE YOU STRENGTH FOR TOMORROW
COME ON AND GET ONE

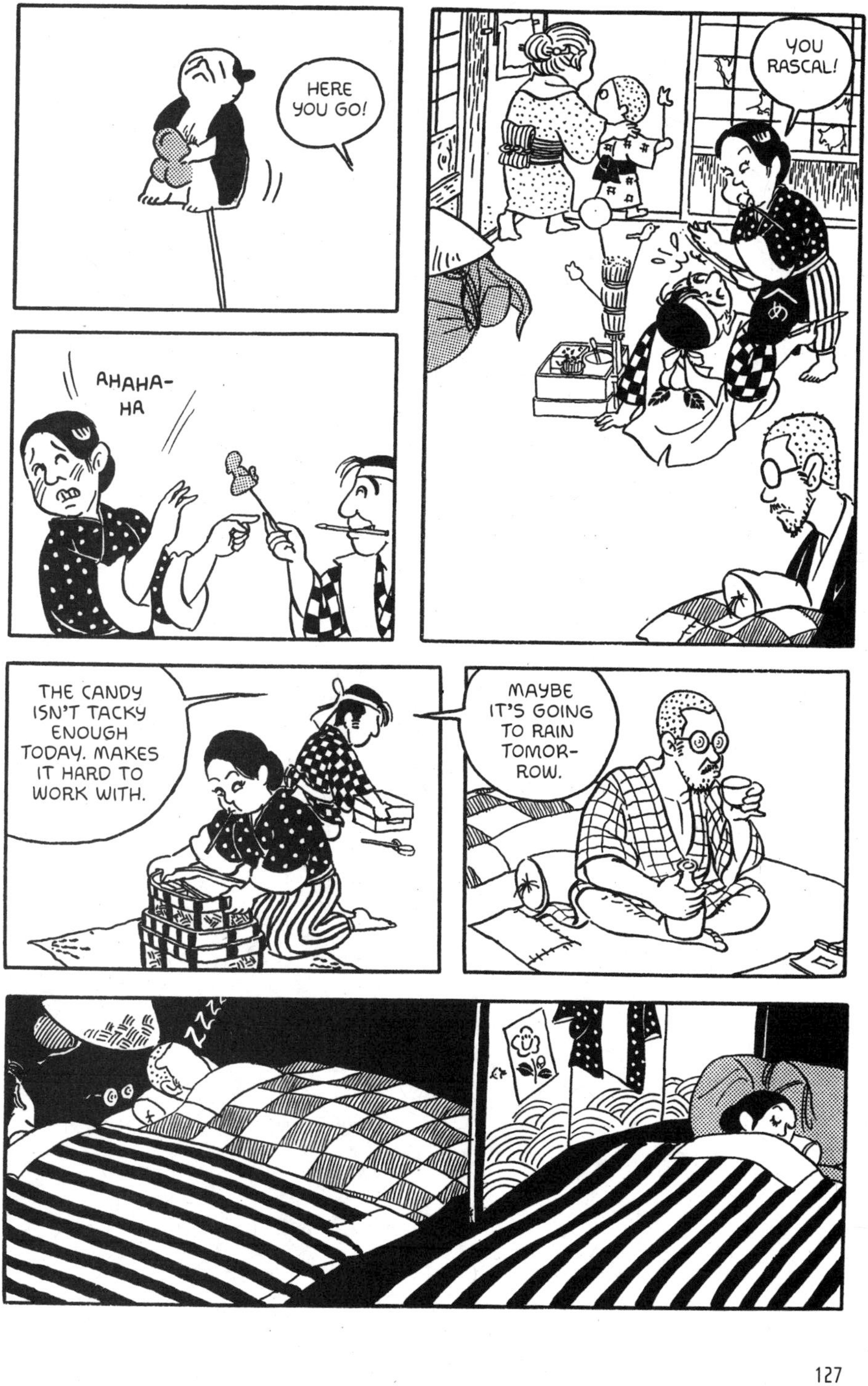
HERE YOU GO!
AHAHA-HA
YOU RASCAL!
THE CANDY ISN'T TACKY ENOUGH TODAY. MAKES IT HARD TO WORK WITH.
MAYBE IT'S GOING TO RAIN TOMOR-ROW.

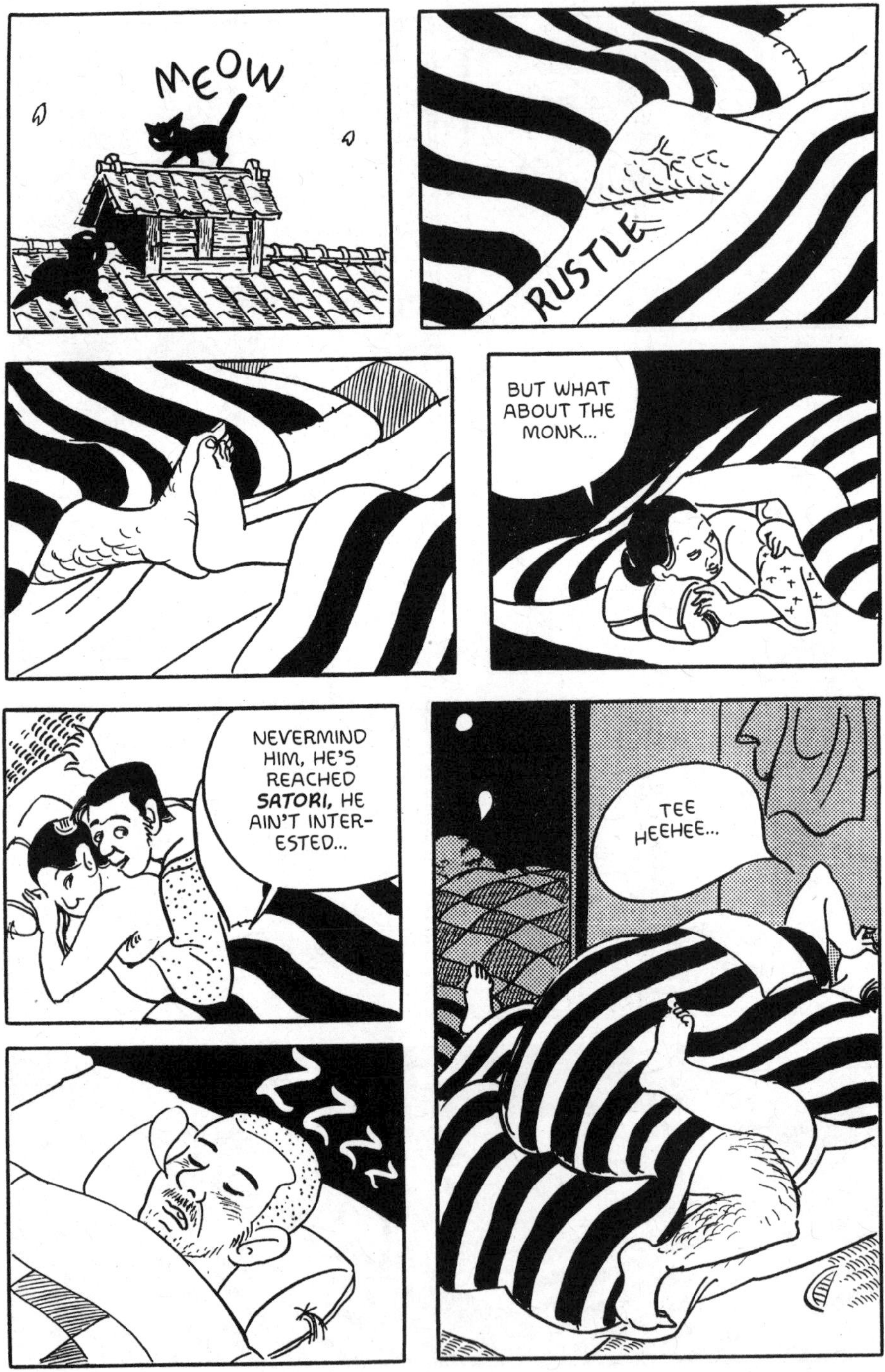
MEOW
RUSTLE
BUT WHAT ABOUT THE MONK...
NEVERMIND HIM, HE'S REACHED **SATORI**, HE AIN'T INTER-ESTED...
ZZZZ
TEE HEEHEE...

MIN MIN MINMI

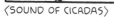
〈SOUND OF CICADAS〉

SNIFF SNIFF

129

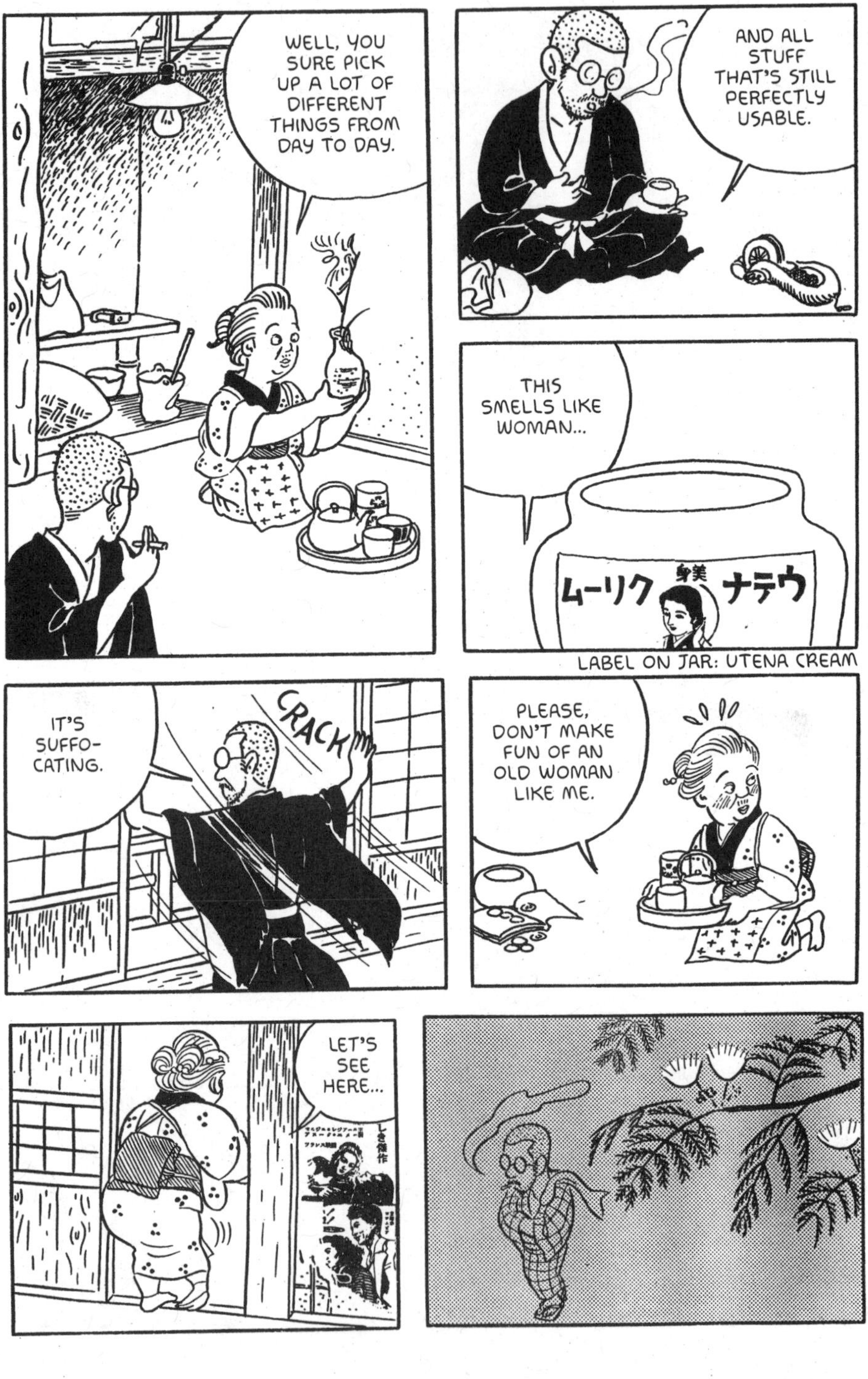
WELL, YOU SURE PICK UP A LOT OF DIFFERENT THINGS FROM DAY TO DAY.
AND ALL STUFF THAT'S STILL PERFECTLY USABLE.
THIS SMELLS LIKE WOMAN...
ウテナ クリーム
LABEL ON JAR: UTENA CREAM
IT'S SUFFO-CATING.
CRACK
PLEASE, DON'T MAKE FUN OF AN OLD WOMAN LIKE ME.
LET'S SEE HERE...

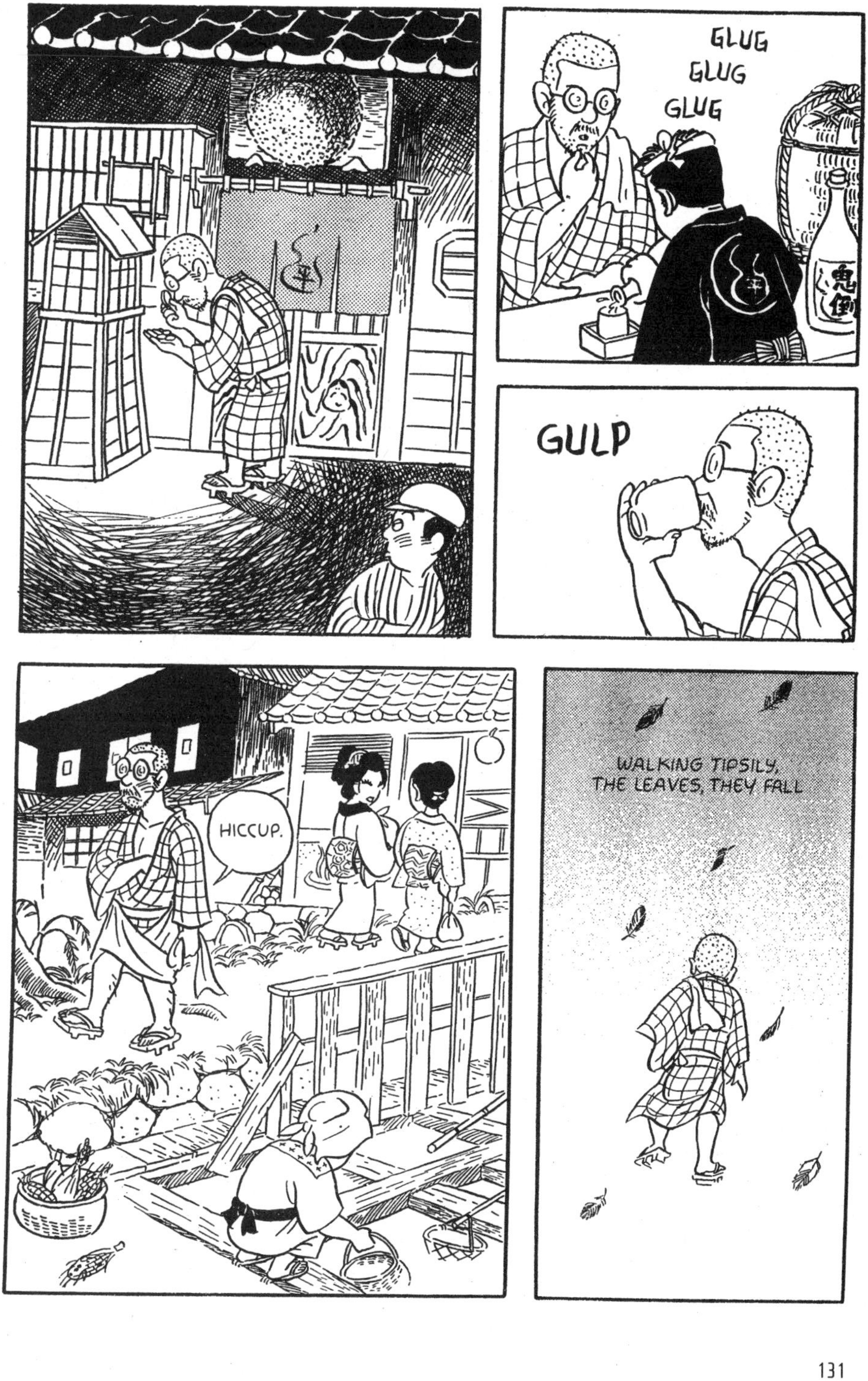
GLUG
GLUG
GLUG
GULP
HICCUP.
WALKING TIPSILY,
THE LEAVES, THEY FALL

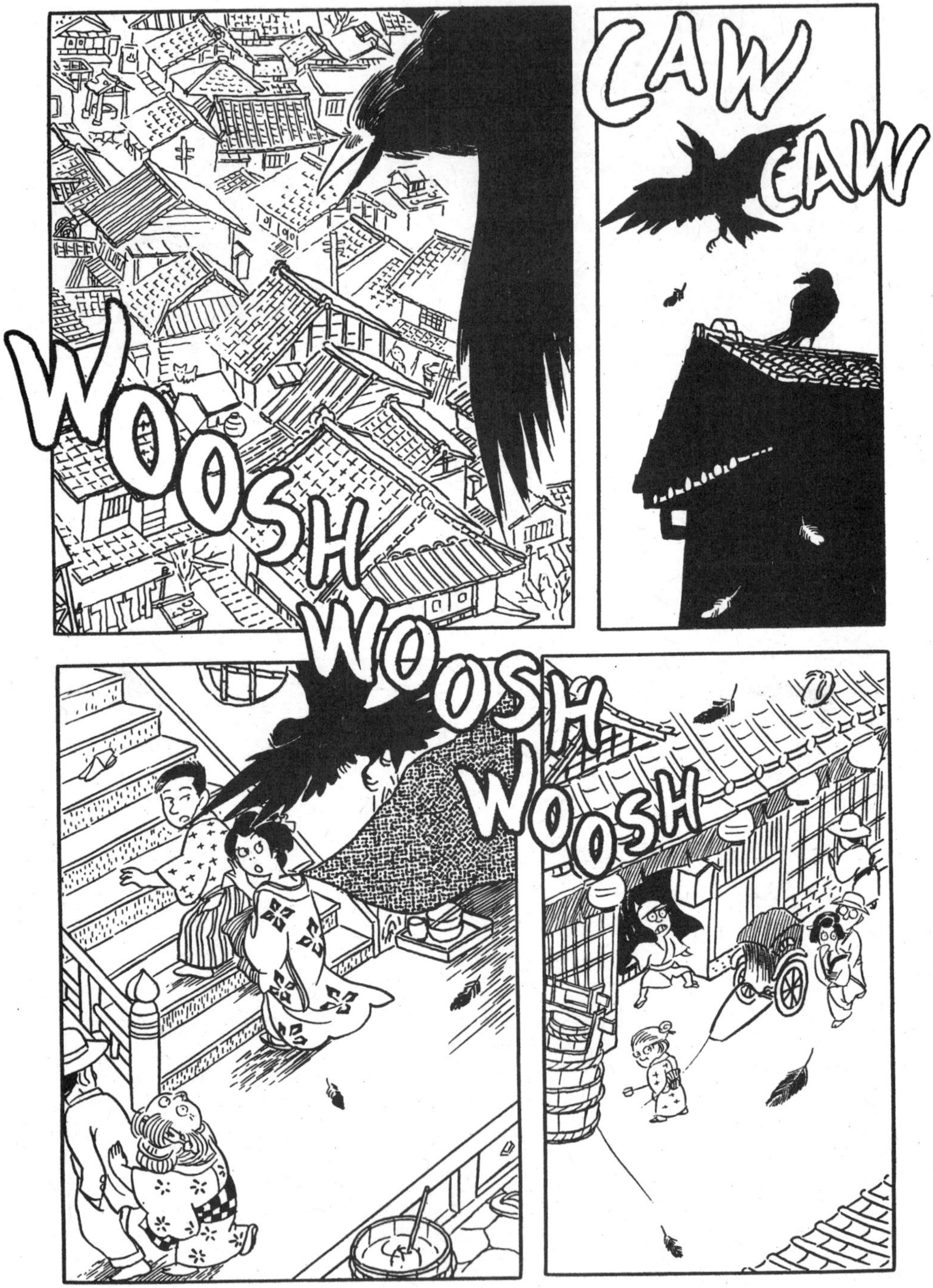
WOOSH
CAW
CAW
WOOSH
WOOSH

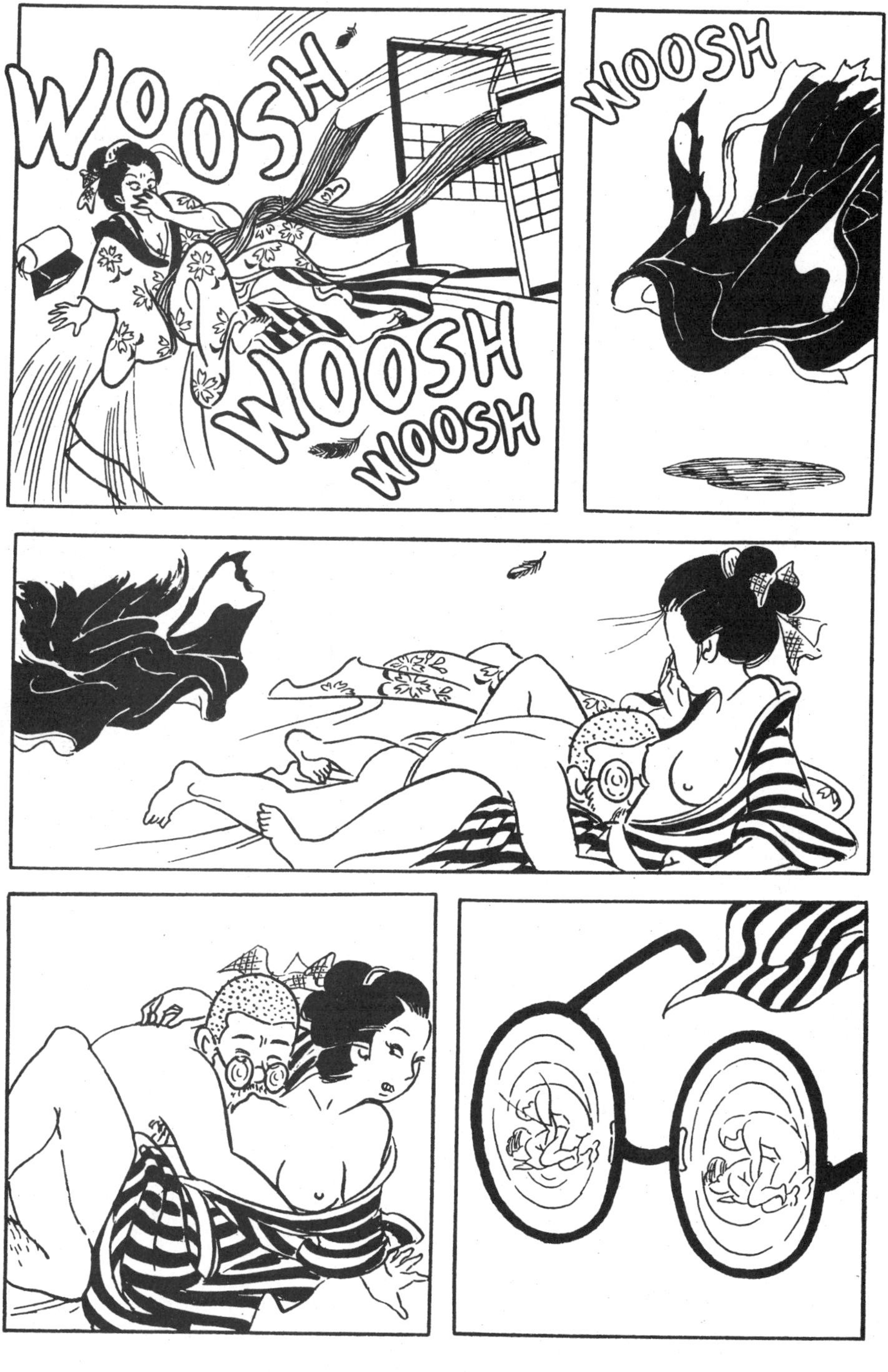
WOOSH
WOOSH
WOOSH
WOOSH

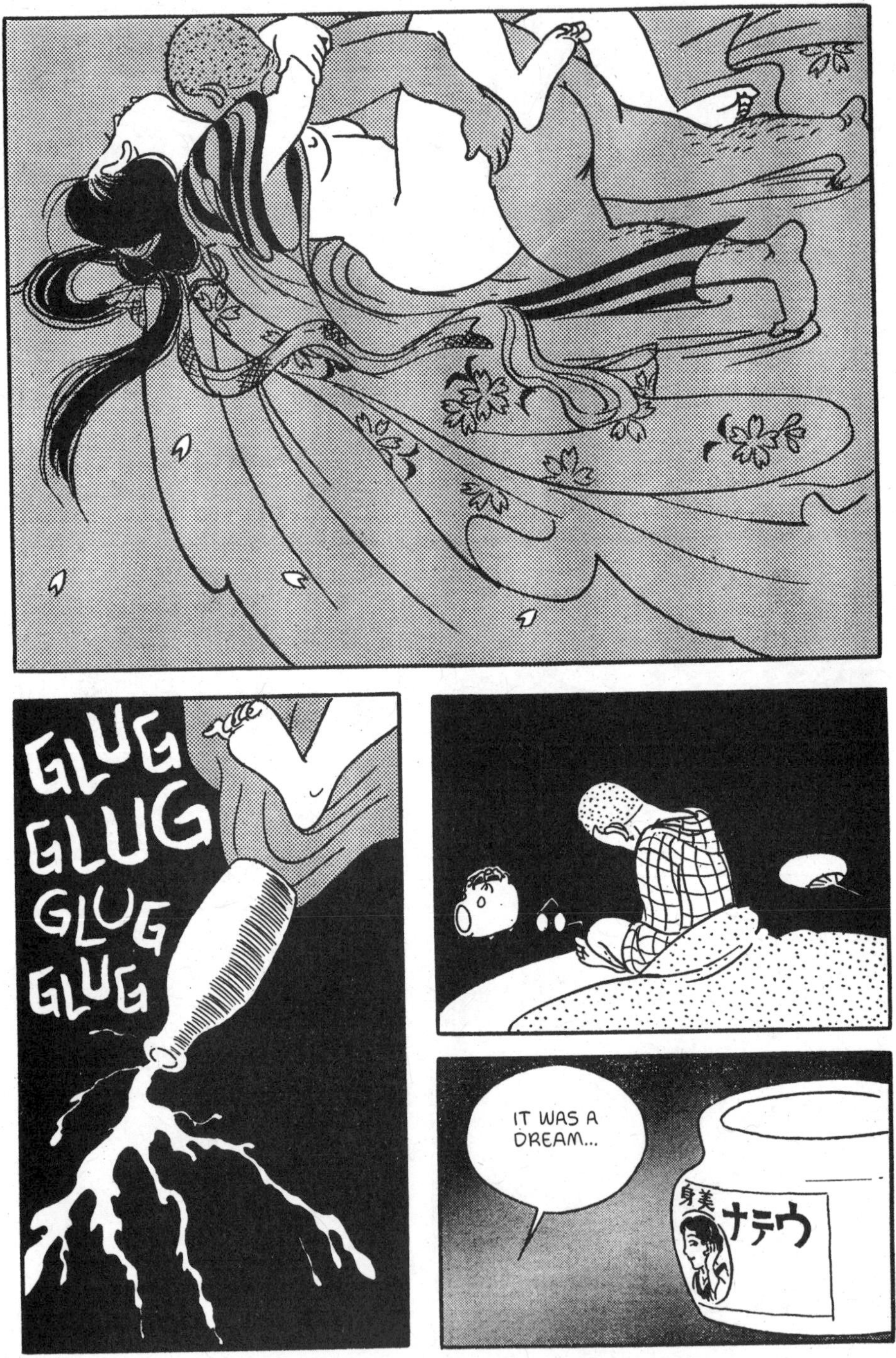
GLUG
GLUG
GLUG
GLUG
IT WAS A DREAM...
美身
ウテナ

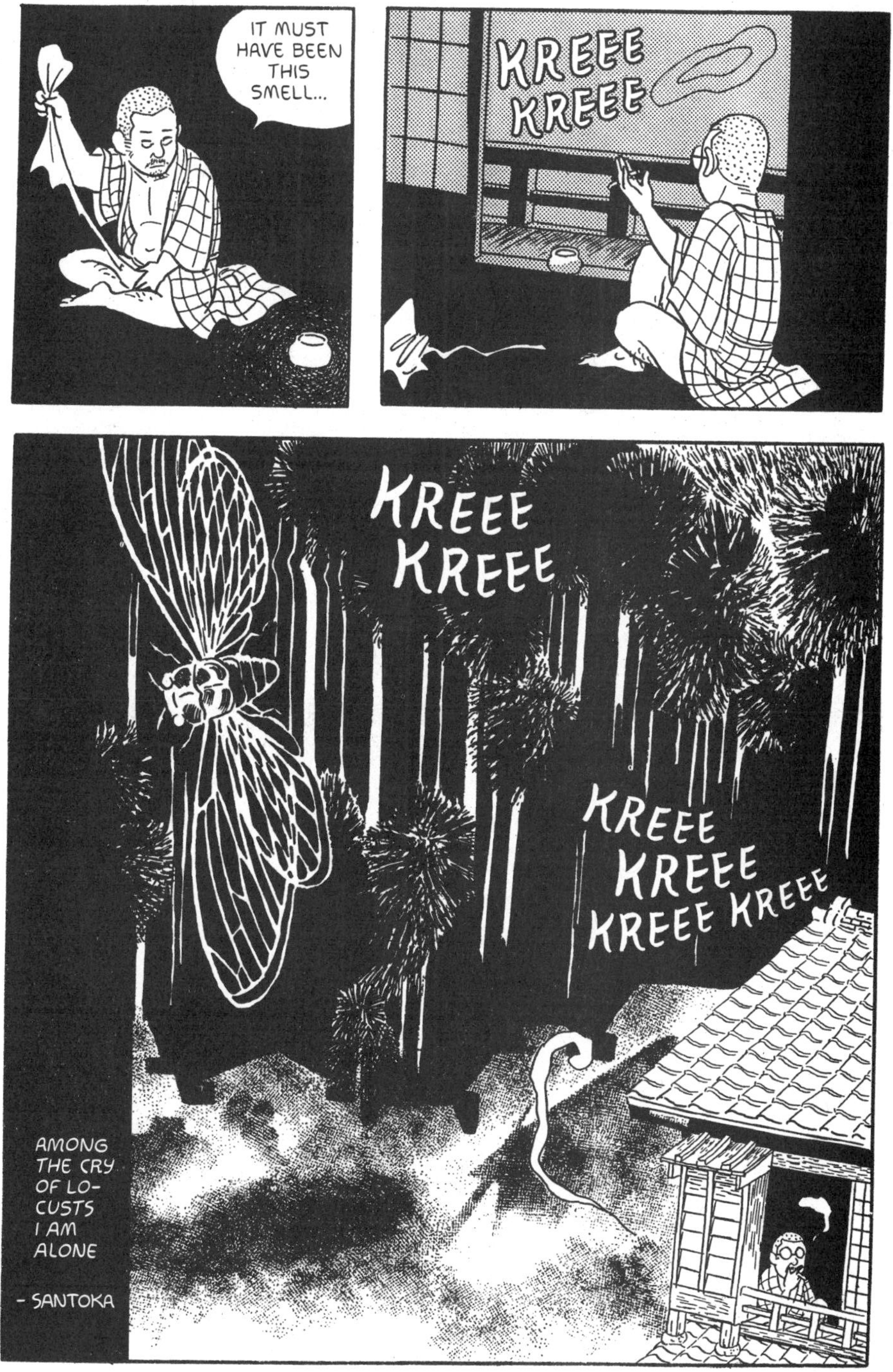
IT MUST HAVE BEEN THIS SMELL...
KREEE KREEE
KREEE KREEE
KREEE KREEE KREEE KREEE
AMONG THE CRY OF LO- CUSTS I AM ALONE
- SANTOKA

SPECTER

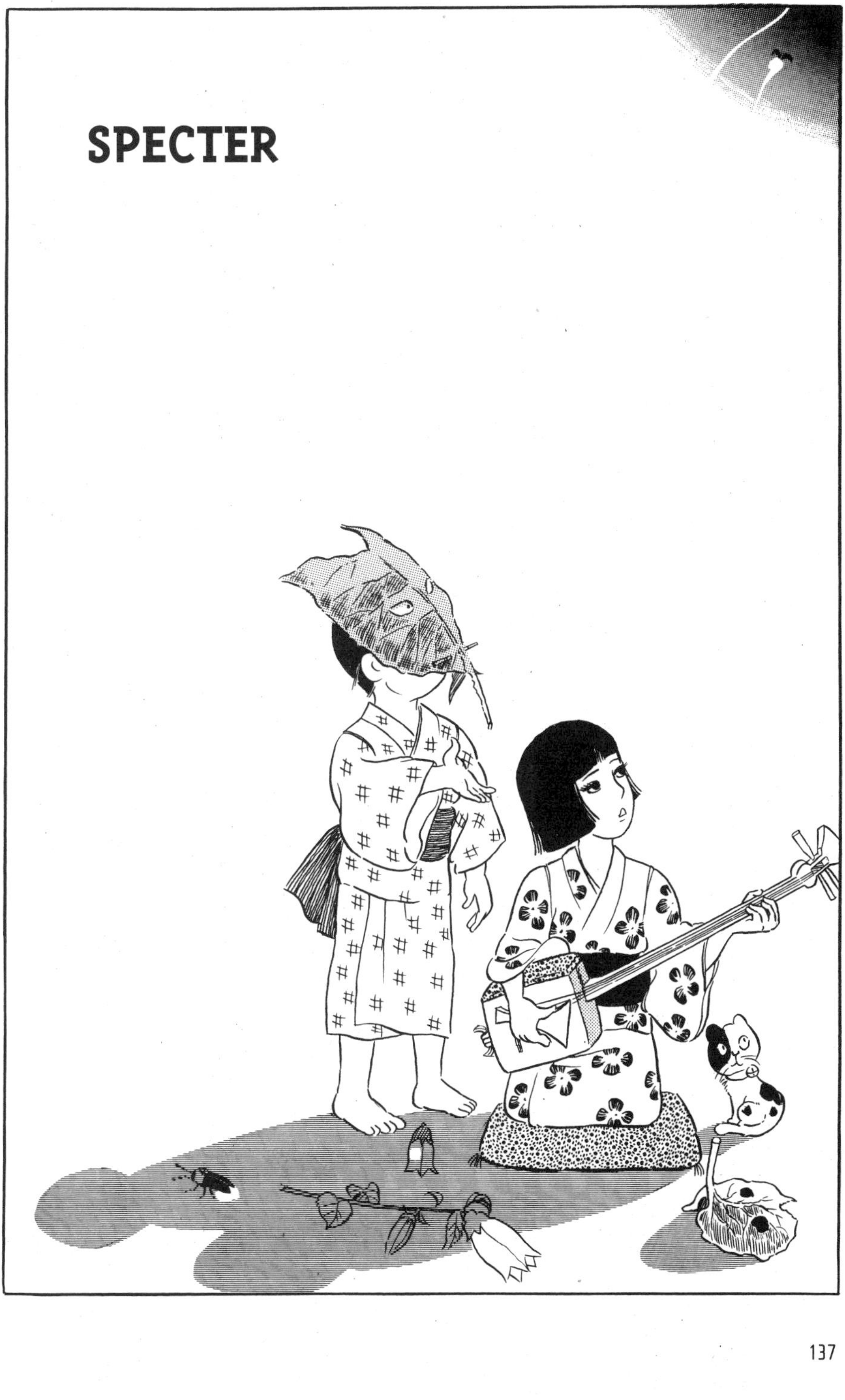

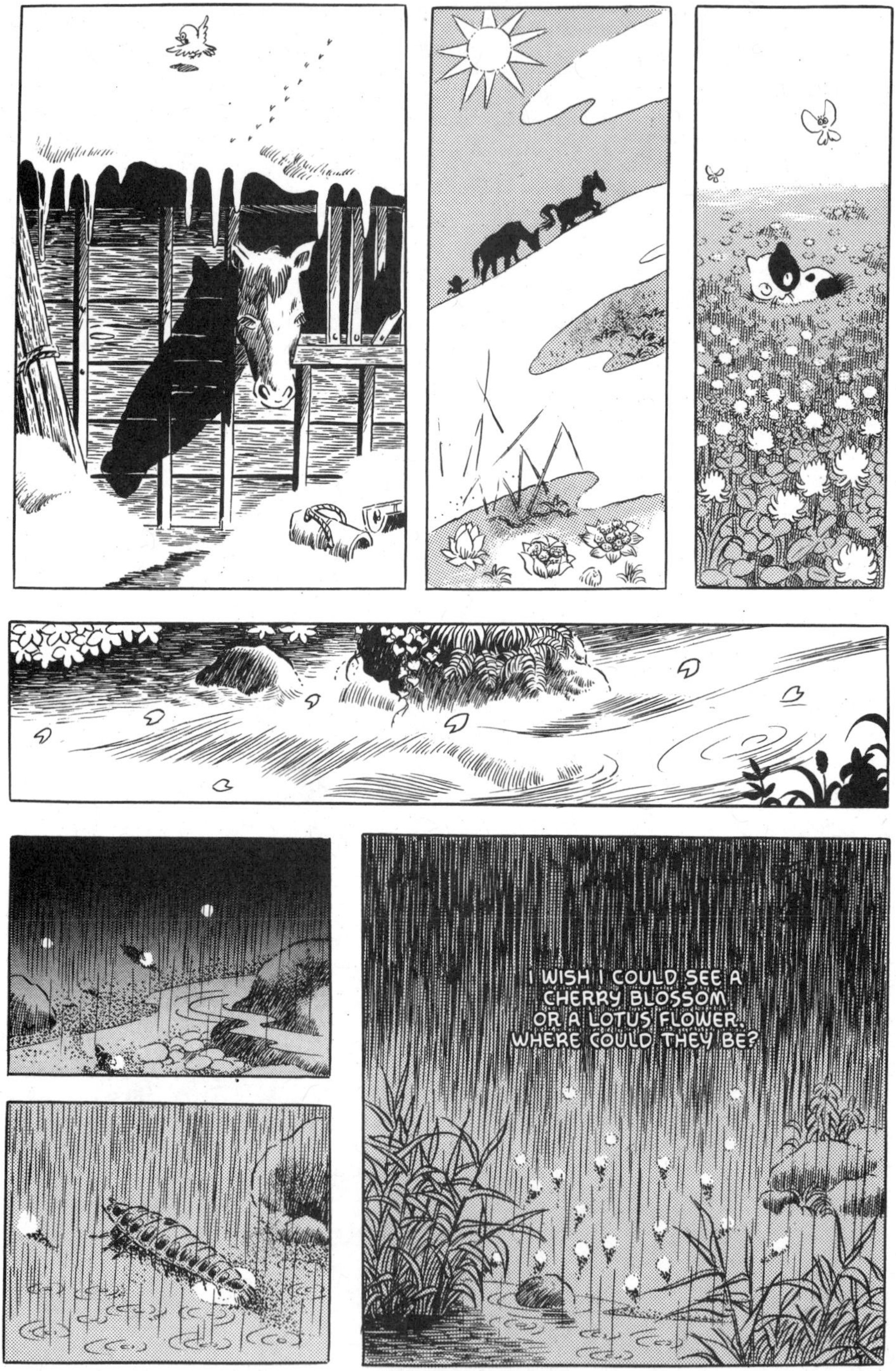
I WISH I COULD SEE A
CHERRY BLOSSOM
OR A LOTUS FLOWER.
WHERE COULD THEY BE?

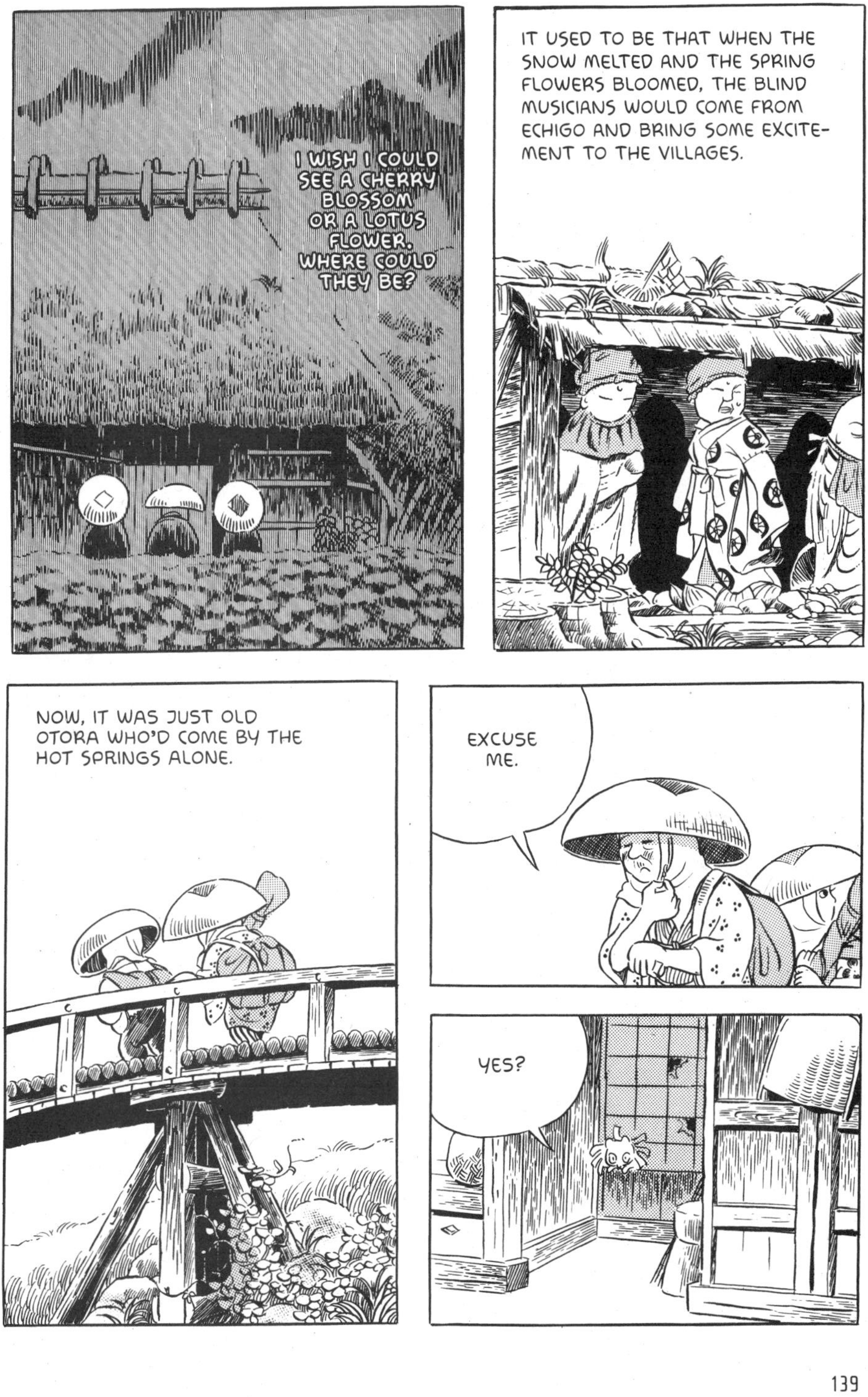
I WISH I COULD SEE A CHERRY BLOSSOM OR A LOTUS FLOWER. WHERE COULD THEY BE?
IT USED TO BE THAT WHEN THE SNOW MELTED AND THE SPRING FLOWERS BLOOMED, THE BLIND MUSICIANS WOULD COME FROM ECHIGO AND BRING SOME EXCITEMENT TO THE VILLAGES.
NOW, IT WAS JUST OLD OTORA WHO'D COME BY THE HOT SPRINGS ALONE.
EXCUSE ME.
YES?

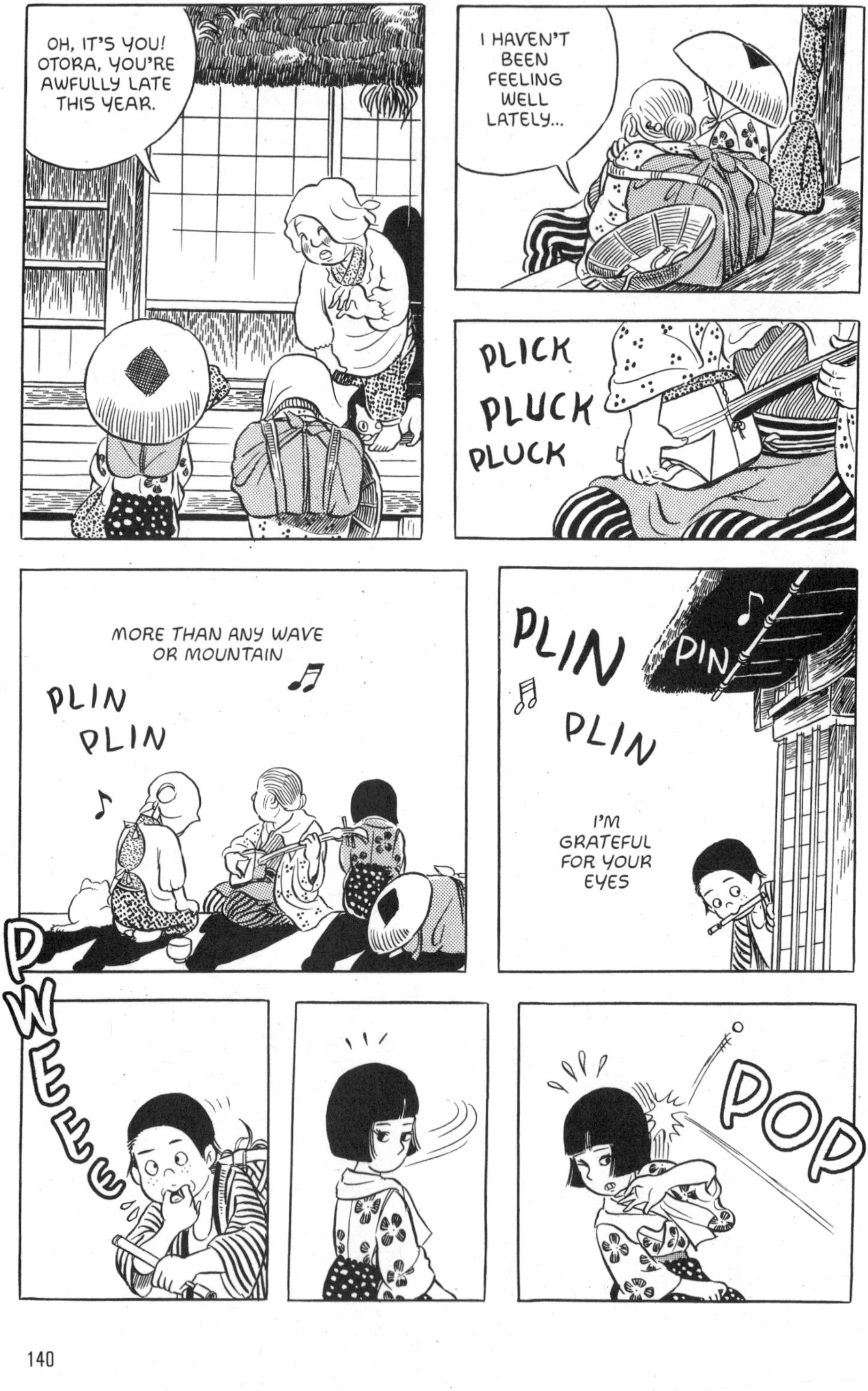
OH, IT'S YOU! OTORA, YOU'RE AWFULLY LATE THIS YEAR.
I HAVEN'T BEEN FEELING WELL LATELY...
PLICK
PLUCK
PLUCK
MORE THAN ANY WAVE OR MOUNTAIN
PLIN
PLIN
PLIN
PIN
PLIN
I'M GRATEFUL FOR YOUR EYES
PWEEEE
POP

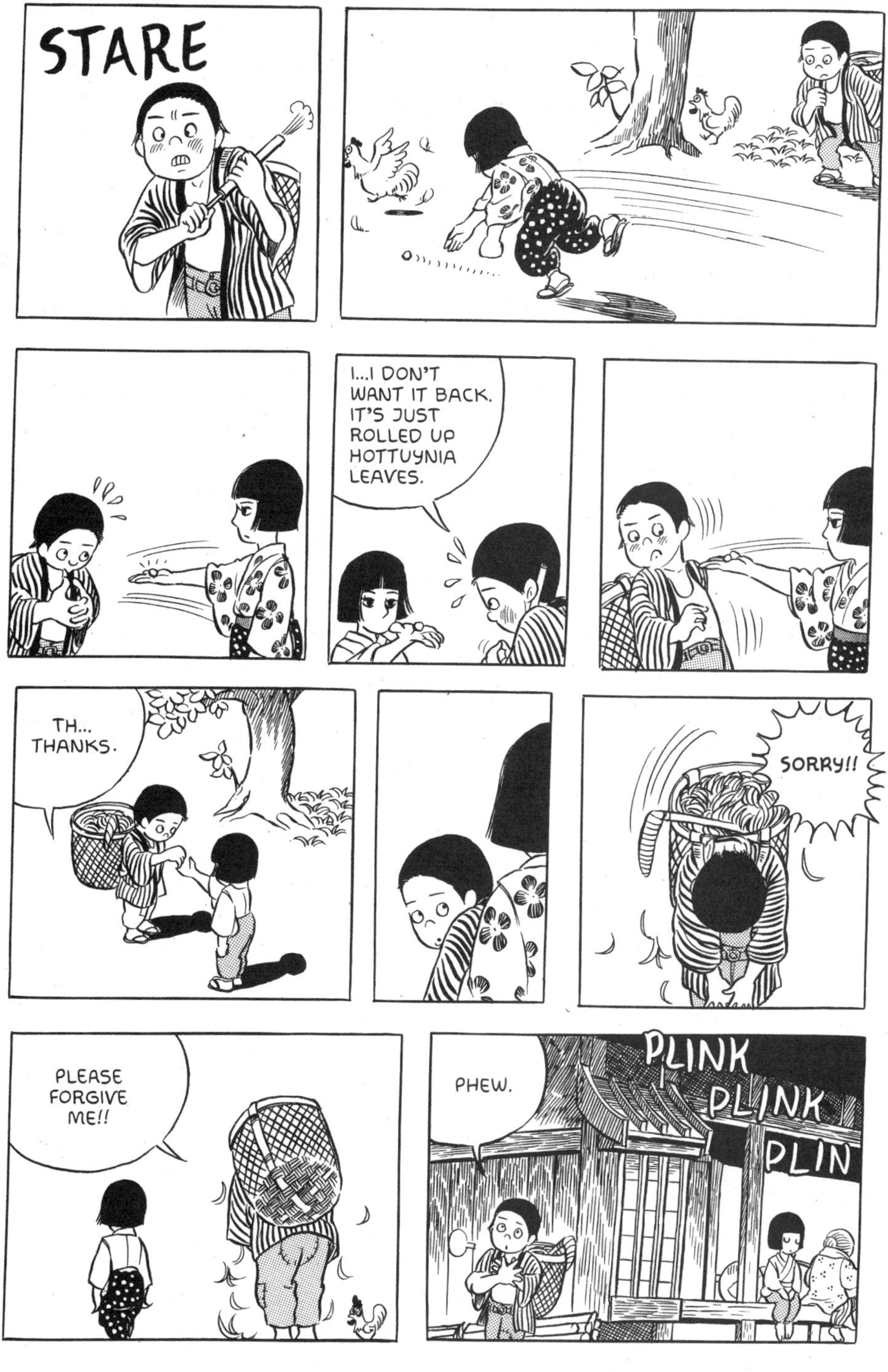
STARE
I...I DON'T WANT IT BACK. IT'S JUST ROLLED UP HOTTUYNIA LEAVES.
TH... THANKS.
SORRY!!
PLEASE FORGIVE ME!!
PHEW.
PLINK
PLINK
PLIN

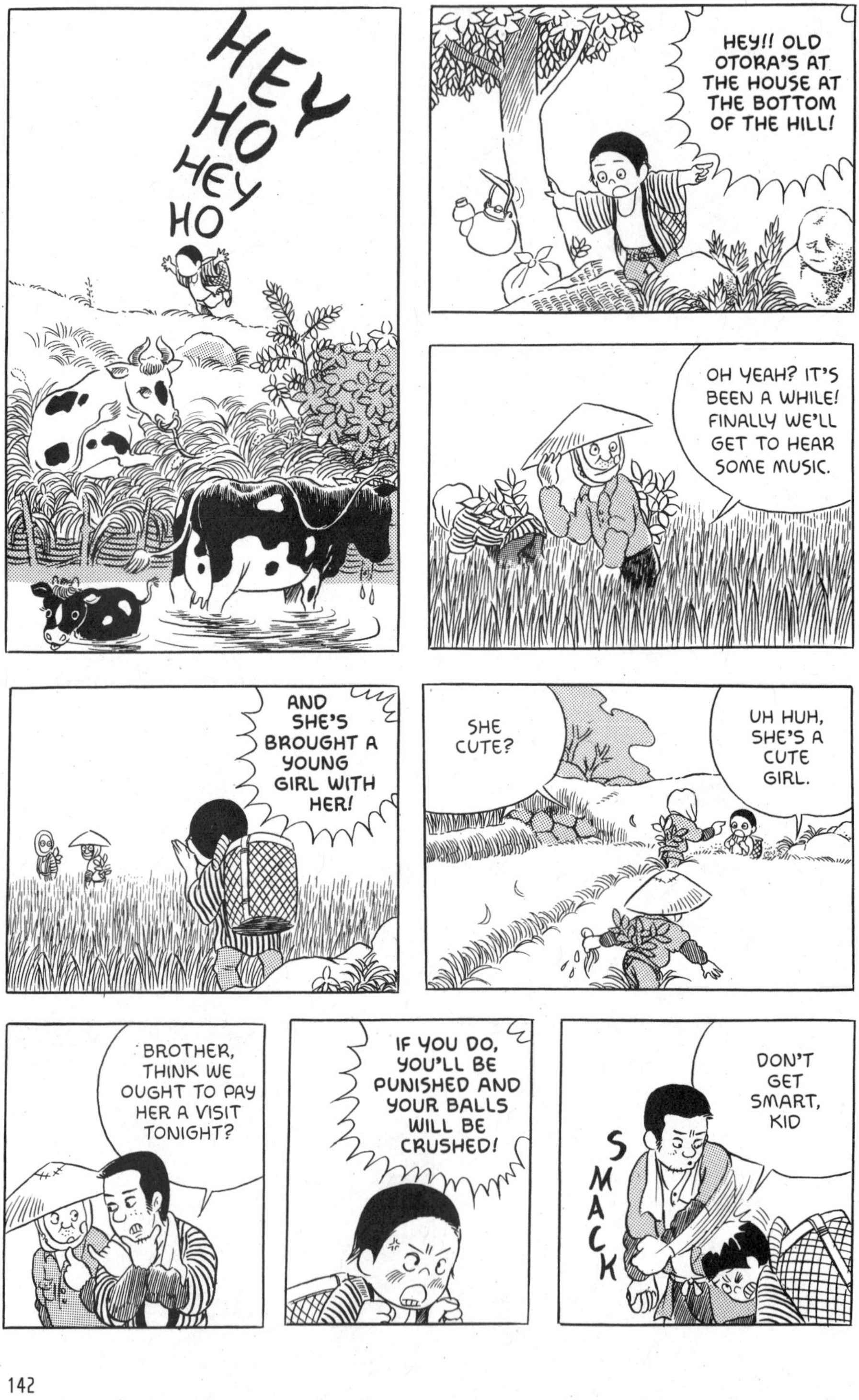
HEY HO HEY HO
HEY!! OLD OTORA'S AT THE HOUSE AT THE BOTTOM OF THE HILL!
OH YEAH? IT'S BEEN A WHILE! FINALLY WE'LL GET TO HEAR SOME MUSIC.
AND SHE'S BROUGHT A YOUNG GIRL WITH HER!
SHE CUTE?
UH HUH, SHE'S A CUTE GIRL.
BROTHER, THINK WE OUGHT TO PAY HER A VISIT TONIGHT?
IF YOU DO, YOU'LL BE PUNISHED AND YOUR BALLS WILL BE CRUSHED!
DON'T GET SMART, KID
SMACK

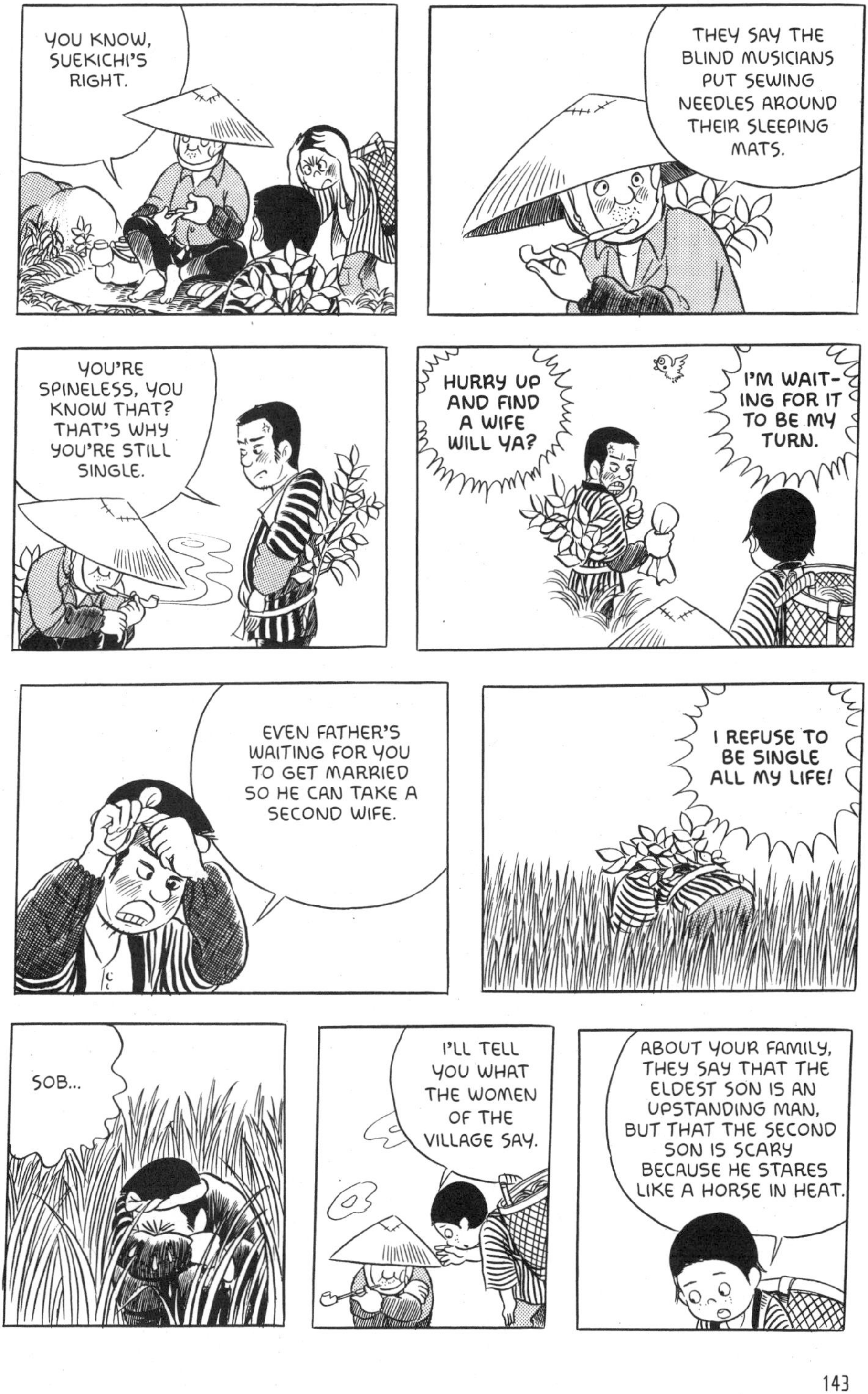
YOU KNOW, SUEKICHI'S RIGHT.
THEY SAY THE BLIND MUSICIANS PUT SEWING NEEDLES AROUND THEIR SLEEPING MATS.
YOU'RE SPINELESS, YOU KNOW THAT? THAT'S WHY YOU'RE STILL SINGLE.
HURRY UP AND FIND A WIFE WILL YA?
I'M WAIT-ING FOR IT TO BE MY TURN.
EVEN FATHER'S WAITING FOR YOU TO GET MARRIED SO HE CAN TAKE A SECOND WIFE.
I REFUSE TO BE SINGLE ALL MY LIFE!
SOB...
I'LL TELL YOU WHAT THE WOMEN OF THE VILLAGE SAY.
ABOUT YOUR FAMILY, THEY SAY THAT THE ELDEST SON IS AN UPSTANDING MAN, BUT THAT THE SECOND SON IS SCARY BECAUSE HE STARES LIKE A HORSE IN HEAT.

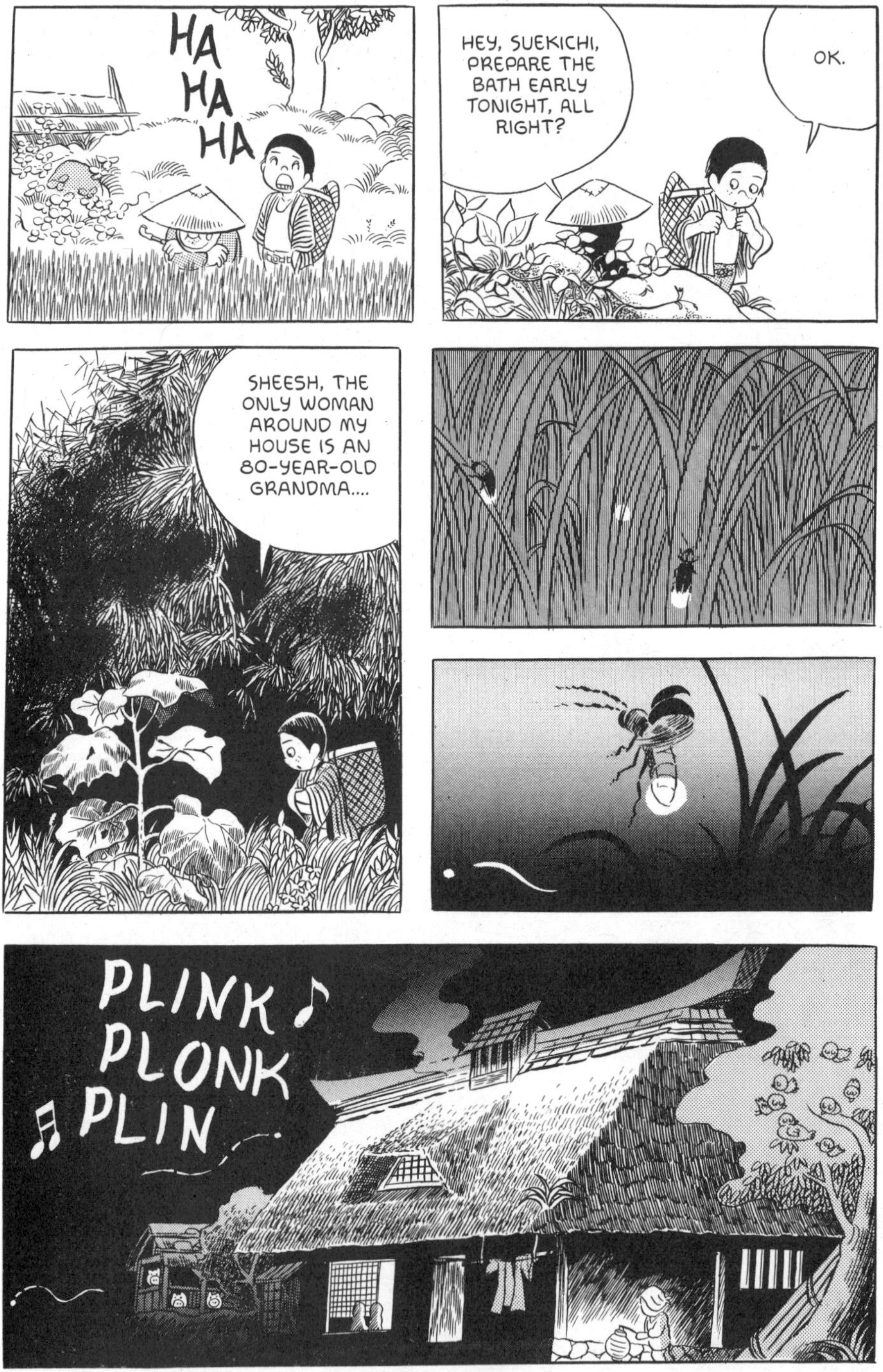
HA HA HA
HEY, SUEKICHI, PREPARE THE BATH EARLY TONIGHT, ALL RIGHT?
OK.
SHEESH, THE ONLY WOMAN AROUND MY HOUSE IS AN 80-YEAR-OLD GRANDMA....
PLINK PLONK PLIN

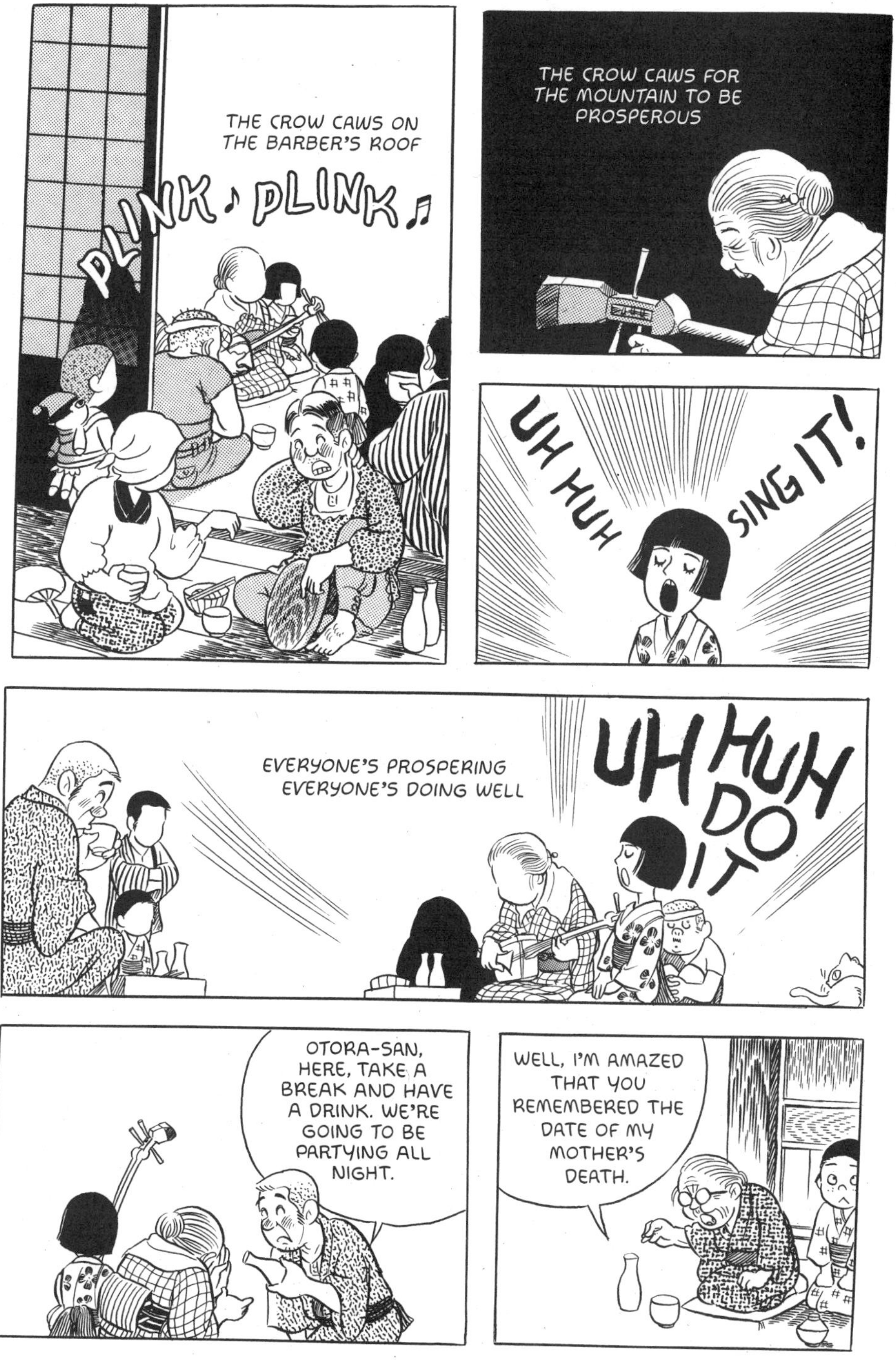
THE CROW CAWS ON THE BARBER'S ROOF
PLINK ♪ PLINK ♫
THE CROW CAWS FOR THE MOUNTAIN TO BE PROSPEROUS
UH HUH
SING IT!
EVERYONE'S PROSPERING EVERYONE'S DOING WELL
UH HUH
DO IT
OTORA-SAN, HERE, TAKE A BREAK AND HAVE A DRINK. WE'RE GOING TO BE PARTYING ALL NIGHT.
WELL, I'M AMAZED THAT YOU REMEMBERED THE DATE OF MY MOTHER'S DEATH.

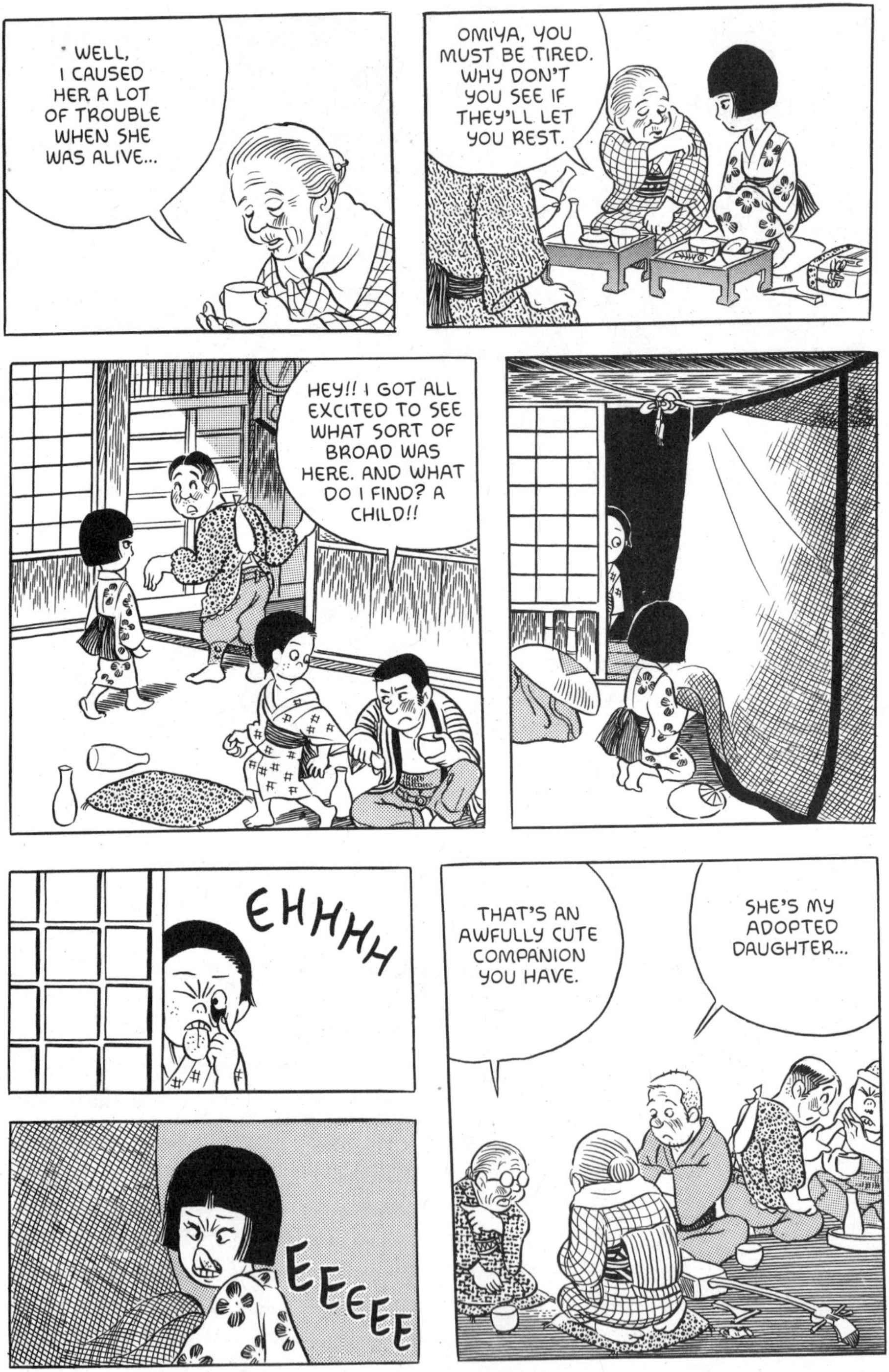
WELL, I CAUSED HER A LOT OF TROUBLE WHEN SHE WAS ALIVE...
OMIYA, YOU MUST BE TIRED. WHY DON'T YOU SEE IF THEY'LL LET YOU REST.
HEY!! I GOT ALL EXCITED TO SEE WHAT SORT OF BROAD WAS HERE. AND WHAT DO I FIND? A CHILD!!
EHHHH
EEEEEE
THAT'S AN AWFULLY CUTE COMPANION YOU HAVE.
SHE'S MY ADOPTED DAUGHTER...

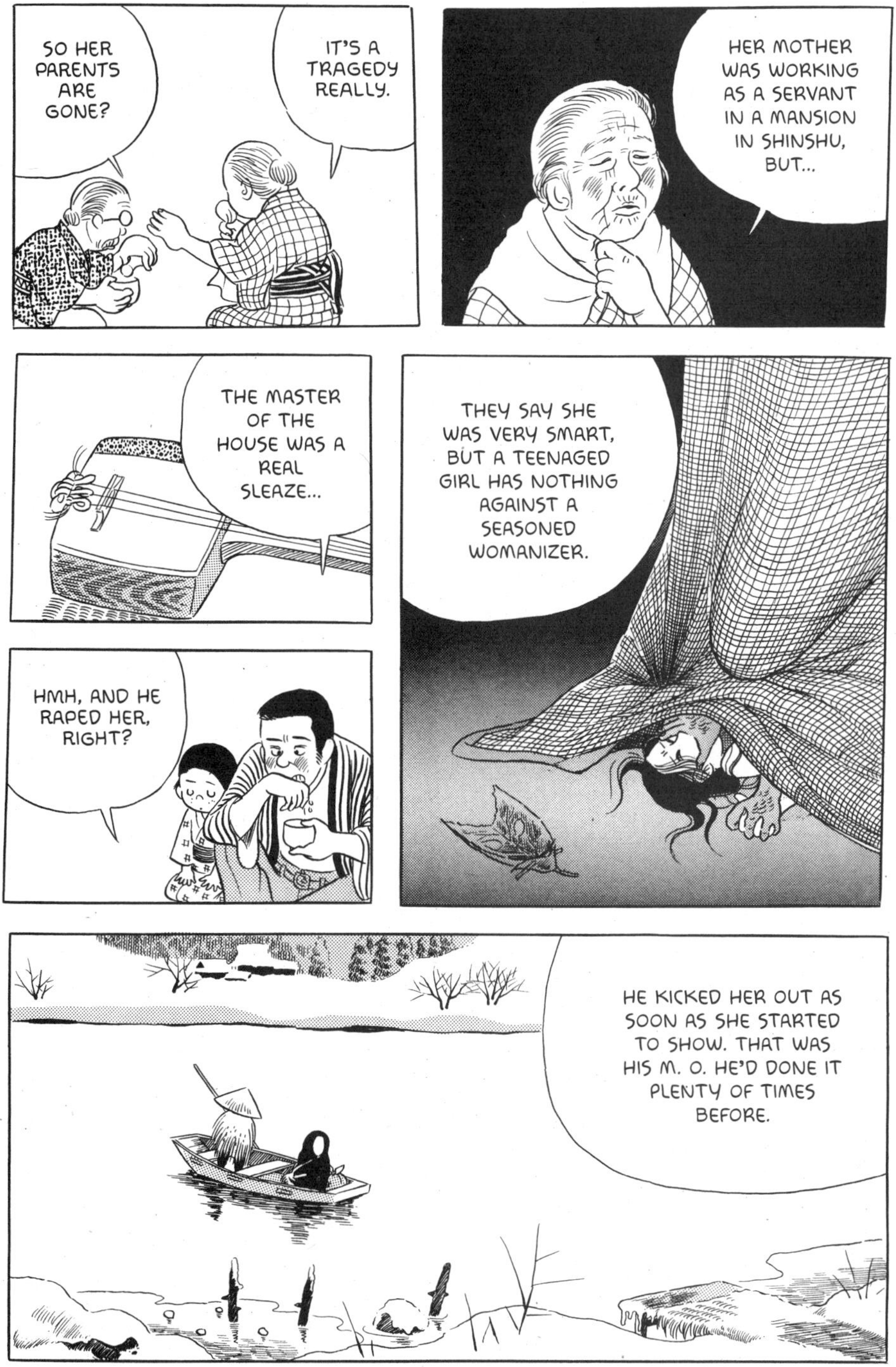
SO HER PARENTS ARE GONE?
IT'S A TRAGEDY REALLY.
HER MOTHER WAS WORKING AS A SERVANT IN A MANSION IN SHINSHU, BUT...
THE MASTER OF THE HOUSE WAS A REAL SLEAZE...
HMH, AND HE RAPED HER, RIGHT?
THEY SAY SHE WAS VERY SMART, BUT A TEENAGED GIRL HAS NOTHING AGAINST A SEASONED WOMANIZER.
HE KICKED HER OUT AS SOON AS SHE STARTED TO SHOW. THAT WAS HIS M. O. HE'D DONE IT PLENTY OF TIMES BEFORE.

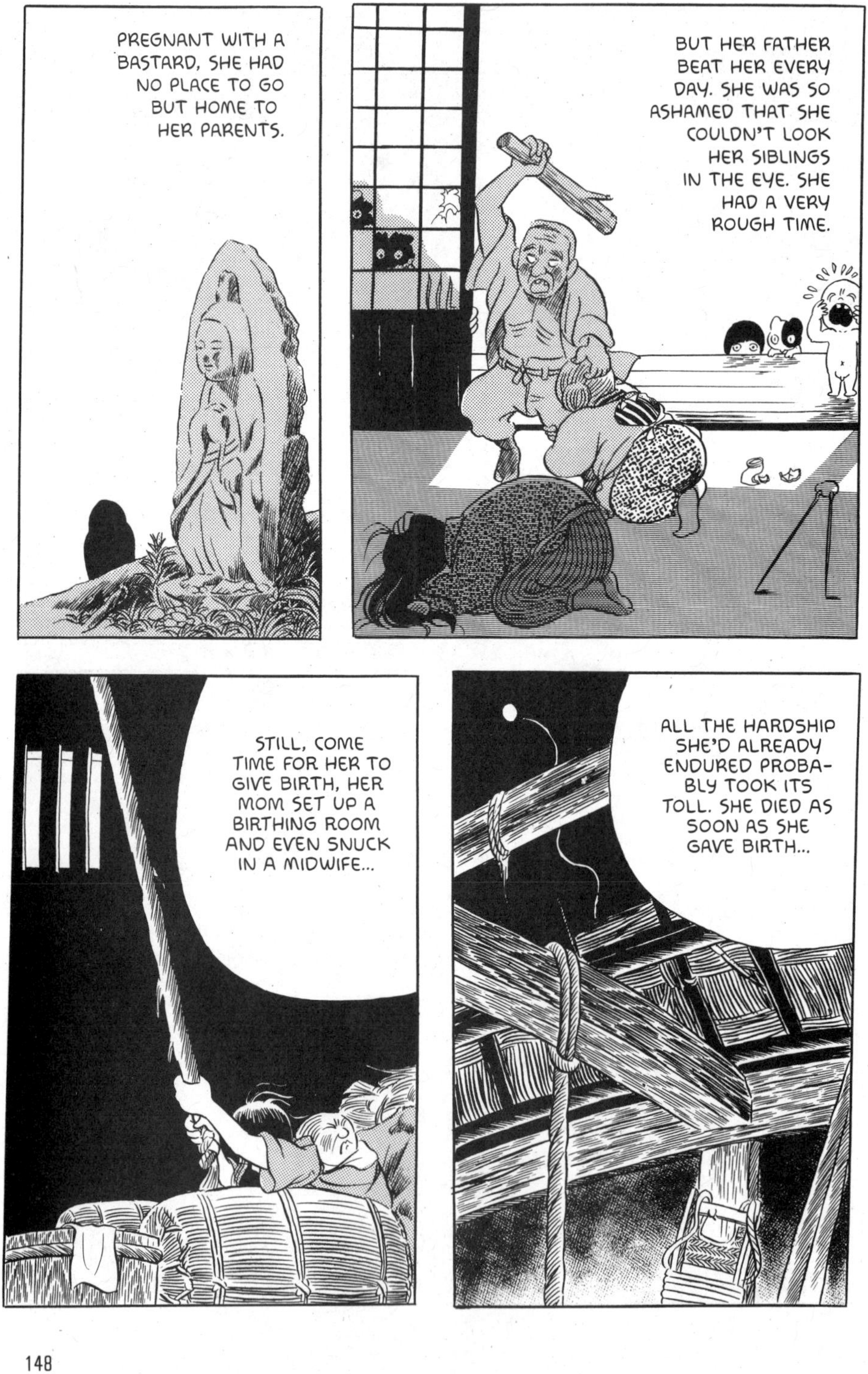
PREGNANT WITH A BASTARD, SHE HAD NO PLACE TO GO BUT HOME TO HER PARENTS.
BUT HER FATHER BEAT HER EVERY DAY. SHE WAS SO ASHAMED THAT SHE COULDN'T LOOK HER SIBLINGS IN THE EYE. SHE HAD A VERY ROUGH TIME.
STILL, COME TIME FOR HER TO GIVE BIRTH, HER MOM SET UP A BIRTHING ROOM AND EVEN SNUCK IN A MIDWIFE...
ALL THE HARDSHIP SHE'D ALREADY ENDURED PROBA-BLY TOOK ITS TOLL. SHE DIED AS SOON AS SHE GAVE BIRTH...

THERE ARE SOME AWFUL MEN IN THIS WORLD.

I CAN'T NAME NAMES, BUT...

UH HUH.

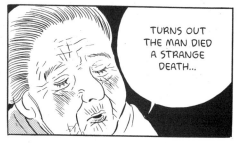

TURNS OUT THE MAN DIED A STRANGE DEATH...

OH YEAH?

HERE, HAVE SOME MORE, PLEASE.

GULP

AND?

IT WAS A HOT AND HUMID NIGHT, JUST LIKE TONIGHT.

A WHOLE MESS OF FIREFLIES APPEARED AT THE MANSION.

THEY TRIED TO SEND THE FIREFLIES AWAY, BUT THEY JUST KEPT ON COMING... AND THEY WENT AND SETTLED INTO THE MASTER'S ROOM...

HIS ROOM WAS COVERED IN FIREFLIES. THE SMELL OF DEATH WAS SO STRONG, IT WAS SUFFOCATING.

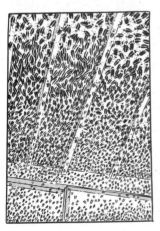

AT NIGHT, THE FIREFLIES...

THE FIREFLIES...?

ALL FLEW UP AT ONCE...

TO FORM THE SHAPE OF A WOMAN.

AND THIS SPECTER HAUNTED THE MAN NIGHT AFTER NIGHT.

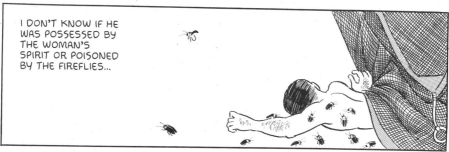

I DON'T KNOW IF HE WAS POSSESSED BY THE WOMAN'S SPIRIT OR POISONED BY THE FIREFLIES...

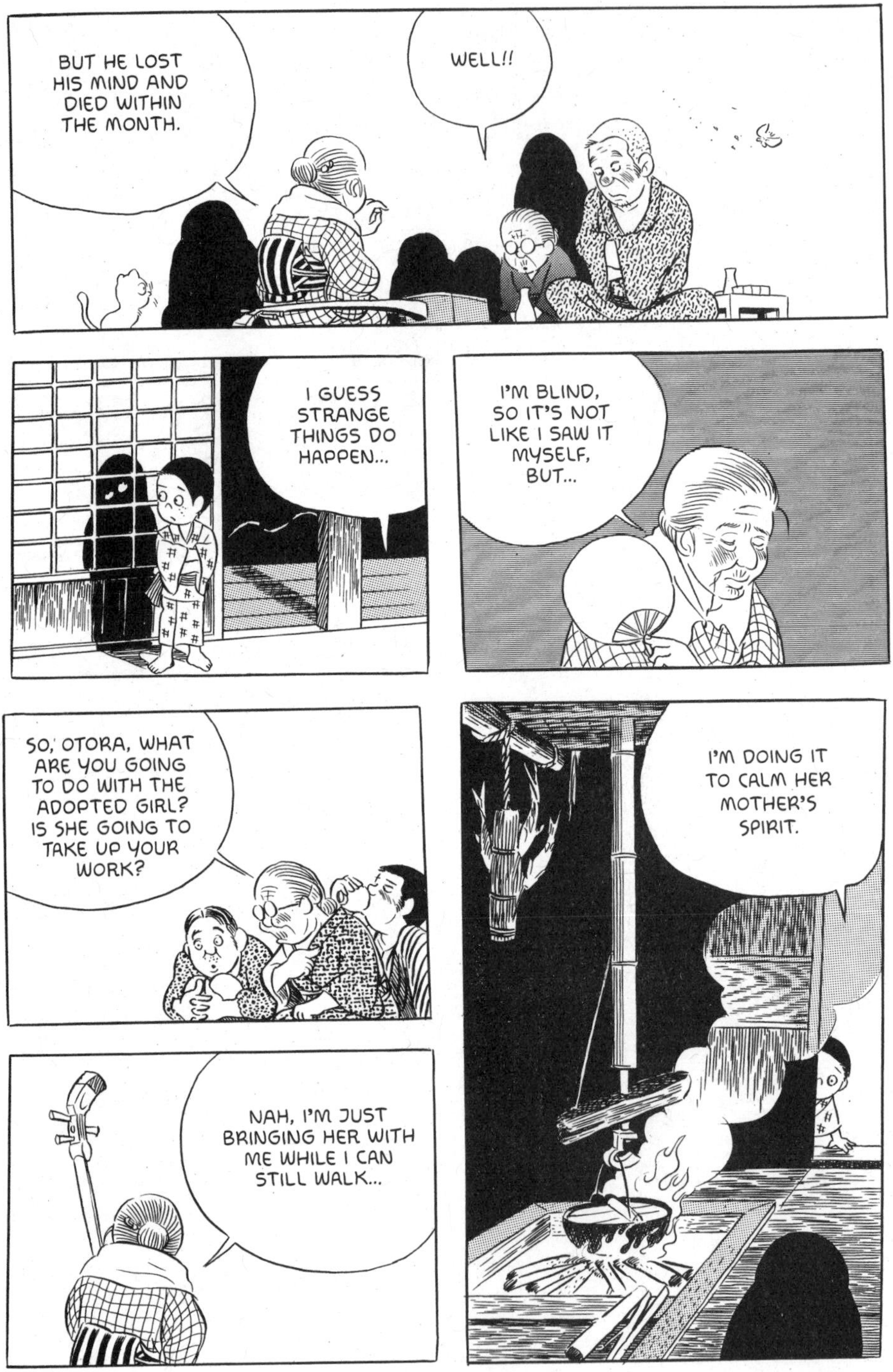
BUT HE LOST HIS MIND AND DIED WITHIN THE MONTH.
WELL!!
I GUESS STRANGE THINGS DO HAPPEN...
I'M BLIND, SO IT'S NOT LIKE I SAW IT MYSELF, BUT...
SO, OTORA, WHAT ARE YOU GOING TO DO WITH THE ADOPTED GIRL? IS SHE GOING TO TAKE UP YOUR WORK?
NAH, I'M JUST BRINGING HER WITH ME WHILE I CAN STILL WALK...
I'M DOING IT TO CALM HER MOTHER'S SPIRIT.

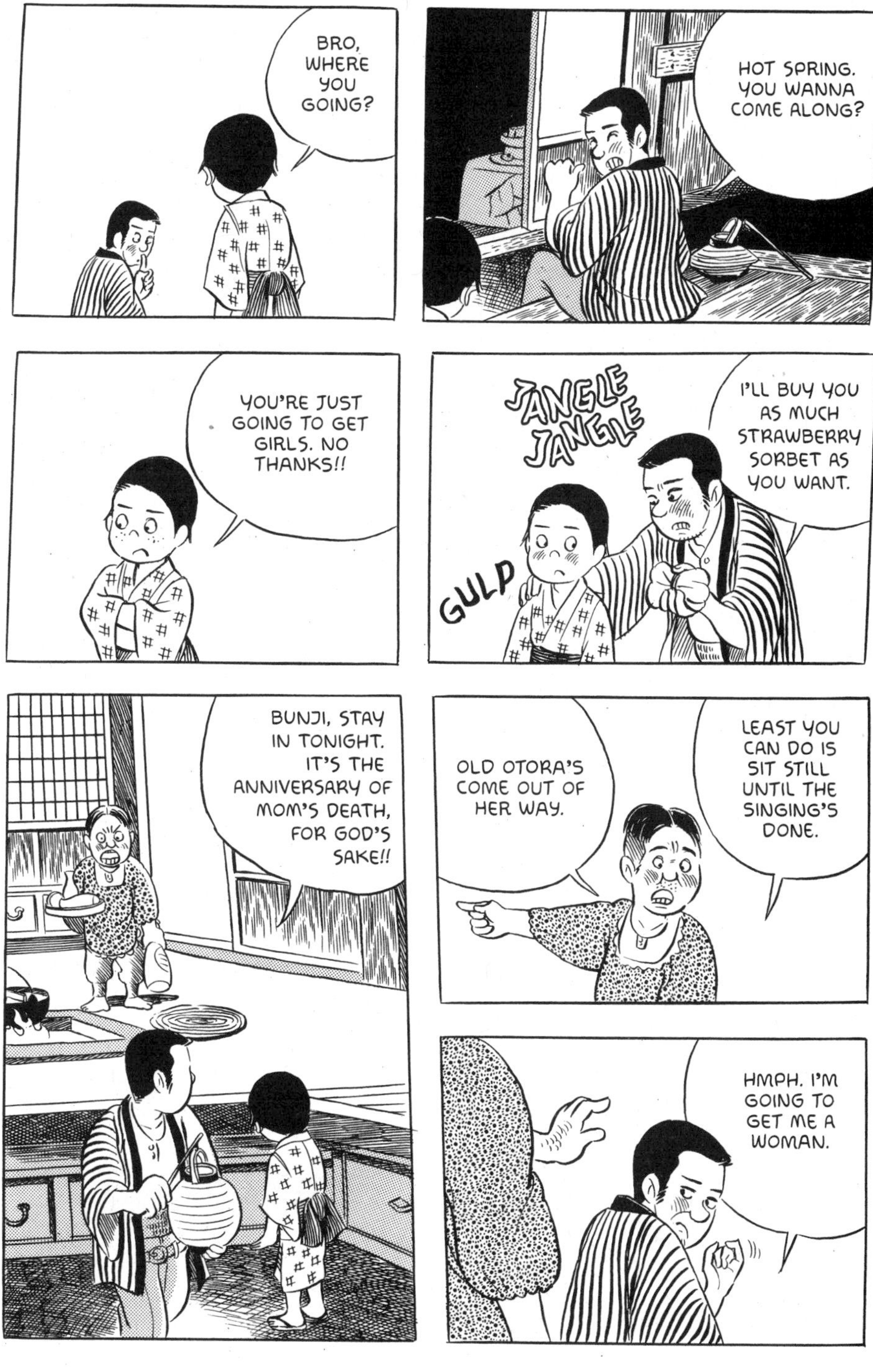
BRO, WHERE YOU GOING?
HOT SPRING. YOU WANNA COME ALONG?
YOU'RE JUST GOING TO GET GIRLS. NO THANKS!!
JANGLE JANGLE
I'LL BUY YOU AS MUCH STRAWBERRY SORBET AS YOU WANT.
GULP
BUNJI, STAY IN TONIGHT. IT'S THE ANNIVERSARY OF MOM'S DEATH, FOR GOD'S SAKE!!
OLD OTORA'S COME OUT OF HER WAY.
LEAST YOU CAN DO IS SIT STILL UNTIL THE SINGING'S DONE.
HMPH. I'M GOING TO GET ME A WOMAN.

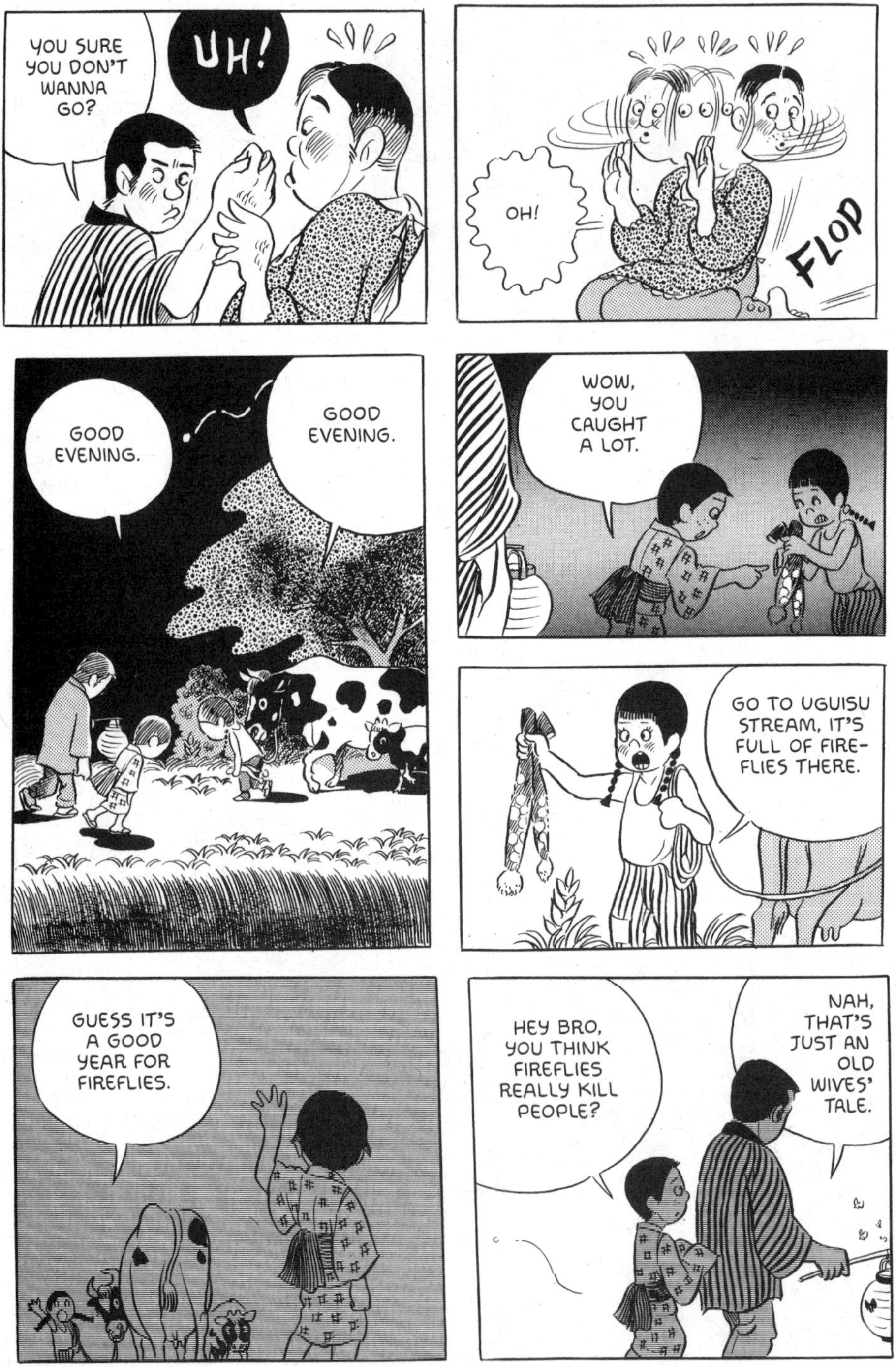
YOU SURE YOU DON'T WANNA GO?
UH!
OH!
FLOP
GOOD EVENING.
GOOD EVENING.
WOW, YOU CAUGHT A LOT.
GO TO UGUISU STREAM, IT'S FULL OF FIRE-FLIES THERE.
GUESS IT'S A GOOD YEAR FOR FIREFLIES.
HEY BRO, YOU THINK FIREFLIES REALLY KILL PEOPLE?
NAH, THAT'S JUST AN OLD WIVES' TALE.

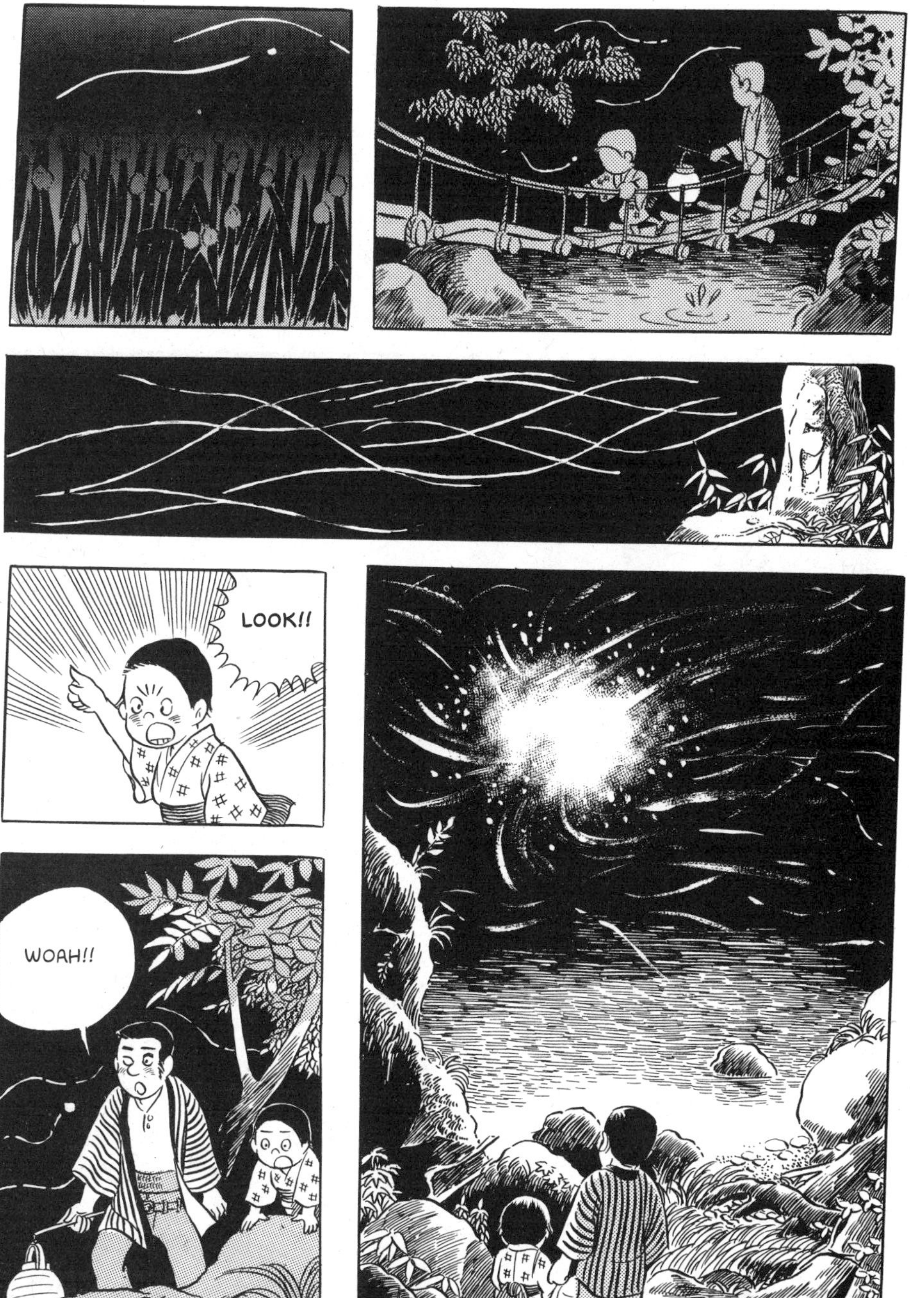
LOOK!!
WOAH!!

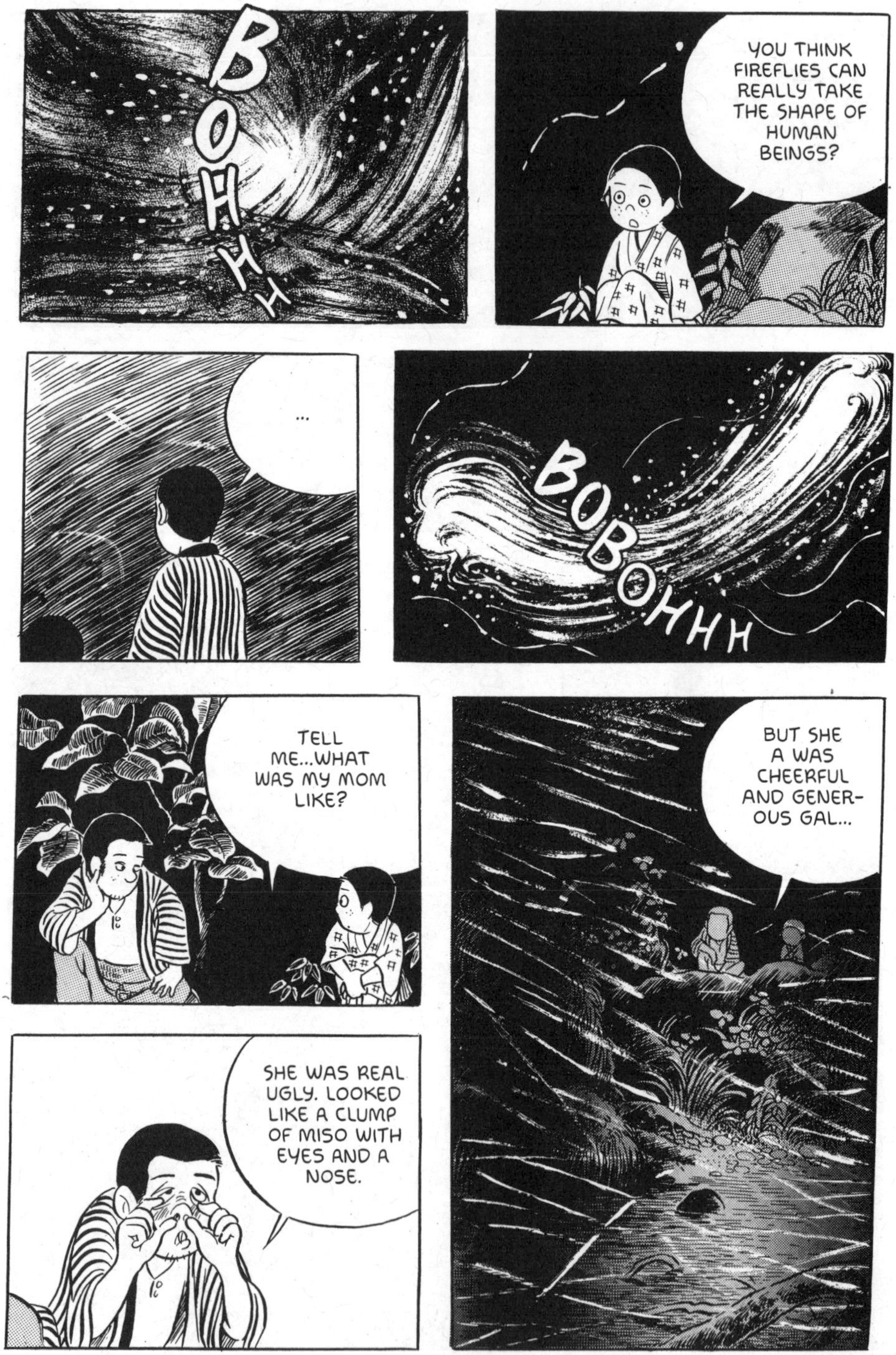
BOHHH
YOU THINK FIREFLIES CAN REALLY TAKE THE SHAPE OF HUMAN BEINGS?
...
BOBOHHHH
TELL ME...WHAT WAS MY MOM LIKE?
SHE WAS REAL UGLY. LOOKED LIKE A CLUMP OF MISO WITH EYES AND A NOSE.
BUT SHE A WAS CHEERFUL AND GENER-OUS GAL...

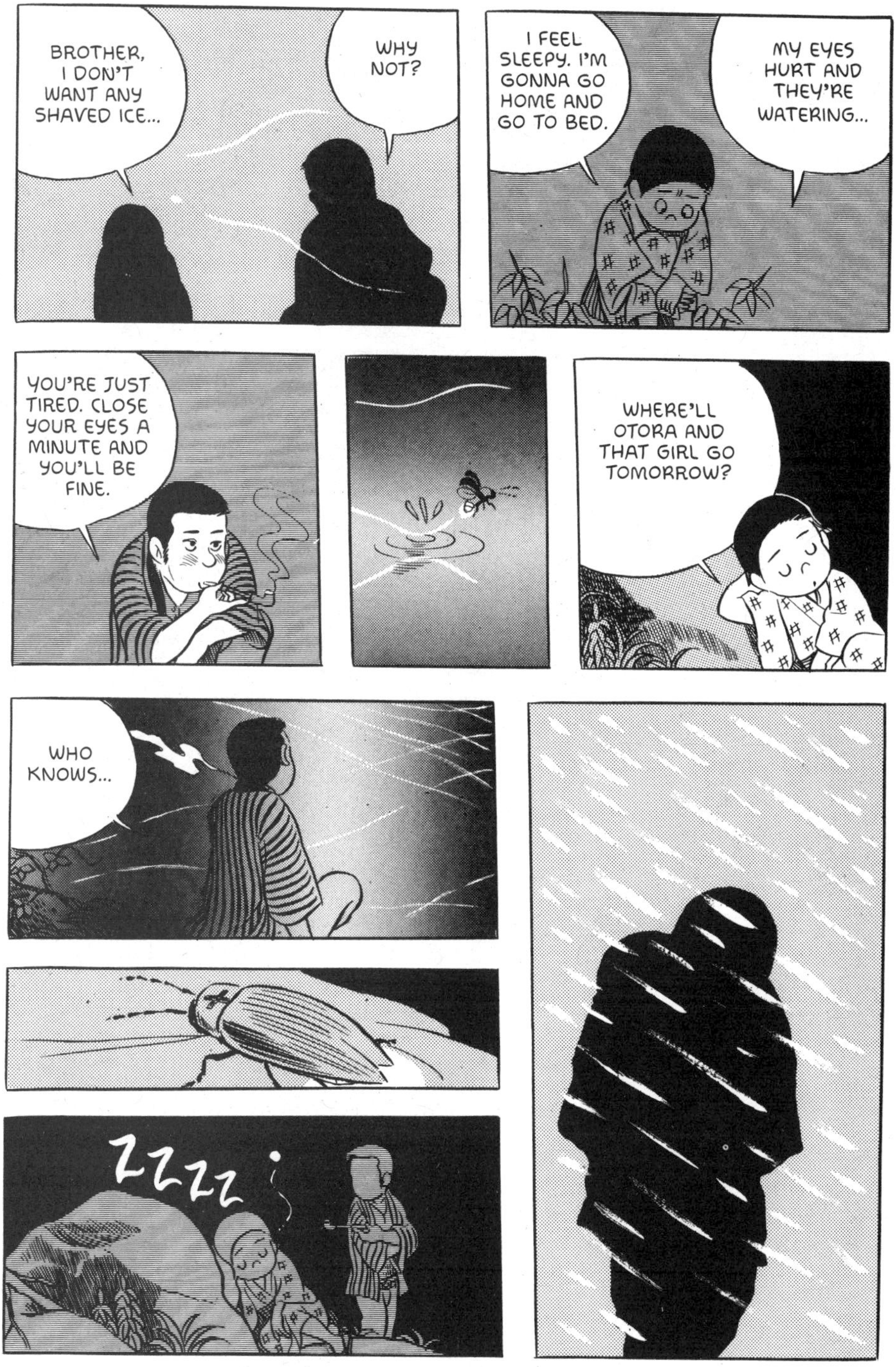
BROTHER, I DON'T WANT ANY SHAVED ICE...
WHY NOT?
I FEEL SLEEPY. I'M GONNA GO HOME AND GO TO BED.
MY EYES HURT AND THEY'RE WATERING...
YOU'RE JUST TIRED. CLOSE YOUR EYES A MINUTE AND YOU'LL BE FINE.
WHERE'LL OTORA AND THAT GIRL GO TOMORROW?
WHO KNOWS...
ZZZZZ

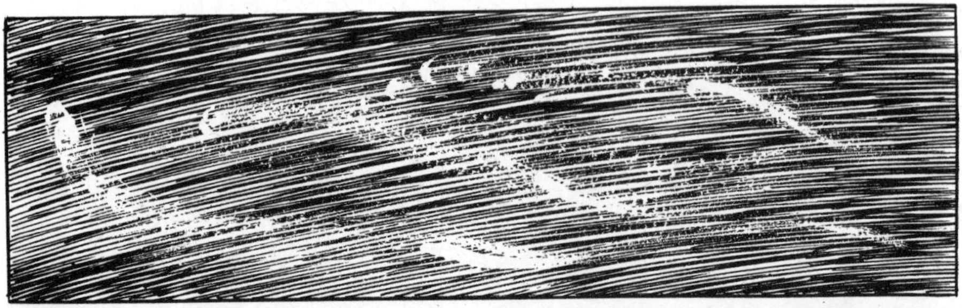

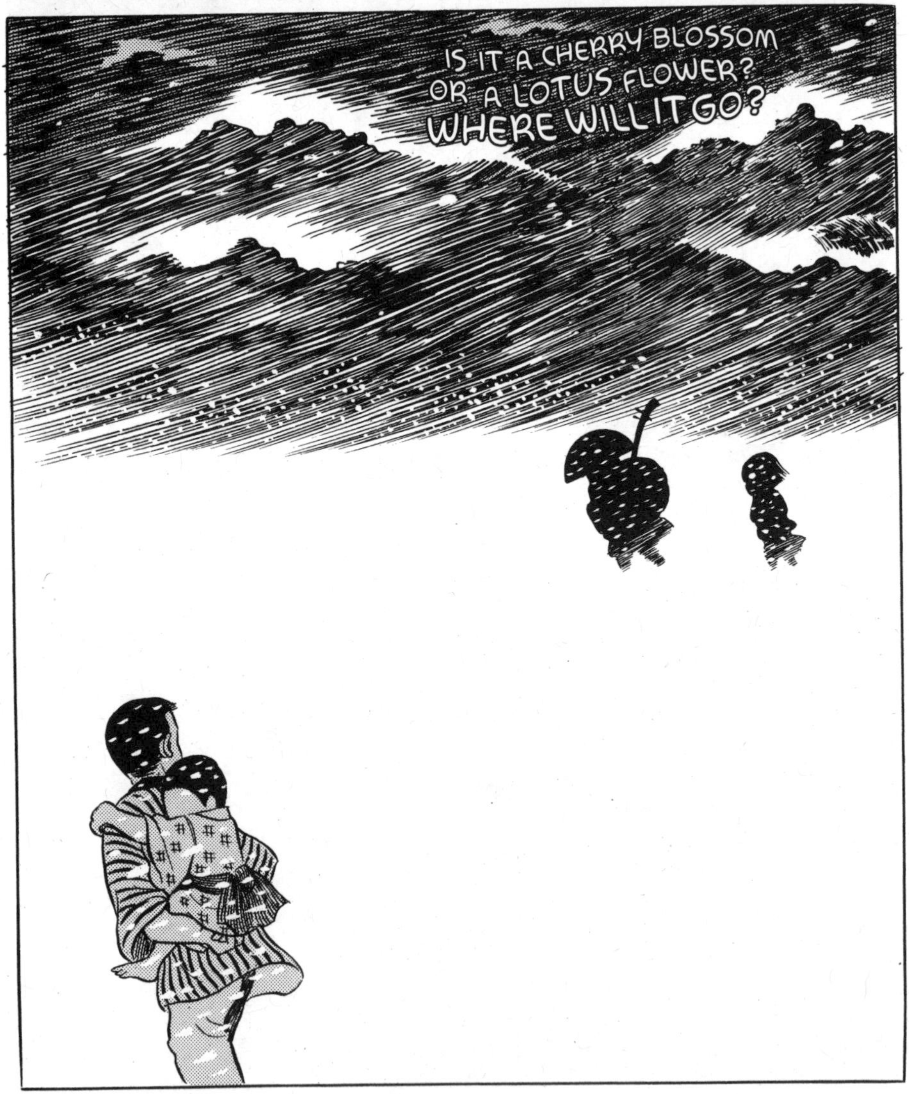
IS IT A CHERRY BLOSSOM
OR A LOTUS FLOWER?
WHERE WILL IT GO?

TORAJIRO
KAPPA

KAPPA: AN IMAGINARY ANIMAL
FREQUENTLY APPEARING IN JAPA-
NESE MYTHS AND FOLK TALES.
KAPPA ARE THE SIZE AND SHAPE OF
CHILDREN, BUT HAVE SHARP BEAKS,
AND SHELLS ON THEIR BACKS. THEY
LIVE IN THE WATER, BUT CAN ROAM
ON LAND AS LONG AS THEY HAVE
WATER IN THE PLATES ON TOP OF
THEIR HEADS. IT IS SAID THAT THE
KAPPA COME ONTO DRY LAND TO
DRAG ANIMALS AND PEOPLE INTO
THE WATER AND SUCK THEIR BLOOD.

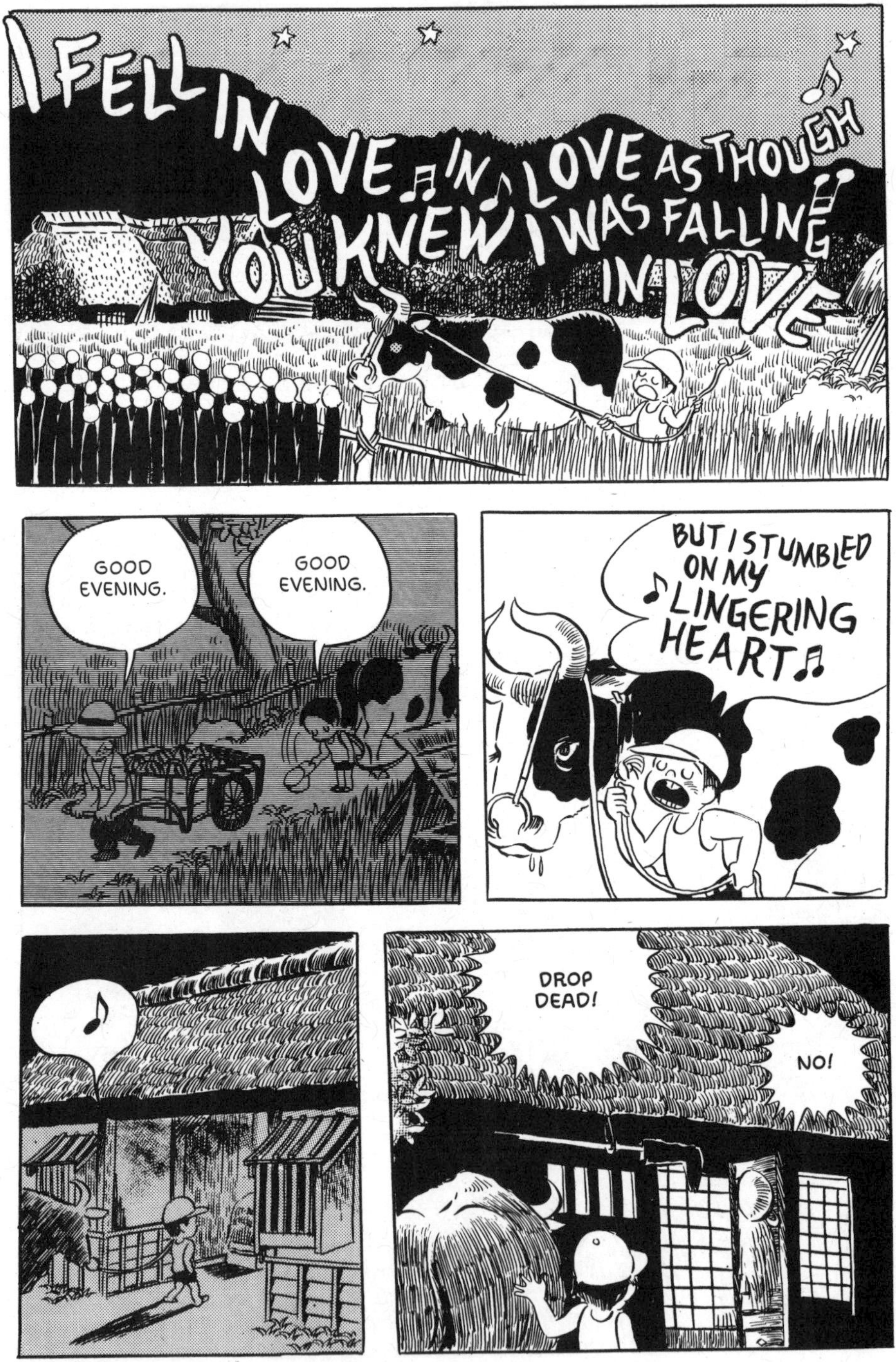
I FELL IN LOVE ♬ IN ♪ LOVE AS THOUGH YOU KNEW I WAS FALLING IN LOVE
GOOD EVENING.
GOOD EVENING.
BUT I STUMBLED ON MY ♪ LINGERING HEART ♬
♪
DROP DEAD!
NO!

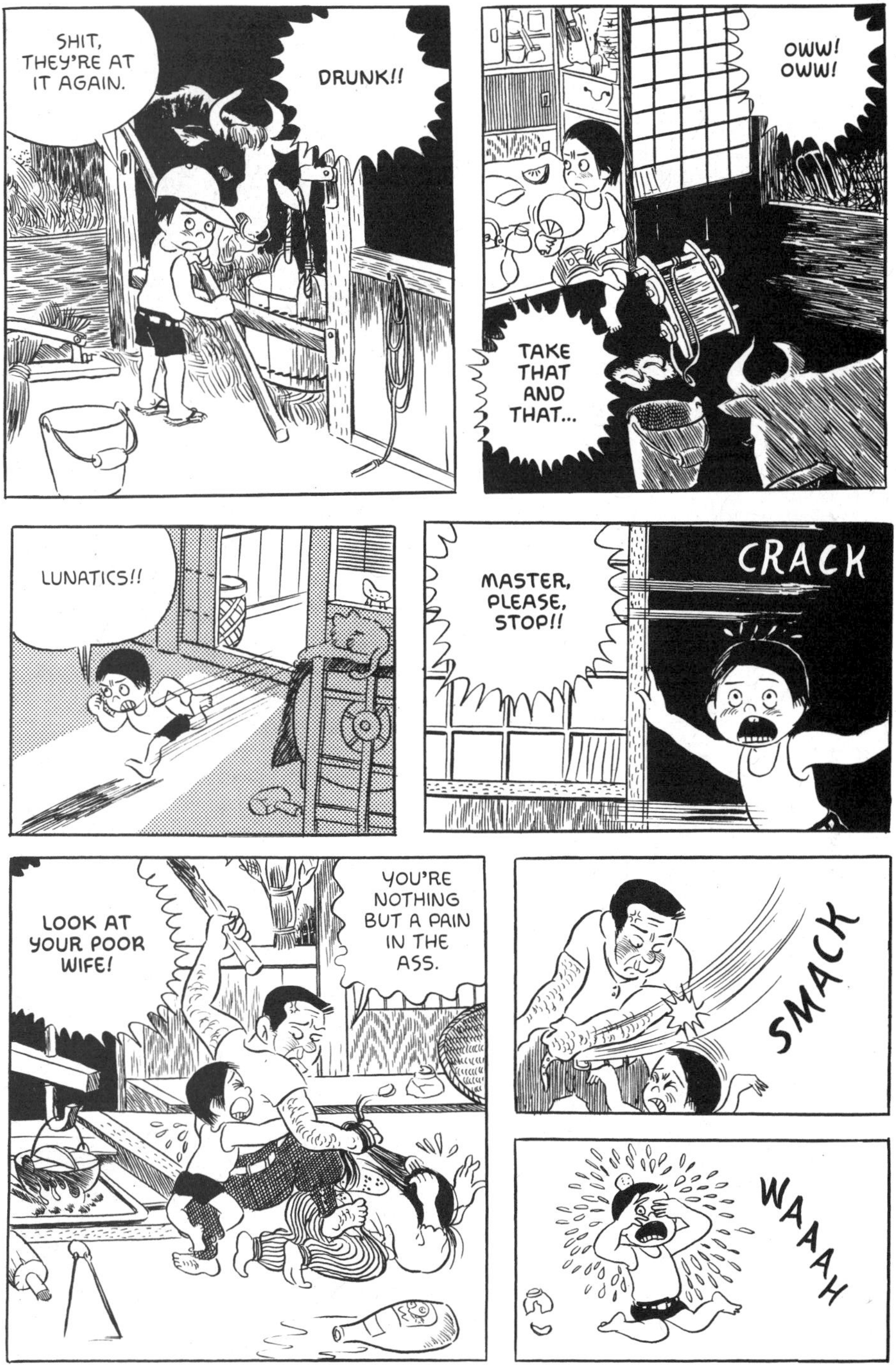
SHIT, THEY'RE AT IT AGAIN.
DRUNK!!
OWW! OWW!
TAKE THAT AND THAT...
LUNATICS!!
MASTER, PLEASE, STOP!!
CRACK
LOOK AT YOUR POOR WIFE!
YOU'RE NOTHING BUT A PAIN IN THE ASS.
SMACK
WAAAH

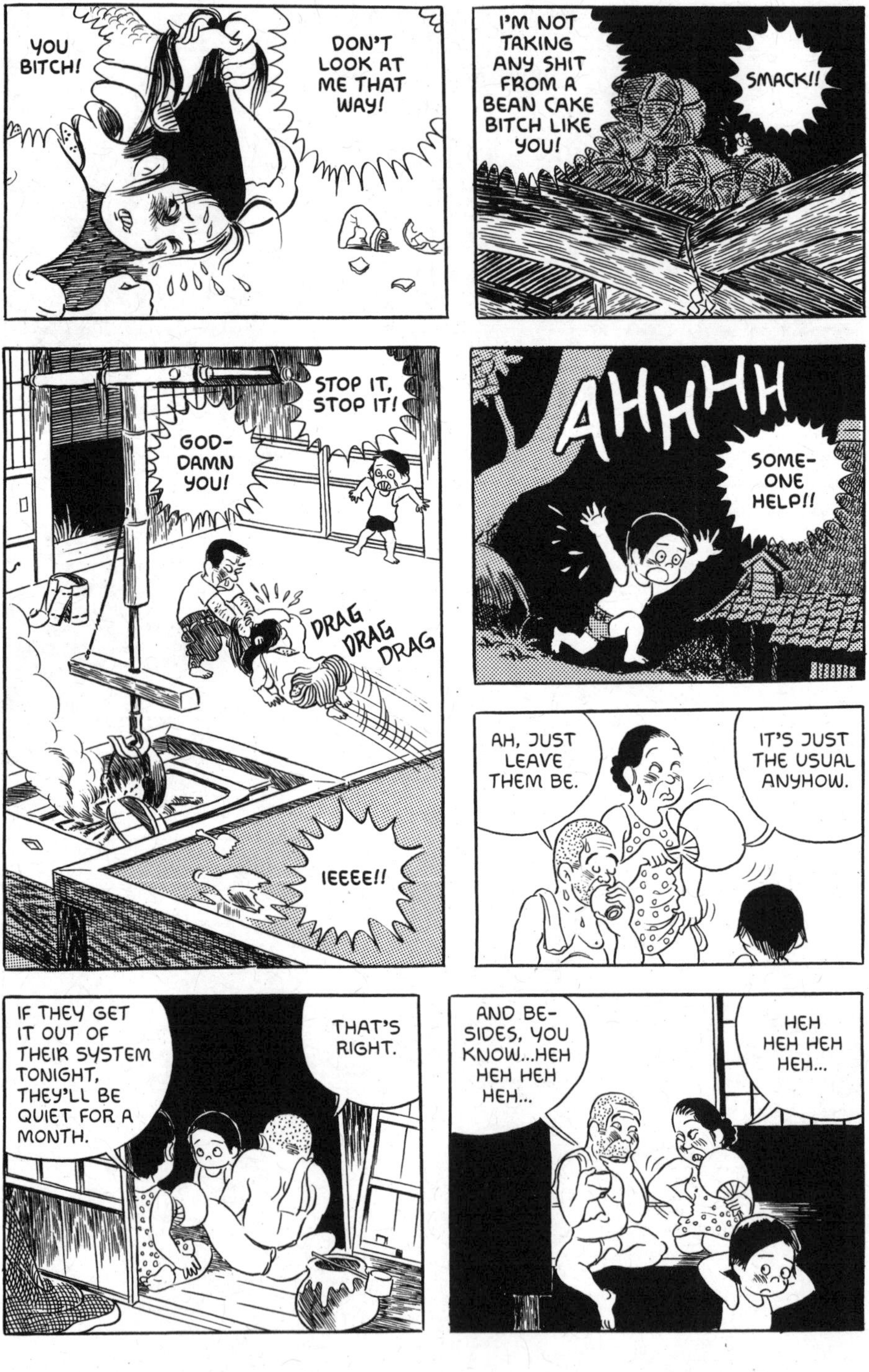
YOU BITCH!
DON'T LOOK AT ME THAT WAY!
I'M NOT TAKING ANY SHIT FROM A BEAN CAKE BITCH LIKE YOU!
SMACK!!
STOP IT, STOP IT!
GOD-DAMN YOU!
DRAG DRAG DRAG
IEEEE!!
AHHHH
SOME-ONE HELP!!
AH, JUST LEAVE THEM BE.
IT'S JUST THE USUAL ANYHOW.
IF THEY GET IT OUT OF THEIR SYSTEM TONIGHT, THEY'LL BE QUIET FOR A MONTH.
THAT'S RIGHT.
AND BE-SIDES, YOU KNOW...HEH HEH HEH HEH...
HEH HEH HEH HEH...

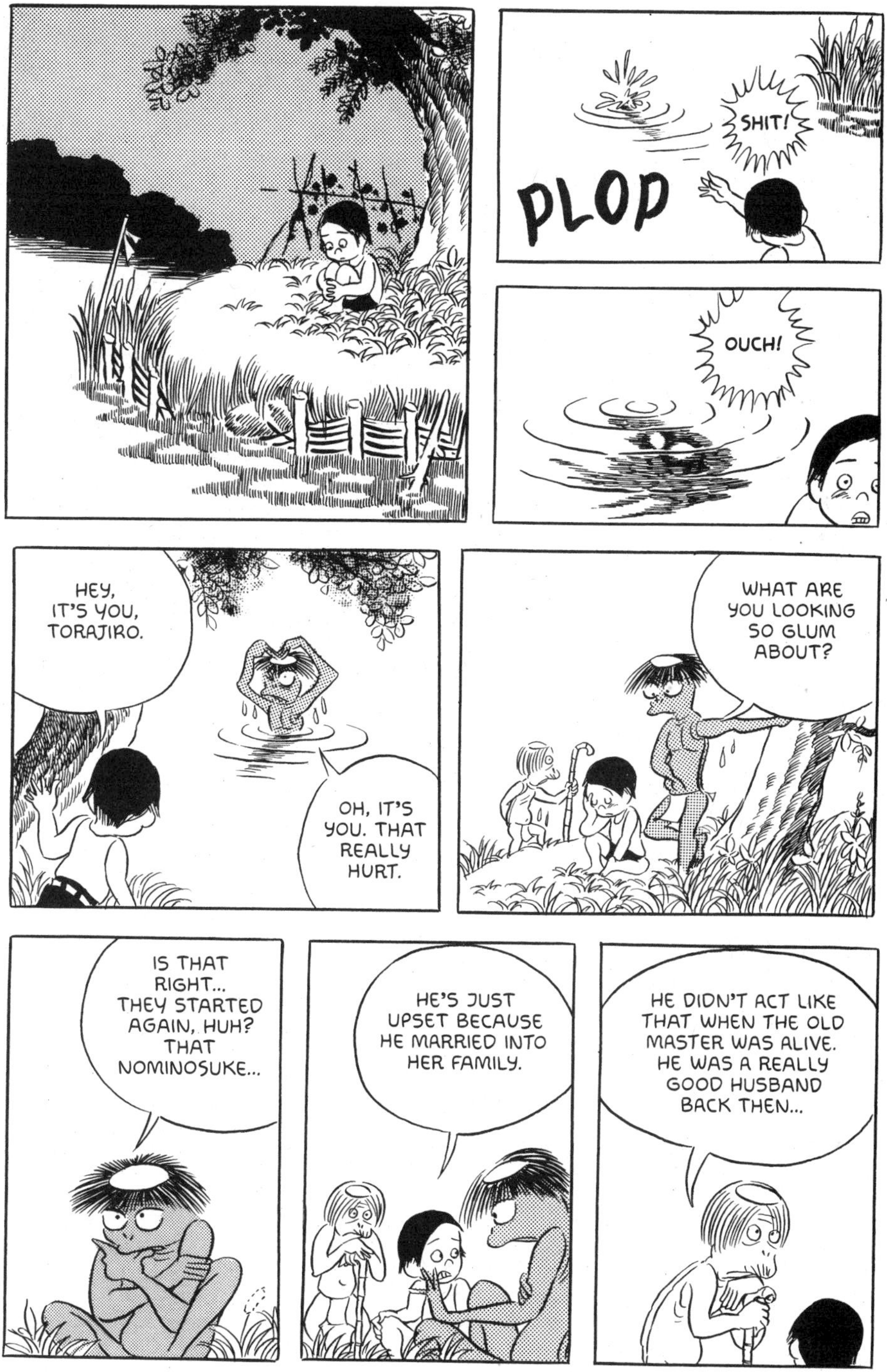
SHIT!
PLOP
OUCH!
HEY, IT'S YOU, TORAJIRO.
OH, IT'S YOU. THAT REALLY HURT.
WHAT ARE YOU LOOKING SO GLUM ABOUT?
IS THAT RIGHT... THEY STARTED AGAIN, HUH? THAT NOMINOSUKE...
HE'S JUST UPSET BECAUSE HE MARRIED INTO HER FAMILY.
HE DIDN'T ACT LIKE THAT WHEN THE OLD MASTER WAS ALIVE. HE WAS A REALLY GOOD HUSBAND BACK THEN...

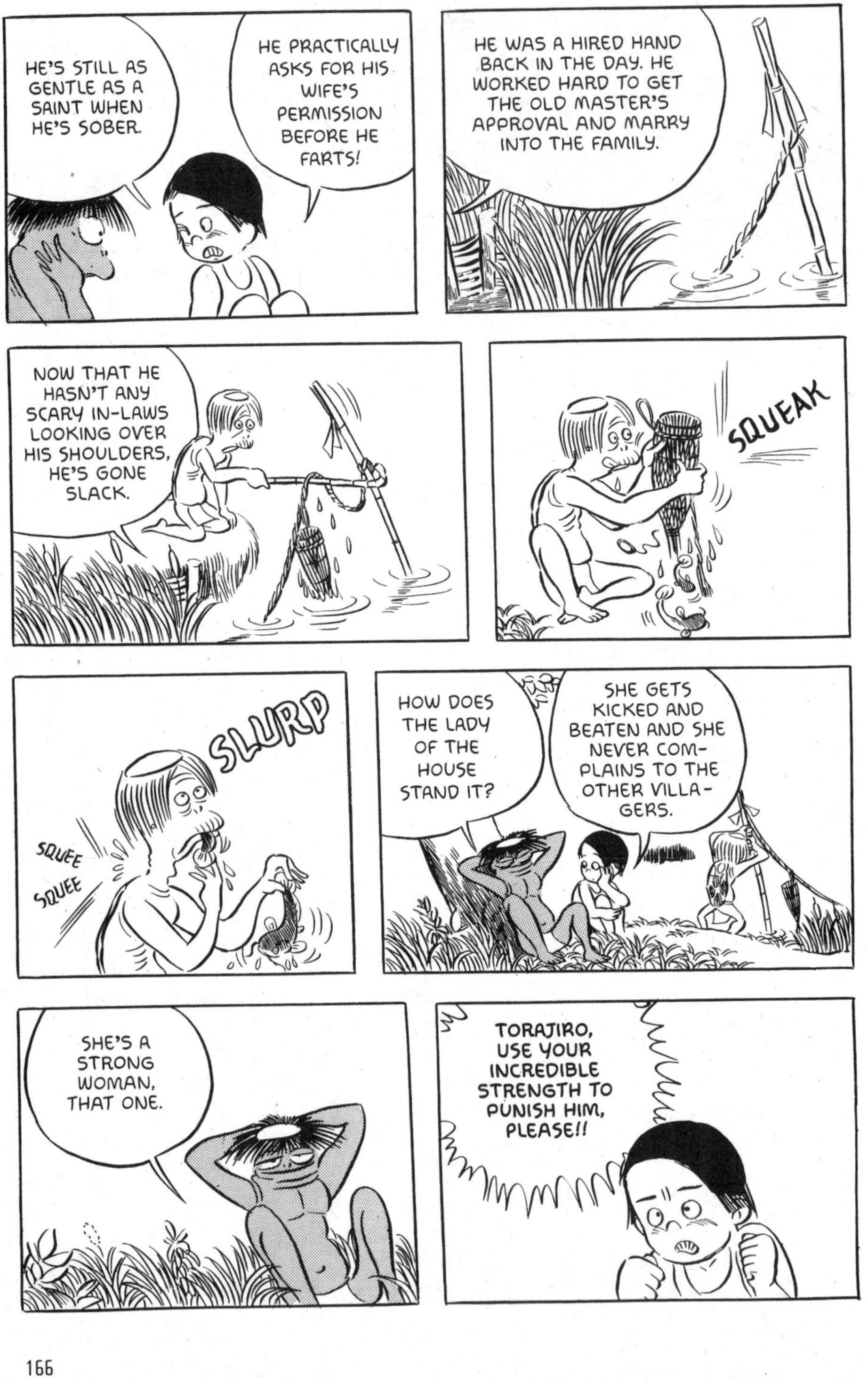
HE'S STILL AS GENTLE AS A SAINT WHEN HE'S SOBER.
HE PRACTICALLY ASKS FOR HIS WIFE'S PERMISSION BEFORE HE FARTS!
HE WAS A HIRED HAND BACK IN THE DAY. HE WORKED HARD TO GET THE OLD MASTER'S APPROVAL AND MARRY INTO THE FAMILY.
NOW THAT HE HASN'T ANY SCARY IN-LAWS LOOKING OVER HIS SHOULDERS, HE'S GONE SLACK.
SQUEAK
SLURP
SQUEE
SQUEE
HOW DOES THE LADY OF THE HOUSE STAND IT?
SHE GETS KICKED AND BEATEN AND SHE NEVER COM-PLAINS TO THE OTHER VILLA-GERS.
SHE'S A STRONG WOMAN, THAT ONE.
TORAJIRO, USE YOUR INCREDIBLE STRENGTH TO PUNISH HIM, PLEASE!!

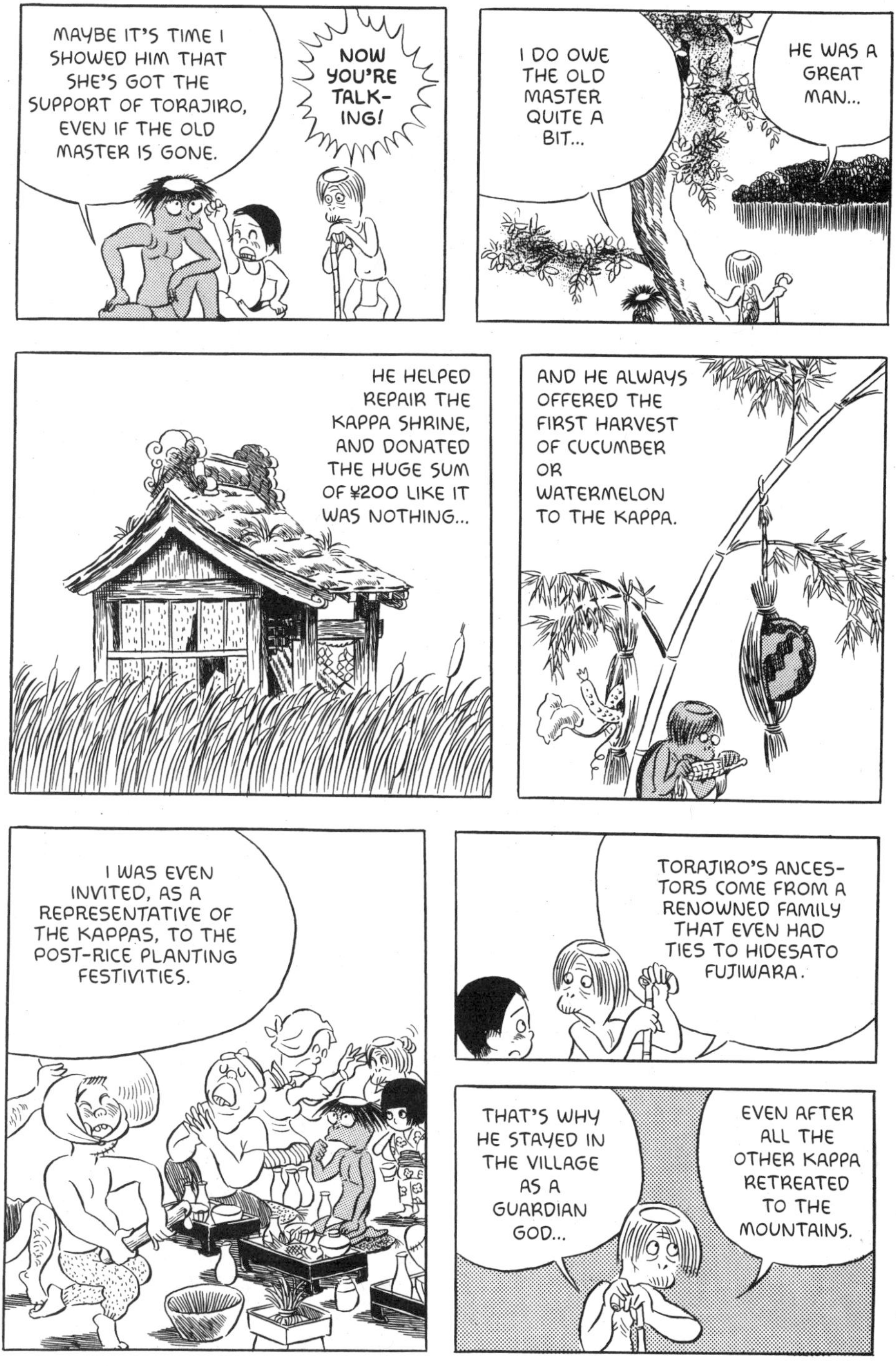
MAYBE IT'S TIME I SHOWED HIM THAT SHE'S GOT THE SUPPORT OF TORAJIRO, EVEN IF THE OLD MASTER IS GONE.
NOW YOU'RE TALK-ING!
I DO OWE THE OLD MASTER QUITE A BIT...
HE WAS A GREAT MAN...
HE HELPED REPAIR THE KAPPA SHRINE, AND DONATED THE HUGE SUM OF ¥200 LIKE IT WAS NOTHING...
AND HE ALWAYS OFFERED THE FIRST HARVEST OF CUCUMBER OR WATERMELON TO THE KAPPA.
I WAS EVEN INVITED, AS A REPRESENTATIVE OF THE KAPPAS, TO THE POST-RICE PLANTING FESTIVITIES.
TORAJIRO'S ANCES-TORS COME FROM A RENOWNED FAMILY THAT EVEN HAD TIES TO HIDESATO FUJIWARA.
THAT'S WHY HE STAYED IN THE VILLAGE AS A GUARDIAN GOD...
EVEN AFTER ALL THE OTHER KAPPA RETREATED TO THE MOUNTAINS.

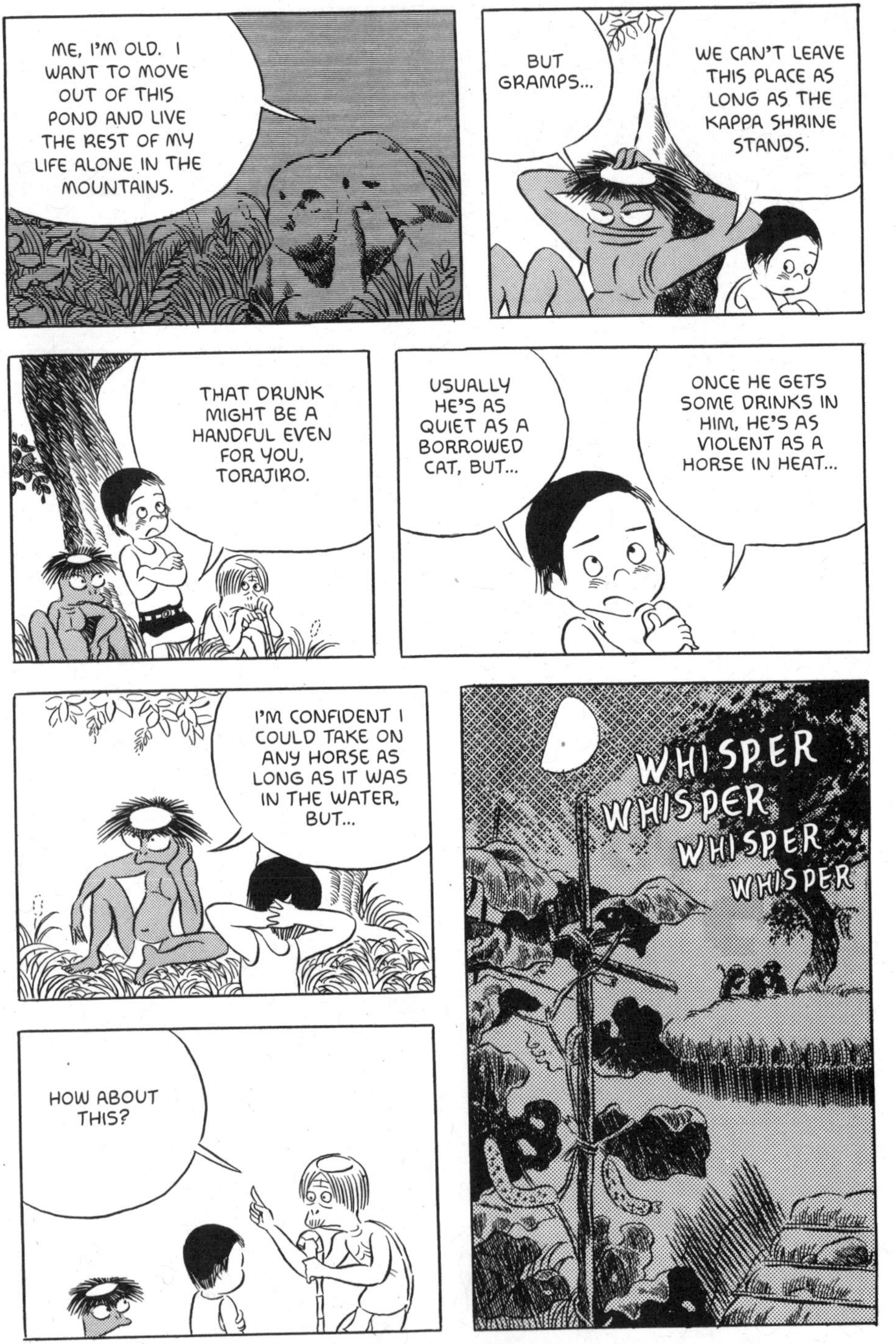
ME, I'M OLD. I WANT TO MOVE OUT OF THIS POND AND LIVE THE REST OF MY LIFE ALONE IN THE MOUNTAINS.
BUT GRAMPS...
WE CAN'T LEAVE THIS PLACE AS LONG AS THE KAPPA SHRINE STANDS.
THAT DRUNK MIGHT BE A HANDFUL EVEN FOR YOU, TORAJIRO.
USUALLY HE'S AS QUIET AS A BORROWED CAT, BUT...
ONCE HE GETS SOME DRINKS IN HIM, HE'S AS VIOLENT AS A HORSE IN HEAT...
I'M CONFIDENT I COULD TAKE ON ANY HORSE AS LONG AS IT WAS IN THE WATER, BUT...
HOW ABOUT THIS?
WHISPER
WHISPER
WHISPER
WHISPER

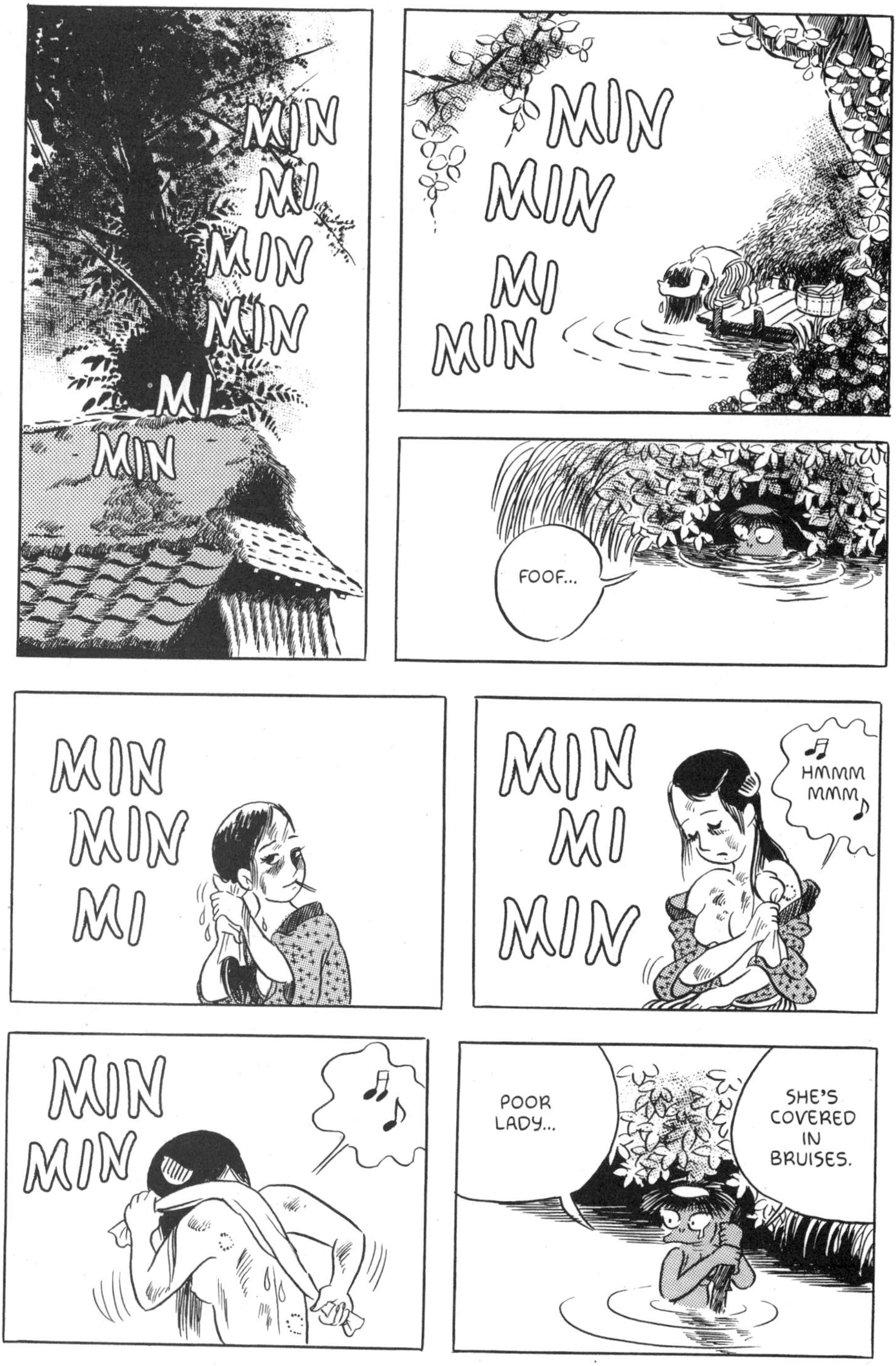
MIN
MI
MIN
MIN
MI
MIN
MIN
MIN
MI
MIN
FOOF...
MIN
MIN
MI
MIN
MI
MIN
HMMM MMM
MIN
MIN
POOR LADY...
SHE'S COVERED IN BRUISES.

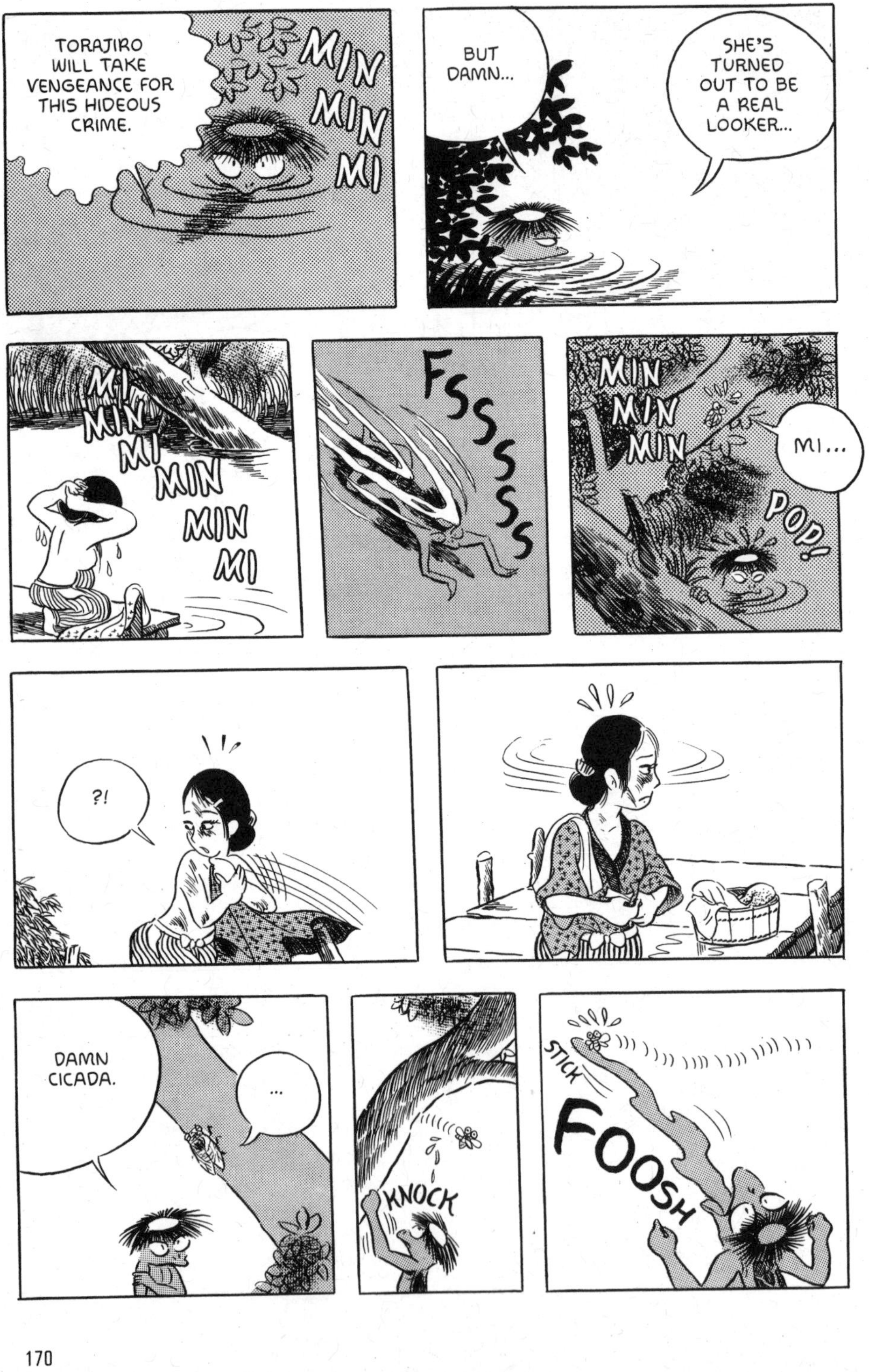
TORAJIRO WILL TAKE VENGEANCE FOR THIS HIDEOUS CRIME.
MIN MIN MI
BUT DAMN...
SHE'S TURNED OUT TO BE A REAL LOOKER...
MI MIN MI MIN MIN MI
FSSSSS
MIN MIN MIN
MI...
POP!
?!
DAMN CICADA.
...
KNOCK
STICK
FOOSH

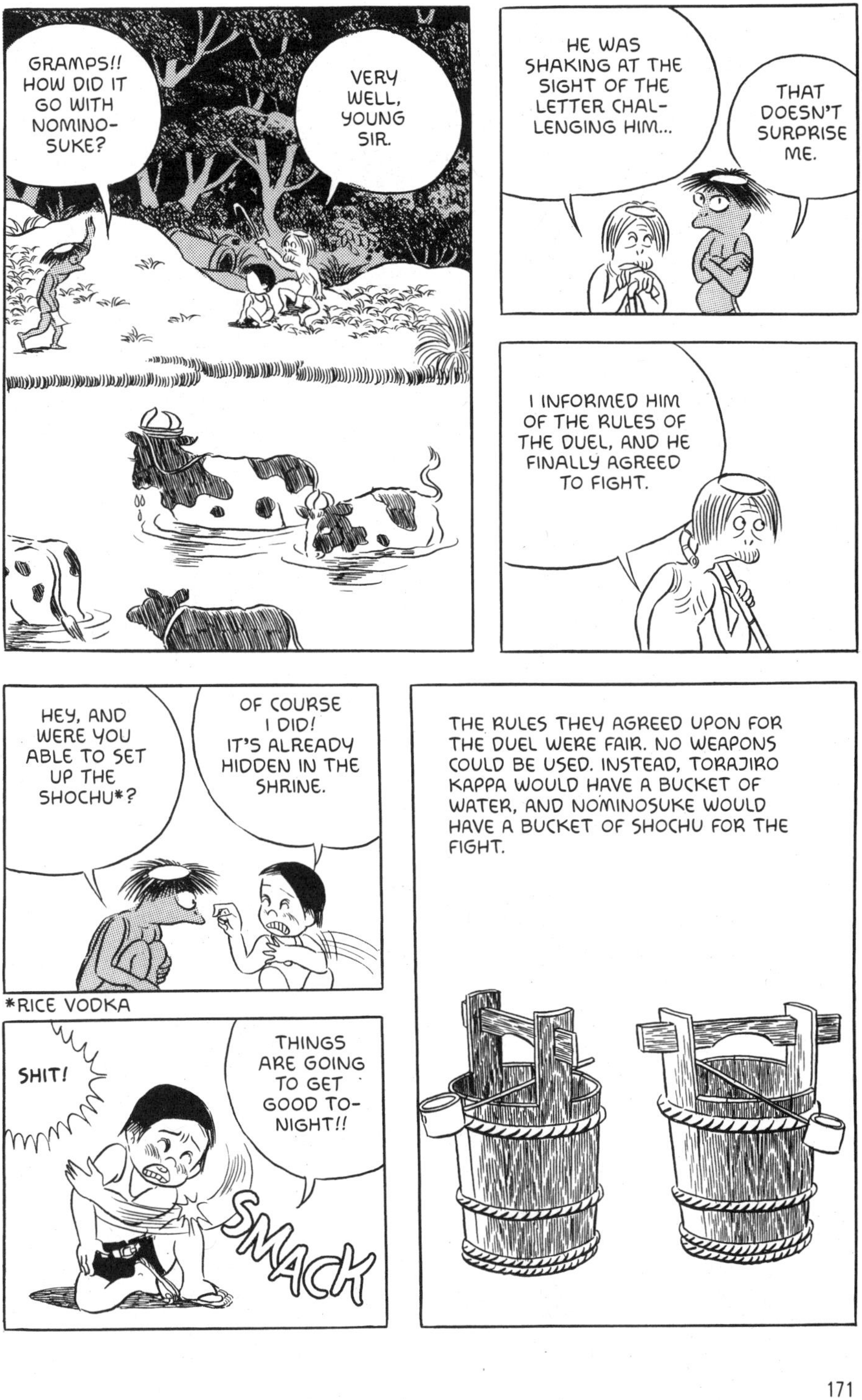
GRAMPS!! HOW DID IT GO WITH NOMINO-SUKE?
VERY WELL, YOUNG SIR.
HE WAS SHAKING AT THE SIGHT OF THE LETTER CHAL-LENGING HIM...
THAT DOESN'T SURPRISE ME.
I INFORMED HIM OF THE RULES OF THE DUEL, AND HE FINALLY AGREED TO FIGHT.
HEY, AND WERE YOU ABLE TO SET UP THE SHOCHU*?
OF COURSE I DID! IT'S ALREADY HIDDEN IN THE SHRINE.
*RICE VODKA
SHIT!
THINGS ARE GOING TO GET GOOD TO-NIGHT!!
SMACK
THE RULES THEY AGREED UPON FOR THE DUEL WERE FAIR. NO WEAPONS COULD BE USED. INSTEAD, TORAJIRO KAPPA WOULD HAVE A BUCKET OF WATER, AND NOMINOSUKE WOULD HAVE A BUCKET OF SHOCHU FOR THE FIGHT.

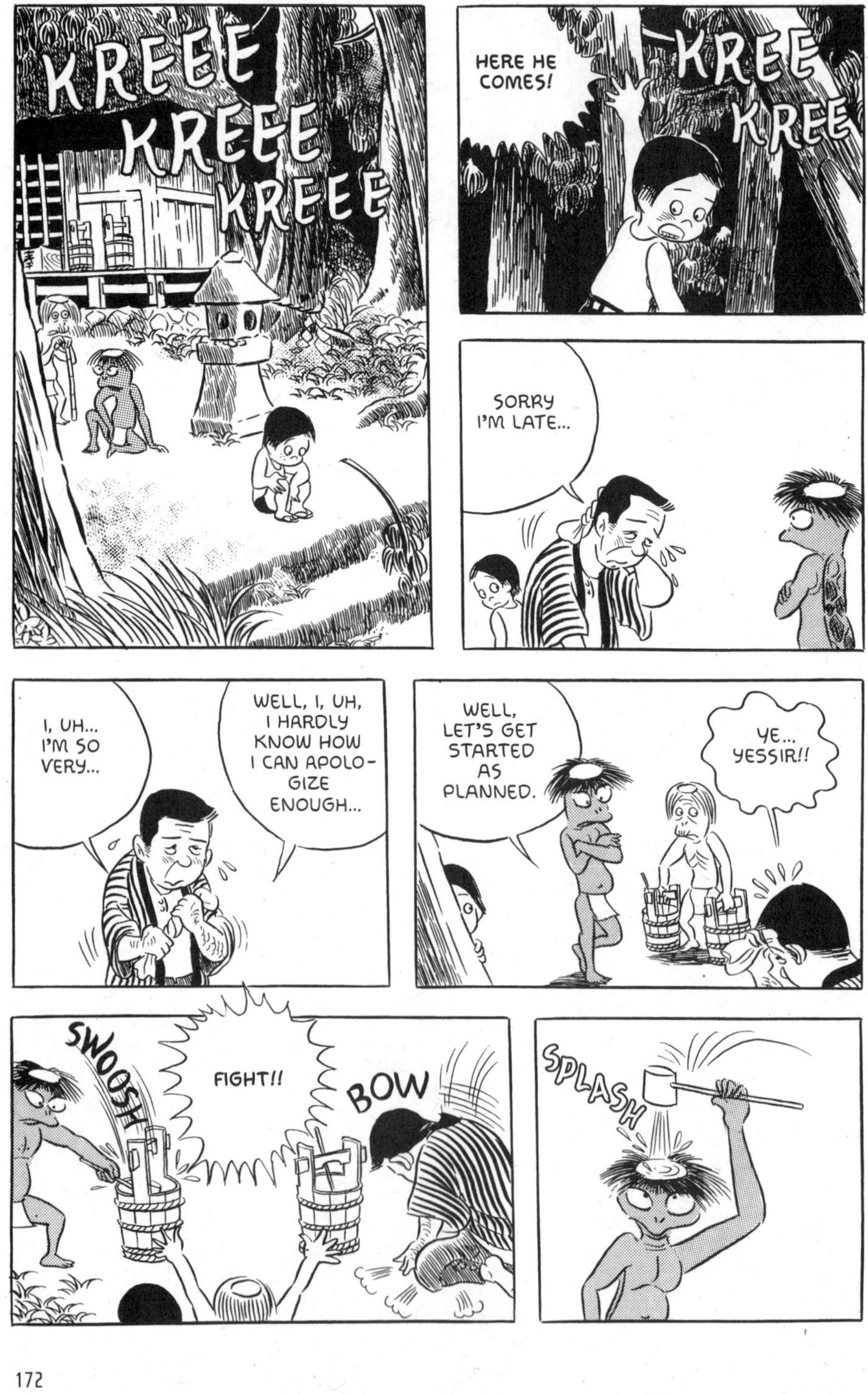
KREEE
KREEE
KREEE
HERE HE COMES!
KREE
KREE
SORRY I'M LATE...
I, UH... I'M SO VERY...
WELL, I, UH, I HARDLY KNOW HOW I CAN APOLOGIZE ENOUGH...
WELL, LET'S GET STARTED AS PLANNED.
YE... YESSIR!!
SWOOSH
FIGHT!!
BOW
SPLASH

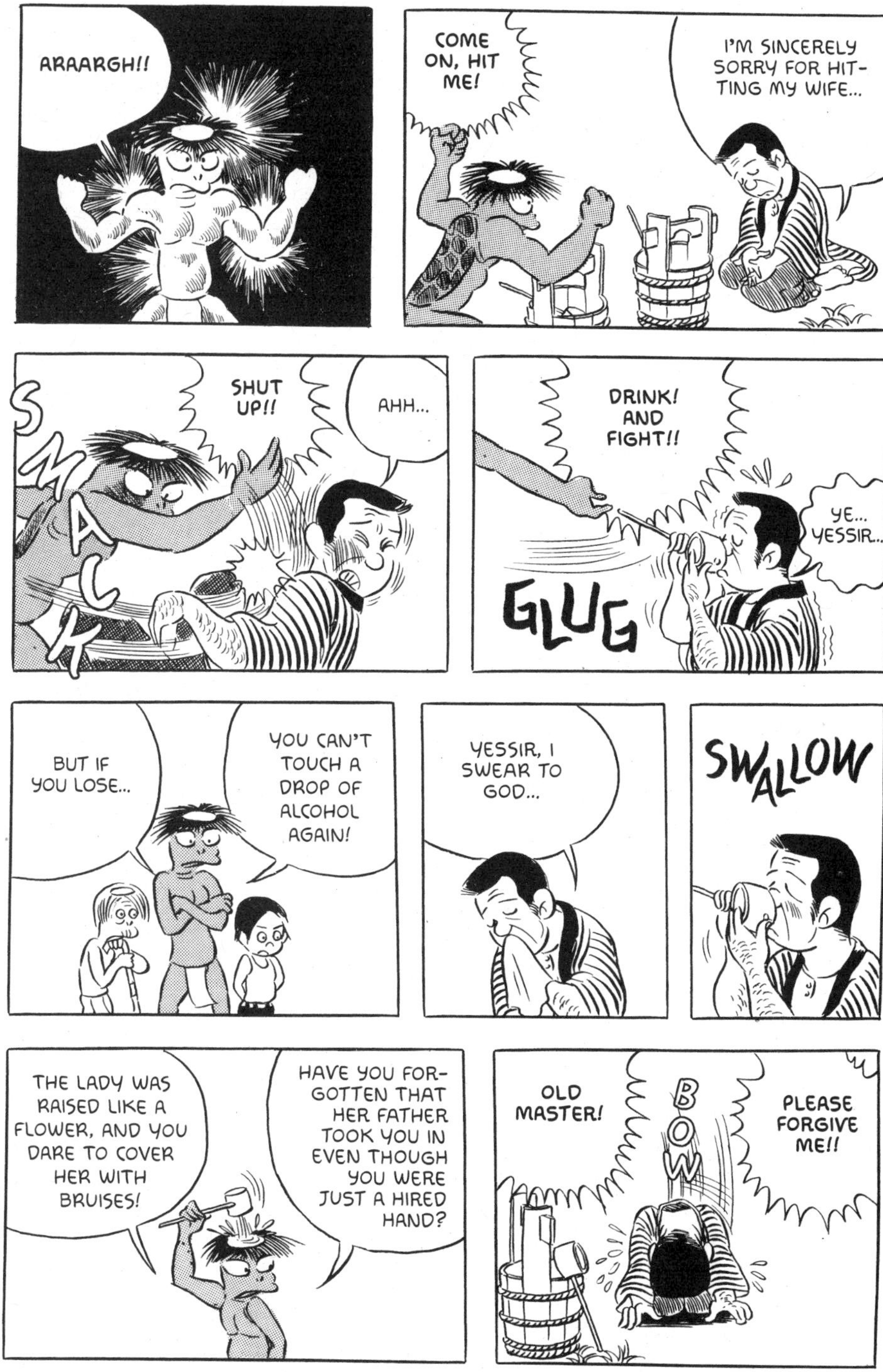
ARAAARGH!!
COME ON, HIT ME!
I'M SINCERELY SORRY FOR HIT-TING MY WIFE...
SMACK
SHUT UP!!
AHH...
DRINK! AND FIGHT!!
YE... YESSIR...
GLUG
BUT IF YOU LOSE...
YOU CAN'T TOUCH A DROP OF ALCOHOL AGAIN!
YESSIR, I SWEAR TO GOD...
SWALLOW
THE LADY WAS RAISED LIKE A FLOWER, AND YOU DARE TO COVER HER WITH BRUISES!
HAVE YOU FOR-GOTTEN THAT HER FATHER TOOK YOU IN EVEN THOUGH YOU WERE JUST A HIRED HAND?
OLD MASTER!
BOW
PLEASE FORGIVE ME!!

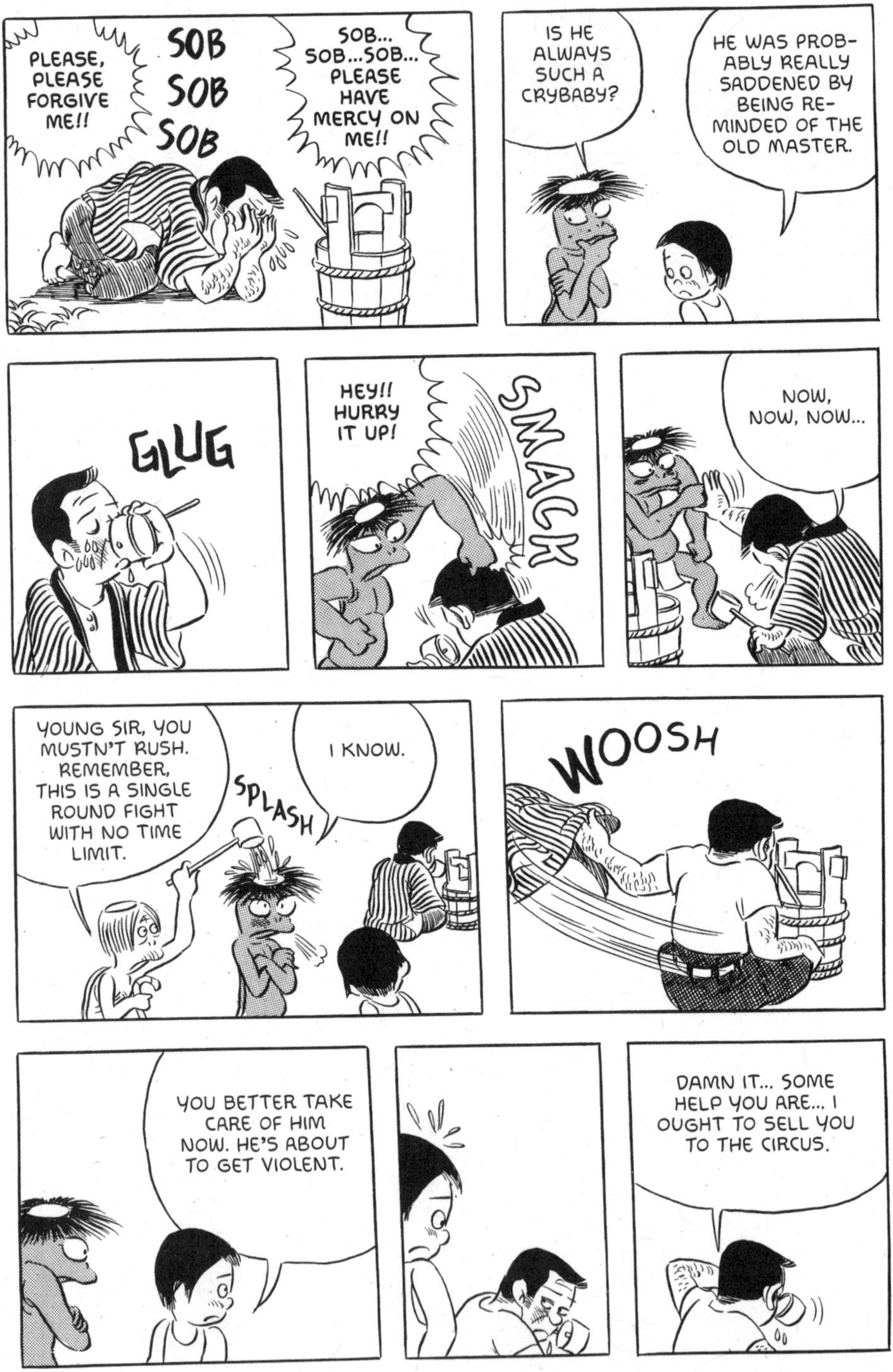
PLEASE, PLEASE FORGIVE ME!!
SOB SOB SOB
SOB... SOB...SOB... PLEASE HAVE MERCY ON ME!!
IS HE ALWAYS SUCH A CRYBABY?
HE WAS PROBABLY REALLY SADDENED BY BEING REMINDED OF THE OLD MASTER.
GLUG
HEY!! HURRY IT UP!
SMACK
NOW, NOW, NOW...
YOUNG SIR, YOU MUSTN'T RUSH. REMEMBER, THIS IS A SINGLE ROUND FIGHT WITH NO TIME LIMIT.
SPLASH
I KNOW.
WOOSH
YOU BETTER TAKE CARE OF HIM NOW. HE'S ABOUT TO GET VIOLENT.
DAMN IT... SOME HELP YOU ARE... I OUGHT TO SELL YOU TO THE CIRCUS.

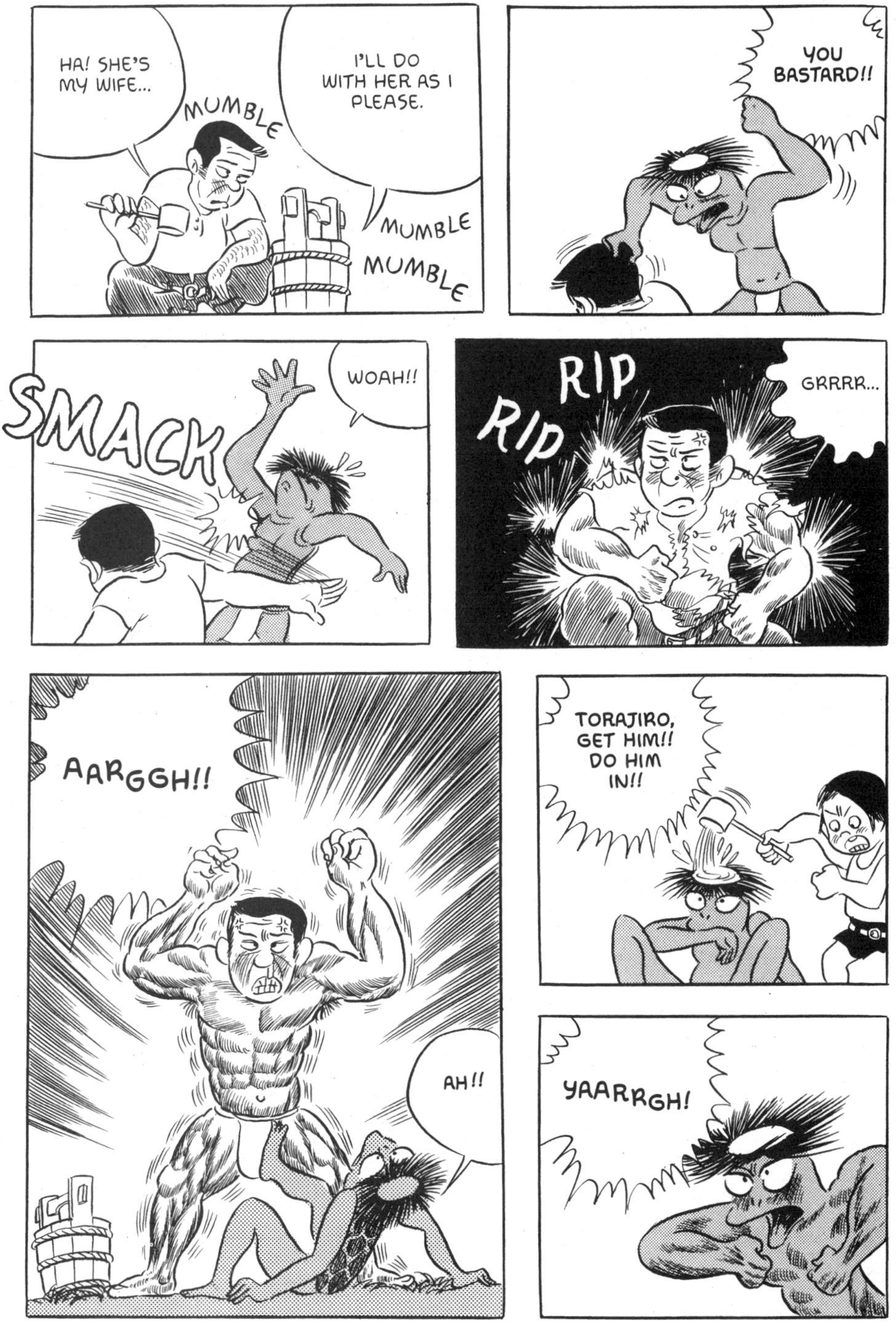
HA! SHE'S MY WIFE...
MUMBLE
I'LL DO WITH HER AS I PLEASE.
MUMBLE
MUMBLE
YOU BASTARD!!
SMACK
WOAH!!
RIP
RIP
GRRRR...
AARGGH!!
AH!!
TORAJIRO, GET HIM!! DO HIM IN!!
YAARRGH!

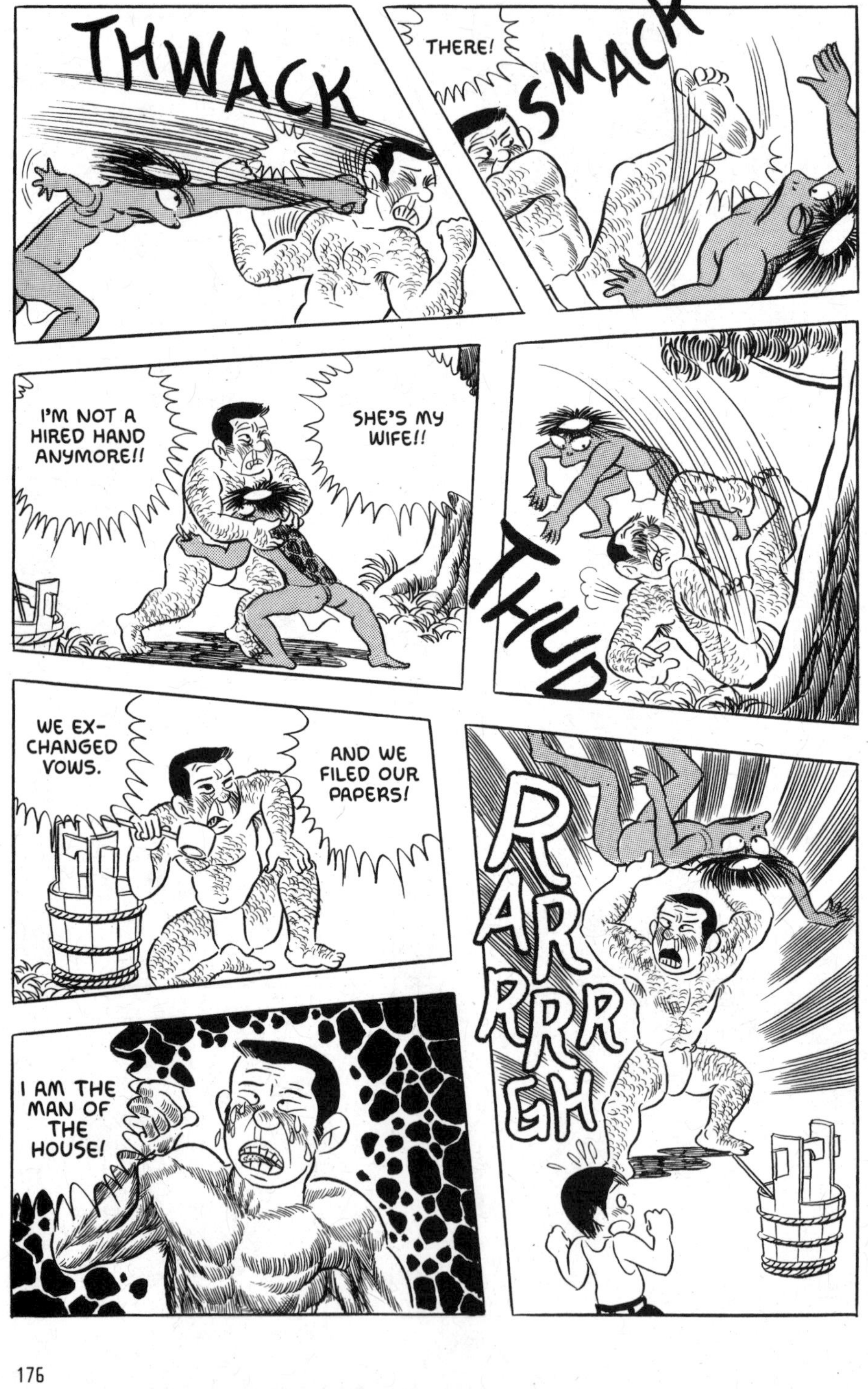
THWACK
THERE!
SMACK
I'M NOT A HIRED HAND ANYMORE!!
SHE'S MY WIFE!!
THUD
WE EX-CHANGED VOWS.
AND WE FILED OUR PAPERS!
I AM THE MAN OF THE HOUSE!
RARRRRRGH

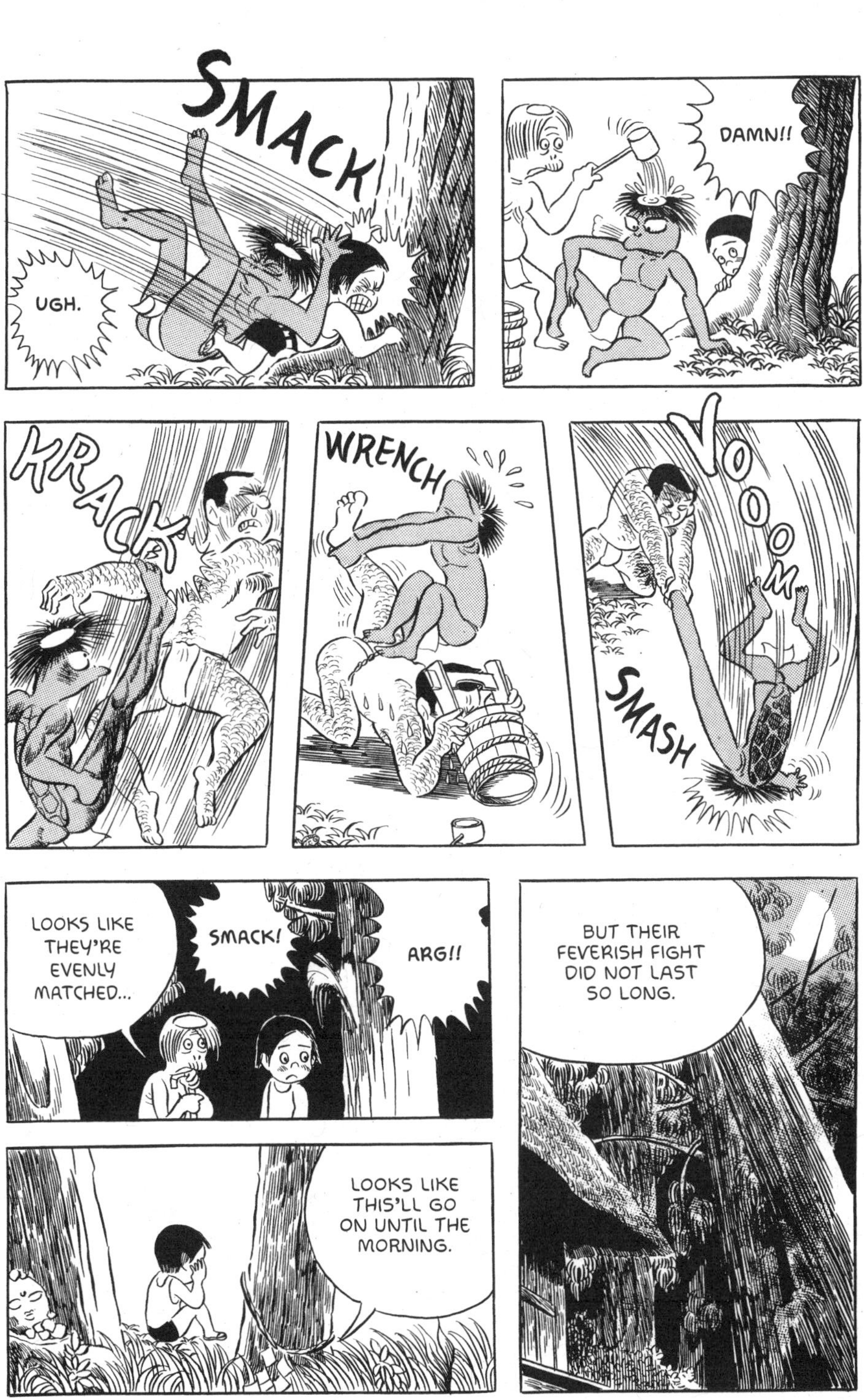
SMACK
UGH.
DAMN!!
KRACK
WRENCH
VOOOM
SMASH
LOOKS LIKE THEY'RE EVENLY MATCHED...
SMACK!
ARG!!
LOOKS LIKE THIS'LL GO ON UNTIL THE MORNING.
BUT THEIR FEVERISH FIGHT DID NOT LAST SO LONG.

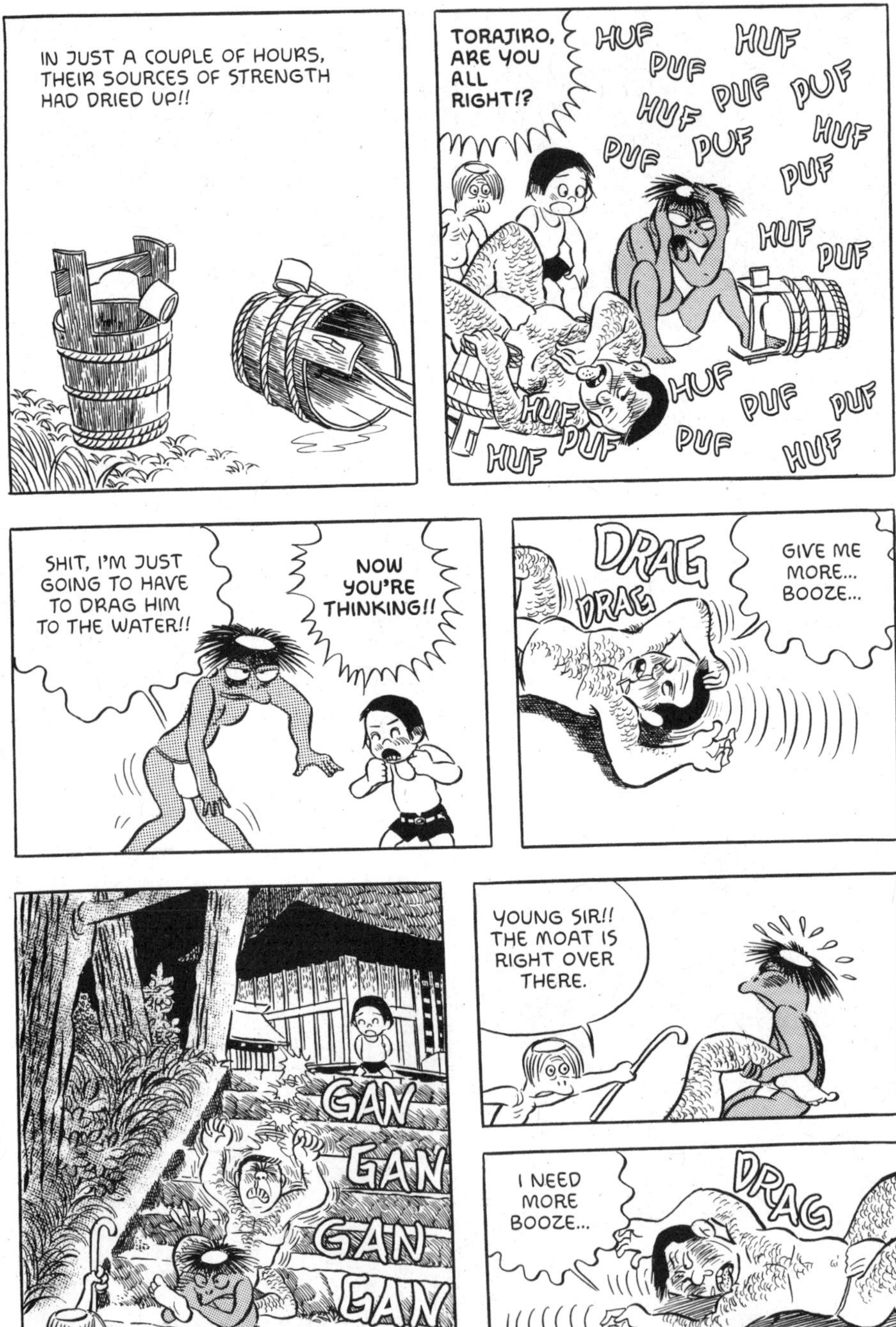
IN JUST A COUPLE OF HOURS, THEIR SOURCES OF STRENGTH HAD DRIED UP!!
TORAJIRO, ARE YOU ALL RIGHT!?
HUF HUF PUF PUF PUF HUF HUF PUF PUF HUF PUF HUF PUF HUF PUF PUF HUF PUF PUF HUF
SHIT, I'M JUST GOING TO HAVE TO DRAG HIM TO THE WATER!!
NOW YOU'RE THINKING!!
DRAG DRAG
GIVE ME MORE... BOOZE...
GAN GAN GAN GAN
YOUNG SIR!! THE MOAT IS RIGHT OVER THERE.
I NEED MORE BOOZE...
DRAG

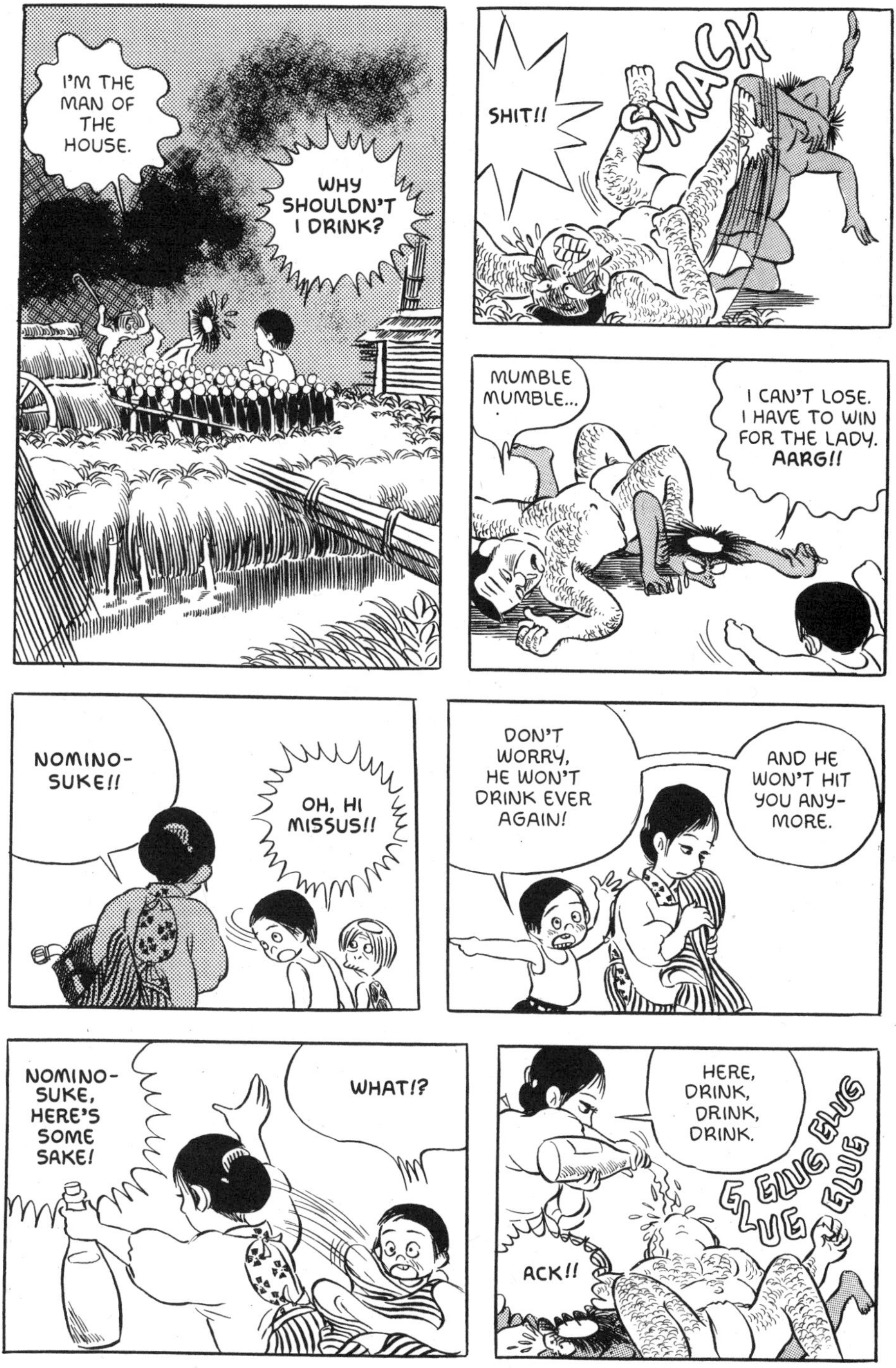
I'M THE MAN OF THE HOUSE.
WHY SHOULDN'T I DRINK?
SHIT!!
SMACK
MUMBLE MUMBLE...
I CAN'T LOSE. I HAVE TO WIN FOR THE LADY. AARG!!
NOMINO-SUKE!!
OH, HI MISSUS!!
DON'T WORRY, HE WON'T DRINK EVER AGAIN!
AND HE WON'T HIT YOU ANY-MORE.
NOMINO-SUKE, HERE'S SOME SAKE!
WHAT!?
HERE, DRINK, DRINK, DRINK.
GLUG GLUG
GLUG GLUG
ACK!!

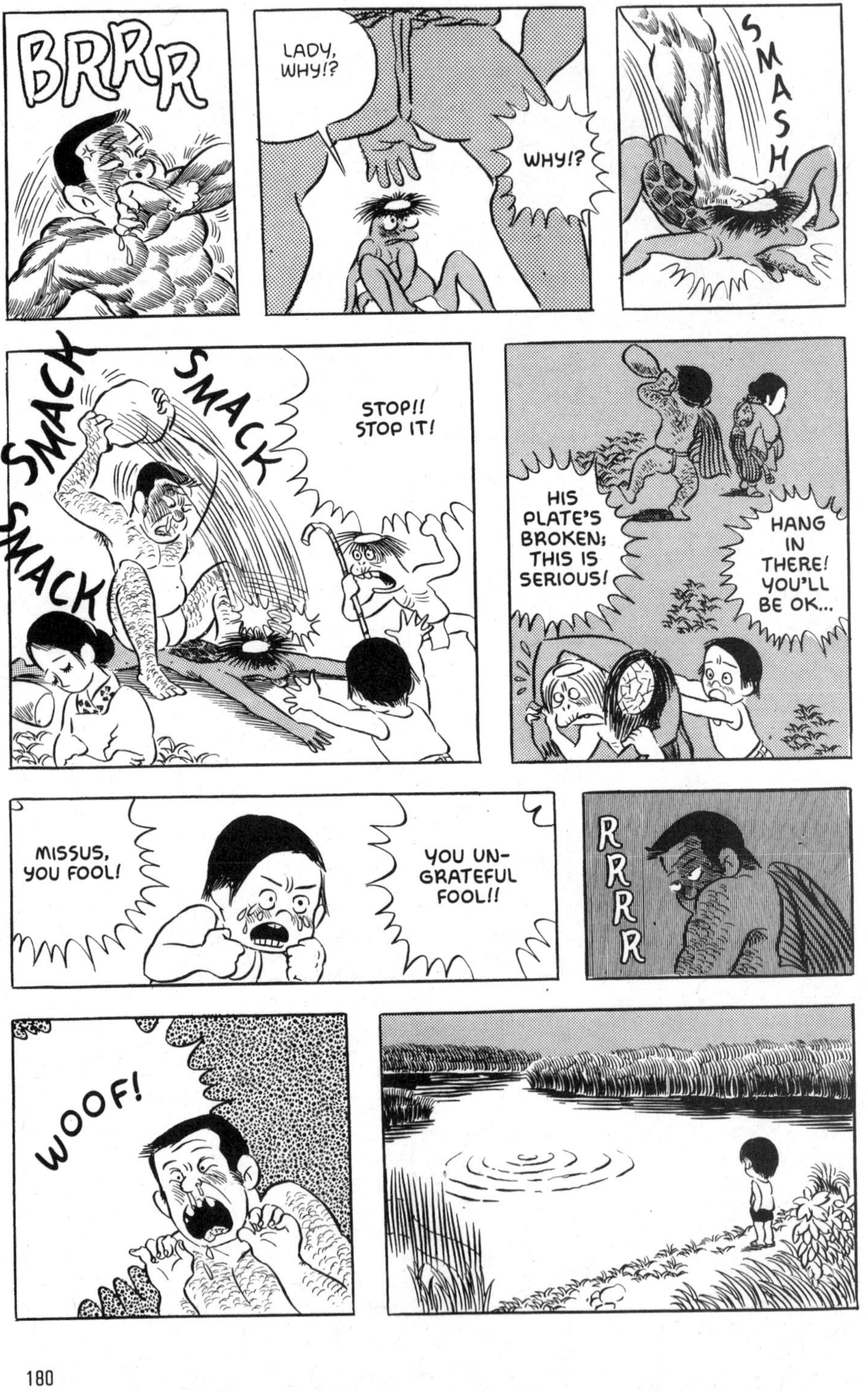
BRRR
LADY, WHY!?
WHY!?
SMASH
SMACK
SMACK
SMACK
STOP!! STOP IT!
HIS PLATE'S BROKEN; THIS IS SERIOUS!
HANG IN THERE! YOU'LL BE OK...
MISSUS, YOU FOOL!
YOU UN-GRATEFUL FOOL!!
RRRR
WOOF!

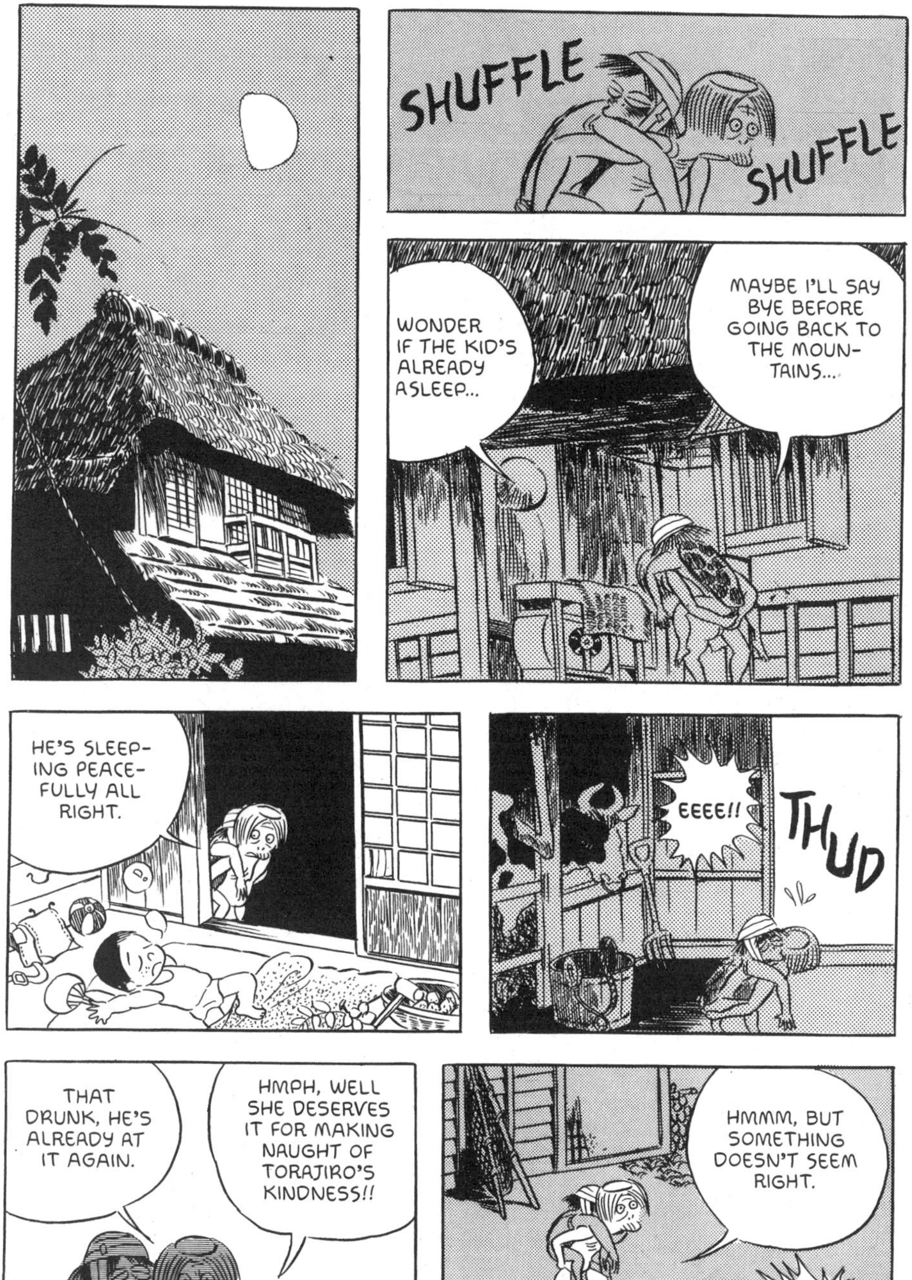
SHUFFLE
SHUFFLE
WONDER IF THE KID'S ALREADY ASLEEP...
MAYBE I'LL SAY BYE BEFORE GOING BACK TO THE MOUN-TAINS...
HE'S SLEEP-ING PEACE-FULLY ALL RIGHT.
EEEE!!
THUD
THAT DRUNK, HE'S ALREADY AT IT AGAIN.
HMPH, WELL SHE DESERVES IT FOR MAKING NAUGHT OF TORAJIRO'S KINDNESS!!
HMMM, BUT SOMETHING DOESN'T SEEM RIGHT.
THERE! THERE!

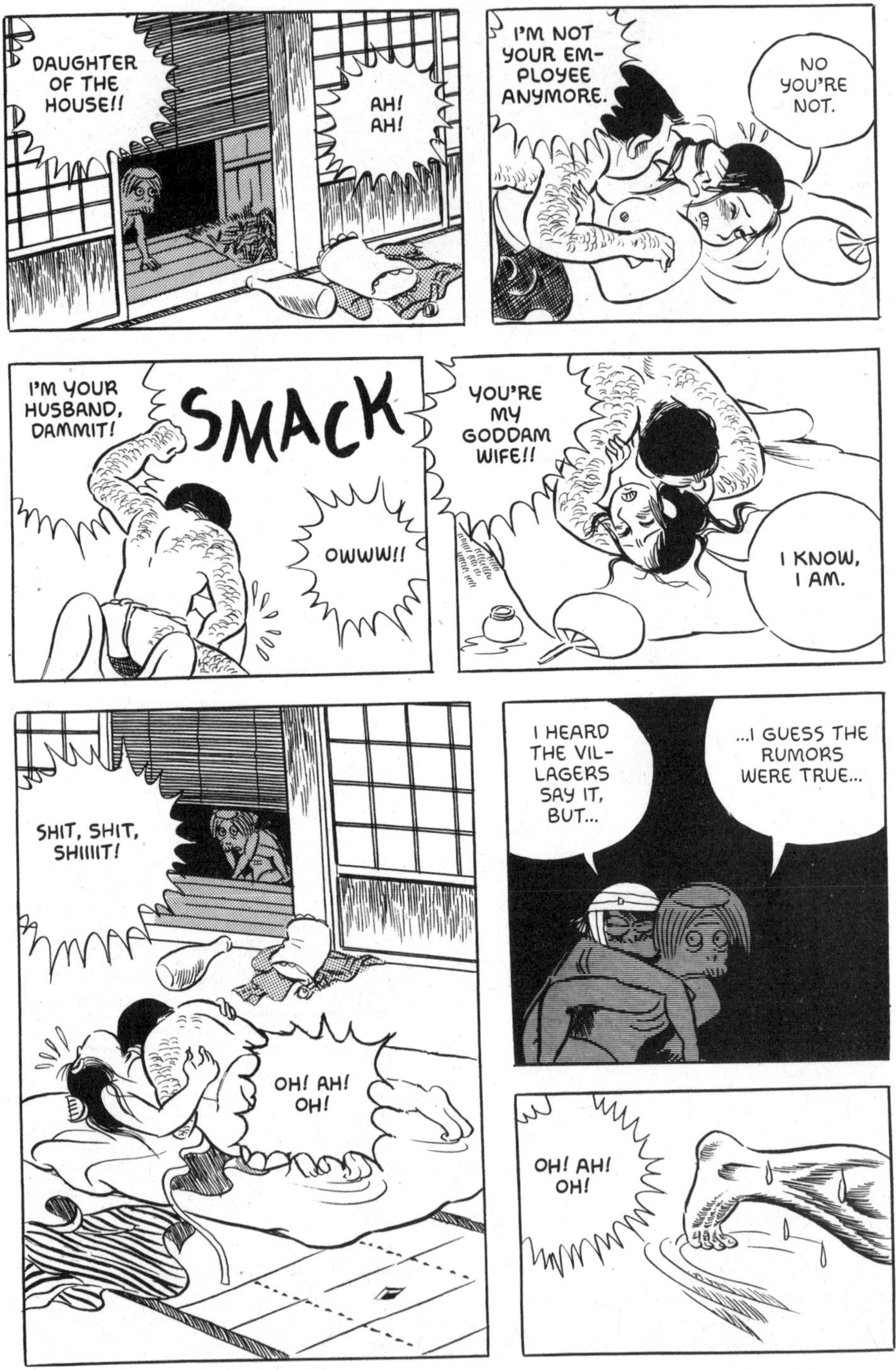
DAUGHTER OF THE HOUSE!!
AH! AH!
I'M NOT YOUR EMPLOYEE ANYMORE.
NO YOU'RE NOT.
I'M YOUR HUSBAND, DAMMIT!
SMACK
OWWW!!
YOU'RE MY GODDAM WIFE!!
I KNOW, I AM.
SHIT, SHIT, SHIIIIT!
OH! AH! OH!
I HEARD THE VILLAGERS SAY IT, BUT...
...I GUESS THE RUMORS WERE TRUE...
OH! AH! OH!

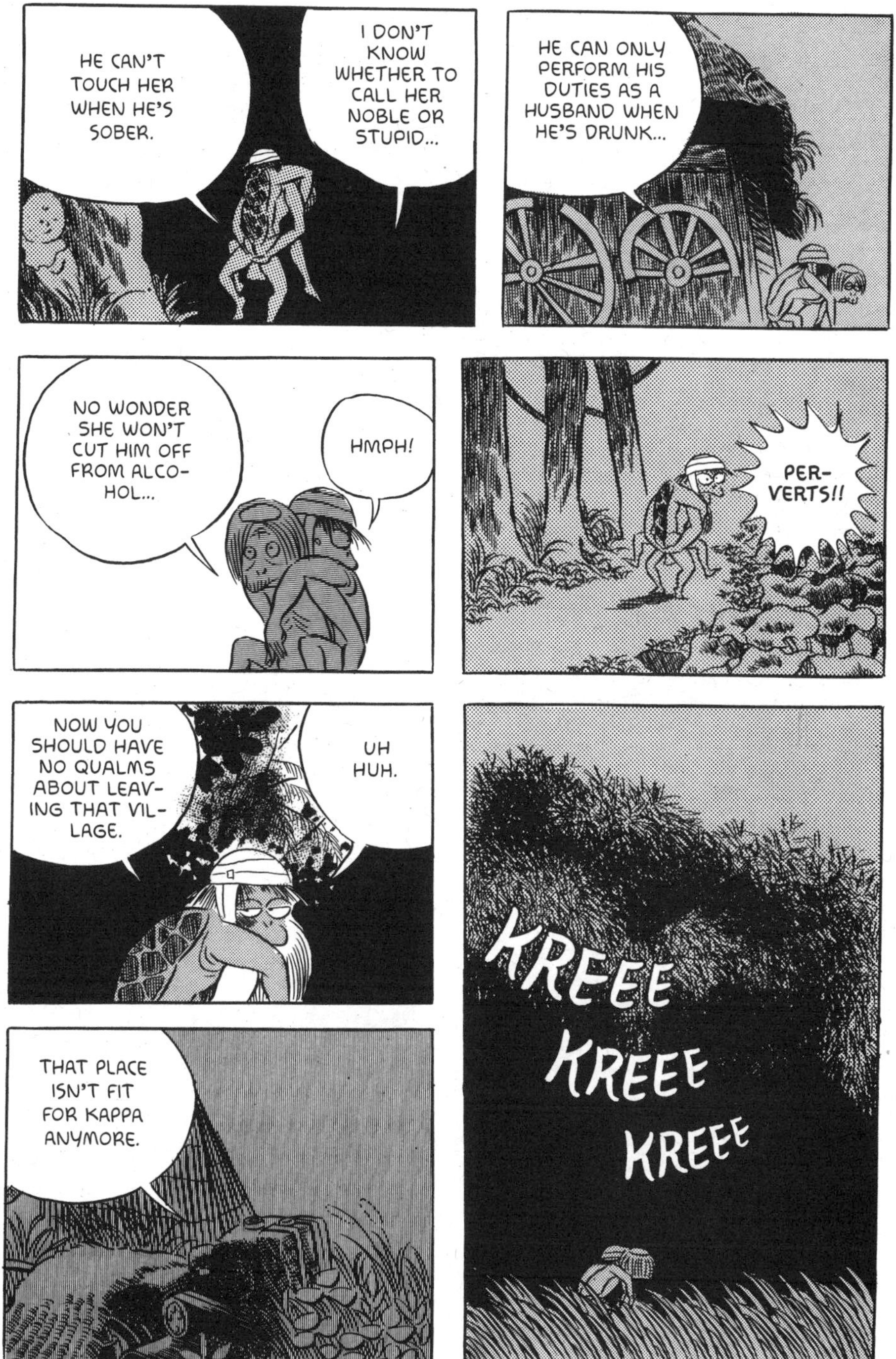
HE CAN'T TOUCH HER WHEN HE'S SOBER.
I DON'T KNOW WHETHER TO CALL HER NOBLE OR STUPID...
HE CAN ONLY PERFORM HIS DUTIES AS A HUSBAND WHEN HE'S DRUNK...
NO WONDER SHE WON'T CUT HIM OFF FROM ALCO-HOL...
HMPH!
PER-VERTS!!
NOW YOU SHOULD HAVE NO QUALMS ABOUT LEAV-ING THAT VIL-LAGE.
UH HUH.
THAT PLACE ISN'T FIT FOR KAPPA ANYMORE.
KREEE
KREEE
KREEE

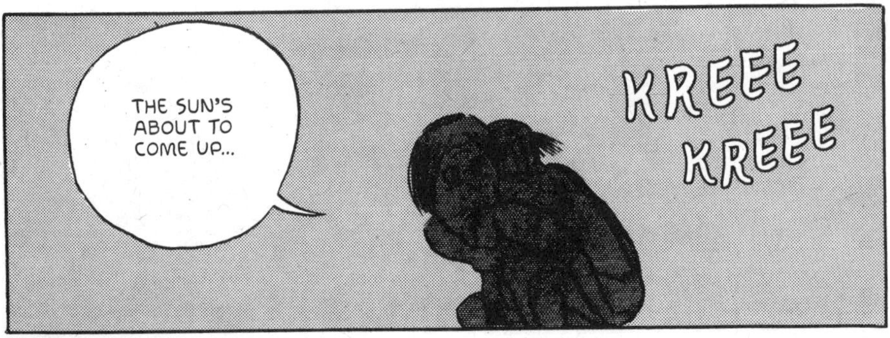
THE SUN'S ABOUT TO COME UP...
KREEE KREEE

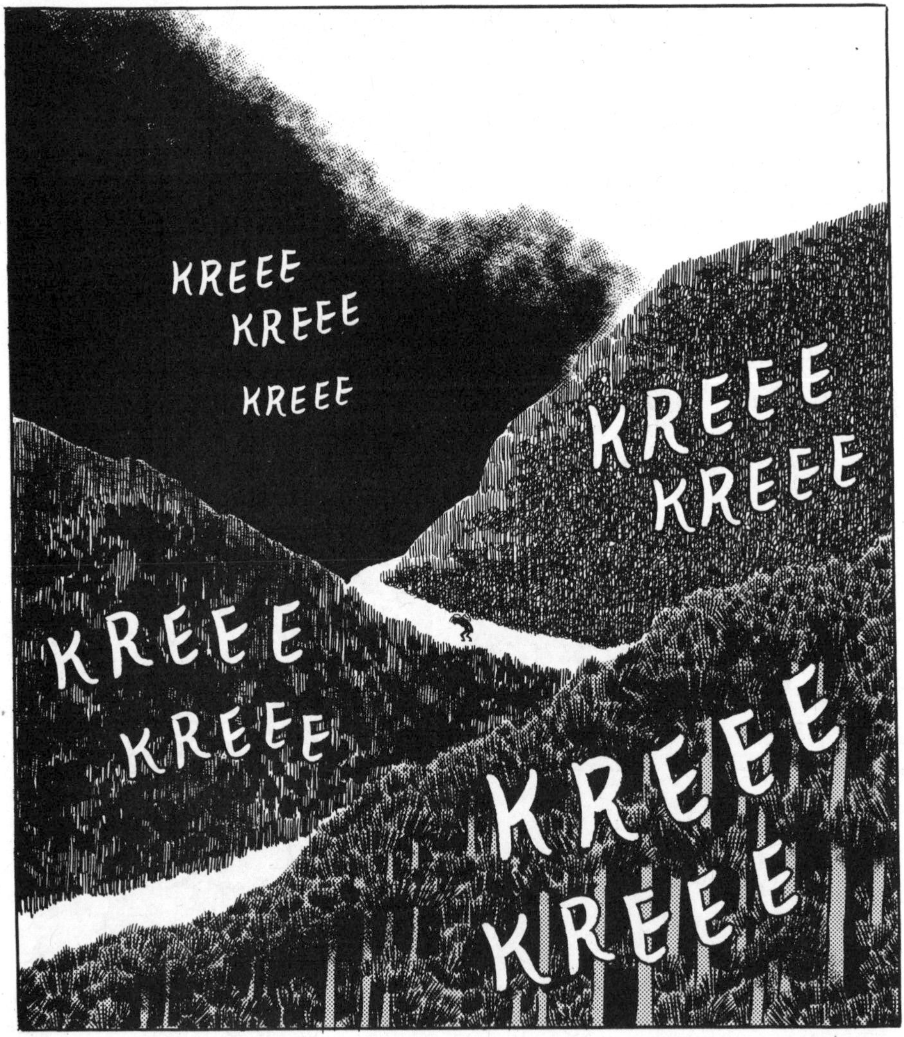
KREEE KREEE KREEE
KREEE KREEE
KREEE KREEE
KREEE KREEE

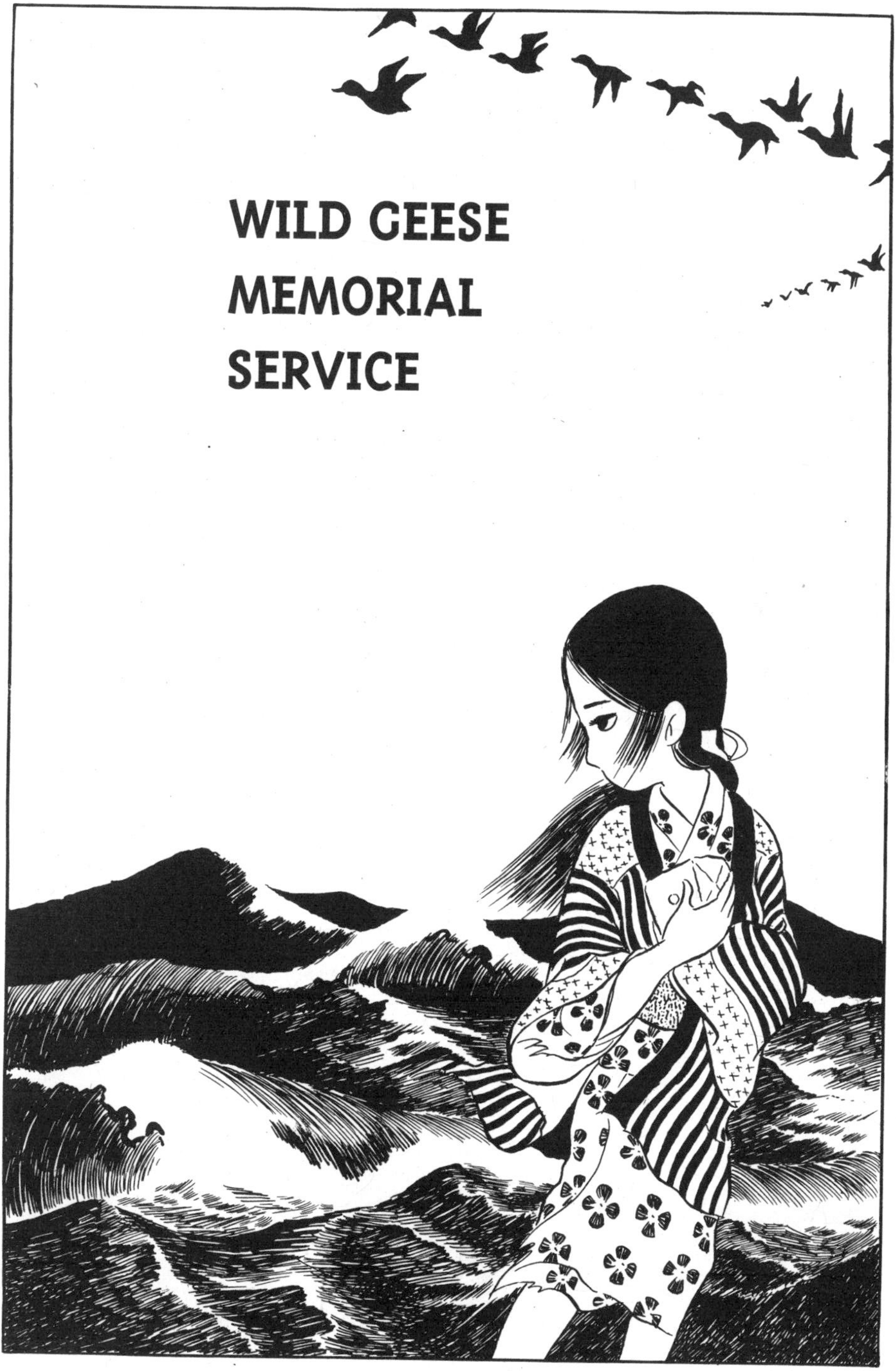
WILD GEESE
MEMORIAL
SERVICE

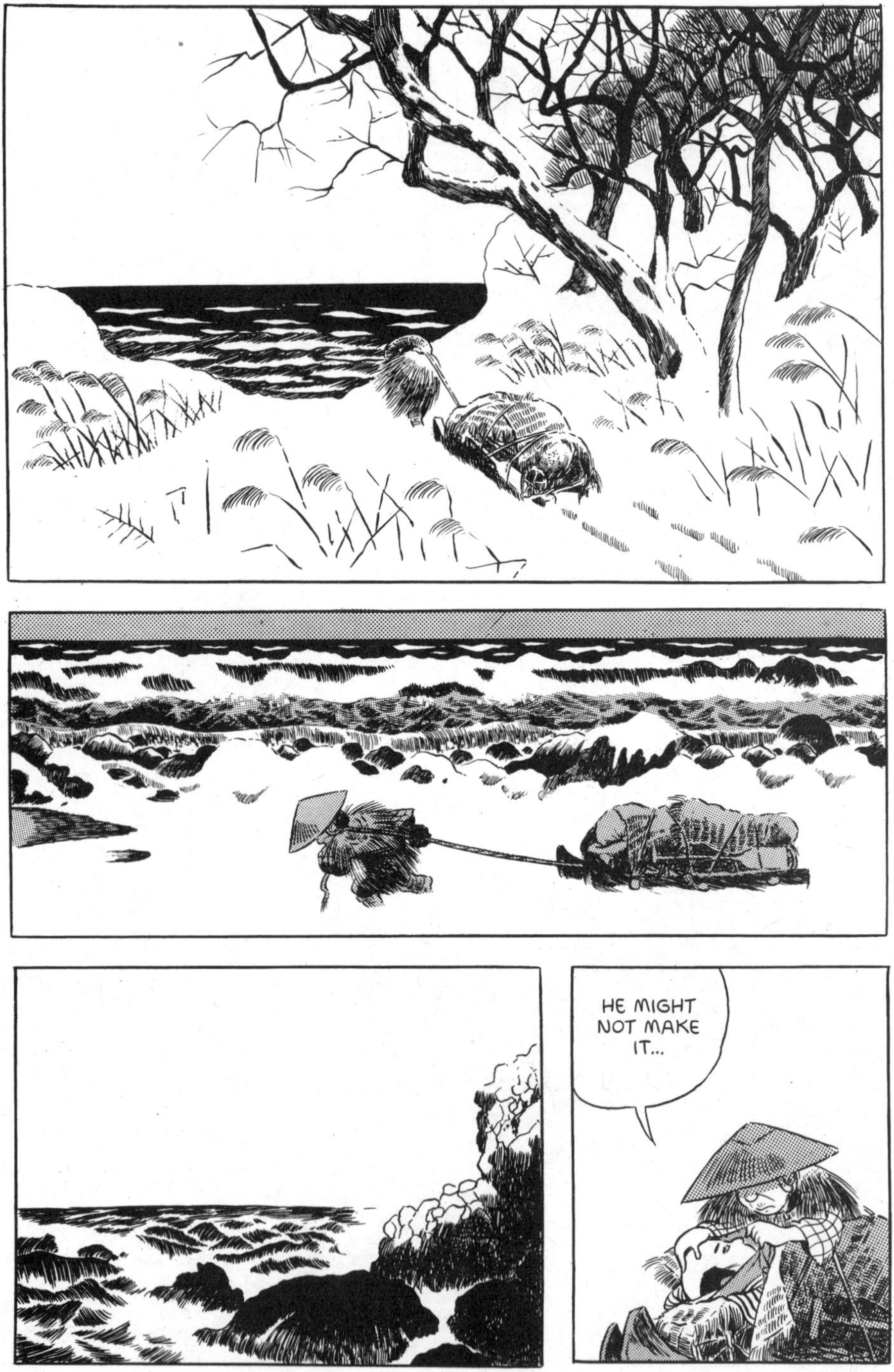
HE MIGHT NOT MAKE IT...

LOOKS LIKE HE GOT CAUGHT IN THE SNOWSTORM THIS MORNING AT TORIGOE PASS.

HE WAS STILL WARM WHEN I DUG HIM OUT OF THE SNOW.

I THOUGHT I MIGHT BE ABLE TO REVIVE HIM...

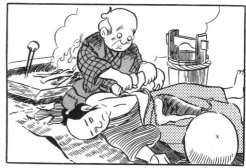

STIR STIR STIR

LOOKS LIKE HE'S A YOUNG HANKONTAN SELLER, BUT HE MUST HAVE LOST HIS WAY IN THE SNOW.

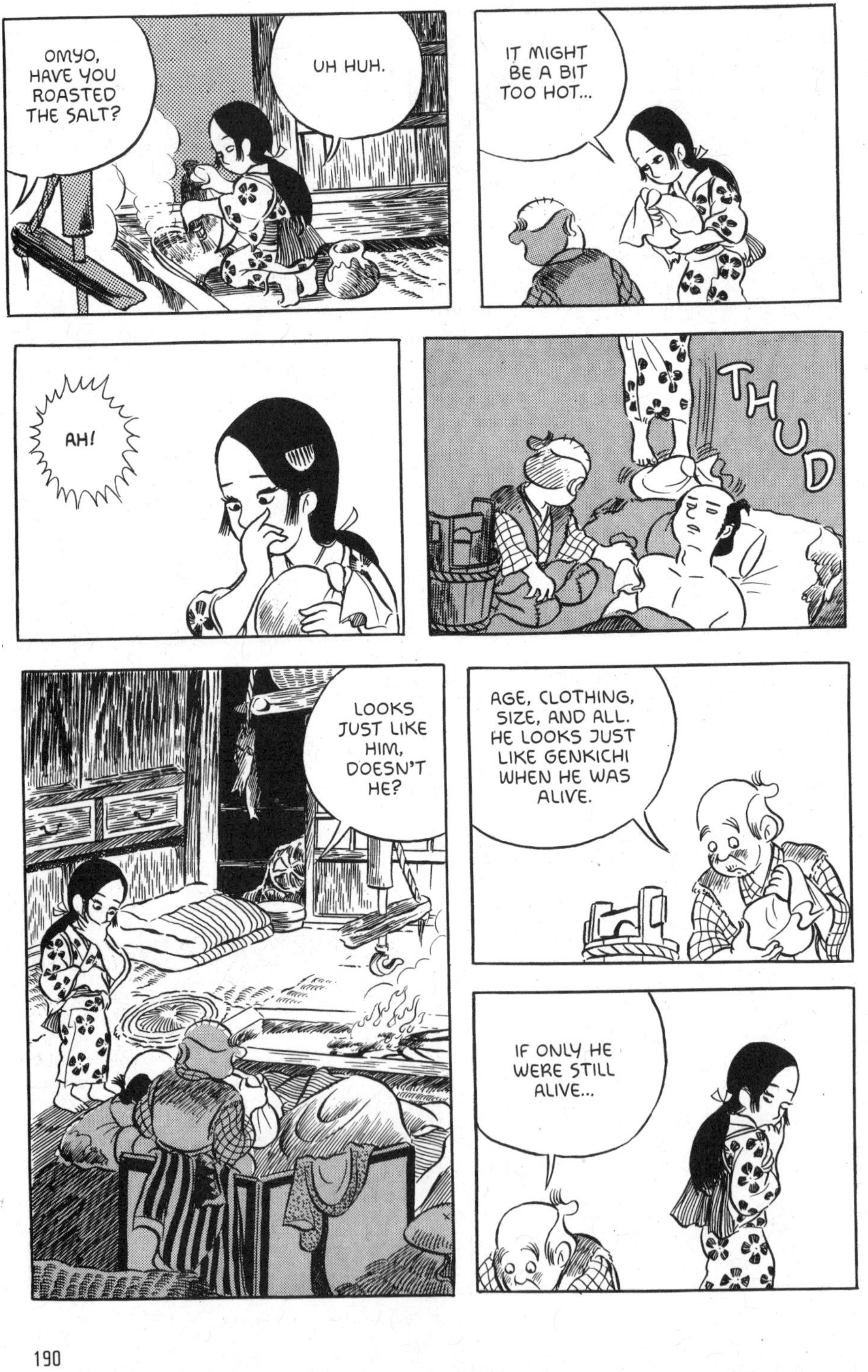
OMYO, HAVE YOU ROASTED THE SALT?
UH HUH.
IT MIGHT BE A BIT TOO HOT...
AH!
THUD
LOOKS JUST LIKE HIM, DOESN'T HE?
AGE, CLOTHING, SIZE, AND ALL. HE LOOKS JUST LIKE GENKICHI WHEN HE WAS ALIVE.
IF ONLY HE WERE STILL ALIVE...

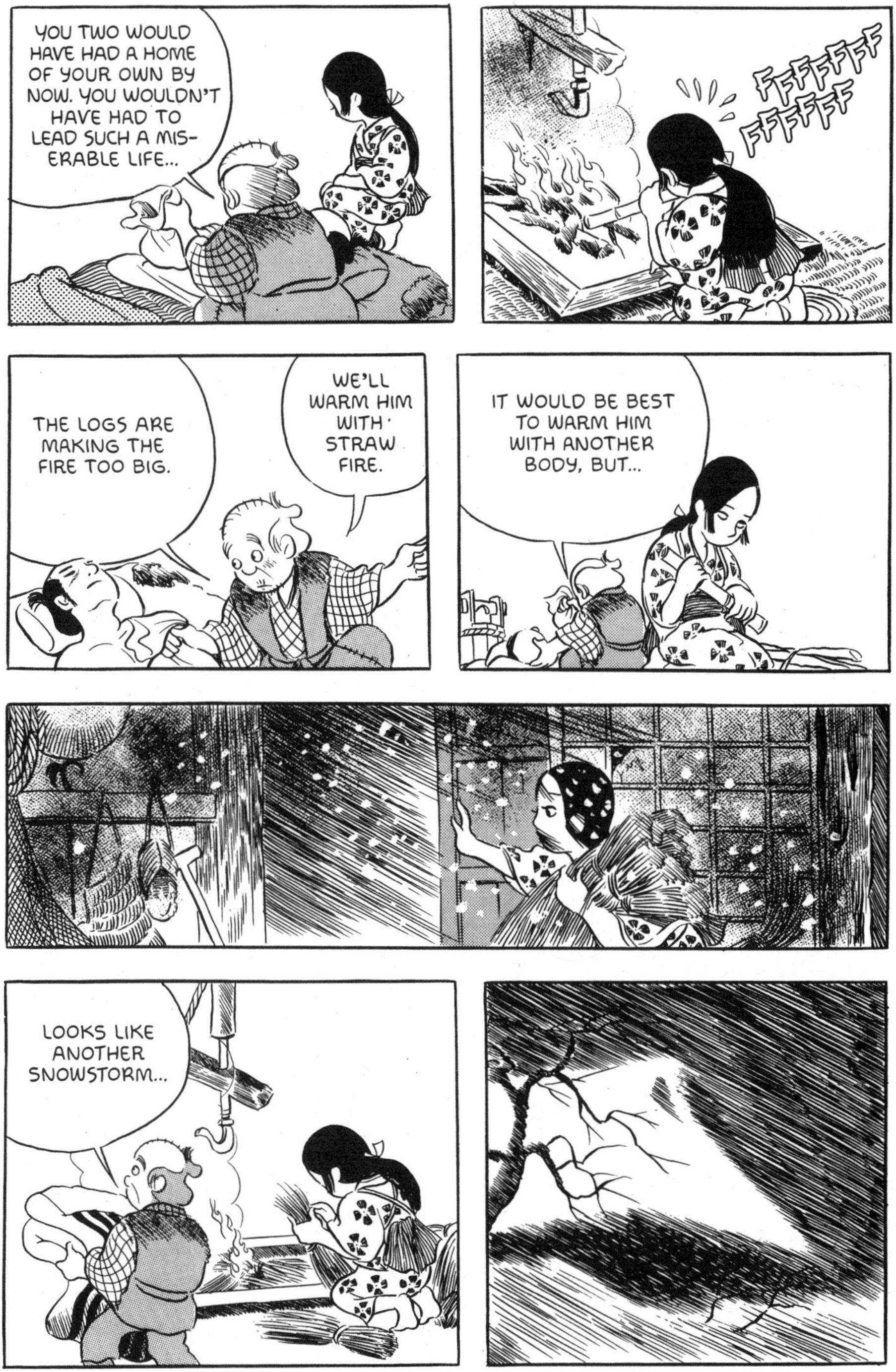
YOU TWO WOULD HAVE HAD A HOME OF YOUR OWN BY NOW. YOU WOULDN'T HAVE HAD TO LEAD SUCH A MIS-ERABLE LIFE...
FFFFFFF FFFFFF
THE LOGS ARE MAKING THE FIRE TOO BIG.
WE'LL WARM HIM WITH STRAW FIRE.
IT WOULD BE BEST TO WARM HIM WITH ANOTHER BODY, BUT...
LOOKS LIKE ANOTHER SNOWSTORM...

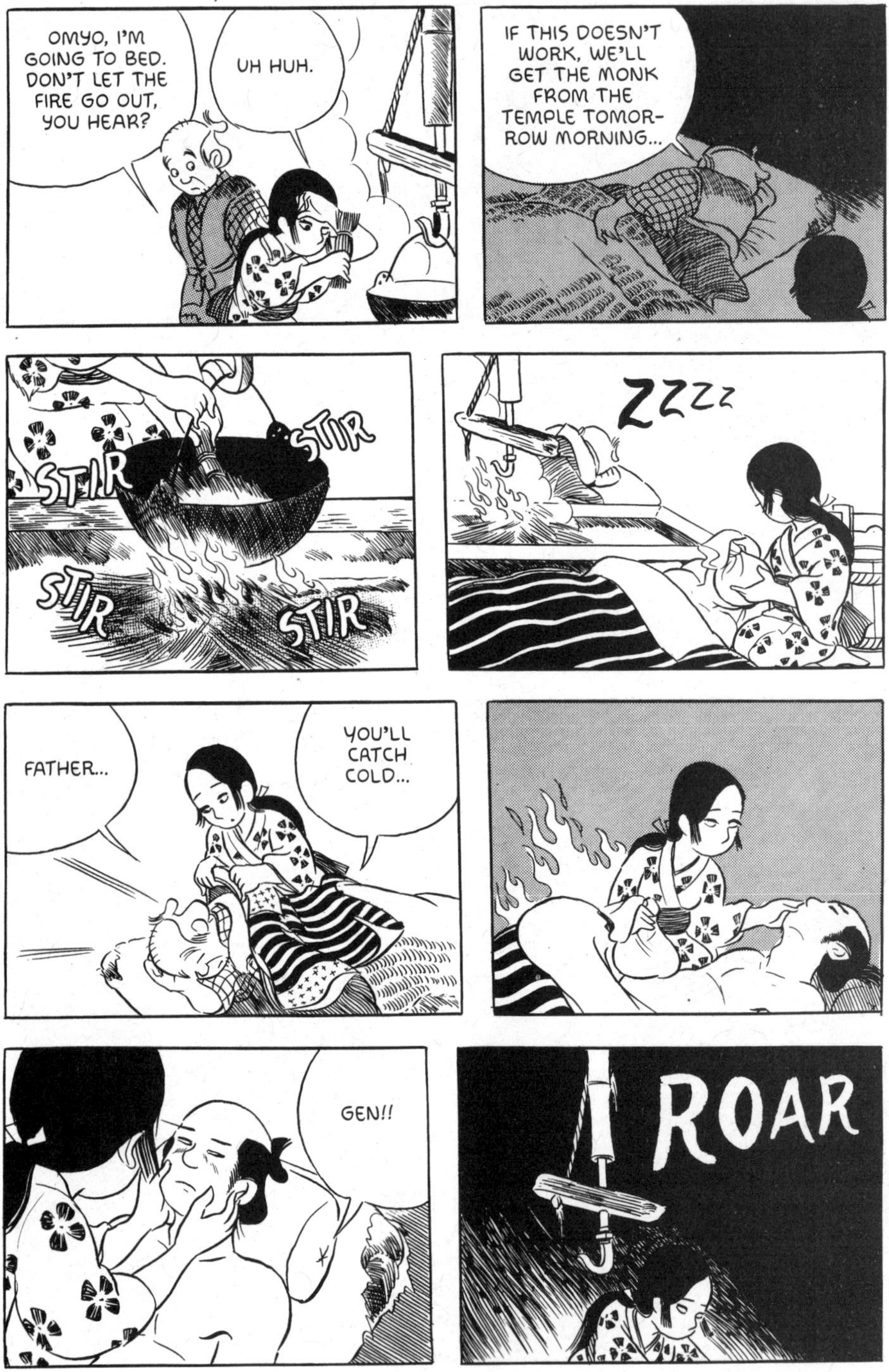
OMYO, I'M GOING TO BED. DON'T LET THE FIRE GO OUT, YOU HEAR?
UH HUH.
IF THIS DOESN'T WORK, WE'LL GET THE MONK FROM THE TEMPLE TOMOR-ROW MORNING...
STIR
STIR
STIR
STIR
ZZZZ
FATHER...
YOU'LL CATCH COLD...
GEN!!
ROAR

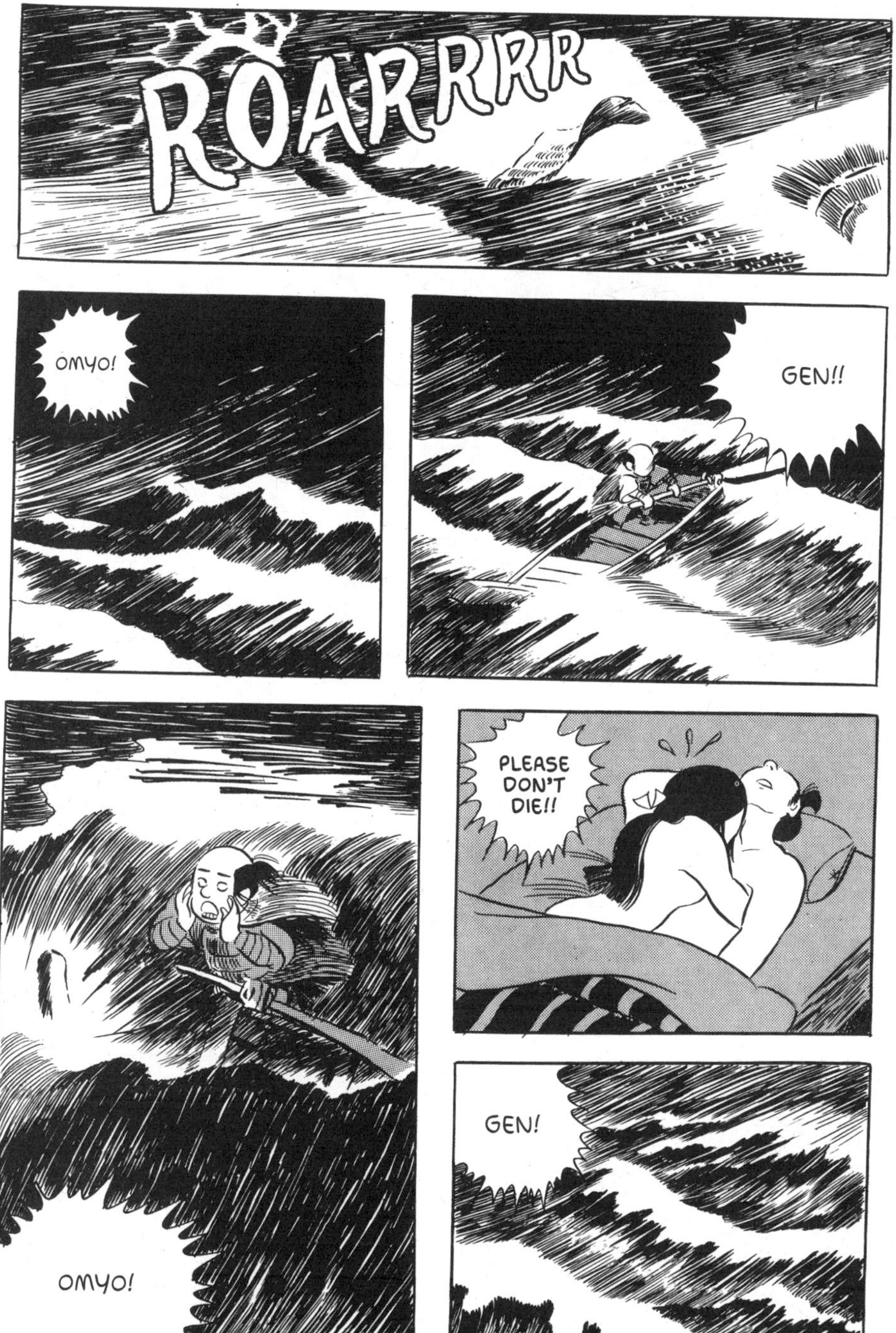
ROARRRR
OMYO!
GEN!!
OMYO!
PLEASE DON'T DIE!!
GEN!

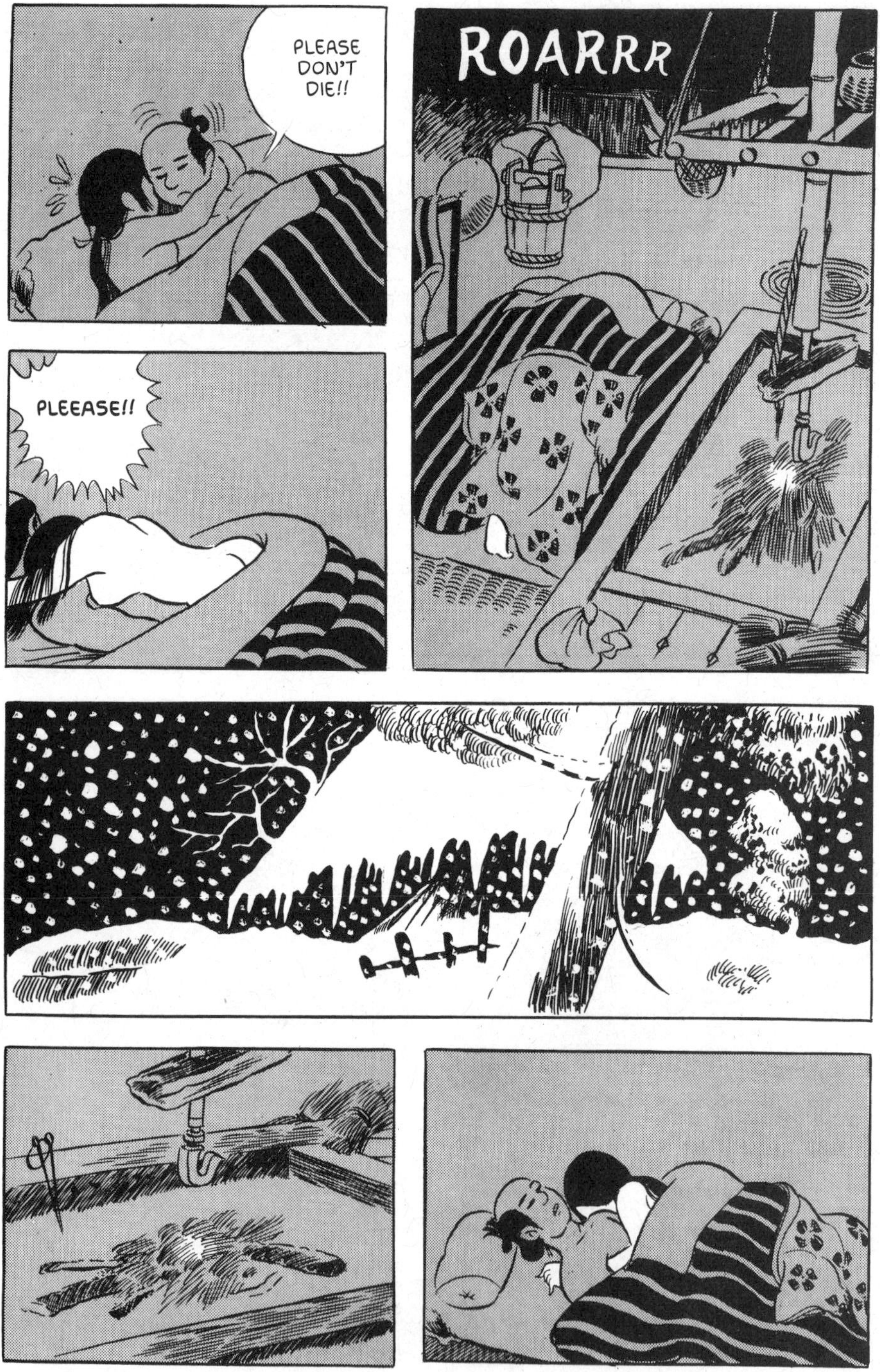
PLEASE DON'T DIE!!
ROARRR
PLEEASE!!

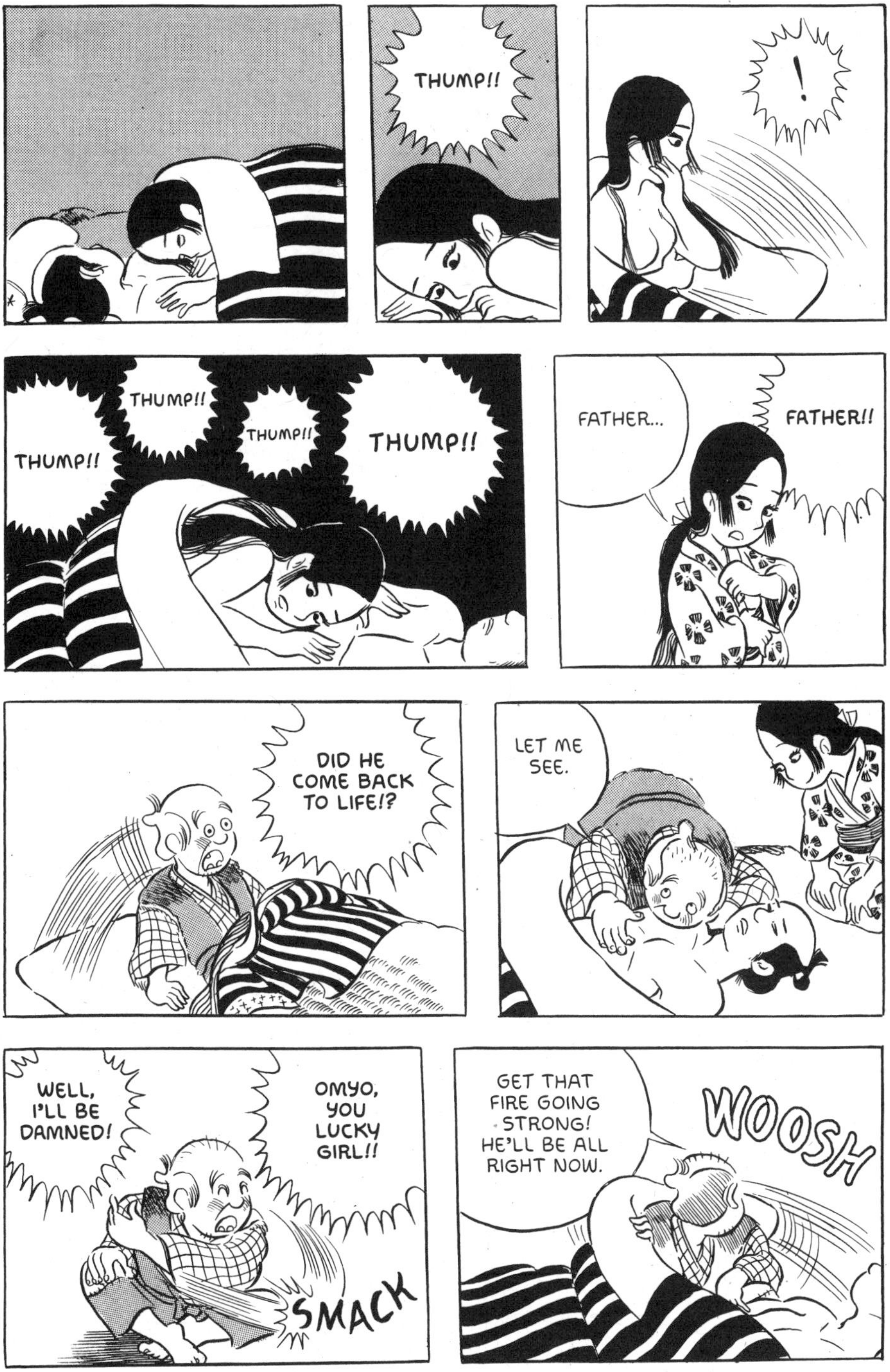
THUMP!!
!
THUMP!!
THUMP!!
THUMP!!
THUMP!!
FATHER...
FATHER!!
DID HE COME BACK TO LIFE!?
LET ME SEE.
WELL, I'LL BE DAMNED!
OMYO, YOU LUCKY GIRL!!
SMACK
GET THAT FIRE GOING STRONG! HE'LL BE ALL RIGHT NOW.
WOOSH

GLIMPSE

GRAB

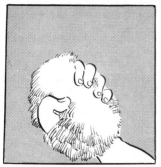

WRAPPED HIS BALLS IN COTTON.

BEING FROM ECCHU, MAKES SENSE HE KNOWS WHAT TO DO IN THE SNOW.

PROBABLY WOULDN'T HAVE MADE IT IF HIS SPERM HAD FROZEN.

GOOD JOB, OMYO.

THE MAN VOMITED A LITTLE THAT MORNING, BUT HIS CONDITION IMPROVED. THANKS TO HIS RESCUERS, HE STEADILY REGAINED HIS STRENGTH, AND WAS UP AND ABOUT IN TWENTY DAYS.

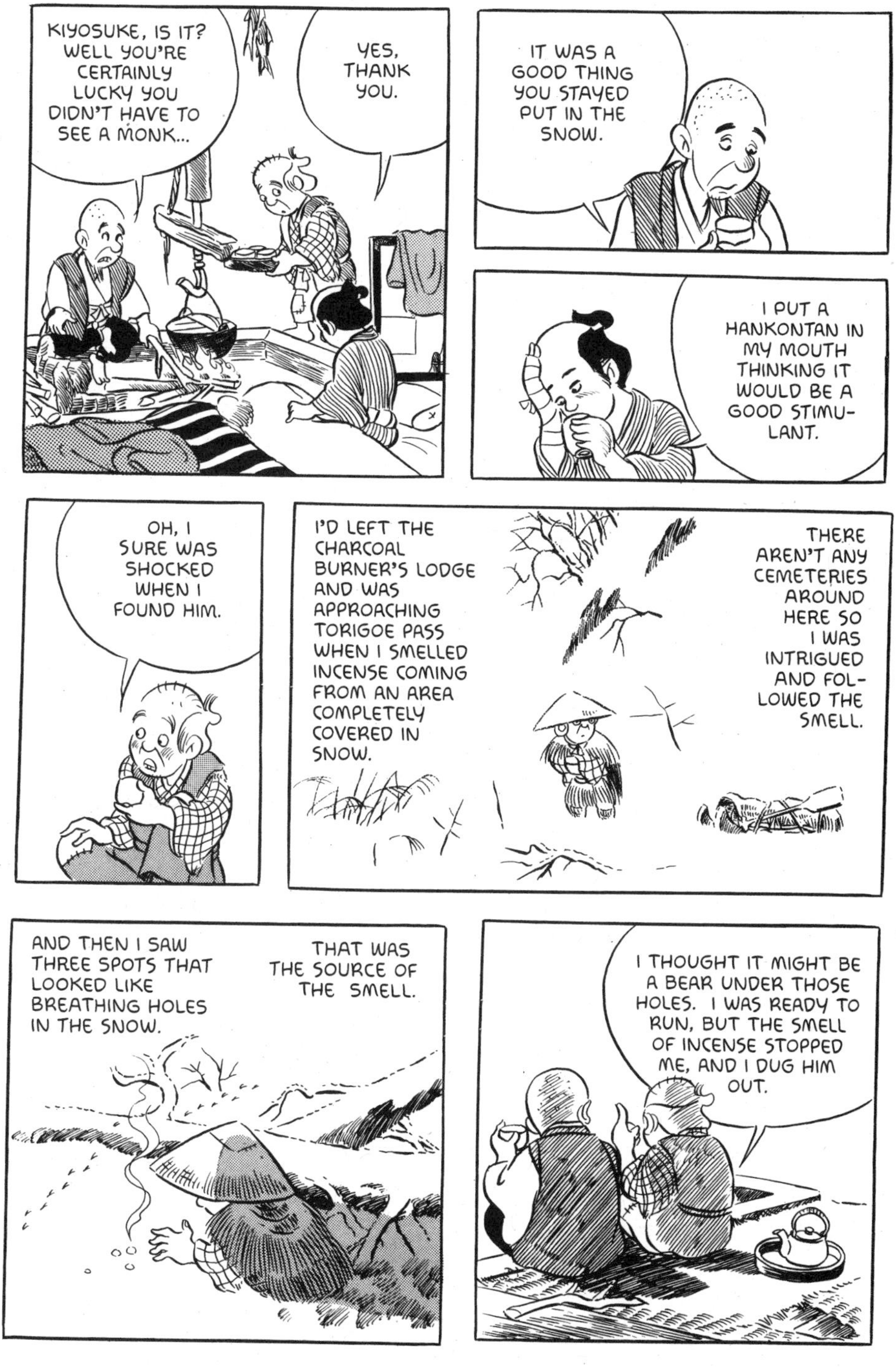
KIYOSUKE, IS IT? WELL YOU'RE CERTAINLY LUCKY YOU DIDN'T HAVE TO SEE A MONK...
YES, THANK YOU.
IT WAS A GOOD THING YOU STAYED PUT IN THE SNOW.
I PUT A HANKONTAN IN MY MOUTH THINKING IT WOULD BE A GOOD STIMU-LANT.
OH, I SURE WAS SHOCKED WHEN I FOUND HIM.
I'D LEFT THE CHARCOAL BURNER'S LODGE AND WAS APPROACHING TORIGOE PASS WHEN I SMELLED INCENSE COMING FROM AN AREA COMPLETELY COVERED IN SNOW.
THERE AREN'T ANY CEMETERIES AROUND HERE SO I WAS INTRIGUED AND FOL-LOWED THE SMELL.
AND THEN I SAW THREE SPOTS THAT LOOKED LIKE BREATHING HOLES IN THE SNOW.
THAT WAS THE SOURCE OF THE SMELL.
I THOUGHT IT MIGHT BE A BEAR UNDER THOSE HOLES. I WAS READY TO RUN, BUT THE SMELL OF INCENSE STOPPED ME, AND I DUG HIM OUT.

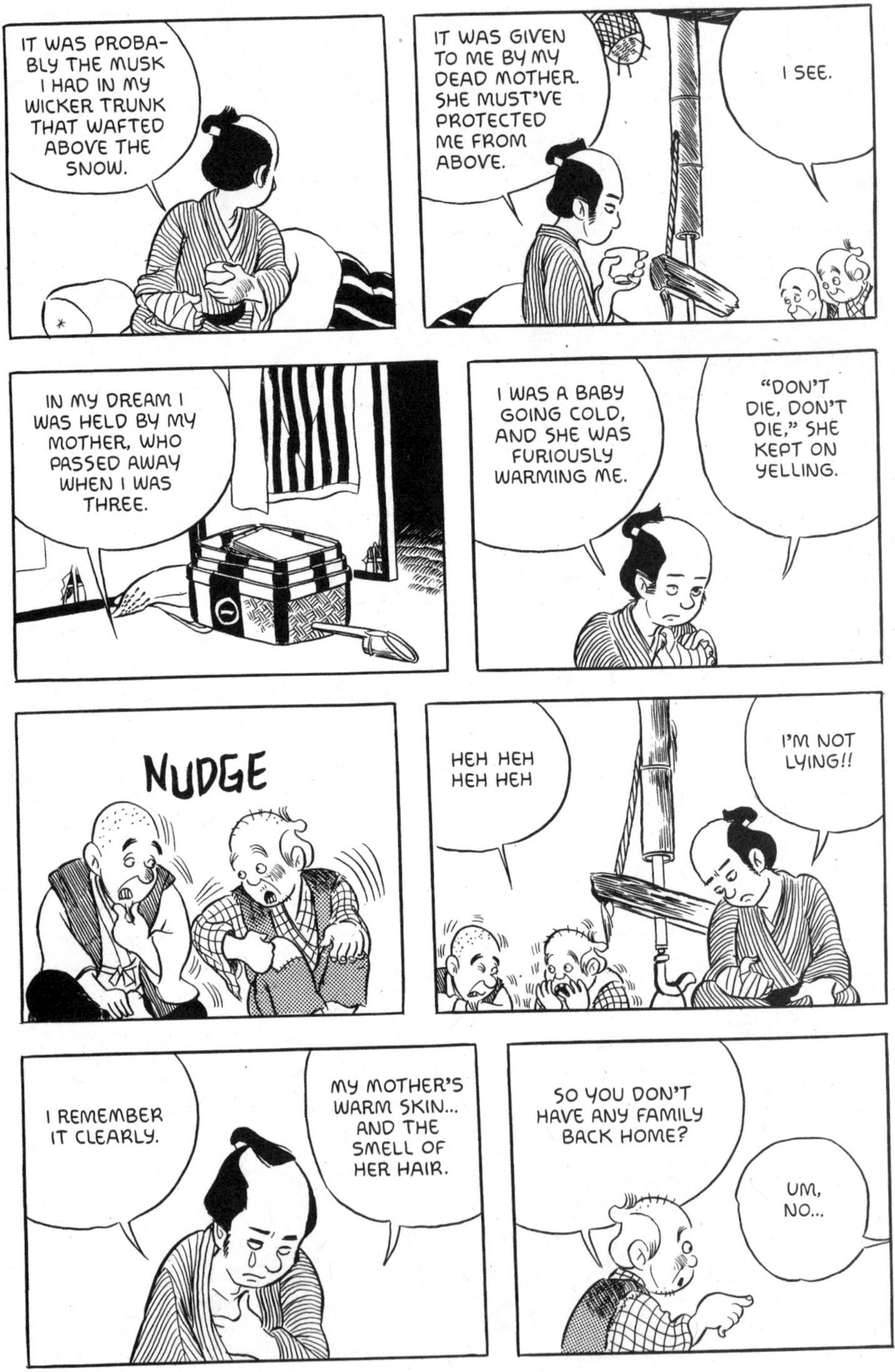
IT WAS PROBA-BLY THE MUSK I HAD IN MY WICKER TRUNK THAT WAFTED ABOVE THE SNOW.
IT WAS GIVEN TO ME BY MY DEAD MOTHER. SHE MUST'VE PROTECTED ME FROM ABOVE.
I SEE.
IN MY DREAM I WAS HELD BY MY MOTHER, WHO PASSED AWAY WHEN I WAS THREE.
I WAS A BABY GOING COLD, AND SHE WAS FURIOUSLY WARMING ME.
"DON'T DIE, DON'T DIE," SHE KEPT ON YELLING.
NUDGE
HEH HEH HEH HEH
I'M NOT LYING!!
I REMEMBER IT CLEARLY.
MY MOTHER'S WARM SKIN... AND THE SMELL OF HER HAIR.
SO YOU DON'T HAVE ANY FAMILY BACK HOME?
UM, NO...

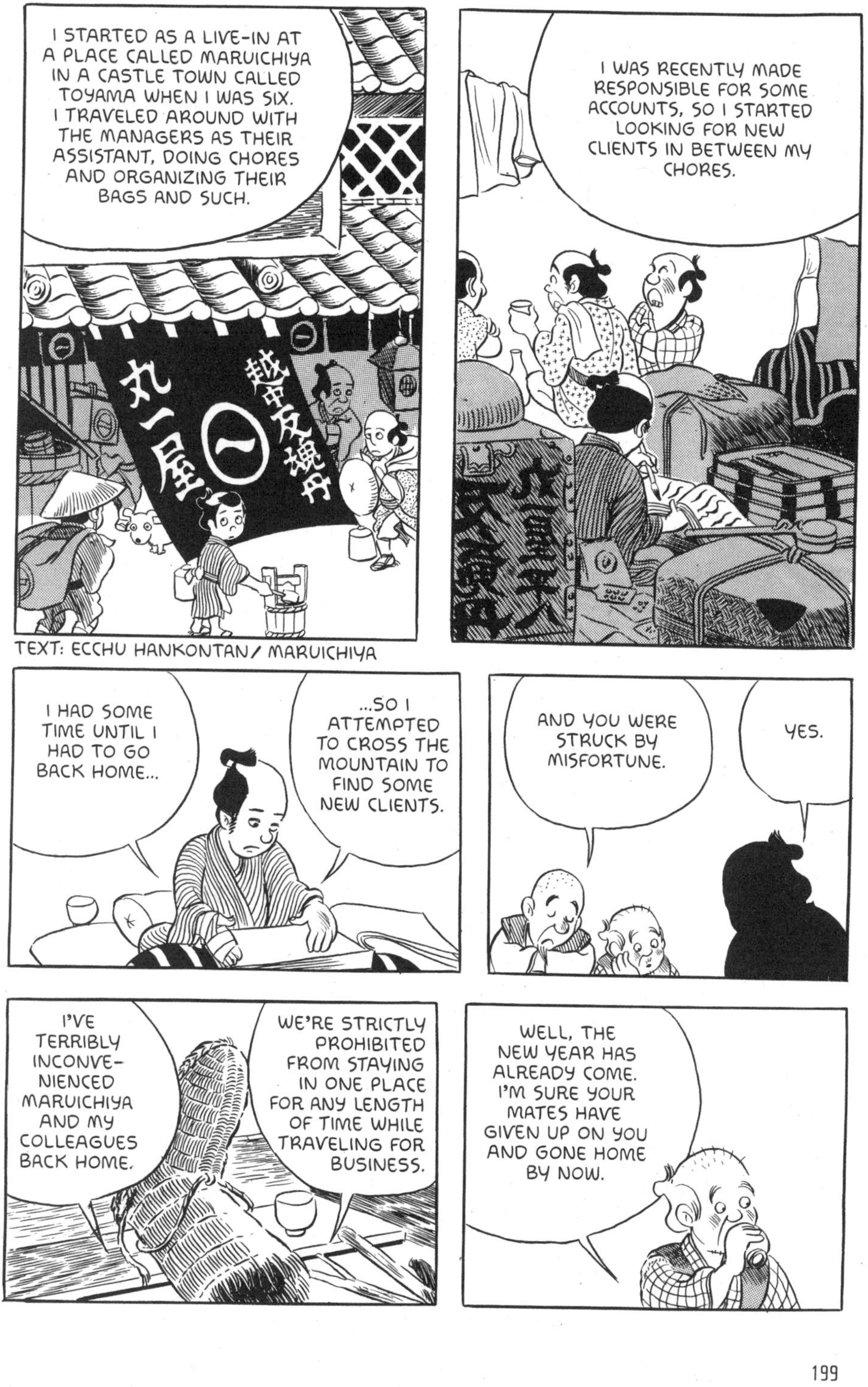
I STARTED AS A LIVE-IN AT A PLACE CALLED MARUICHIYA IN A CASTLE TOWN CALLED TOYAMA WHEN I WAS SIX. I TRAVELED AROUND WITH THE MANAGERS AS THEIR ASSISTANT, DOING CHORES AND ORGANIZING THEIR BAGS AND SUCH.
越中反魂丹
丸一屋
TEXT: ECCHU HANKONTAN/ MARUICHIYA
I WAS RECENTLY MADE RESPONSIBLE FOR SOME ACCOUNTS, SO I STARTED LOOKING FOR NEW CLIENTS IN BETWEEN MY CHORES.
I HAD SOME TIME UNTIL I HAD TO GO BACK HOME...
...SO I ATTEMPTED TO CROSS THE MOUNTAIN TO FIND SOME NEW CLIENTS.
AND YOU WERE STRUCK BY MISFORTUNE.
YES.
I'VE TERRIBLY INCONVE-NIENCED MARUICHIYA AND MY COLLEAGUES BACK HOME.
WE'RE STRICTLY PROHIBITED FROM STAYING IN ONE PLACE FOR ANY LENGTH OF TIME WHILE TRAVELING FOR BUSINESS.
WELL, THE NEW YEAR HAS ALREADY COME. I'M SURE YOUR MATES HAVE GIVEN UP ON YOU AND GONE HOME BY NOW.

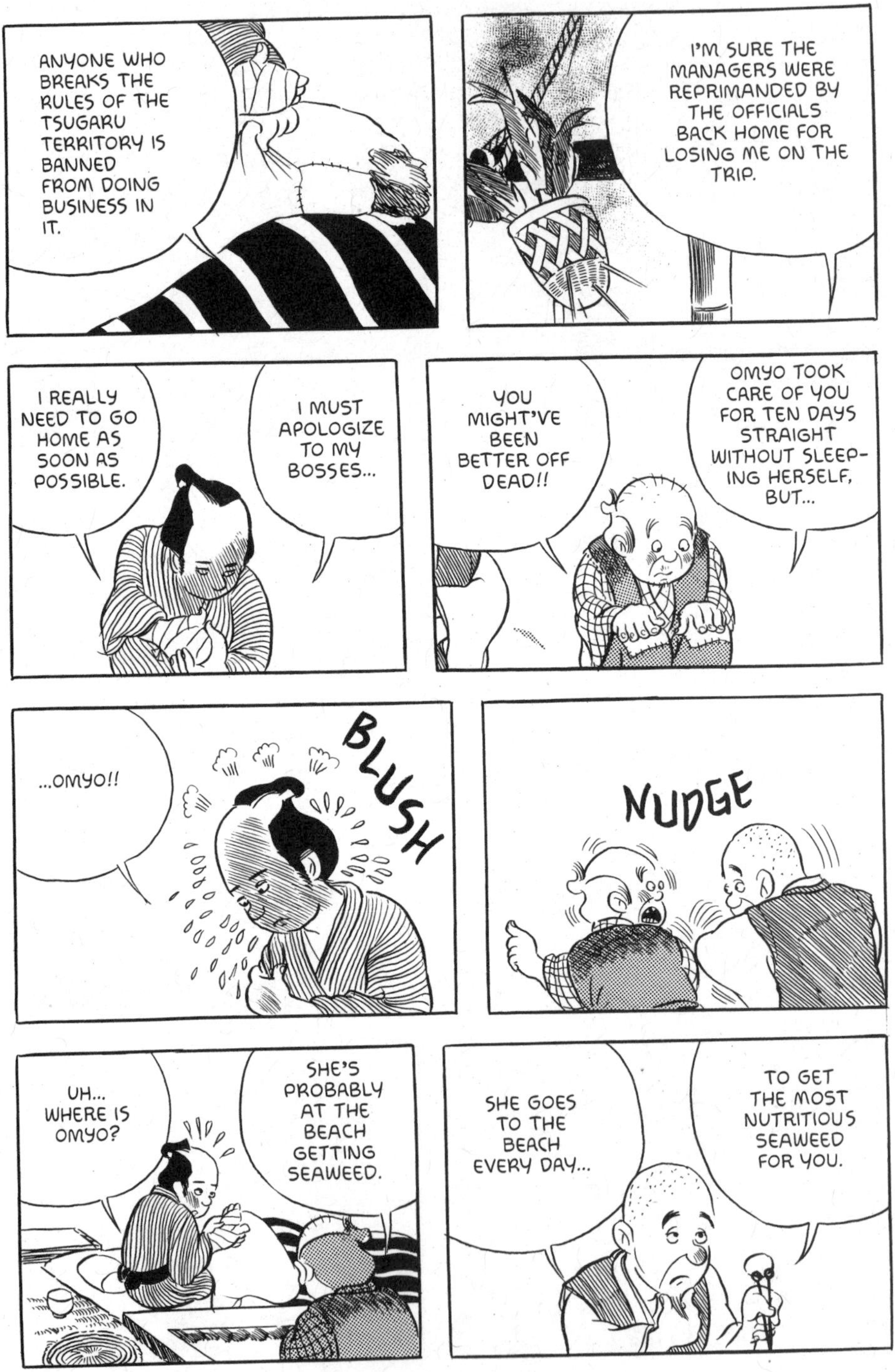
ANYONE WHO BREAKS THE RULES OF THE TSUGARU TERRITORY IS BANNED FROM DOING BUSINESS IN IT.
I'M SURE THE MANAGERS WERE REPRIMANDED BY THE OFFICIALS BACK HOME FOR LOSING ME ON THE TRIP.
I REALLY NEED TO GO HOME AS SOON AS POSSIBLE.
I MUST APOLOGIZE TO MY BOSSES...
YOU MIGHT'VE BEEN BETTER OFF DEAD!!
OMYO TOOK CARE OF YOU FOR TEN DAYS STRAIGHT WITHOUT SLEEPING HERSELF, BUT...
...OMYO!!
BLUSH
NUDGE
UH... WHERE IS OMYO?
SHE'S PROBABLY AT THE BEACH GETTING SEAWEED.
SHE GOES TO THE BEACH EVERY DAY...
TO GET THE MOST NUTRITIOUS SEAWEED FOR YOU.

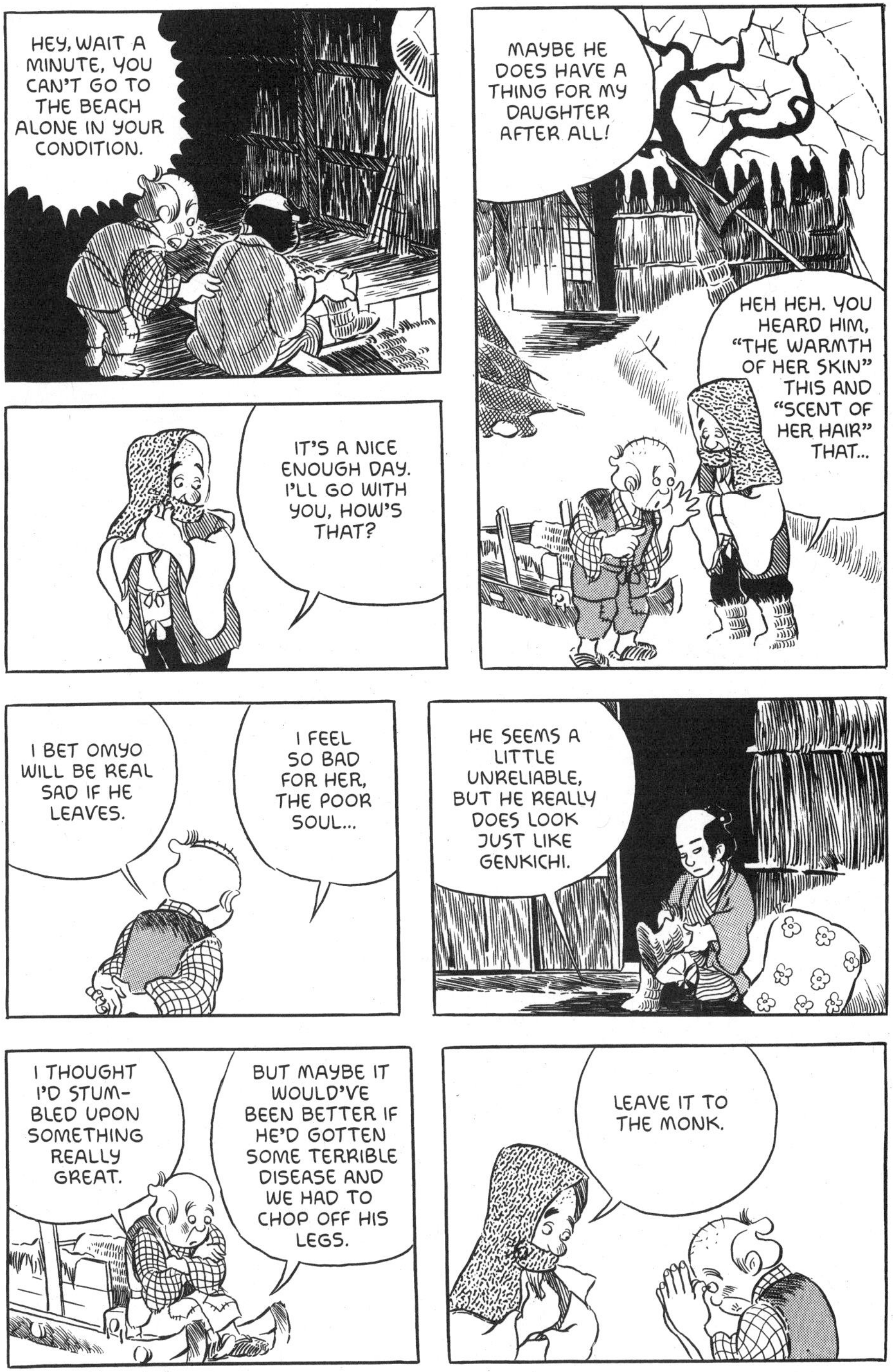

HEY, WAIT A MINUTE, YOU CAN'T GO TO THE BEACH ALONE IN YOUR CONDITION.
MAYBE HE DOES HAVE A THING FOR MY DAUGHTER AFTER ALL!
HEH HEH. YOU HEARD HIM, "THE WARMTH OF HER SKIN" THIS AND "SCENT OF HER HAIR" THAT...
IT'S A NICE ENOUGH DAY. I'LL GO WITH YOU, HOW'S THAT?
I BET OMYO WILL BE REAL SAD IF HE LEAVES.
I FEEL SO BAD FOR HER, THE POOR SOUL...
HE SEEMS A LITTLE UNRELIABLE, BUT HE REALLY DOES LOOK JUST LIKE GENKICHI.
I THOUGHT I'D STUM-BLED UPON SOMETHING REALLY GREAT.
BUT MAYBE IT WOULD'VE BEEN BETTER IF HE'D GOTTEN SOME TERRIBLE DISEASE AND WE HAD TO CHOP OFF HIS LEGS.
LEAVE IT TO THE MONK.

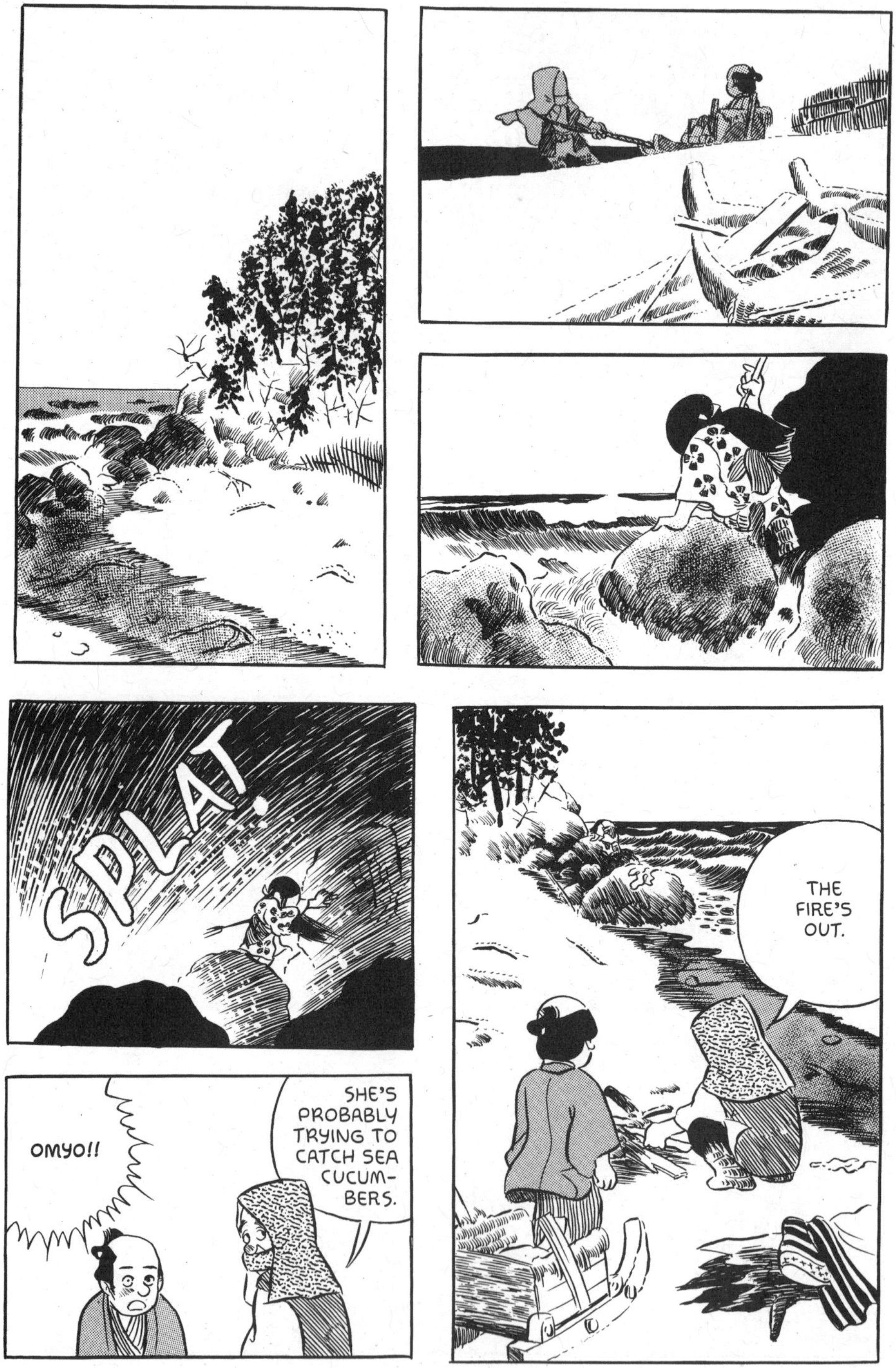
SPLAT
OMYO!!
SHE'S PROBABLY TRYING TO CATCH SEA CUCUMBERS.
THE FIRE'S OUT.

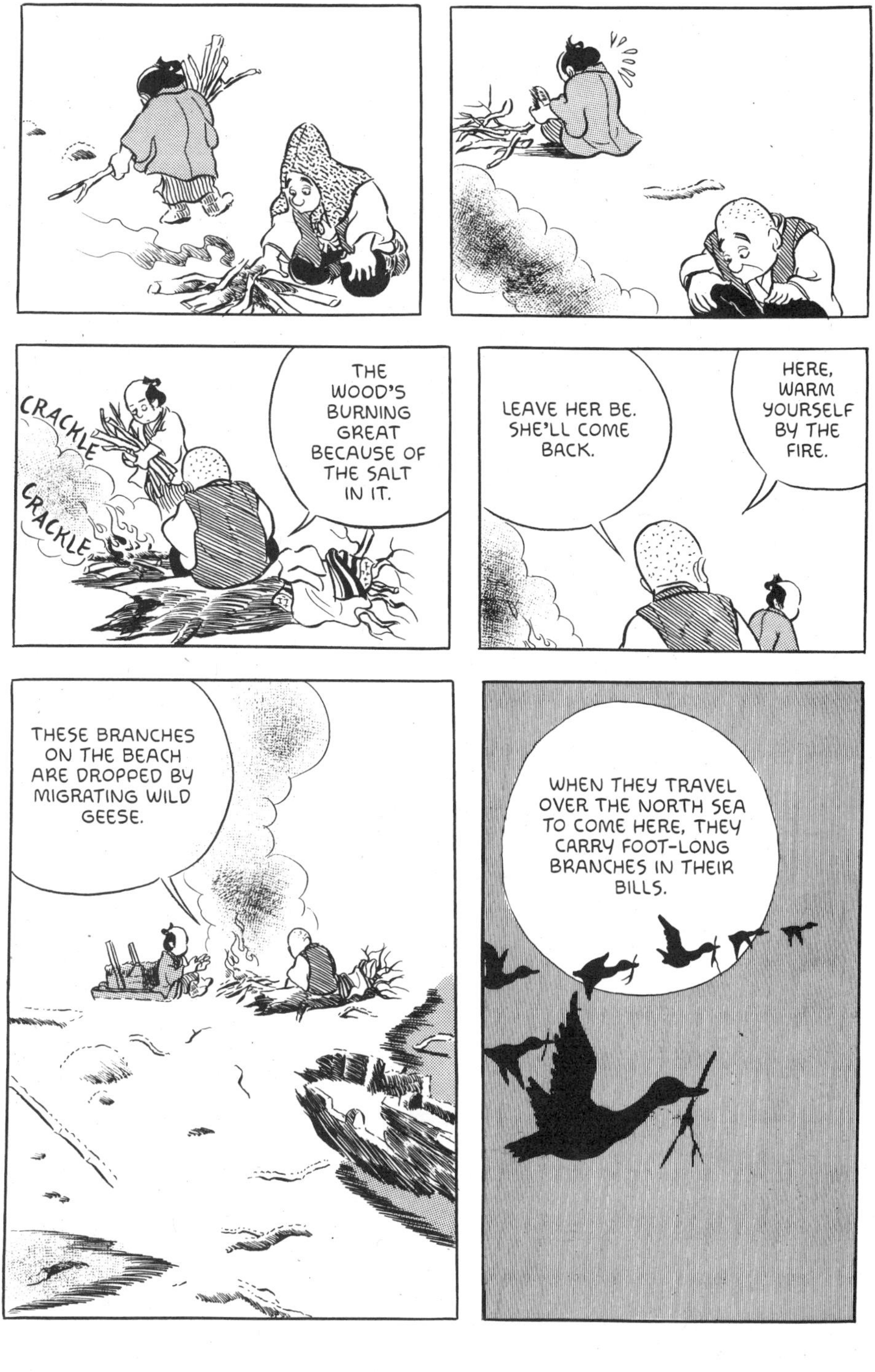
CRACKLE CRACKLE
THE WOOD'S BURNING GREAT BECAUSE OF THE SALT IN IT.
LEAVE HER BE. SHE'LL COME BACK.
HERE, WARM YOURSELF BY THE FIRE.
THESE BRANCHES ON THE BEACH ARE DROPPED BY MIGRATING WILD GEESE.
WHEN THEY TRAVEL OVER THE NORTH SEA TO COME HERE, THEY CARRY FOOT-LONG BRANCHES IN THEIR BILLS.

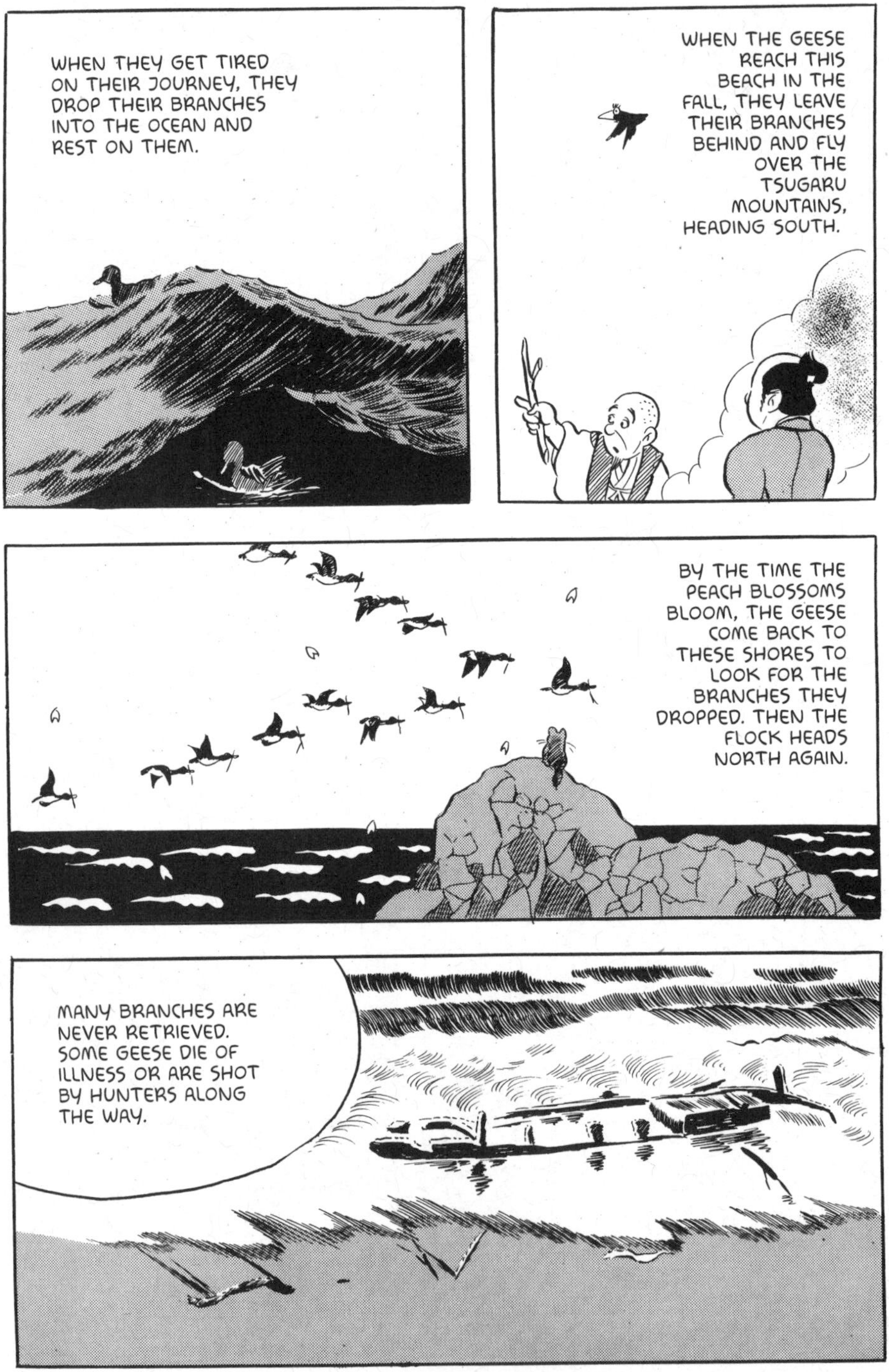
WHEN THEY GET TIRED ON THEIR JOURNEY, THEY DROP THEIR BRANCHES INTO THE OCEAN AND REST ON THEM.
WHEN THE GEESE REACH THIS BEACH IN THE FALL, THEY LEAVE THEIR BRANCHES BEHIND AND FLY OVER THE TSUGARU MOUNTAINS, HEADING SOUTH.
BY THE TIME THE PEACH BLOSSOMS BLOOM, THE GEESE COME BACK TO THESE SHORES TO LOOK FOR THE BRANCHES THEY DROPPED. THEN THE FLOCK HEADS NORTH AGAIN.
MANY BRANCHES ARE NEVER RETRIEVED. SOME GEESE DIE OF ILLNESS OR ARE SHOT BY HUNTERS ALONG THE WAY.

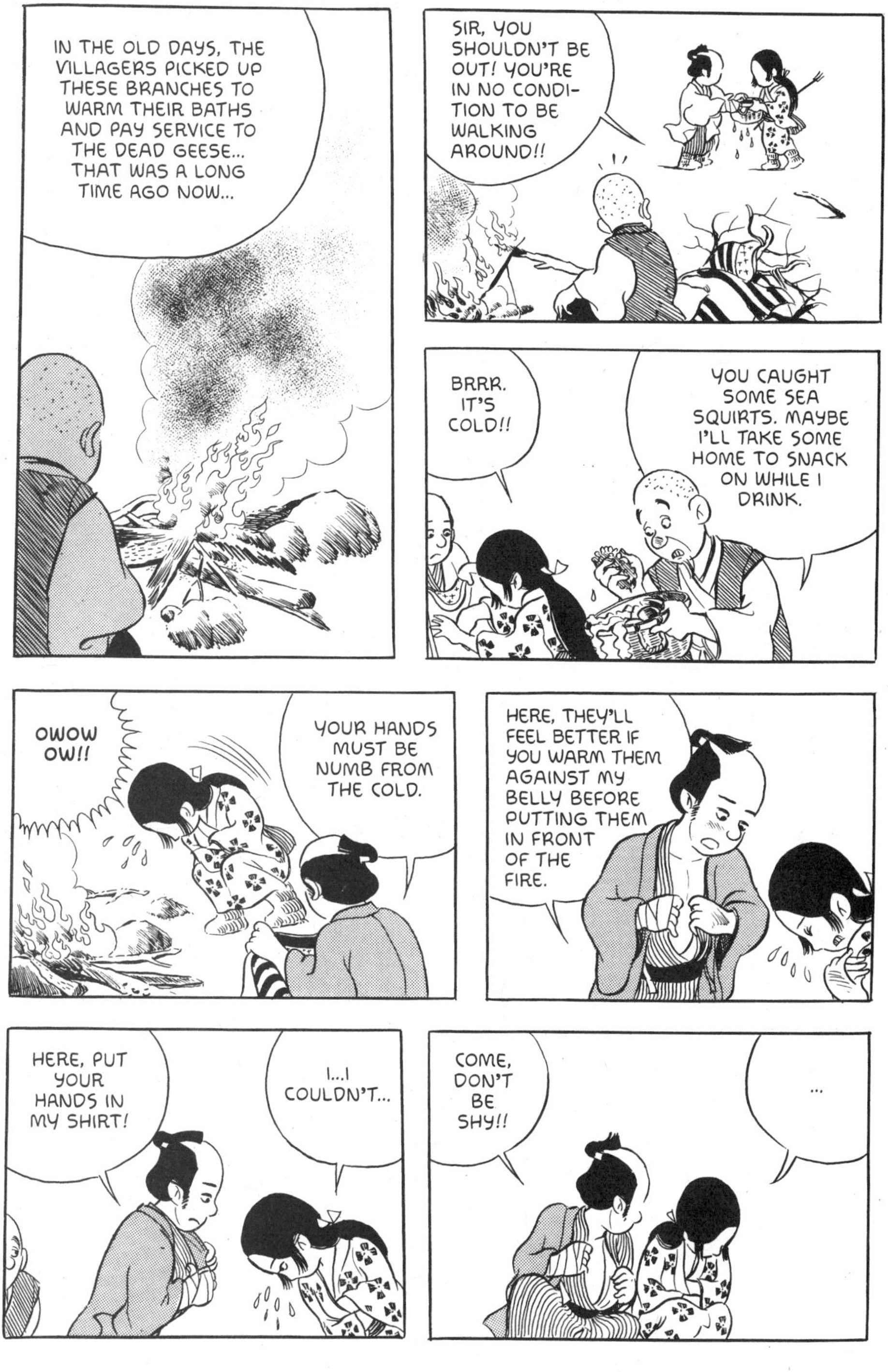
IN THE OLD DAYS, THE VILLAGERS PICKED UP THESE BRANCHES TO WARM THEIR BATHS AND PAY SERVICE TO THE DEAD GEESE... THAT WAS A LONG TIME AGO NOW...
SIR, YOU SHOULDN'T BE OUT! YOU'RE IN NO CONDITION TO BE WALKING AROUND!!
BRRR. IT'S COLD!!
YOU CAUGHT SOME SEA SQUIRTS. MAYBE I'LL TAKE SOME HOME TO SNACK ON WHILE I DRINK.
OWOW OW!!
YOUR HANDS MUST BE NUMB FROM THE COLD.
HERE, THEY'LL FEEL BETTER IF YOU WARM THEM AGAINST MY BELLY BEFORE PUTTING THEM IN FRONT OF THE FIRE.
HERE, PUT YOUR HANDS IN MY SHIRT!
I...I COULDN'T...
COME, DON'T BE SHY!!
...

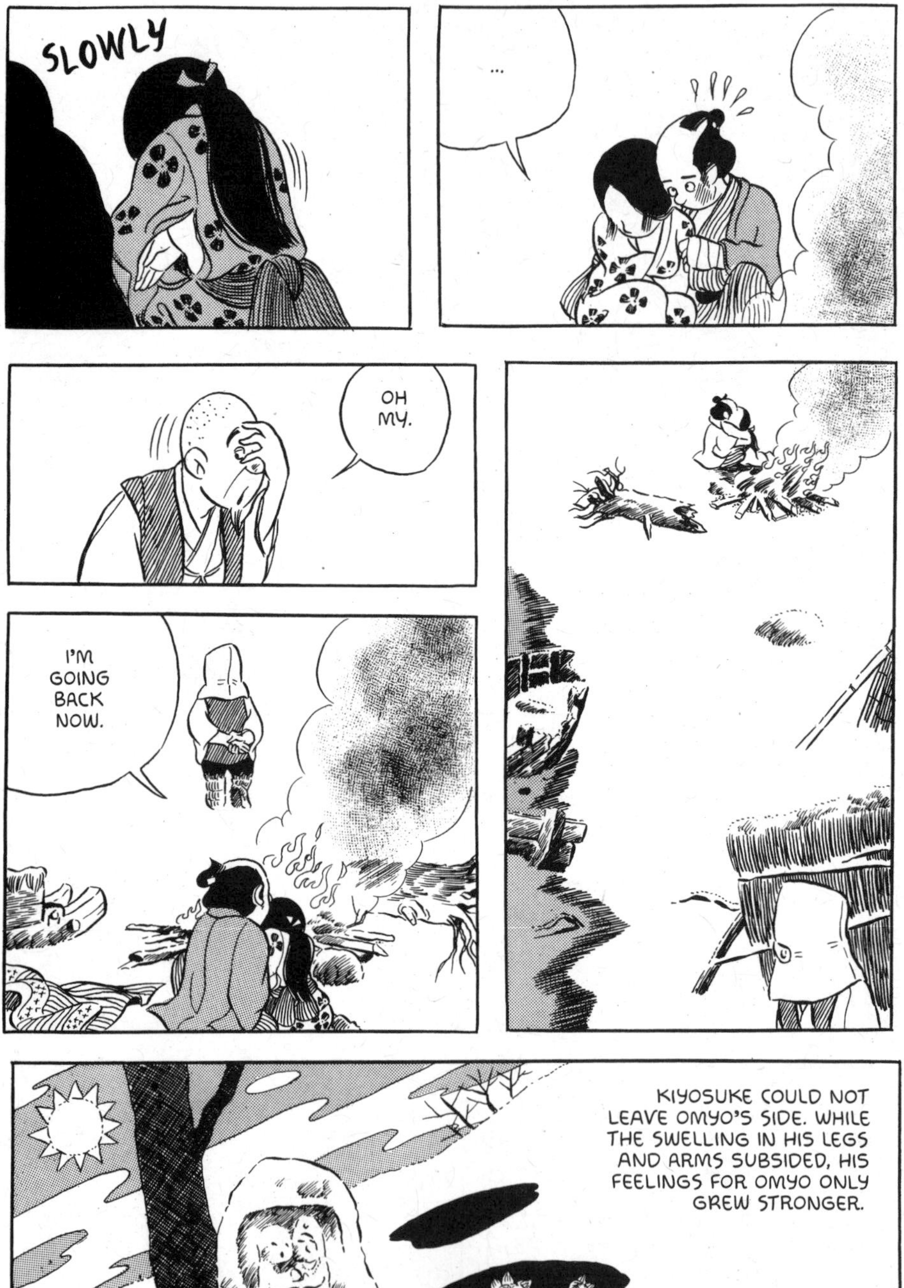
SLOWLY
...
OH MY.
I'M GOING BACK NOW.
KIYOSUKE COULD NOT LEAVE OMYO'S SIDE. WHILE THE SWELLING IN HIS LEGS AND ARMS SUBSIDED, HIS FEELINGS FOR OMYO ONLY GREW STRONGER.

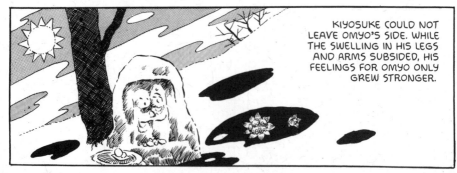

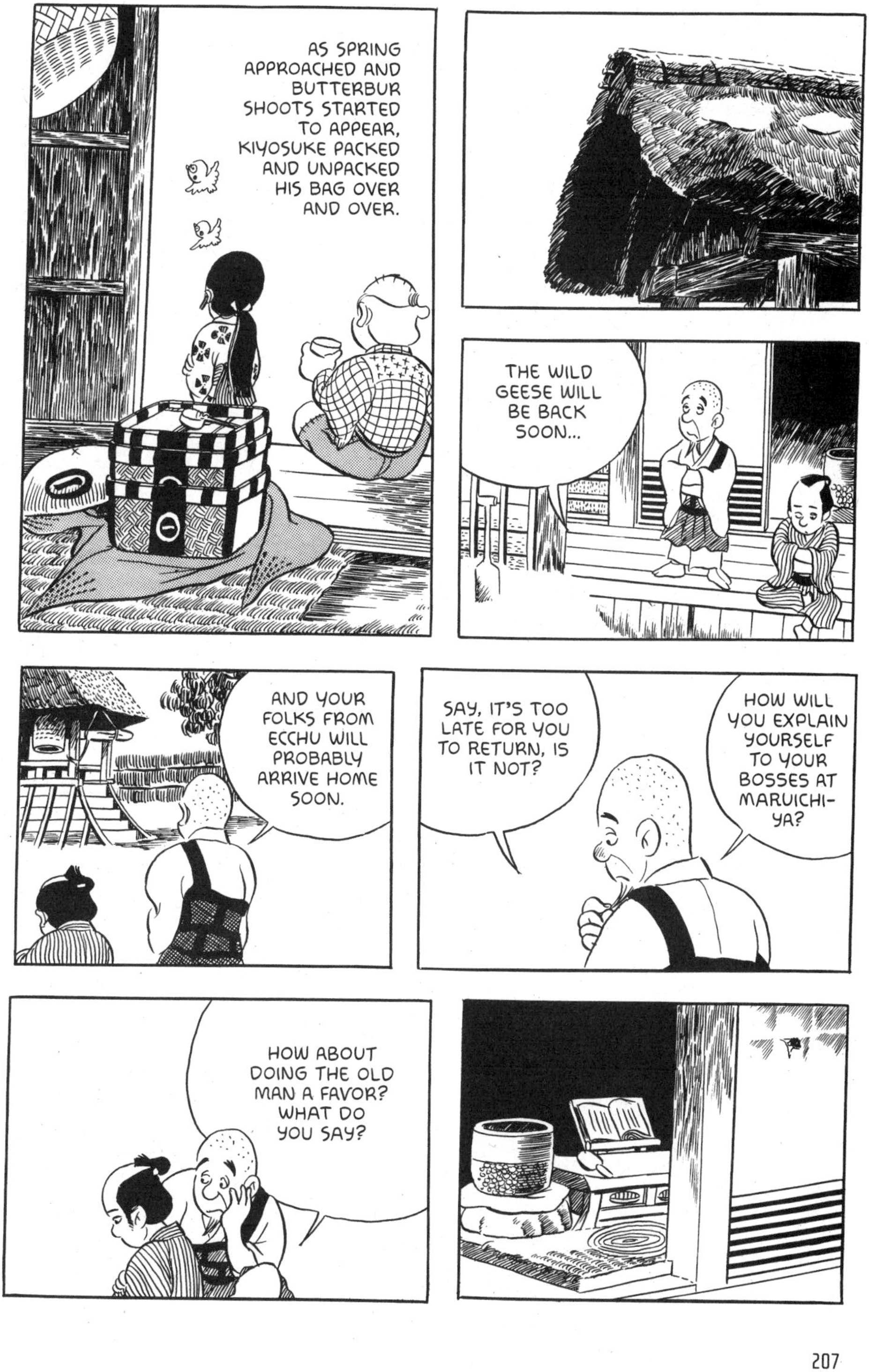
AS SPRING APPROACHED AND BUTTERBUR SHOOTS STARTED TO APPEAR, KIYOSUKE PACKED AND UNPACKED HIS BAG OVER AND OVER.
THE WILD GEESE WILL BE BACK SOON...
AND YOUR FOLKS FROM ECCHU WILL PROBABLY ARRIVE HOME SOON.
SAY, IT'S TOO LATE FOR YOU TO RETURN, IS IT NOT?
HOW WILL YOU EXPLAIN YOURSELF TO YOUR BOSSES AT MARUICHI-YA?
HOW ABOUT DOING THE OLD MAN A FAVOR? WHAT DO YOU SAY?

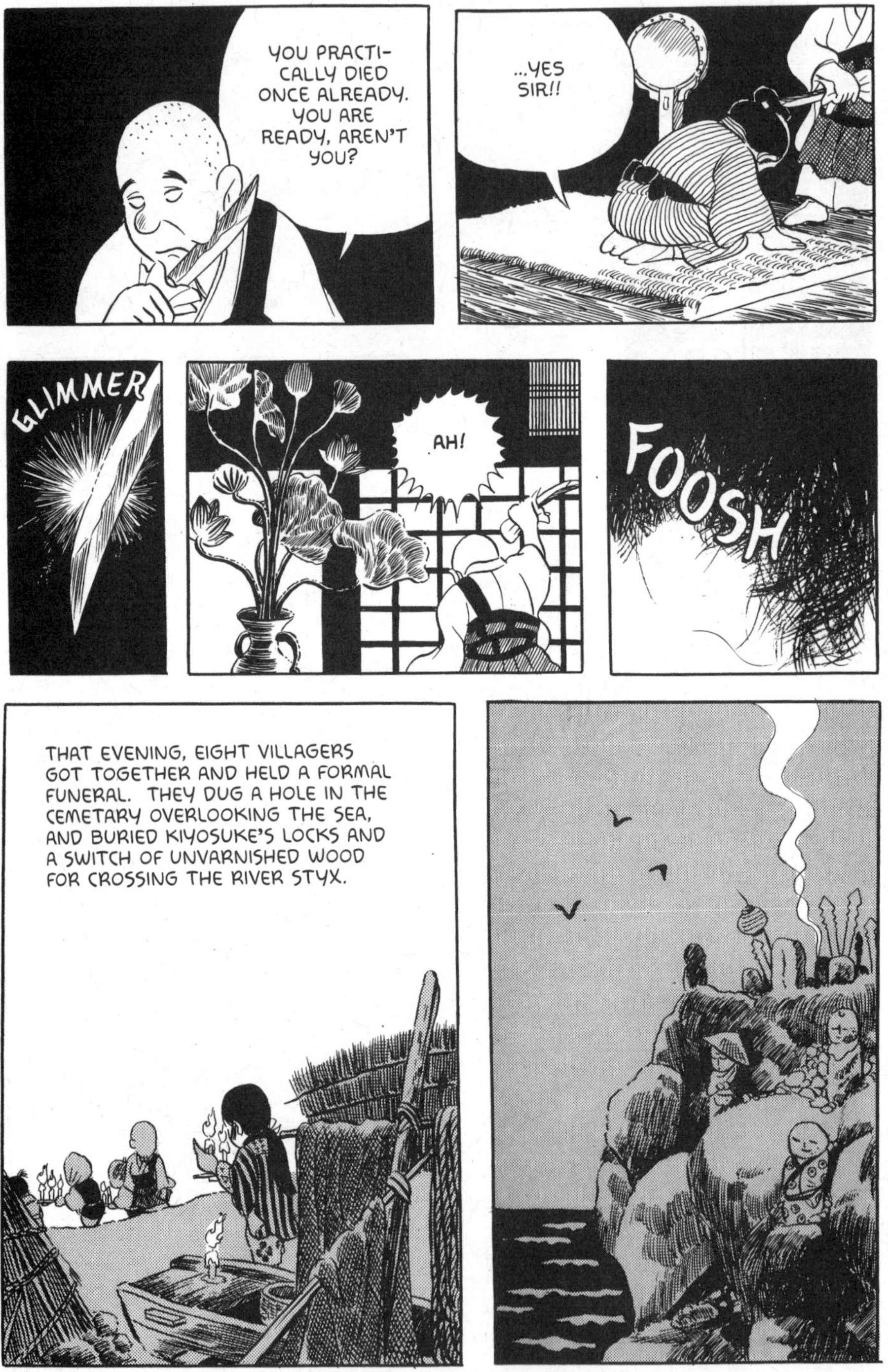
YOU PRACTI-
CALLY DIED
ONCE ALREADY.
YOU ARE
READY, AREN'T
YOU?
...YES
SIR!!
GLIMMER
AH!
FOOSH
THAT EVENING, EIGHT VILLAGERS GOT TOGETHER AND HELD A FORMAL FUNERAL. THEY DUG A HOLE IN THE CEMETARY OVERLOOKING THE SEA, AND BURIED KIYOSUKE'S LOCKS AND A SWITCH OF UNVARNISHED WOOD FOR CROSSING THE RIVER STYX.

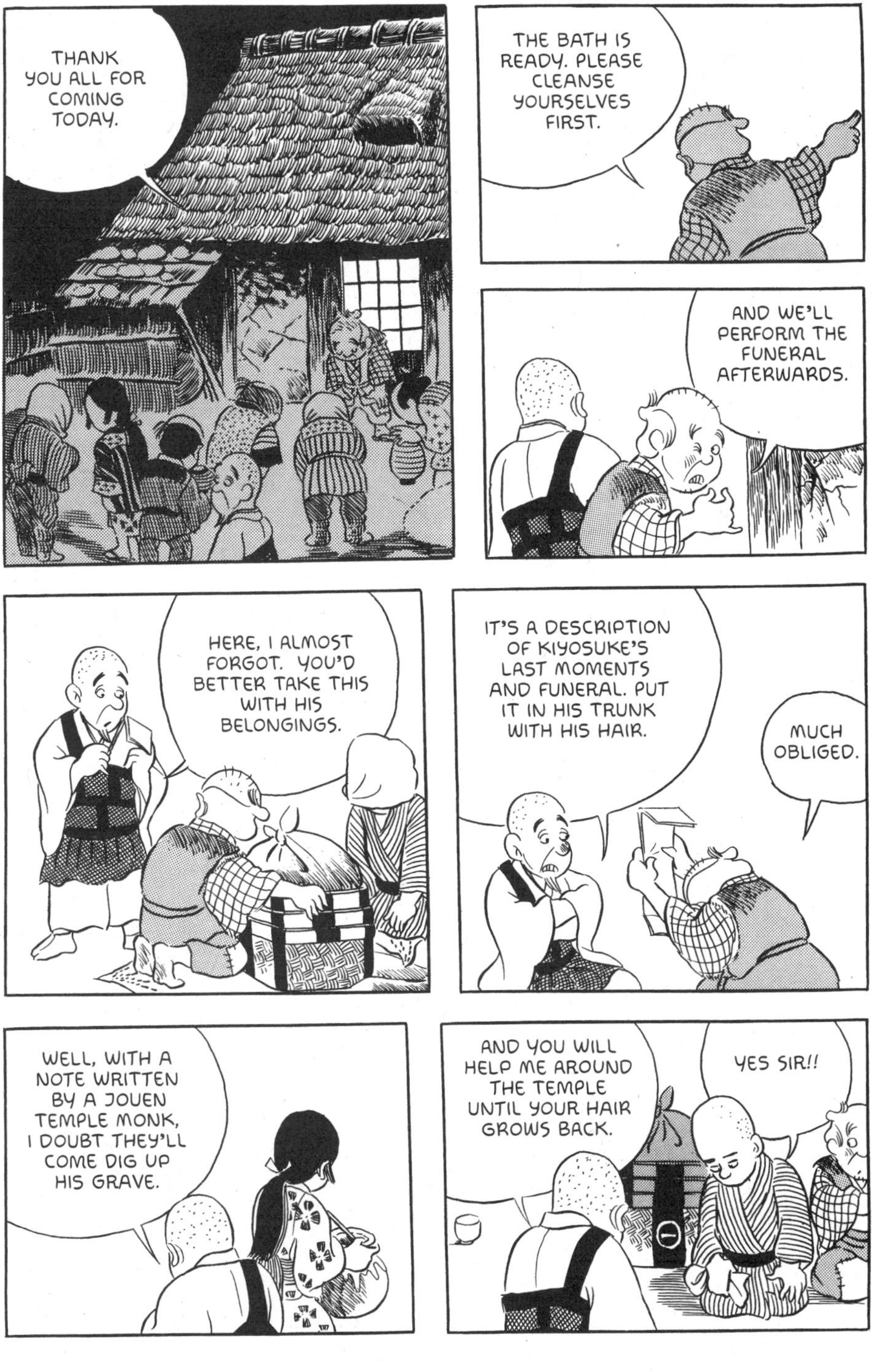
THANK YOU ALL FOR COMING TODAY.
THE BATH IS READY. PLEASE CLEANSE YOURSELVES FIRST.
AND WE'LL PERFORM THE FUNERAL AFTERWARDS.
HERE, I ALMOST FORGOT. YOU'D BETTER TAKE THIS WITH HIS BELONGINGS.
IT'S A DESCRIPTION OF KIYOSUKE'S LAST MOMENTS AND FUNERAL. PUT IT IN HIS TRUNK WITH HIS HAIR.
MUCH OBLIGED.
WELL, WITH A NOTE WRITTEN BY A JOUEN TEMPLE MONK, I DOUBT THEY'LL COME DIG UP HIS GRAVE.
AND YOU WILL HELP ME AROUND THE TEMPLE UNTIL YOUR HAIR GROWS BACK.
YES SIR!!

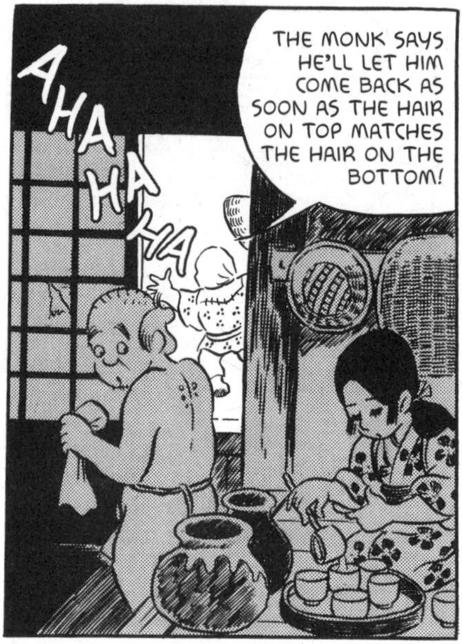
AHAHAHAHA
THE MONK SAYS HE'LL LET HIM COME BACK AS SOON AS THE HAIR ON TOP MATCHES THE HAIR ON THE BOTTOM!
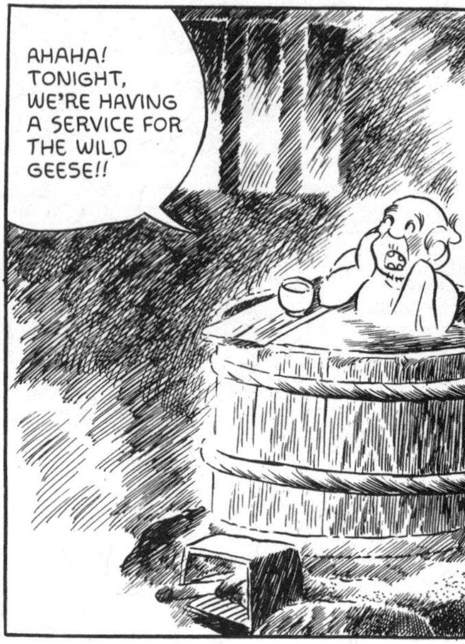
AHAHA! TONIGHT, WE'RE HAVING A SERVICE FOR THE WILD GEESE!!
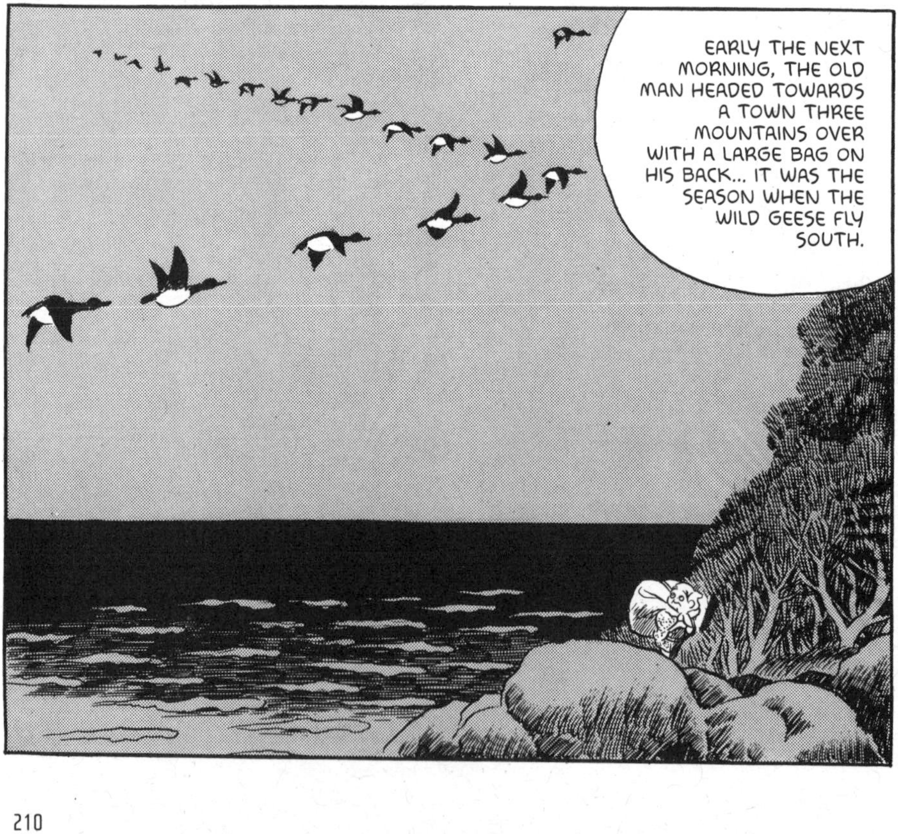
EARLY THE NEXT MORNING, THE OLD MAN HEADED TOWARDS A TOWN THREE MOUNTAINS OVER WITH A LARGE BAG ON HIS BACK... IT WAS THE SEASON WHEN THE WILD GEESE FLY SOUTH.

RED SNOW

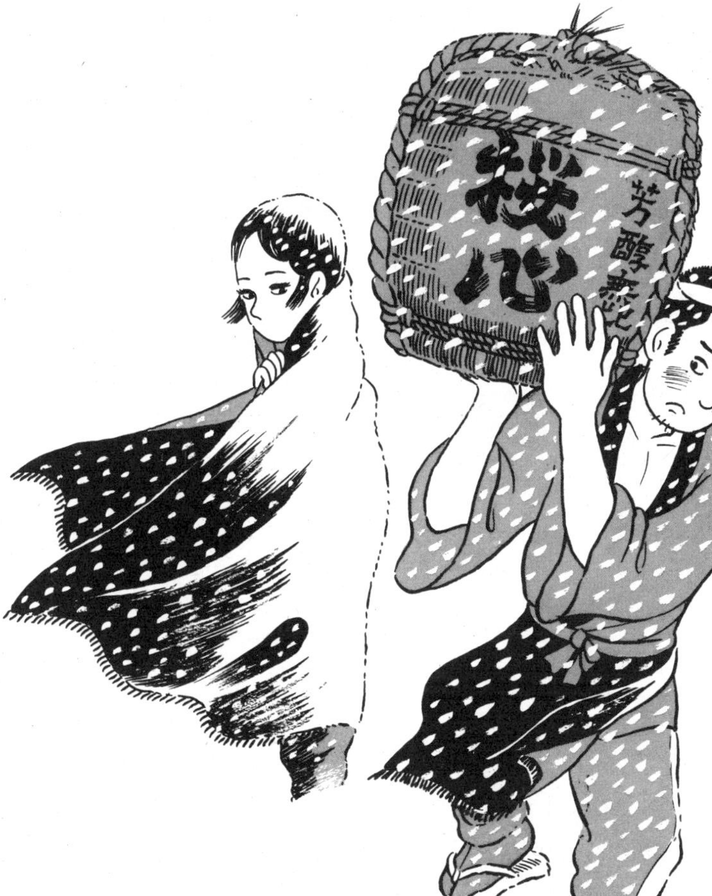
桜心
芳醇

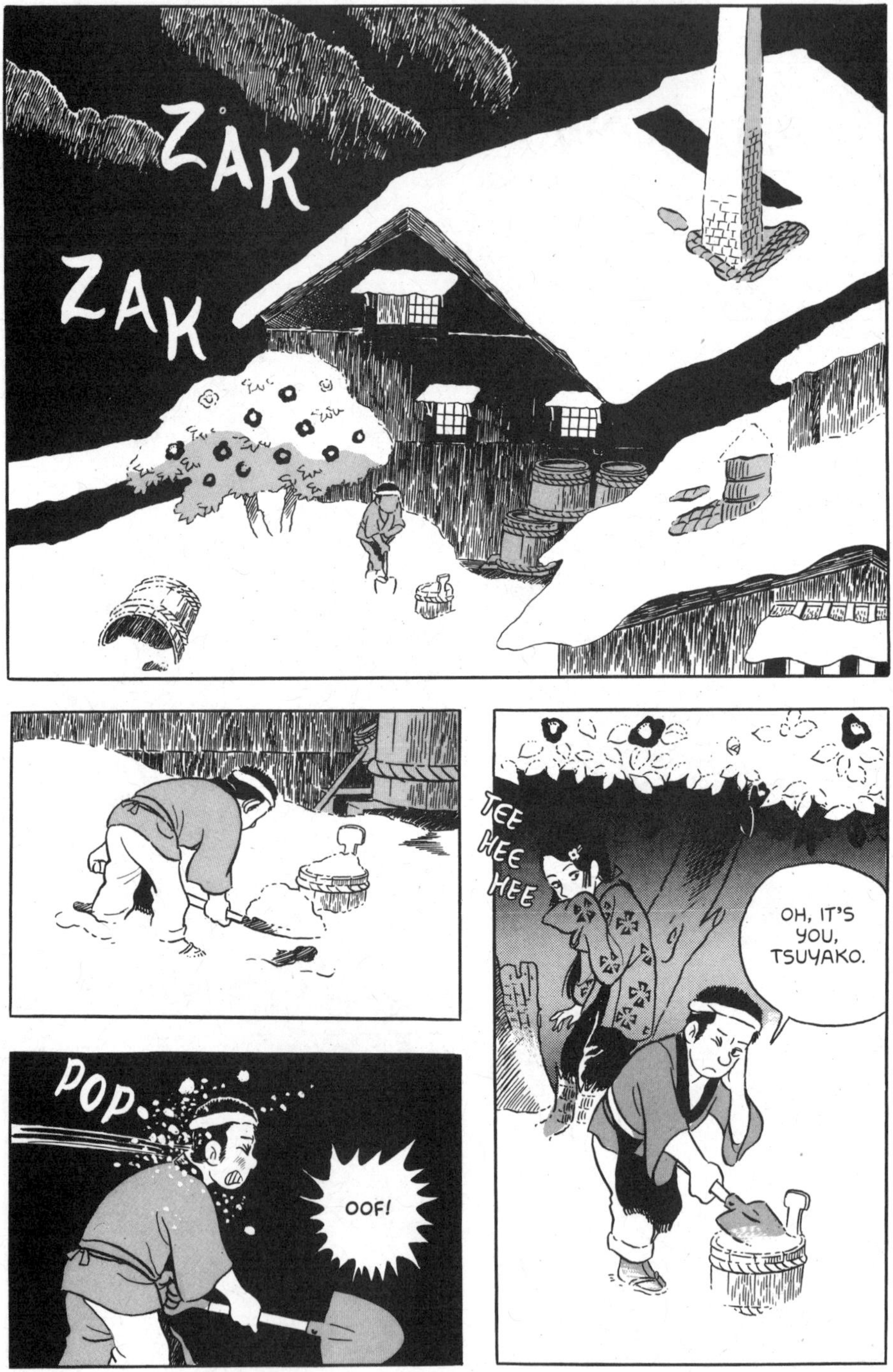
ZAK
ZAK
POP
OOF!
TEE HEE HEE
OH, IT'S YOU, TSUYAKO.

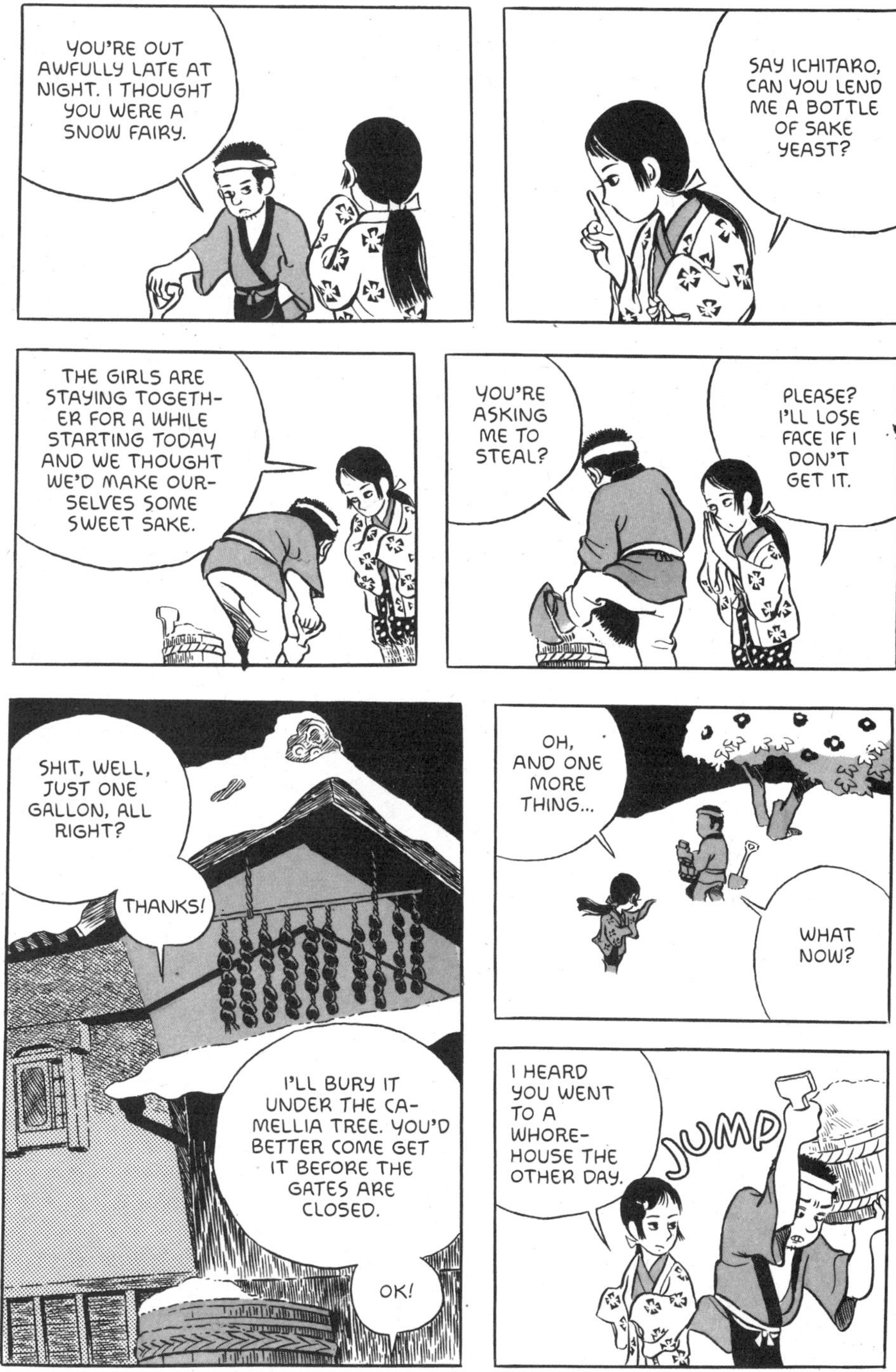
YOU'RE OUT AWFULLY LATE AT NIGHT. I THOUGHT YOU WERE A SNOW FAIRY.
SAY ICHITARO, CAN YOU LEND ME A BOTTLE OF SAKE YEAST?
THE GIRLS ARE STAYING TOGETHER FOR A WHILE STARTING TODAY AND WE THOUGHT WE'D MAKE OURSELVES SOME SWEET SAKE.
YOU'RE ASKING ME TO STEAL?
PLEASE? I'LL LOSE FACE IF I DON'T GET IT.
SHIT, WELL, JUST ONE GALLON, ALL RIGHT?
THANKS!
I'LL BURY IT UNDER THE CAMELLIA TREE. YOU'D BETTER COME GET IT BEFORE THE GATES ARE CLOSED.
OK!
OH, AND ONE MORE THING...
WHAT NOW?
I HEARD YOU WENT TO A WHOREHOUSE THE OTHER DAY.
JUMP

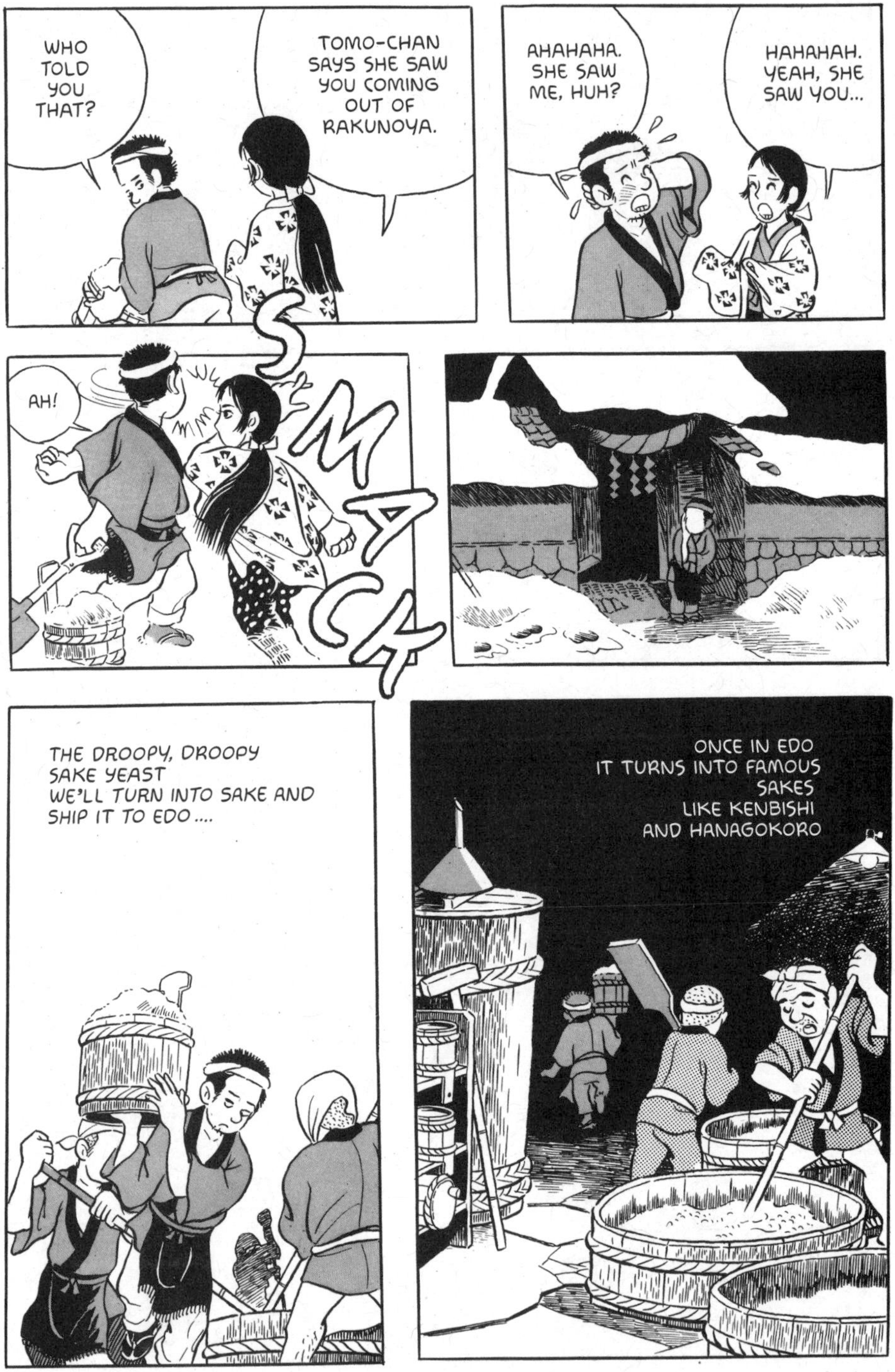
WHO TOLD YOU THAT?
TOMO-CHAN SAYS SHE SAW YOU COMING OUT OF RAKUNOYA.
AHAHAHA. SHE SAW ME, HUH?
HAHAHAH. YEAH, SHE SAW YOU...
AH!
SMACK
THE DROOPY, DROOPY SAKE YEAST WE'LL TURN INTO SAKE AND SHIP IT TO EDO....
ONCE IN EDO IT TURNS INTO FAMOUS SAKES LIKE KENBISHI AND HANAGOKORO

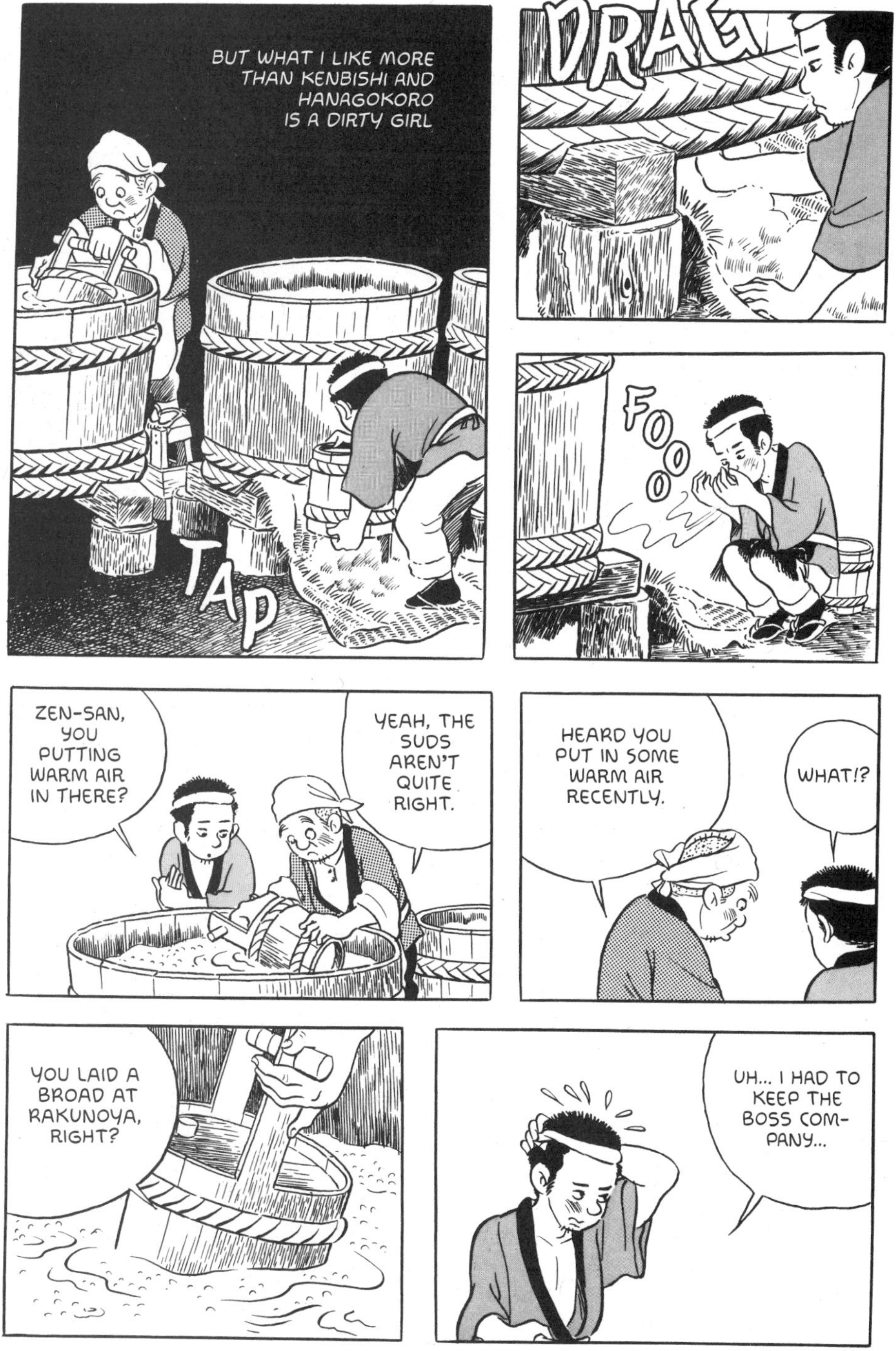
BUT WHAT I LIKE MORE THAN KENBISHI AND HANAGOKORO IS A DIRTY GIRL
TAP
DRAG
FOOOO
ZEN-SAN, YOU PUTTING WARM AIR IN THERE?
YEAH, THE SUDS AREN'T QUITE RIGHT.
HEARD YOU PUT IN SOME WARM AIR RECENTLY.
WHAT!?
YOU LAID A BROAD AT RAKUNOYA, RIGHT?
UH... I HAD TO KEEP THE BOSS COM-PANY...

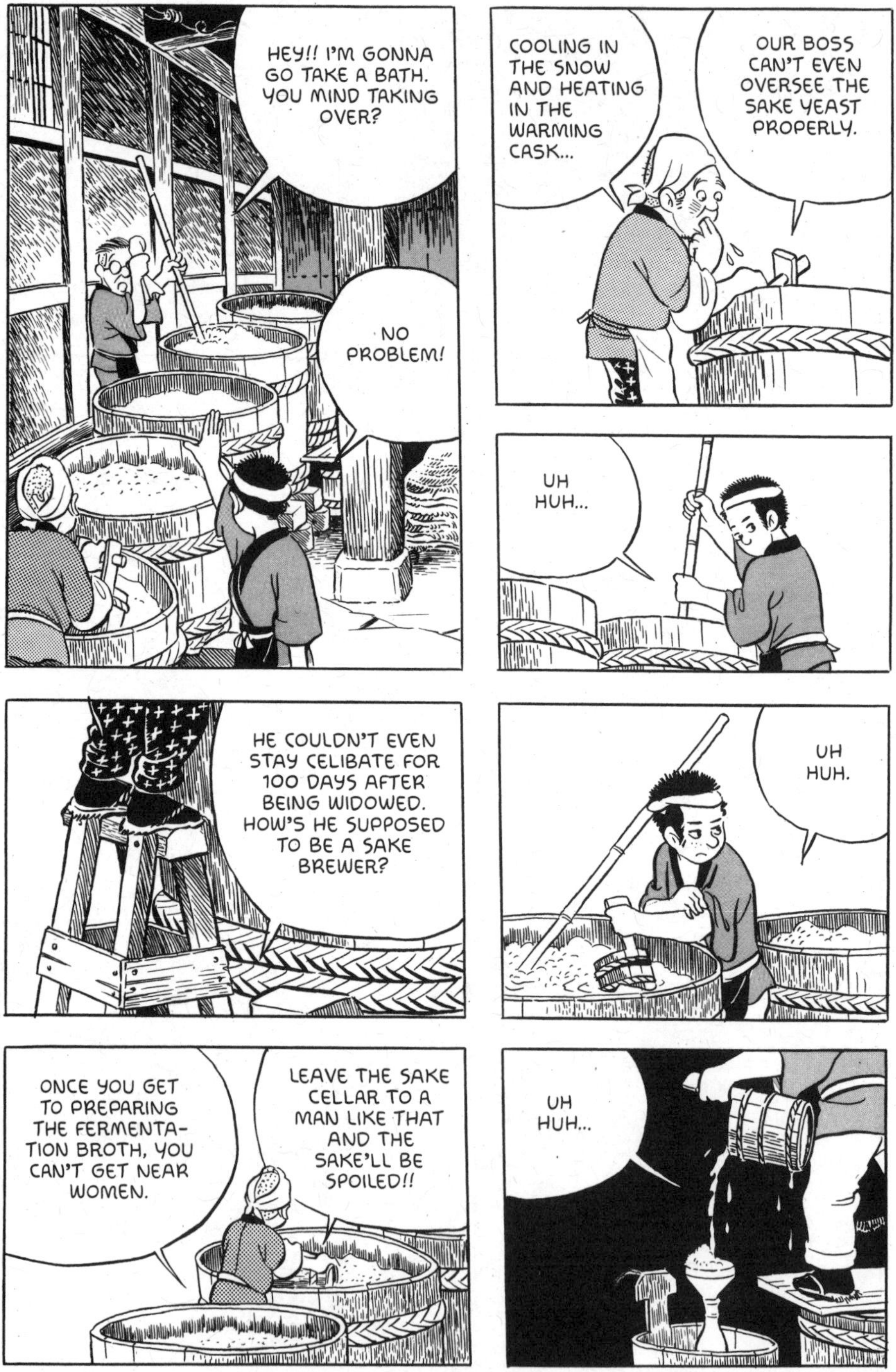
HEY!! I'M GONNA GO TAKE A BATH. YOU MIND TAKING OVER?
NO PROBLEM!
COOLING IN THE SNOW AND HEATING IN THE WARMING CASK...
OUR BOSS CAN'T EVEN OVERSEE THE SAKE YEAST PROPERLY.
UH HUH...
HE COULDN'T EVEN STAY CELIBATE FOR 100 DAYS AFTER BEING WIDOWED. HOW'S HE SUPPOSED TO BE A SAKE BREWER?
UH HUH.
ONCE YOU GET TO PREPARING THE FERMENTATION BROTH, YOU CAN'T GET NEAR WOMEN.
LEAVE THE SAKE CELLAR TO A MAN LIKE THAT AND THE SAKE'LL BE SPOILED!!
UH HUH...

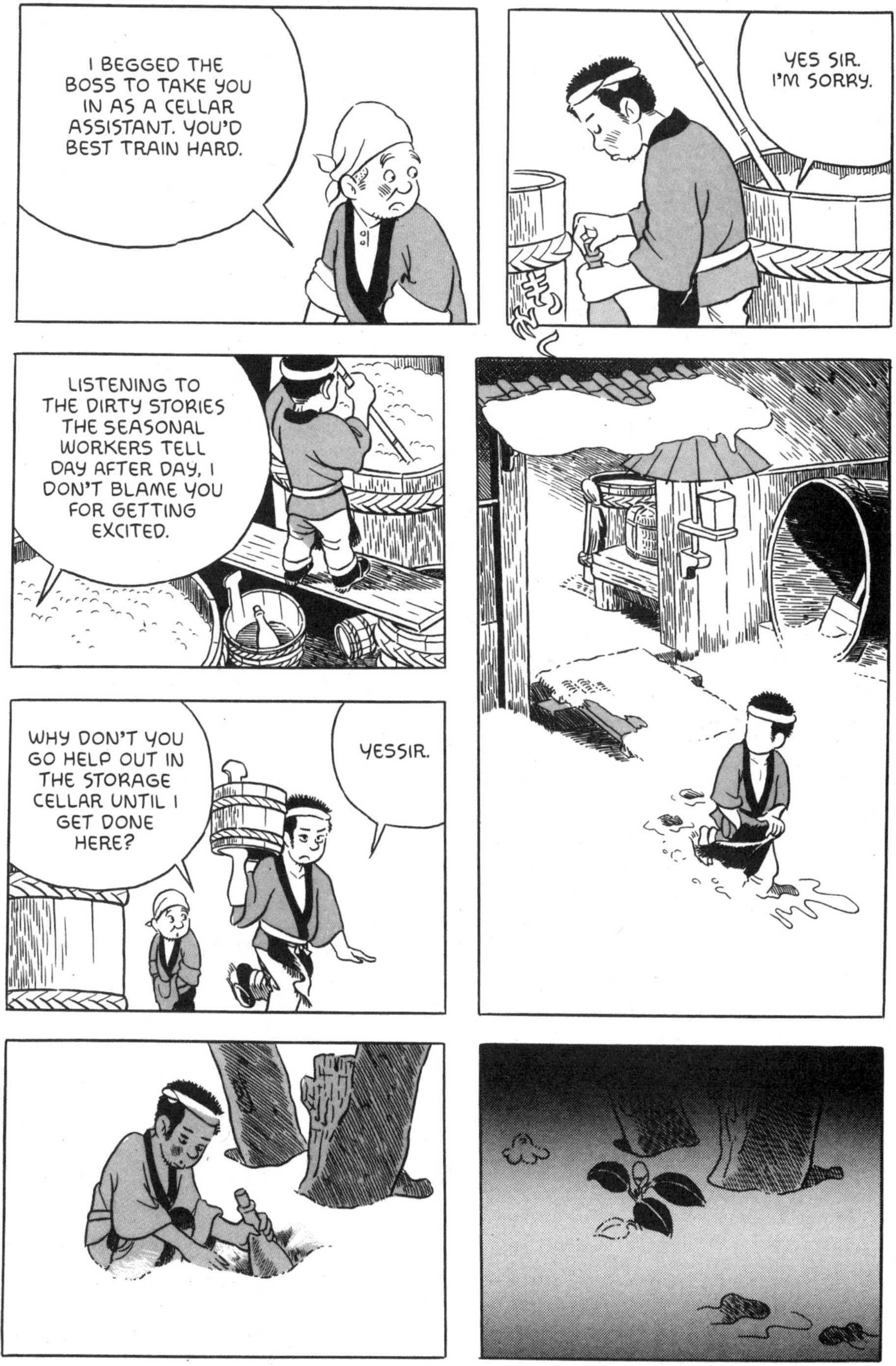
I BEGGED THE BOSS TO TAKE YOU IN AS A CELLAR ASSISTANT. YOU'D BEST TRAIN HARD.
YES SIR. I'M SORRY.
LISTENING TO THE DIRTY STORIES THE SEASONAL WORKERS TELL DAY AFTER DAY, I DON'T BLAME YOU FOR GETTING EXCITED.
WHY DON'T YOU GO HELP OUT IN THE STORAGE CELLAR UNTIL I GET DONE HERE?
YESSIR.

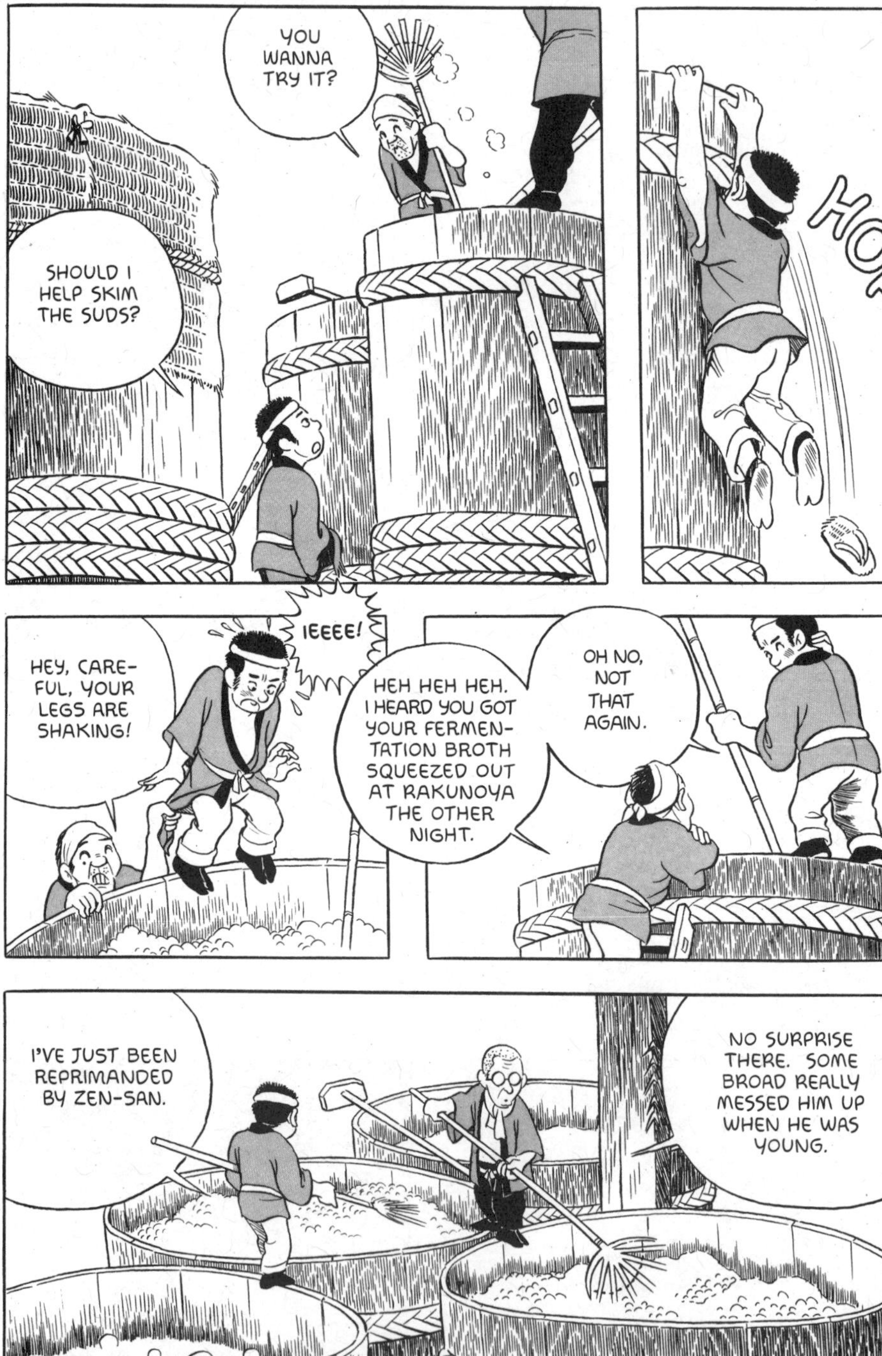
YOU WANNA TRY IT?
SHOULD I HELP SKIM THE SUDS?
HOP
HEY, CAREFUL, YOUR LEGS ARE SHAKING!
IEEEE!
HEH HEH HEH. I HEARD YOU GOT YOUR FERMENTATION BROTH SQUEEZED OUT AT RAKUNOYA THE OTHER NIGHT.
OH NO, NOT THAT AGAIN.
I'VE JUST BEEN REPRIMANDED BY ZEN-SAN.
NO SURPRISE THERE. SOME BROAD REALLY MESSED HIM UP WHEN HE WAS YOUNG.

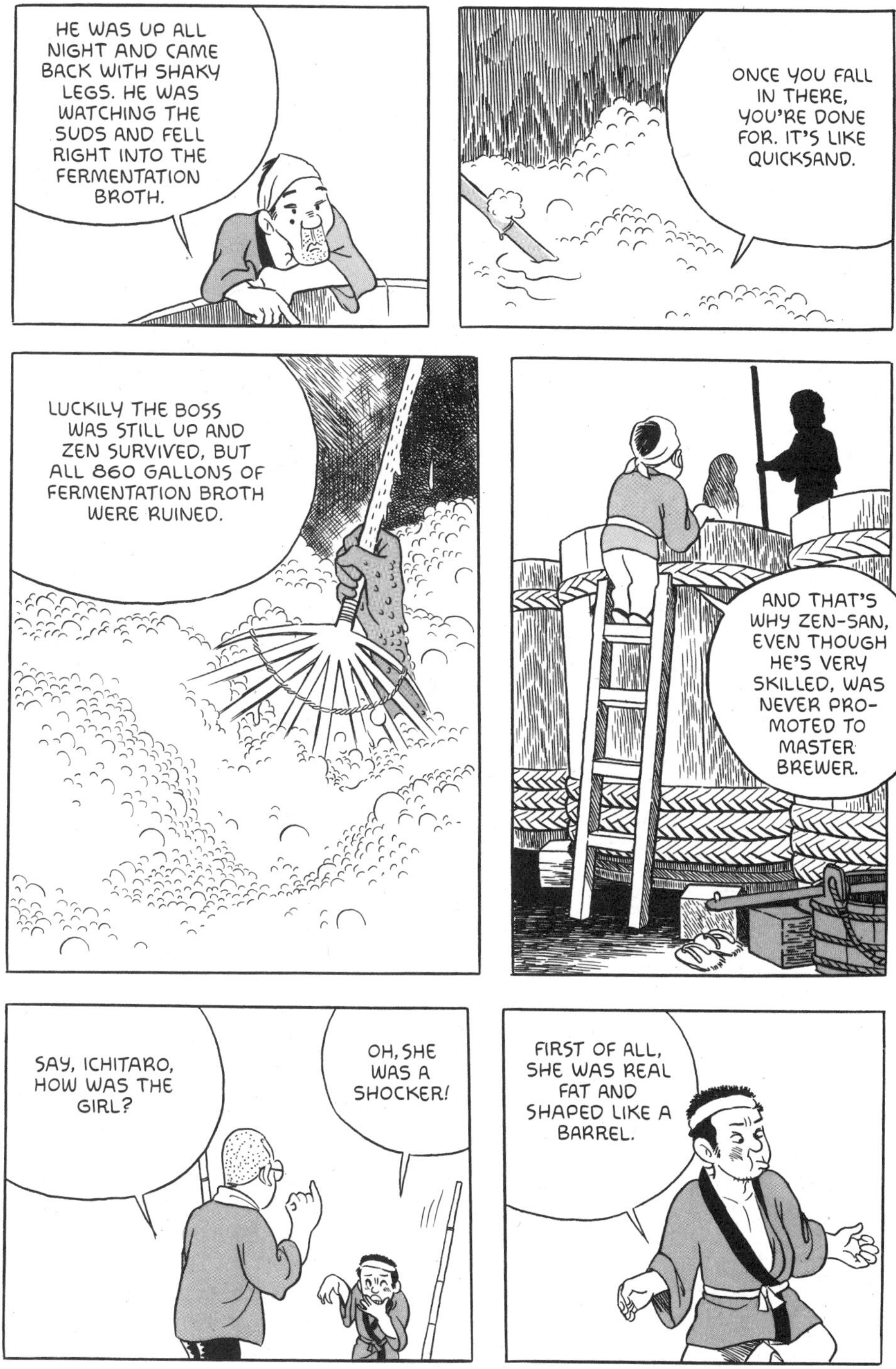
HE WAS UP ALL NIGHT AND CAME BACK WITH SHAKY LEGS. HE WAS WATCHING THE SUDS AND FELL RIGHT INTO THE FERMENTATION BROTH.
ONCE YOU FALL IN THERE, YOU'RE DONE FOR. IT'S LIKE QUICKSAND.
LUCKILY THE BOSS WAS STILL UP AND ZEN SURVIVED, BUT ALL 860 GALLONS OF FERMENTATION BROTH WERE RUINED.
AND THAT'S WHY ZEN-SAN, EVEN THOUGH HE'S VERY SKILLED, WAS NEVER PRO-MOTED TO MASTER BREWER.
SAY, ICHITARO, HOW WAS THE GIRL?
OH, SHE WAS A SHOCKER!
FIRST OF ALL, SHE WAS REAL FAT AND SHAPED LIKE A BARREL.

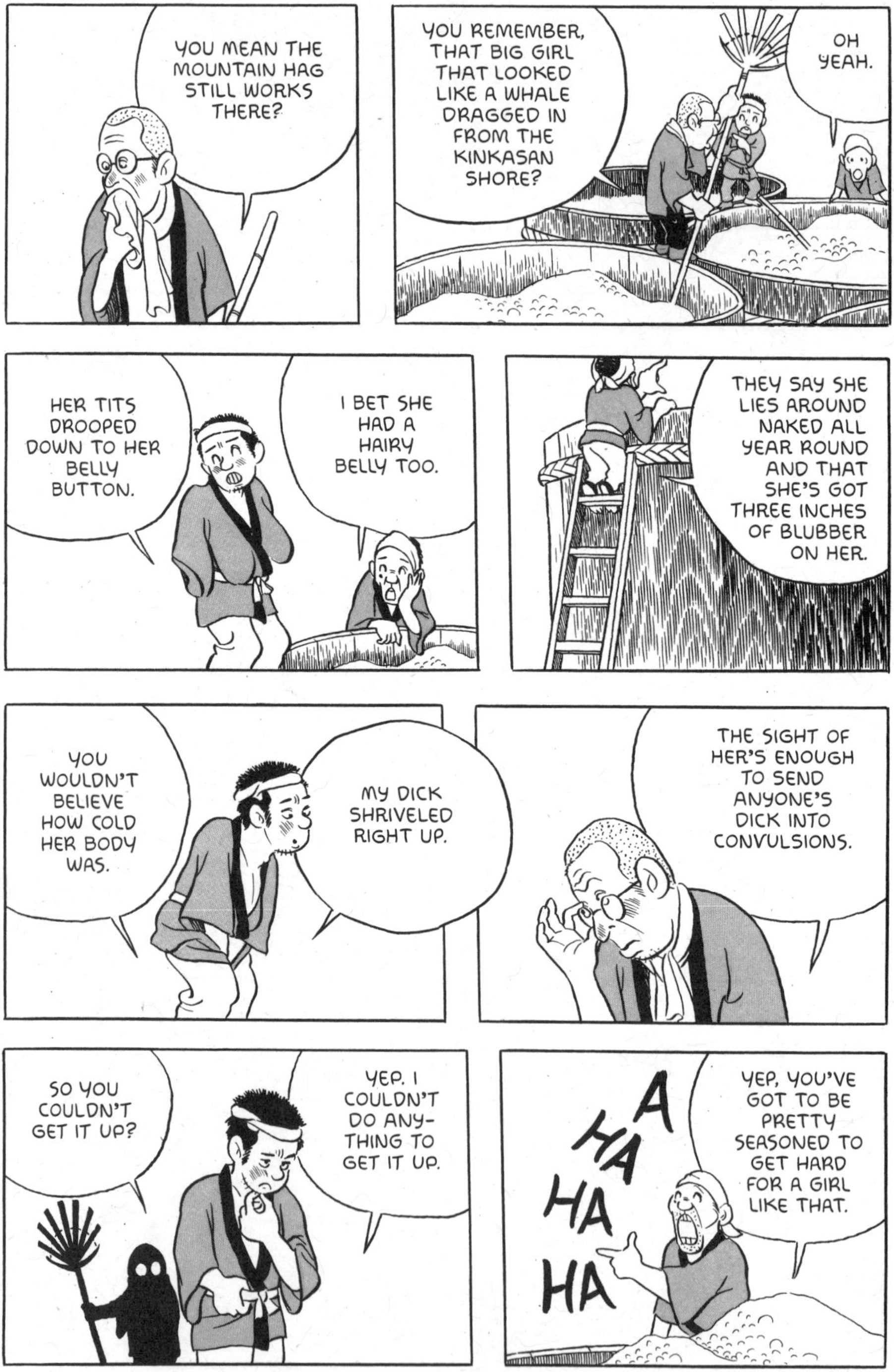
YOU MEAN THE MOUNTAIN HAG STILL WORKS THERE?
YOU REMEMBER, THAT BIG GIRL THAT LOOKED LIKE A WHALE DRAGGED IN FROM THE KINKASAN SHORE?
OH YEAH.
HER TITS DROOPED DOWN TO HER BELLY BUTTON.
I BET SHE HAD A HAIRY BELLY TOO.
THEY SAY SHE LIES AROUND NAKED ALL YEAR ROUND AND THAT SHE'S GOT THREE INCHES OF BLUBBER ON HER.
YOU WOULDN'T BELIEVE HOW COLD HER BODY WAS.
MY DICK SHRIVELED RIGHT UP.
THE SIGHT OF HER'S ENOUGH TO SEND ANYONE'S DICK INTO CONVULSIONS.
SO YOU COULDN'T GET IT UP?
YEP. I COULDN'T DO ANY-THING TO GET IT UP.
A HA HA HA HA
YEP, YOU'VE GOT TO BE PRETTY SEASONED TO GET HARD FOR A GIRL LIKE THAT.

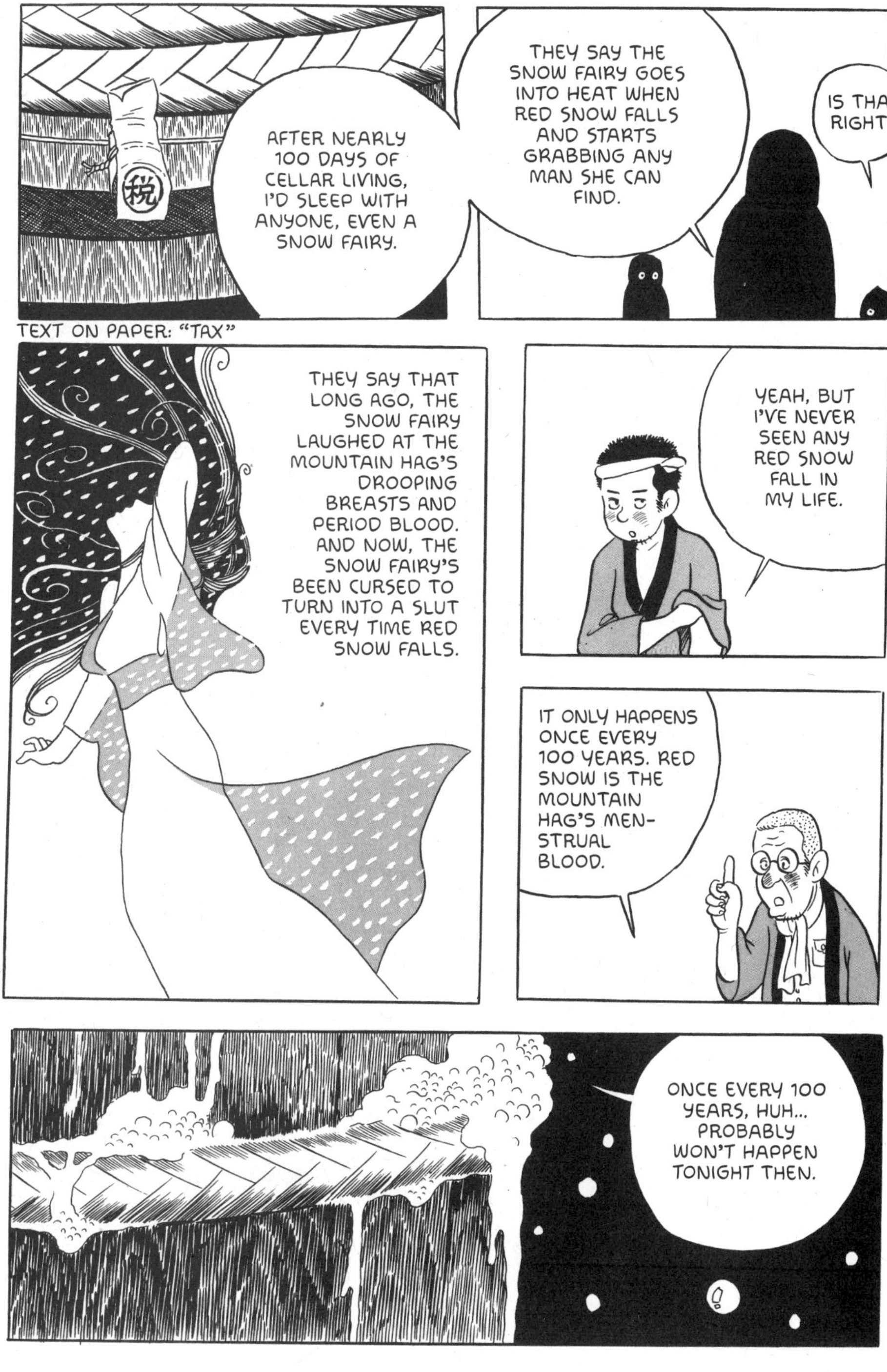
AFTER NEARLY 100 DAYS OF CELLAR LIVING, I'D SLEEP WITH ANYONE, EVEN A SNOW FAIRY.
THEY SAY THE SNOW FAIRY GOES INTO HEAT WHEN RED SNOW FALLS AND STARTS GRABBING ANY MAN SHE CAN FIND.
IS THAT RIGHT?
TEXT ON PAPER: "TAX"
THEY SAY THAT LONG AGO, THE SNOW FAIRY LAUGHED AT THE MOUNTAIN HAG'S DROOPING BREASTS AND PERIOD BLOOD. AND NOW, THE SNOW FAIRY'S BEEN CURSED TO TURN INTO A SLUT EVERY TIME RED SNOW FALLS.
YEAH, BUT I'VE NEVER SEEN ANY RED SNOW FALL IN MY LIFE.
IT ONLY HAPPENS ONCE EVERY 100 YEARS. RED SNOW IS THE MOUNTAIN HAG'S MEN-STRUAL BLOOD.
ONCE EVERY 100 YEARS, HUH... PROBABLY WON'T HAPPEN TONIGHT THEN.

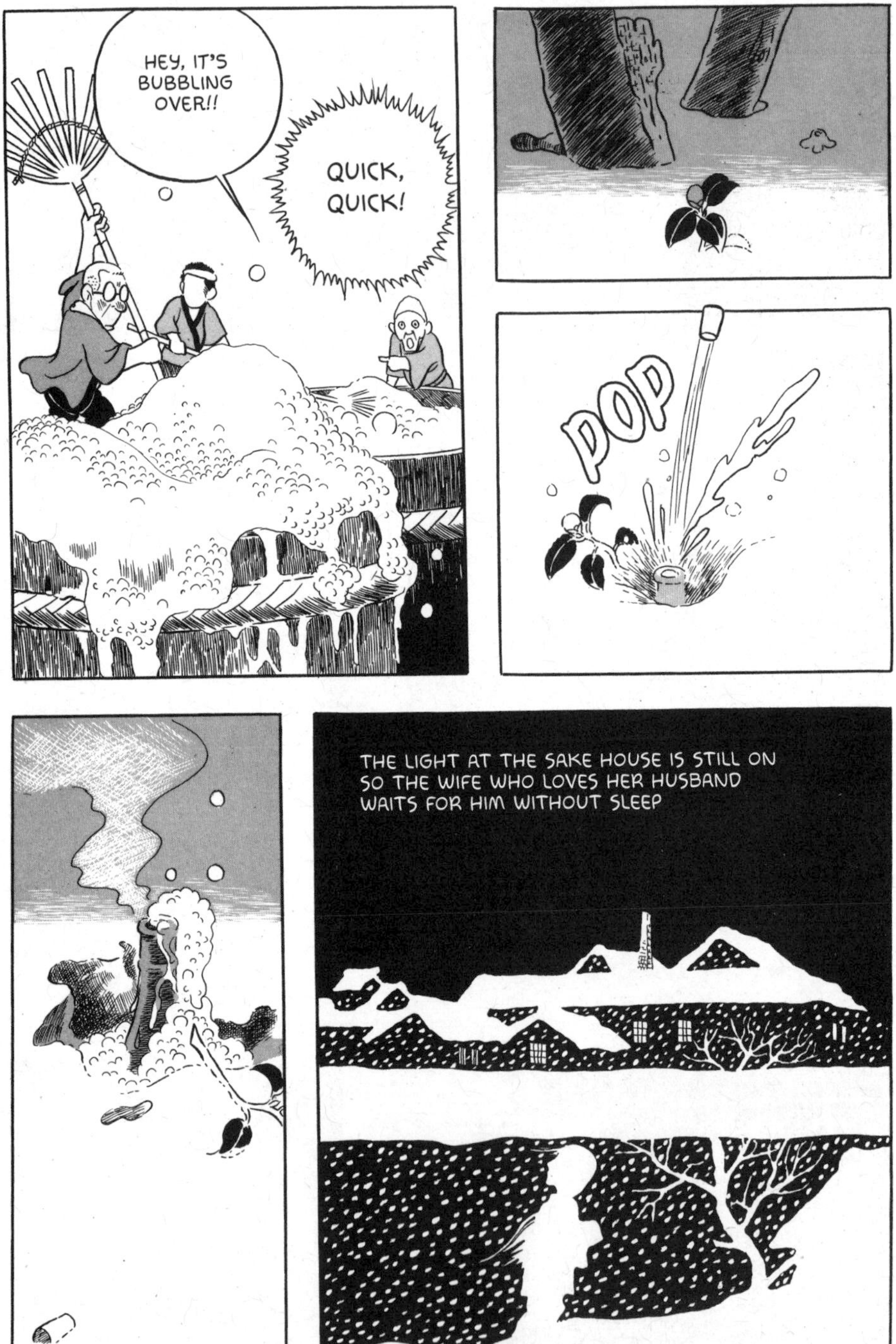
HEY, IT'S BUBBLING OVER!!
QUICK, QUICK!
POP
THE LIGHT AT THE SAKE HOUSE IS STILL ON SO THE WIFE WHO LOVES HER HUSBAND WAITS FOR HIM WITHOUT SLEEP

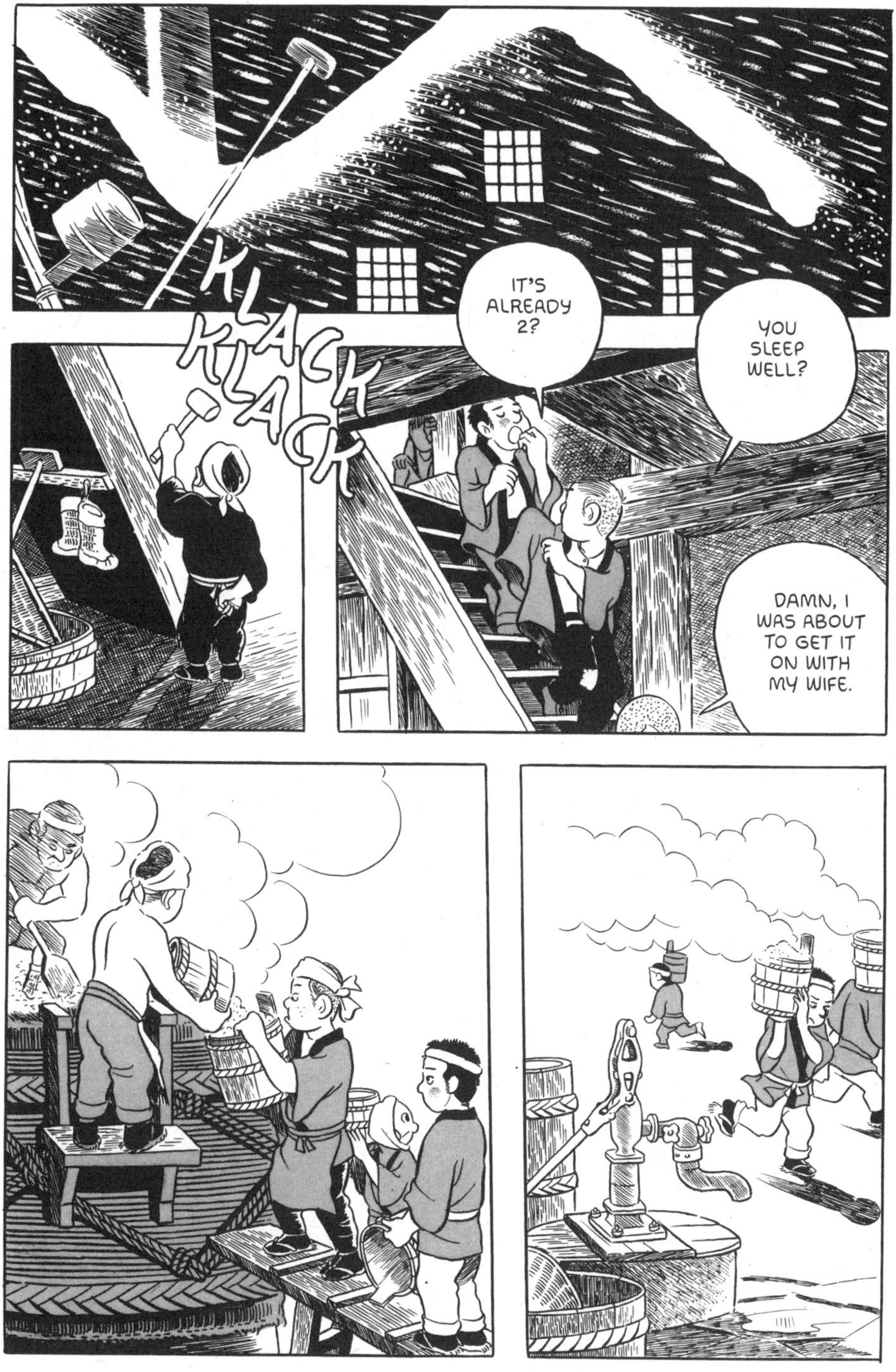
KLACK KLACK
IT'S ALREADY 2?
YOU SLEEP WELL?
DAMN, I WAS ABOUT TO GET IT ON WITH MY WIFE.

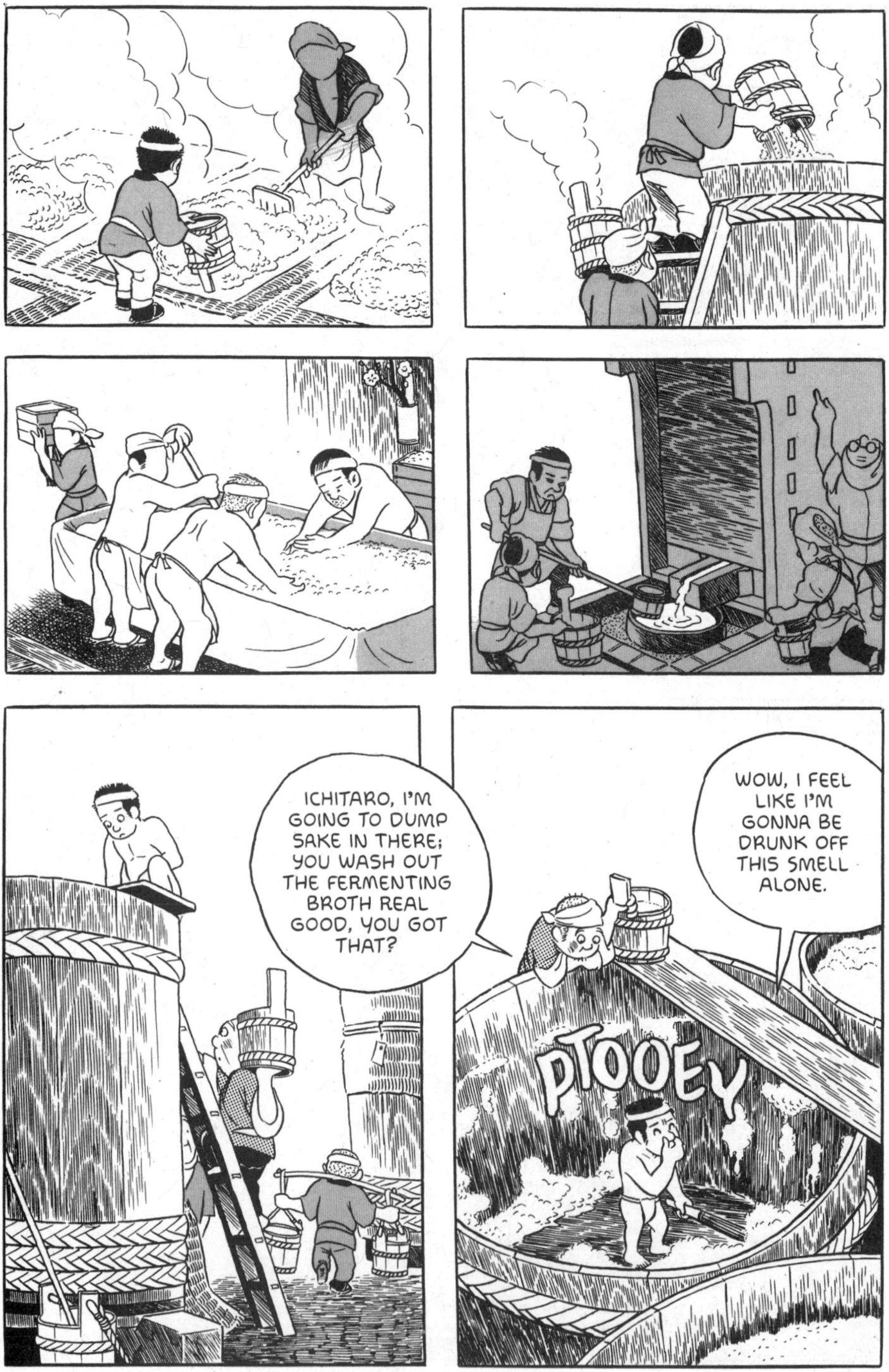
ICHITARO, I'M GOING TO DUMP SAKE IN THERE; YOU WASH OUT THE FERMENTING BROTH REAL GOOD, YOU GOT THAT?
WOW, I FEEL LIKE I'M GONNA BE DRUNK OFF THIS SMELL ALONE.
PTOOEY

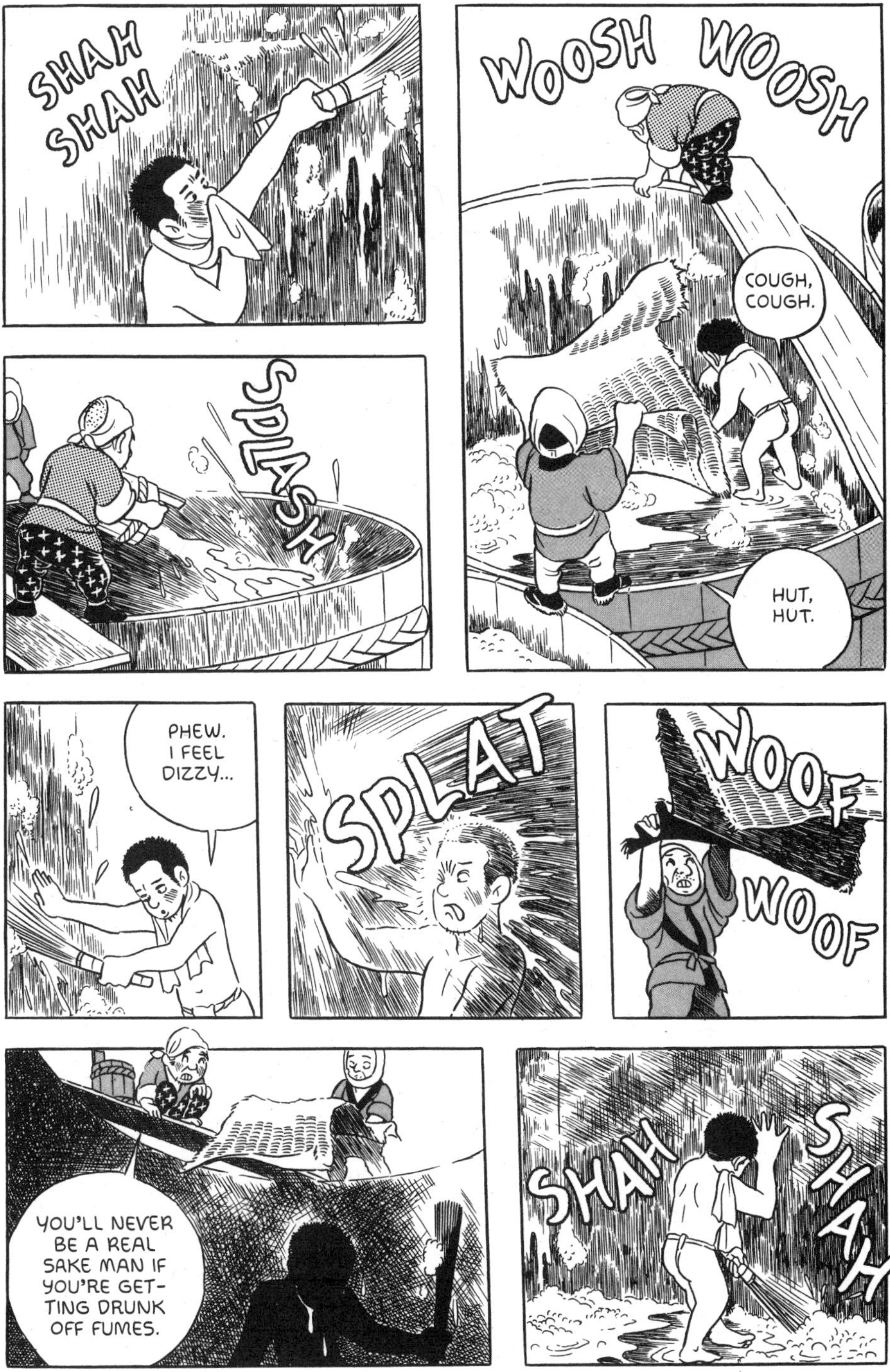
SHAH SHAH
WOOSH WOOSH
COUGH, COUGH.
SPLASH
HUT, HUT.
PHEW. I FEEL DIZZY...
SPLAT
WOOF WOOF
YOU'LL NEVER BE A REAL SAKE MAN IF YOU'RE GETTING DRUNK OFF FUMES.
SHAH SHAH

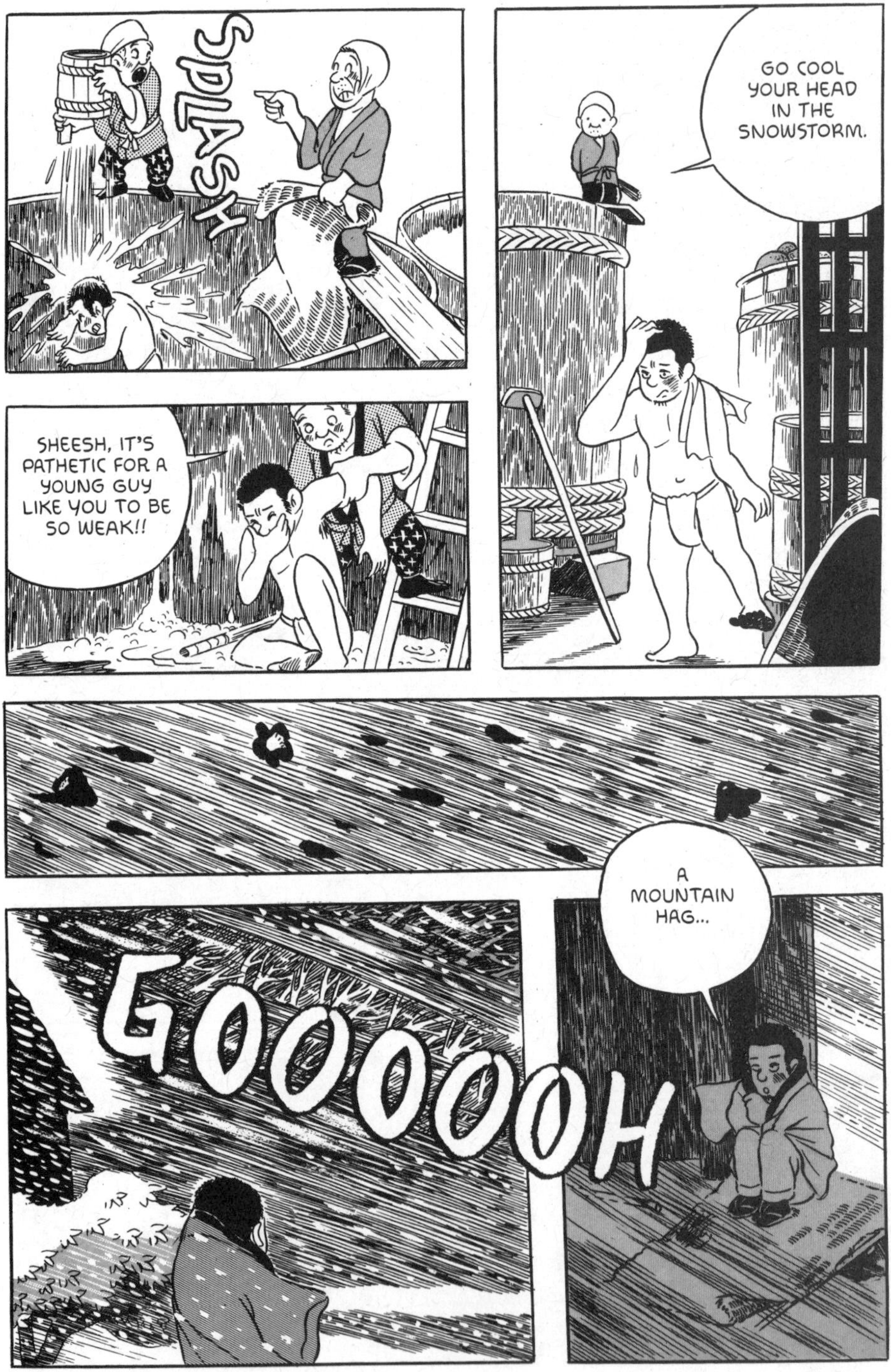
SPLASH
GO COOL YOUR HEAD IN THE SNOWSTORM.
SHEESH, IT'S PATHETIC FOR A YOUNG GUY LIKE YOU TO BE SO WEAK!!
GOOOOOOH
A MOUNTAIN HAG...

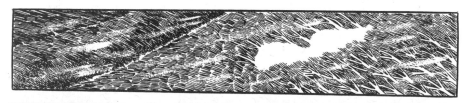

GOOOOOH

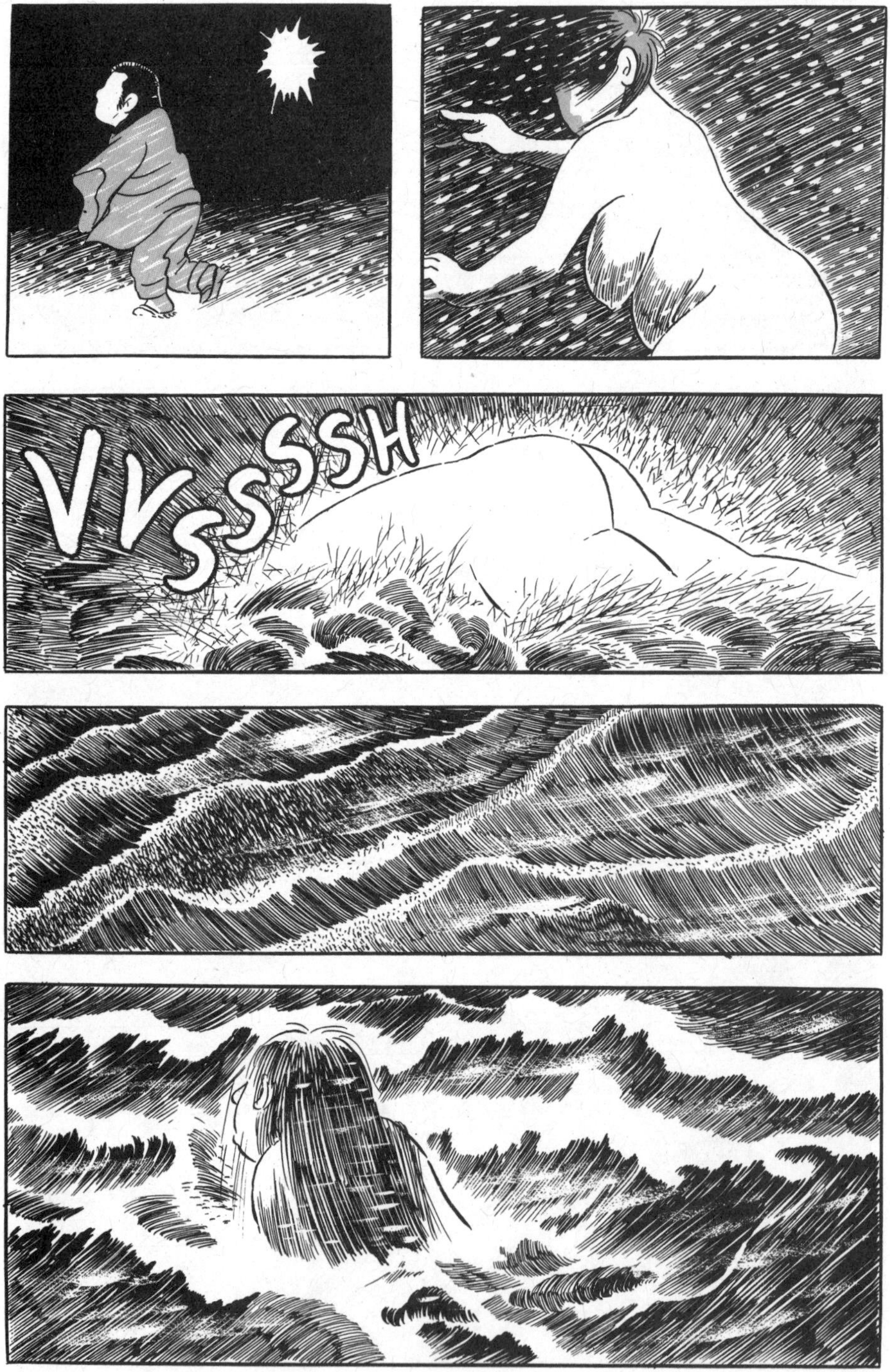
VVSSSSSH

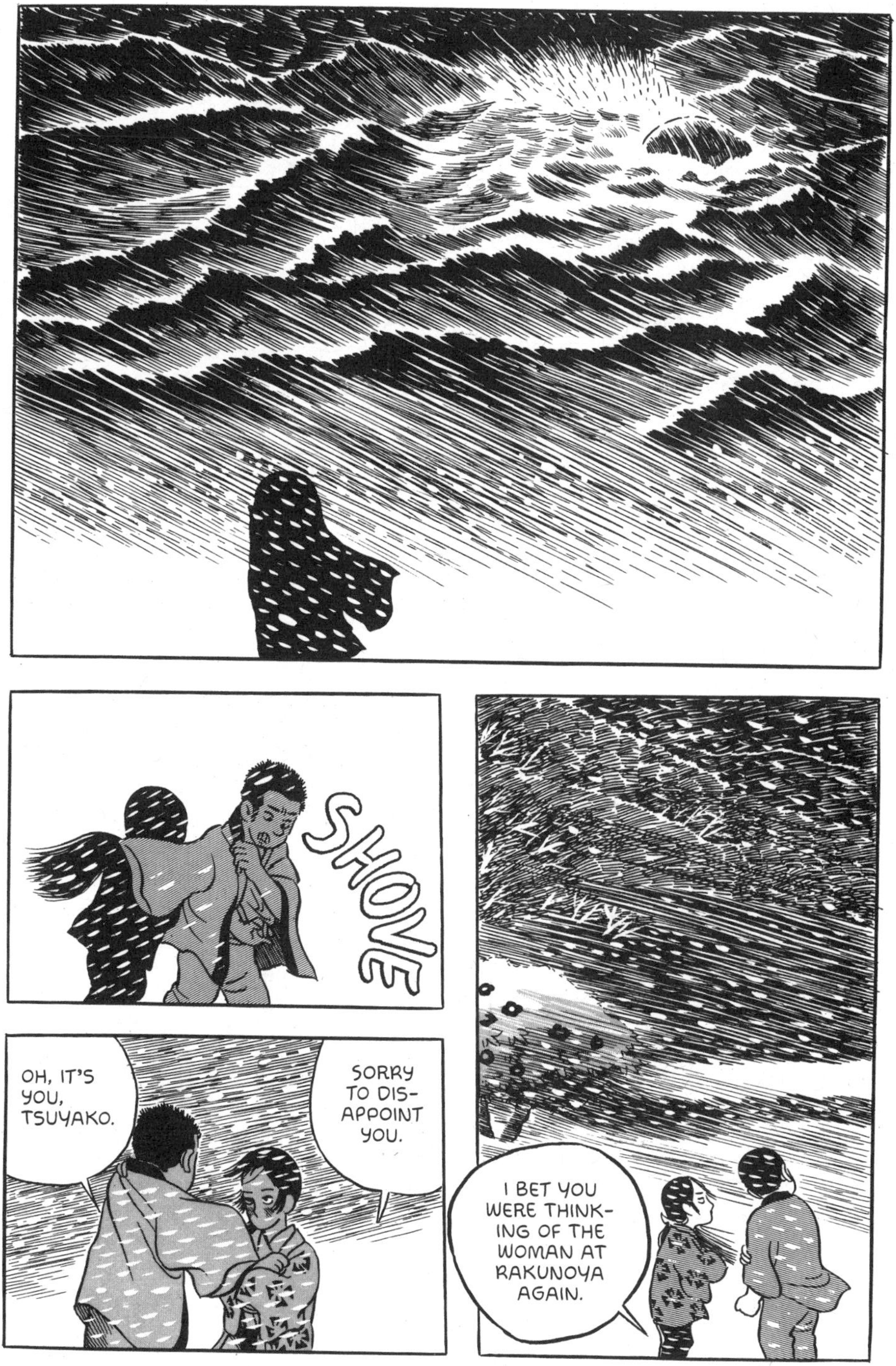
SHOVE
OH, IT'S YOU, TSUYAKO.
SORRY TO DIS-APPOINT YOU.
I BET YOU WERE THINKING OF THE WOMAN AT RAKUNOYA AGAIN.

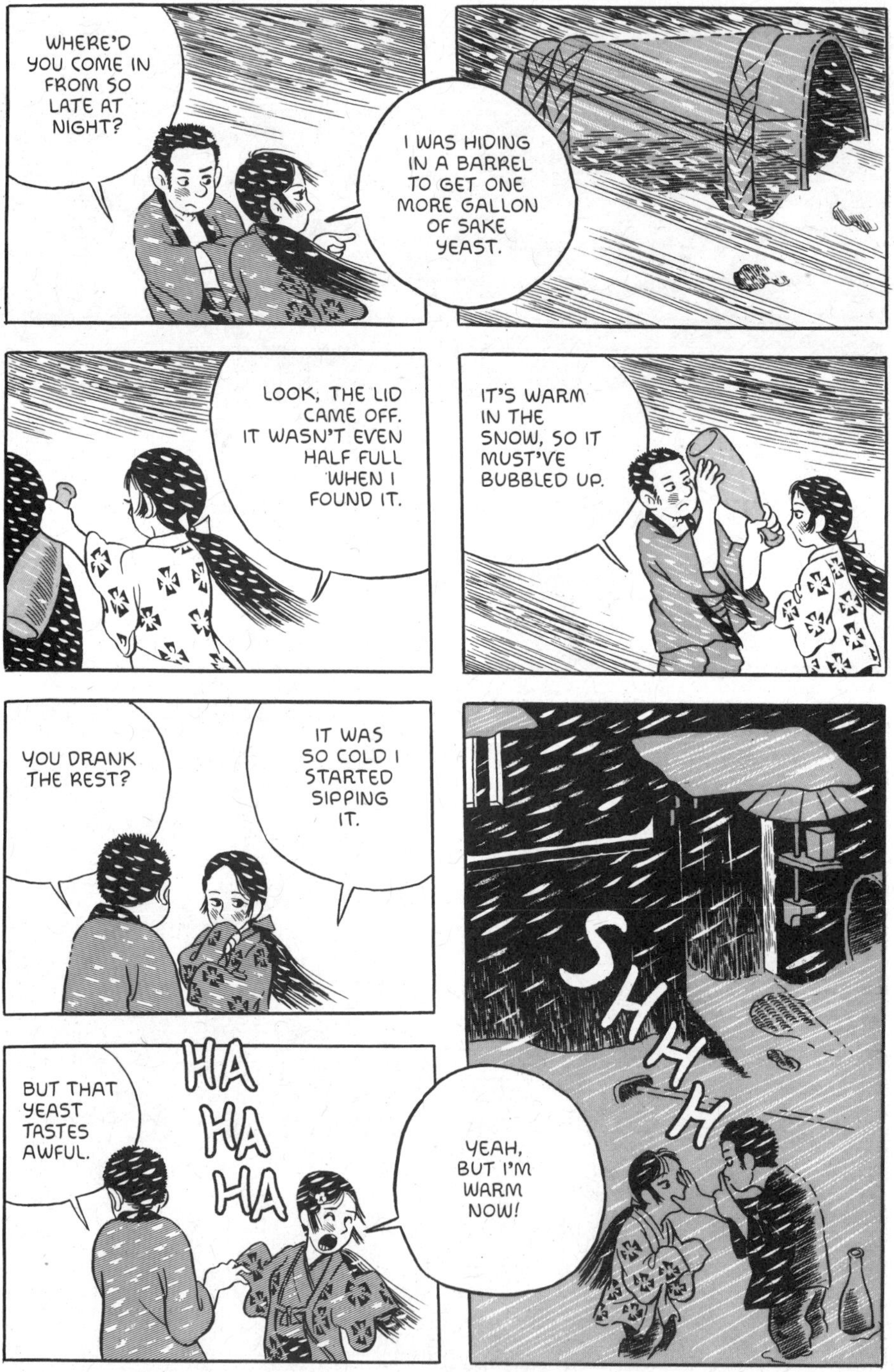
WHERE'D YOU COME IN FROM SO LATE AT NIGHT?
I WAS HIDING IN A BARREL TO GET ONE MORE GALLON OF SAKE YEAST.
LOOK, THE LID CAME OFF. IT WASN'T EVEN HALF FULL WHEN I FOUND IT.
IT'S WARM IN THE SNOW, SO IT MUST'VE BUBBLED UP.
YOU DRANK THE REST?
IT WAS SO COLD I STARTED SIPPING IT.
BUT THAT YEAST TASTES AWFUL.
HA HA HA
YEAH, BUT I'M WARM NOW!
SHHHH

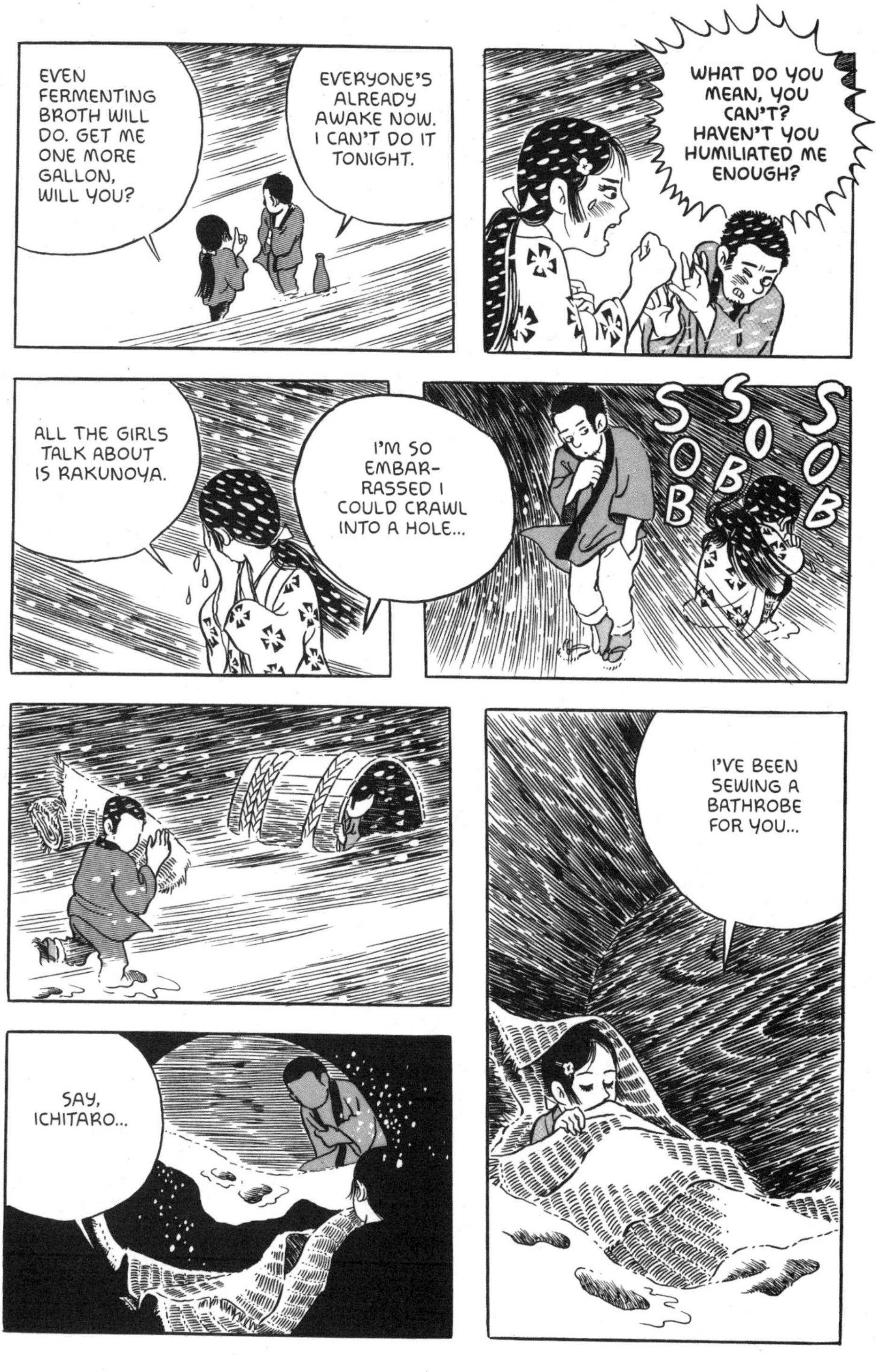
EVEN FERMENTING BROTH WILL DO. GET ME ONE MORE GALLON, WILL YOU?
EVERYONE'S ALREADY AWAKE NOW. I CAN'T DO IT TONIGHT.
WHAT DO YOU MEAN, YOU CAN'T? HAVEN'T YOU HUMILIATED ME ENOUGH?
ALL THE GIRLS TALK ABOUT IS RAKUNOYA.
I'M SO EMBAR-RASSED I COULD CRAWL INTO A HOLE...
SOB SOB SOB
SAY, ICHITARO...
I'VE BEEN SEWING A BATHROBE FOR YOU...

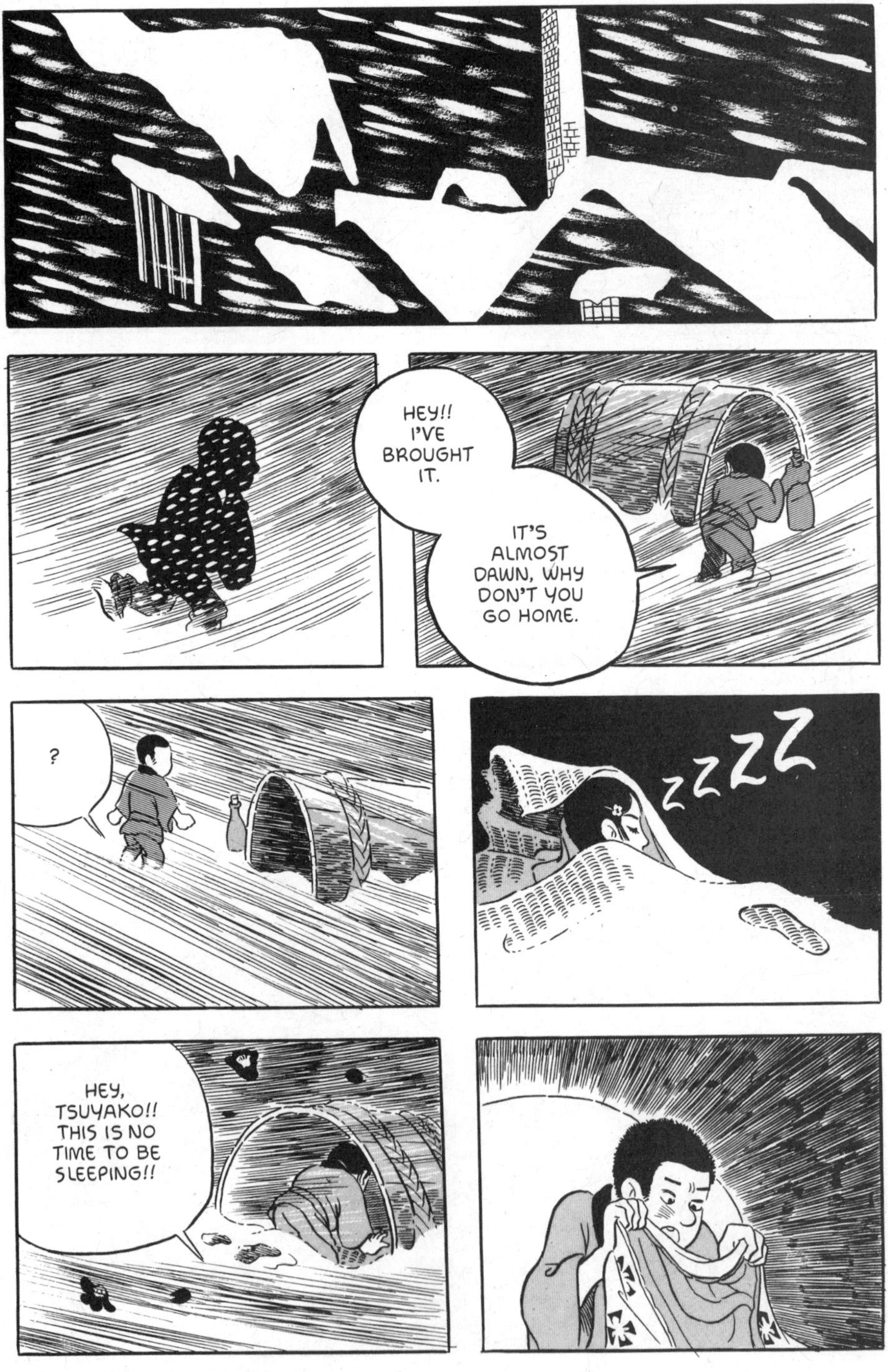
HEY!! I'VE BROUGHT IT.
IT'S ALMOST DAWN, WHY DON'T YOU GO HOME.
?
ZZZZZ
HEY, TSUYAKO!! THIS IS NO TIME TO BE SLEEPING!!

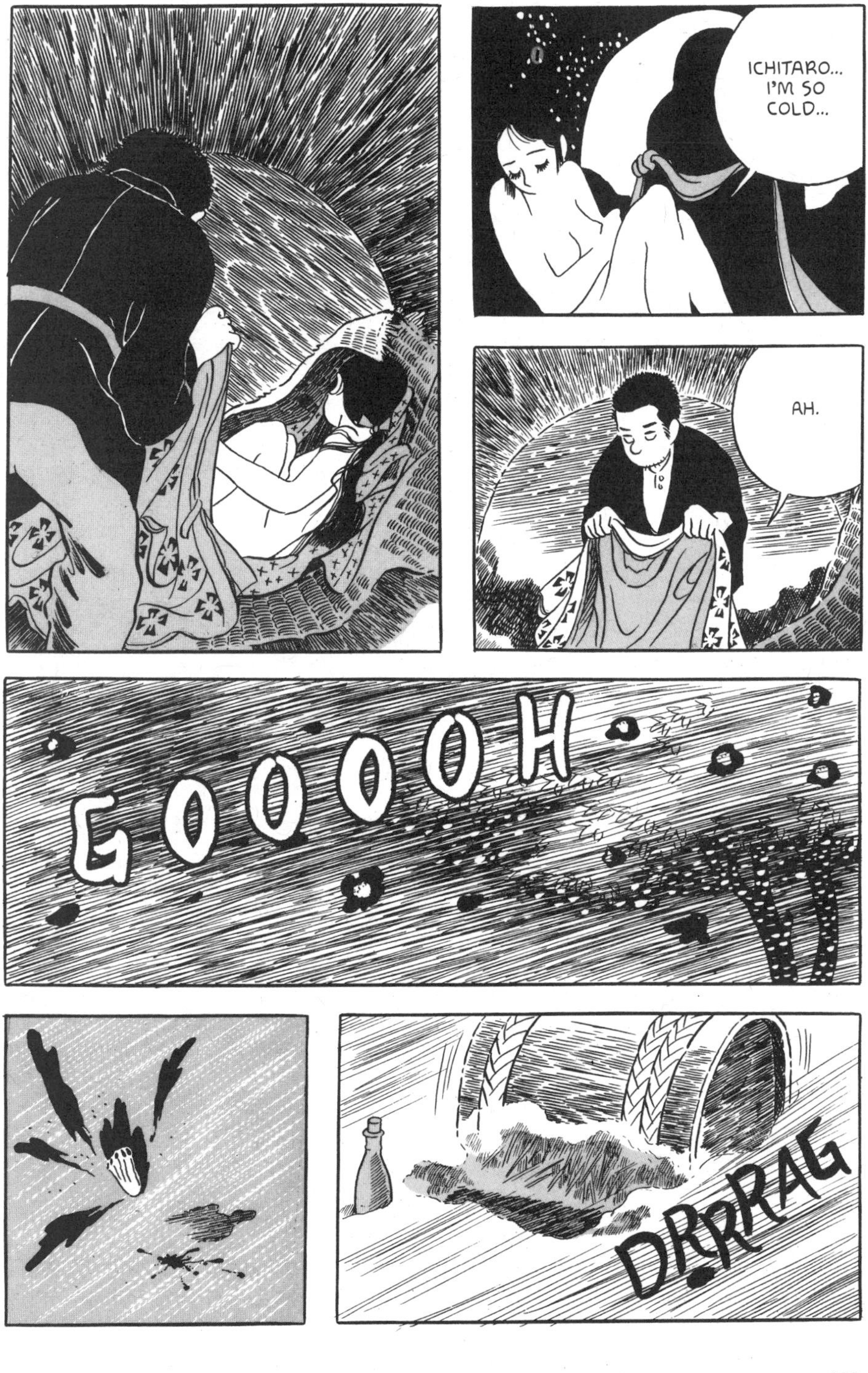
ICHITARO... I'M SO COLD...
AH.
GOOOOOH
DRRRAG

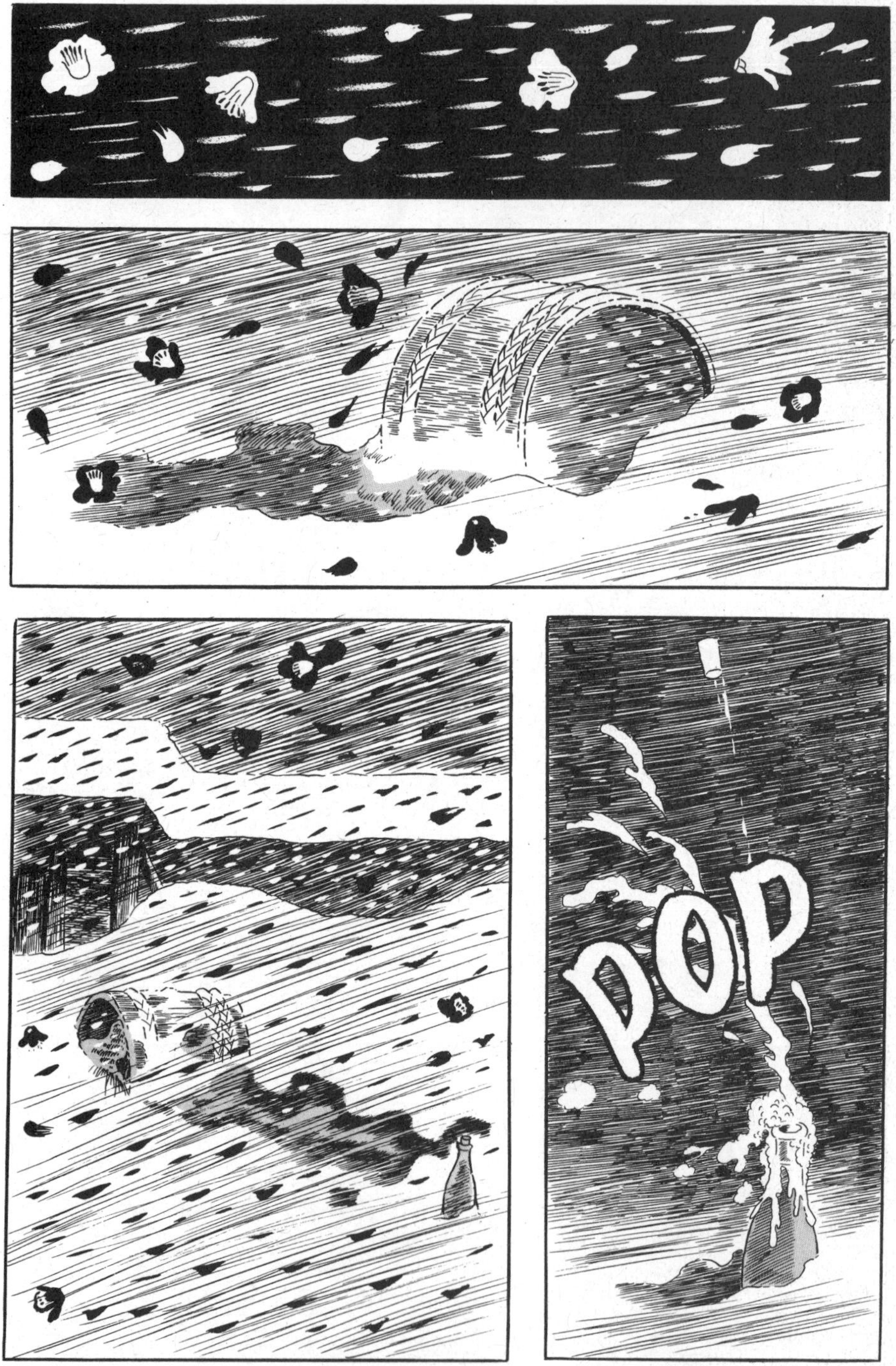
POP

AN INTERVIEW WITH SUSUMU KATSUMATA

Conducted by Seirinkogeisha editor Mitsuhiro Asakawa on the release of the Japanese edition of *Red Snow*, November 10, 2005.

Mitsuhiro Asakawa: Your short stories are being collected as a single volume for the first time in many years with *Red Snow*. I went over the chronology of the book and your career with the goal of getting at the big picture. First of all, your debut: you're known as a four-panel comic artist and I believe your first piece in *Garo* was a four-panel comic.

Susumu Katsumata: Yes, that's right.

MA: Originally, you weren't just drawing four-panel comics, though.

SK: Yes, there were some pretty long pieces in the things I was drawing in elementary school or after that when I started working.

MA: You drew a *manga* about an orphan, called "King of the Forest," during elementary school.

SK: It's the story of a boy living with the animals (laughs). The story was kind of directionless. Accompanied by his animal friends, the protagonist happens across his real father, who turns out to be Nagamasa Yamada, a great samurai! That's sort of an embarrassing story (laughs). I think I copied the animals like the chipmunks and deer from Osamu Tezuka.

MA: I was a bit shocked when suddenly the "real father" appeared. Mr. Katsumata, you were raised from childhood without knowing your father; your mother told you that your father had died. She passed away when you were six, and from then on, you were raised by your older sister.

SK: That's right. I was drawing this kind of *manga* when I was in Grade 5 or 6, a while after my mother passed away.

MA: So how did you first encounter *manga*?

SK: In magazines. I used to read *Omoshiro Book* and *BokenOh*. I also borrowed Shogakukan's learning

series from my friend and I loved Eiichi Fukui's "Chibi Tengu" (Editor's note: Incomplete work serialized in *Shogakko Yonnensei* from April 1953 to March 1954 and in *Shogakko Gonensei* from April to August 1954). I mean, he could fly! If the hero was an orphan or something, of course I liked that too. Also Hifumi Yamane and Shigeru Sugiura. I loved Shigeru Sugiura.

MA: What kind of meaning does the word "hometown" have for you?

SK: Well…I guess it's not just fond memories. For a long time, I didn't want to go back there. There were some unpleasant bits. But the smell of the mountains and the trees in the forest, picking *akebia* and flowers, gathering chestnuts, bracken—I have so many memories like this. So of course I feel some nostalgia, but it's not that simple.

MA: Were you the type who was always playing with friends, or were you more of a loner?

SK: I had a lot of friends at school, but I didn't have time for playing.

MA: Because you were helping at home?

SK: After school, I had to go home pretty early and help with the work there. There was no staying late and playing baseball with everyone else or anything like that.

MA: You said that you were raised not knowing your father. Your mother also passed away early, and you were taken in by your older sister—this kind of experience must have had a huge effect on you. You found out your father's name when you were in high school; he was still alive at the time.

SK: Yes. But I learned this indirectly from the talk of the adults around me before I started high school.

MA: You majored in nuclear physics at the Tokyo University of Education. Didn't you consider continuing on into research?

SK: Part of me wanted to continue, but I gradually

came to understand that continuing with research would be very difficult. Without financial backing, you can only go so far. Of course, I had also come to see the limits of my own abilities. Although I've always been able to lock myself up and work on something alone (laughs)! Around that time, someone asked me what the purpose of studying was, and I had my doubts there too. I was meeting different people and going to demonstrations and so on.

MA: So there was also the activity in the student movement of the time.

SK: I don't think it was unrelated. The general feeling was that it was almost embarrassing to graduate from university.

MA: Now this is much later, but you gave a lecture on the topic "*Ninja Bugeicho* and the Flow of Life" at Furukawa Industrial High School, your alma mater (1986). That's an extremely interesting theme, and I thought you must have been an admirer of Shirato's works for quite some time.

SK: I started reading him after finding *Garo*. *Ninja Bugeicho* shares some things with Osamu Tezuka's *Phoenix*, you know. I find they are quite connected in terms of the depth of their ideas. In *Phoenix*, there is the theme of human civilization being a borrowed form. In the Greece volume, in the Karma volume, the human drama itself is not so different. And I can feel this a little in some places in *Ninja Bugeicho* as well. Kagemaru will die over and over…but even when the body is destroyed, someone will definitely appear to carry on his purpose. And there's Iwana, Zoroku's underling. How did he end up living in the water? Here, too, the explanation is that the history of human evolution was reversed and organs from when we were fish were resurrected. And again, you're made to feel the flow of existence.

MA: So you didn't pick up Shirato's work until you were an adult?

SK: That's right. Around the time I was working at the company, I was drawing pictures of ninjas in the dorm, and this was the type of work I brought when I went to *Garo* for the first time. Mizuki came into Seirindo's Editorial Department, and I blush to think of it now, but Mr. Nagai and Mr. Mizuki both looked at my work. It's embarrassing (laughs). I also brought some four-panel comics, and Mr. Nagai told me, "The

four-panel comics are better."

MA: What were the four-panel comics like?

SK: Really bad (laughs). I thought at the time that that was what four-panel comic pictures should be like.

MA: Relatively simple lines.

SK: Yes.

MA: After that, the first short story you drew was "*Kapparo*", for your own special issue of *Garo*.

SK: I think I felt like taking a little risk.

MA: Your four-panel comics stepped away from the orthodox style of introduction, development, turn and conclusion; they were drawn with a freer hand. They left a strange lingering note, somehow like haiku. "Burial" placed a four-panel comic in the middle of a detailed drawing of scenery using a two-page spread. So I feel like even in your four-panel comics, there were already the signs of your later short stories.

SK: It's true that I wanted to draw pictures around the time I drew "Burial." It was likely Mr. Tsuge's influence. I wanted to try drawing this sort of persuasive picture. This probably developed into the short stories.

MA: After that, while drawing four-panel comics for a variety of places, you began to release short stories mainly in *Garo*. For example, the piece "Winter Sea (*Fuyu no Umi*)" (*Garo*, April 1971). Was this work related to your own upbringing?

SK: Yes, it was. I wanted to draw my mother in that piece. I was having a really hard time then emotionally. And there was also my struggle over whether or not to quit university.

MA: That was the year you got married, wasn't it? So, was it a case of trying to face yourself?

SK: Right. In the end, I think drawing is a good thing. Right now, I'm undergoing homeopathic treatment for an illness. Homeopathy came out of Germany about two hundred years ago, with a philosophy of "treat like with like." In short, you drink a heavily diluted solution, almost to zero percent, of the cause of your illness. With homeopathy, rather than taking fever medication and suppressing the symptoms, you'd treat a cold using medicine that triggers those symptoms. In one treatment, the doctor listens extremely closely to the patient. It's not psychiatry, but the doctor, by listening to the patient, goes down to the depths of the patient's consciousness and, in doing so, raises immunity. So in this sense, writing, storytelling is good. In "Winter Sea (*Fuyu no Umi*)," I wanted to draw my mother since she passed away when I was small and I didn't know what a mother was. And in my own way, I imagined one and created the story. So of course, the story is fiction. But the feeling of a woman who dies leaving behind a small baby, that I can draw.

MA: And your sister is quite a bit older than you.

SK: We have different fathers. Katsumata is the surname of the family my mother married into and I was born quite some time after my mother's husband, my sister's father, passed away. My father had another family and so I was an illegitimate child.

MA: …Did you ever want to meet your father?

SK: No, I was rather scared to…

MA: But it must have been a particular shock to find out during puberty.

SK: Especially since at that time, people were judgmental about those things. In the looks of the adults around me, I felt…how can I say it? That my existence was shameful?

MA: You had the feeling that your very existence was being denied.

SK: So the feeling of wanting to hide was pretty strong.

MA: Do you remember anything about your mother?

SK: I don't remember anything at all…I only remember how busy the funeral was when she died, but I don't recall any conversations with my mother. I don't really have a poor memory, and it may be that I tried to forget at some point.

MA: It could be that it was too heavy an experience and you blocked the memory subconsciously.

SK: When I was a child, I though the world was such an unfair place. Even when I got a certificate in drawing class at school, there was no one to be happy for me.

MA: As far back as you can remember, you felt a disconnect with society…you really had no choice but to feel out of place.

SK: I hated meeting adults. That's why the work of driving cattle was so great. Driving cattle, I could spend time alone so I think I was able to turn out right (laughs). And seeing the fireflies and the small animals relaxed me.

MA: Now, you have a wife and two children.

SK: I was happy when my son was born. That in him, I had a blood relative.

MA: …In your first short stories, I felt like there was a close connection with your past. It wasn't just the pieces that evoked this relatively directly, like "Winter Sea (*Fuyu no Umi*)," "Winter Insect (*Fuyu no Mushi*)," and "Spring Ghost (*Haru no Rei*)." Even in works like "Straw Tales (*Wara Soshi*)" and "The Passing of the Tree's Leaves (*Ki no Kakei*)," your use of non-human creatures evokes a feeling of disconnect.

SK: I suppose so. The *tanuki* and *kappa* who show up in folklore and legends; the *tanuki* in particular, make a show of themselves, looking for some connection to society. But the general pattern is that the disguise comes off (laughs). Maybe I managed something close to that *tanuki*'s feeling. The *kappa* is a half-human creature living in the water, much like a miscarried fetus.

MA: So close to a human being, but…

SK: An amphibian. A being that went into the water instead of becoming human. In certain legends, too, you can feel the connection to something clearly miscarried like this. I imagined "*Kokeshi*", also collected in *Red Snow*, out of that idea. In a way, there's some overlap between a miscarried child and myself.

MA: The development on the last page of "*Kokeshi*" is good. Reading that page, for a moment, I thought the story was grim. Incidentally, the way you draw *kappa* is a little different, isn't it?

SK: My *kappa* with their sharp look are descendants of Akutagawa's. The *kappa* he draws have hard eyes.

Kon Shizumi and others draw sweet-looking *kappa*.

ABOUT RED SNOW

MA: Reading *Red Snow*, I think that many people see similarities to the works of Yoshiharu Tsuge, like the theme of menarche in "Mulberries" and the way you develop your characters. But you have a totally different viewpoint, don't you…I think that the key to all of Tsuge's work is the conflict between the self and society. Shiroyasu Suzuki expresses Choji's role with the words "the indigenous logic of the masses" [Editor's note: Conversation with Yoshiharu Tsuge, "The People, the Language, the *Manga*," *Garo*, April 1969], but in that same conversation, Tsuge said he would have liked to have been able to draw the piece from Choji's point of view. I think that is exactly what your work does. Even if there are similarities at the surface, the deeper points are different. And isn't it for exactly that reason that Tsuge has praised your work so highly? [Editor's note: Refer to the comments on the *obi* for the Japanese edition of *Red Snow* by Yoshiharu Tsuge.]

SK: Well, I can't really see my own work so objectively as that, but I was pleased to be praised by Mr. Tsuge at that time. I was much happier than I would have been winning some prize. After all, he really influenced me so much and writing "Mulberries," images from "Red Flowers" were very strong in my head. And I took the scene where they crush the berries in "Mulberries" from the novella *The Strawberry Season* by the American writer Erskine Caldwell. When they are snacking on strawberries, they play and the boy puts strawberries into the girl's collar and crushes them, and I took a hint from that.

MA: In terms of the collection *Red Snow*, there is a detailed reality, like eating mulberries gives you dysentery ("Mulberries") or fireflies smell like dead people ("Specter"). These days there are not very many places where you can catch fireflies and I have a distant memory of the smell of fireflies, but I felt like I was remembering it for the first time in many years. Also, in the offhand scene where Kumaichi departs at a trot in "Echo" and makes the "ka ka ko ko" sound.

SK: I've actually made charcoal, you know. The sound in that scene is sound of the *kiseru* pipe hitting the *doranko*. [Editor's note: This is formally known as a *doran*, but in the Tohoku dialect, "*ko*" is added to the end to become "*doranko*". Made from the bark of the cherry tree, it is used to hold loose tobacco.) When

you walk, it makes a sound like that.

MA: It's really such a minor scene, but it makes a curious impression. It's natural you would draw these kinds of things from your experience, but you're also extremely thorough in researching the period that is the background for the story and finding materials to set the stage.

SK: The story actually comes to me when I'm looking through the materials. Of course, the overwhelming majority of these things don't end up being much of a reference and it's mostly an exercise in futility, but in there somewhere, there's a tiny clue.

MA: So there's an origin story for "Pulp Novel about a Sack?"

SK: Chanting the praises of Buddha and the wandering praying monk are real. I based the story on the several lines from the picture scroll "Sack Priest Picture Scroll (*Fukuro Hoshi E Kotoba*)" introduced in something written by the author Toko Kon. I also tried to take a look at the scroll, but since I couldn't find the story Toko Kon wrote about, I used the lines from his work.

MA: In particular, although it goes without saying that men will, I feel like women reading the short story "Red Snow" will really be able to empathize. As an author who made his debut in *Garo*, I think that you have some things in common with Hinako Sugiura.

SK: Before she retired, Ms. Sugiura and I wrote letters to each other. She often read my work and once wrote, "Whenever I'm stuck with a *manga*, I re-read Mr. Katsumata's short story collection."

MA: Are you planning a new work?

SK: I want to try drawing the story of the Hokkaido folk song, "*Esashi Oiwake*." Right now, I'm reading materials related to coal mines, herring, and the *Ainu*. I think I'll end up taking my time and draw a series of about eight or ten pieces.

MA: We'll look forward to that then.

SK: This interview is like a job interview for a retired old man trying to re-enter the workforce.

MA: Then I must be the nasty interviewer! ✿

SUSUMU KATSUMATA: THE MAN AND HIS WORK

This additional text corrects and revises the introduction to the life and works of Mr. Katsumata, written by Mitsuhiro Asakawa for *Saiko Comics No. 4* (January 2007), a *manga* magazine published from time to time in South Korea. Since each issue includes information about the author and the author's career, accompanied by an explanation of the situation surrounding Japanese *manga* and *manga*'s history for a Korean audience, parts of the explanation may be redundant. For this, we apologize.

INTRODUCTION

In recent years, the number of artists in the West drawing their personal experiences as comics has swelled, but the majority of these efforts are unimpressive. Naturally, there are some interesting works among them, but most comics like this seem to be nothing more than the author documenting an experience. A diary and a creative work are two different things. Even if the subject is reality, taking an objective look at that reality and picking out new meaning leads to the diary becoming art for the first time. Sinking down to the depths of one's consciousness and giving clear shape to the formless emotions and thoughts there can be painful. But don't we find eternity in exactly those things that can only be reached through such a difficult process?

Susumu Katsumata began drawing *manga* under the influence of the first generation of *gekiga* artists, like Yoshihiro Tatsumi and Yoshiharu Tsuge. Katsumata was part of *gekiga*'s second wave, as it were. Debuting in the latter half of the 1960s, with the decline of the rental *manga* industry, this second generation produced new works drawing on the ideas expressed by its predecessor. The fact that *gekiga* was developed and passed on was due to the efforts of Katsumata's generation taking over the experiment of *gekiga*'s originators. Katsumata's short stories, like the work of Tsuge and Tatsumi, managed a universality independent of his period.

THE DEATH OF RENTAL MANGA

An important distinction between Tatsumi and Tsuge's generation and Katsumata's generation was

their difference in involvement as authors of rental *manga*. Because the world of rental *manga* bypassed the major agencies, authors were able to draw their work with a certain degree of freedom, which became a base for the rise of alternative expression. With a circulation of 8,000 copies in the case of a hit, the scale was small compared with the major publishers, but rental publishers made up for this by publishing numerous books, diverse offerings to suit the tastes of readers: mysteries, period pieces, war stories, girls' stories, horror, humour and comedy, stories for adolescents, and science fiction. For authors, this presented a variety of options: one could draw the *manga* one liked and make a living as long as one didn't fall into a slump.

However, this kind of creative expression began to disappear in the mid-'60s. Rental *manga* as a medium was dying. It was in this period that Katsumata and his colleagues made their debut, with Seirindo's *Garo*, launched in 1964. *Garo* was almost the only magazine printing alternative comics at the time. But payments for manuscripts at *Garo* were extremely low. When its publication stopped, in the '70s, the authors writing for *Garo* were not able to make a living with *manga*. Since then, places accepting alternative expression have appeared intermittently, but a mature market allowing authors to make a real living has still not taken form. The issues surrounding expression and making a living are of utmost importance when considering alternative comics, particularly when authors take on the subject of personal experience. Creative work is born from the friction between one's social role and one's identity as an individual. However, Katsumata has almost never taken such a direct stance in his work.

LONELY CHILDHOOD YEARS

Susumu Katsumata made his debut in *Garo* in June 1966, not long after the magazine's launch. Rather than a short story, like those in the collection *Red Snow* issued by this company, his first published work was a four-panel comic. (This four-panel strip was serialized in *Garo* for about ten years under the title "Writings of Susumu Katsumata.") From then on, Katsumata occasionally released short stories while continuing to write mainly four-panel comics. Before introducing each of his works, let's take a look at Katsumata himself.

Susumu Katsumata was born in 1943 in Miyagi Prefecture as a child who never knew his father's face. His mother died of illness when he was six, and he was raised by his older sister and her husband. Because his sister kept it no secret that Susumu was a foster child, he passed his childhood years in solitude. Skilled at drawing, Katsumata won awards at school, but he had no blood relatives to share his joy in this. After school, once lessons were over, while reading *manga* and driving cattle—part of his daily routine to help with the household work—his only comfort was his contact with these animals. When he went to drive the cattle, Katsumata made sure to bring several *manga* magazines. Once he had finished reading all of them, he'd sing popular songs to himself. In summer, the cows that Katsumata had raised and cared for were big enough to be sold at the market for high prices. The boy's invaluable contact with these animals was, thus, always linked to their inevitable separation. Growing up accepting this contradiction, Katsumata must have become more adult than other children.

In the upper grades of elementary school, Katsumata began to draw *manga*. Among the pieces he drew at this time was "King of the Forest," the story of an orphaned boy living with the animals in the woods, who meets his real father by chance. If creation reclaims something lost by expressing something, then for Katsumata, the act of drawing *manga* likely had cathartic effects from the start, regardless of whether he was aware of it.

In junior high and high school, Katsumata stepped away from *manga* for a while. He found work in sales at an appliance manufacturer after graduating from high school, and spent three years there as an employee. Despite his hope to become financially independent, Katsumata soon discovered that university graduates received more favourable treatment. It became clear that staying with the company would mean compromising his future. He left the company and entered the Tokyo University of Education, where he studied nuclear physics. His passion for art springing up in him again, Katsumata drew *manga* while attending university. He submitted his work to *Garo*, and was accepted.

FROM FOUR-PANEL COMICS TO SHORT STORIES

About the time he started drawing for *Garo*, Katsumata's four-panel comic strips were in the orthodox style. However, they occasionally deviated from the four-panel convention of introduction, development, turn and conclusion to create pieces with a lyric afterglow. With these works and the release of a special Katsumata edition of *Garo*, he gained popularity with readers. The first short story Katsumata drew using the four-panel comic format was "*Kapparo*" (Special Susumu Katsumata edition of *Garo*, October 1969). Featuring the mythical *kappa* as protagonist, the work evoked humour and emotion, and deserves an honourable mention. From then on, Katsumata worked on short stories while drawing his four-panel comics. With sharp humour, he drew *kappa*, *tanuki*, and cats in unpredictable situations strikingly close to those of the human world. At the root of his short stories was the discomfort with and alienation from society Katsumata had felt since childhood. In his work, the joy and sadness of existence were always laid down together.

Meanwhile, he wrote only a few short stories dealing with personal subjects in the brief period from 1971 to 1972. "Winter Insect (*Fuyu no Mushi*)" (*COM*, March 1971), "Winter Sea (*Fuyu no Umi*)" (Fig. 5; *Garo*, April 1971) and "Spring Soul" (*Garo*, March 1972) correspond to this period. In 1971, Katsumata dropped out of graduate school amid the turbulence of student protests against the US-Japan Security Treaty. Widespread skepticism towards authority and values led to Katsumata's decision to leave school as he asked himself about the meaning of scholarship. Additionally, he realized that to continue on later in research as a scholar, he would need connections and financial resources that he simply did not have. When he closed the book on what had been his goal, Katsumata's thoughts turned to the past. In "Winter Sea," Katsumata used his own mother as a model, a woman he had almost no memory of. The story depicts a woman who has given birth to a child with no father. There is none of the humour seen in Katsumata's work up to that point: the pictures, with their solid black printing, are utterly solemn. The story is abstract, and it would be difficult to argue that the piece succeeds as a creative work. However, it seemed that for Katsumata, drawing this work was somehow necessary. Here, he sincerely contemplates the foundation of his own existence. More than the question of artistic merit, it was this motivation that moved me. Isn't one of the fundamental values of art its ability to overcome the past by facing and objectifying it in a creative work?

COMPLETION OF KATSUMATA'S GEKIGA

By 1975, the number of readers drawn to Katsumata's short stories was growing steadily. Requests started to come in from magazines other than *Garo*. Katsumata worked enthusiastically on commissions from weekly magazines oriented towards mainstream entertainment, like *Weekly Manga Goraku*. For these publications, Katsumata drew the lives of the indigenous people in settings reminiscent of the Tohoku region where he was born and raised (Fig. 6). The tendencies seen in the short stories he tested in *Garo*—fantasy with animals and creatures as the subject and stories drawing on personal themes—were deftly blended, and the lives of a variety of people, including their sexuality, were drawn vividly and generously. However, because the portraits were so generous, they were somehow also extremely melancholy. Seen in these works was the knowledge Katsumata gained from bravely confronting his past, and his new viewpoint of affirming all existence. The formation of characters and other parts of his work may give the impression of being similar to the work of Yoshiharu Tsuge, but Tsuge's work was always drawn from the viewpoint of an observer, while Katsumata's was drawn from the point of view of the characters themselves. It was a world that Tsuge, raised in the city, could not have expressed even had he wanted to. Tsuge, who rarely praised the work of other people, was generous with his accolades to Katsumata.

THE TURNING POINT OF THE 1980S: RE-EVALUATED AFTER A QUARTER OF A CENTURY

Highly praised by Yoshiharu Tsuge and Shigeru Mizuki, Katsumata's *gekiga* works did not, however, win over the general public. In the '80s, Katsumata's short stories appeared in *Comic Baku*, the *manga* magazine that Tsuge was regularly writing for, but were not particularly talked about. In the frivolous and light-hearted times on the eve of the economic bubble, there was likely little place for the work of Katsumata, drawing pre-modern indigenous lifestyles. Although the works drawn for *Goraku* and *Custom Comics* were collected in *Mulberry Fruit* (*Kuwa Ichigo*), sadly, the publication of *Custom Comics* was

suspended and the book was quickly out of print.

After this, Katsumata moved away from short *gekiga* stories from the mid-'80s and found a great deal of work in the four-panel comics he had long been doing and in illustrations for children's books. Meanwhile, he illustrated *Why Are We Scared of Nuclear Power?* (*Genpatsu wa Naze Kowai ka?*) (published by Koubunken), a book about nuclear power plants. This experience bore fruit as "Deep-sea Fish (*Shinkaigyo*)" (*Comic Baku 3*, December 1984), a unique short story replete with quiet rage. It was also in the mid-'80s that Katsumata became aware of the problems involved in the Sayama Incident, which shone a spotlight on official discrimination against Japan's *Burakumin* (untouchables), through his work on related illustrations triggered by a request from the *Kaiho Newspaper*. In the middle of the 1990s, he began the serial "*Manga Sayama Incident*" (monthly Sayama Discrimination Trial, Headquarters of the *Buraku* Liberation League, Central Sayama Fight Division), which became a work of over 500 pages (Fig. 7; published as a single volume in 2006 by Nanatsumori Shokan). Katsumata expressed his unmitigated anger at discrimination and irrationality, a reaction bursting from his very heart towards threats to the sanctity of all life.

In 2005, Katsumata was stricken ill and it seemed certain that the time left to him was not long. In November 2005, we published *Red Snow* in Japan. "I'm happy to be called a *gekiga* artist. Up to now, no one's ever said that about me. (laughs)...When I'm able to draw something new, I'd like to send it to Mr. Tsuge and Mr. Mizuki, who were so kind as to write comments for the *obi*. Because I think drawing is a way of saying thank you." Leaving such excellent *gekiga* pieces behind, it's no stretch to say that Katsumata's work absolutely did not receive the attention it deserved. After the book's release, Katsumata needed an operation, so he heard the news of the Japan Cartoonists Association Award in 2006 post-surgery, still groggy in his hospital bed. Even still, he presented himself at the awards ceremony shortly thereafter, showing his enthusiasm for creating new work.

He managed some rough sketches while in hospital, but, regrettably, he had neither the time nor the physical strength to complete these as *manga*. In particular among these were drafts he left for the science picture book *The Mysterious Round Cabbage*

(*Marui Kyabetsu no Fuashigi*), drawn with no real plans for release. The story was complete with underdrawing in pencil, explaining in an easy-to-understand way the process by which the initially straight leaves of the cabbage became the current leaves that are round like an eye, alongside portrayals of the lifestyle and background of early people, among other things, clearly taking advantage of a fair amount of research materials. This work vividly evokes Katsumata's "eyes," looking intently at the mysteriousness of existence and the flow of life from his sickbed.

When the Korean translation of *Red Snow* arrived in February 2007, Katsumata began to study Korean, ambitious as always. He checked the rough cover design for the French edition of *Red Snow*, scheduled to follow the Korean translation, and looked forward to its completion. But Katsumata did not get to see the completed book: the French edition of *Red Snow* arrived in January 2007, one month after he passed away. The book was beautifully done, with every detail meticulously worked out. Several other translations of Katsumata's work are also planned for the future, and readers encountering Katsumata's work for the first time are likely to feel something begin inside them. Katsumata perceived existence not as isolated points of one person after another, but rather as a part of a continuous flow. If this is the case, ceasing to exist is not the end, but rather nothing more than melting into a larger flow. And as long as this flow continues, Katsumata's work will live on. ❊

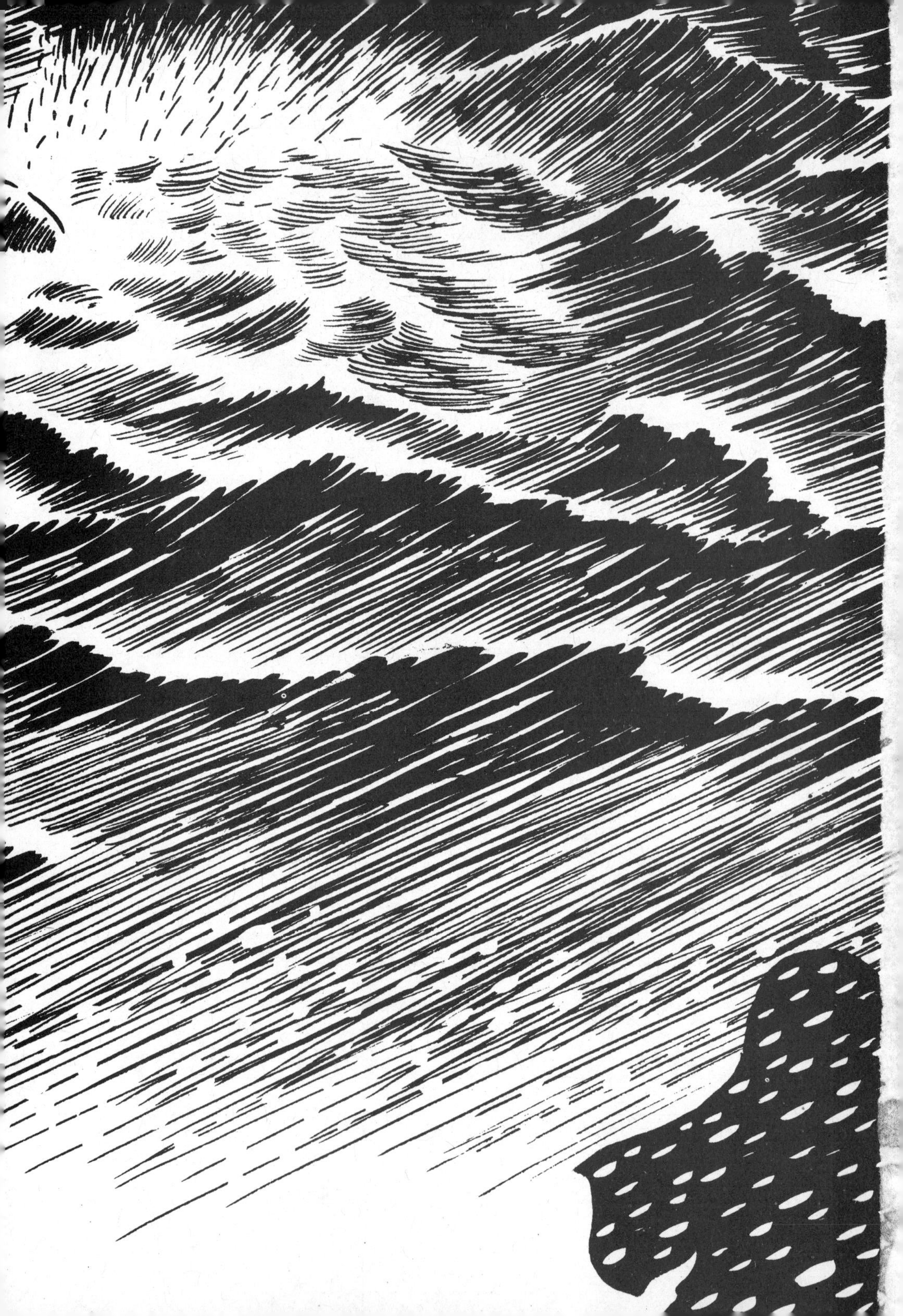

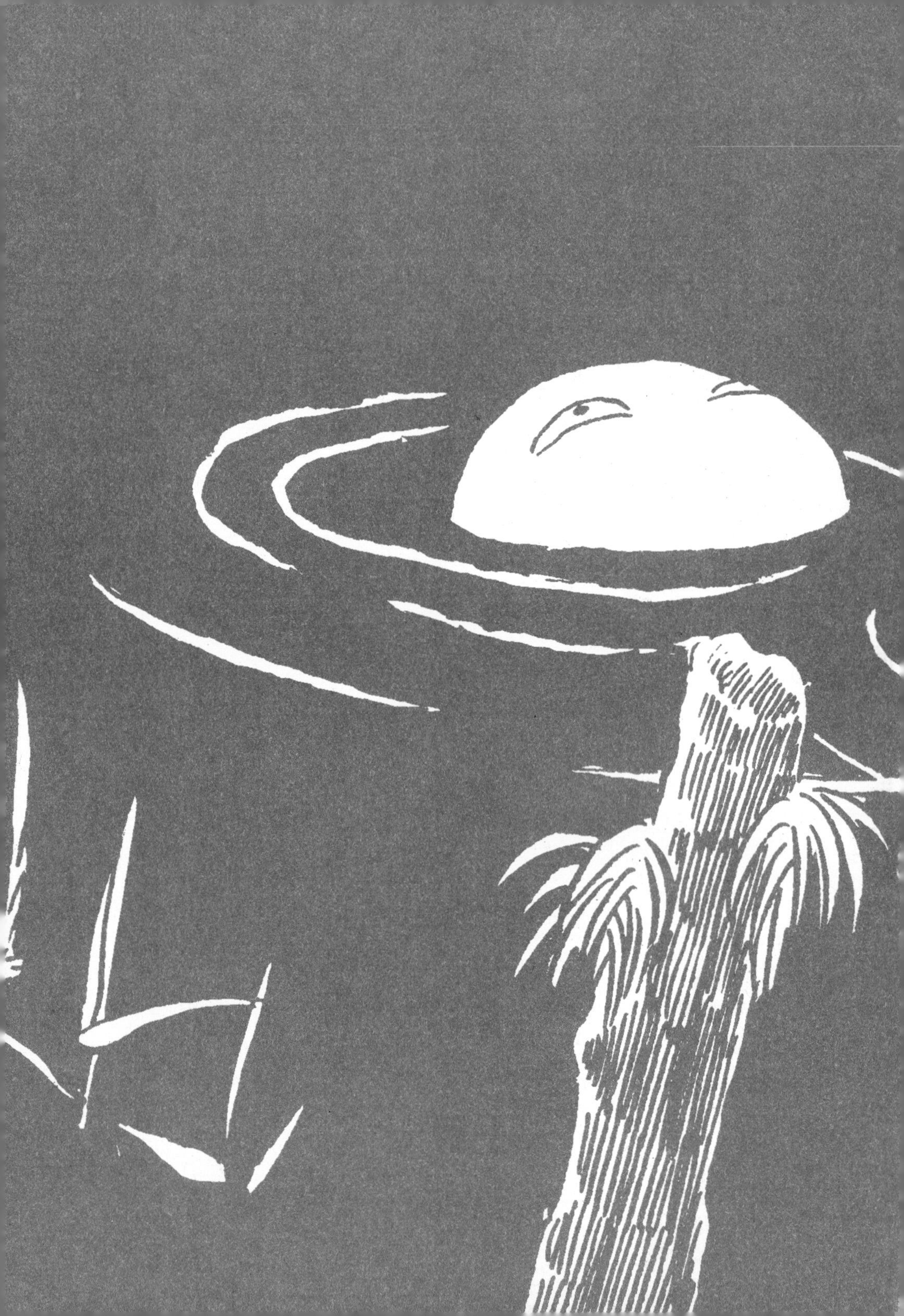